OILHEAT TECHNICIANS MANUAL

SILVER

NATIONAL OILHEAT RESEARCH ALLIANCE

This manual is not intended as a substitute for the manufacturers' installation, operation and/or service instructions, which should always be consulted and considered the first and best reference for installing, commissioning and servicing equipment.

This book describes recommended and well established practices for installing and maintaining oilburners, furnaces, boilers, water heaters, and heating oil tanks and piping. Additionally, it describes how venting and chimneys affect the equipment's operation. However, the "correct" way of doing things may change over time due to new technologies, new research or safety issues that become better understood. Therefore, you must continue your education after reading this book, take continuing education classes and communicate with manufacturers and local authorities regarding changes.

We describe building and installation codes, and we discuss manufacturers' instructions. Of necessity, each of these is important to install equipment, but unfortunately, the relationships between them are not always synchronized, and therefore, sometimes they appear to conflict.

The book relies on well established model codes. NFPA 31, Standard for the Installation of Oil Burning Equipment, is the predominant model code for oil equipment installations. Many states adopt this code and use it in their jurisdiction. Unfortunately, sometimes it takes time for a jurisdiction to adopt changes that are made to the code; they may use old editions, or may use competing model codes. Additionally, some NFPA changes may occur between editions of this book. Unless your county or state adopts these model codes, they are not "legally" required. However, they generally reflect best practices, and customers will expect that from you. And if you are sued and you have ignored best practices, you will almost certainly lose.

Each state, county, or city may adopt a local building or fire code. Usually these will be based on uniform national codes (NFPA 31), but occasionally there will be variances or changes to suit local problems or issues.

Some areas may rely on a different model code than NFPA 31, or their code may not be based on a national model. These codes are the law in the area in which you are working and you must follow them.

Finally, each manufacturer provides instructions on how to install his equipment. The codes generally defer to the manufacturer, and state, but the manufacturer must be specific. For example, if the manufacturer says, "Use a draft regulator if necessary," and the codebook says, "draft regulators are required," then you must use a draft regulator. In describing draft regulators, NFPA says they must be used "unless the appliance design, conditions of installation, or combinations thereof preclude excessive chimney draft, or the appliance is listed for use without one." Thus, NFPA says that a draft regulator must be used unless you can determine that the final installation will not allow excessive draft or the appliance is listed for use without the draft regulator.

—*Bob Hedden, Editor-in-Chief*

We want to express our deepest gratitude to the following people who spent untold hours checking over the material in this book for accuracy:

Jerry Herron—*RW Beckett Corp.*
Tom Tubman, Chuck Feldman, Marc Bryden, Walter Hadank, Mark Leclerc, Rich Newberry, Jim Ratcliffe, Dave Rousayne, and Mike Shayda—
    Carlin Combustion Technology
John Jones—*Delavan Spray Technologies*
Chris Jordyn—*ICPA*
    (Independent Connecticut Petroleum Assn.)
Roger Mitchell—*MODA (Maine Oil Dealers Assn.)*
Mike Szentesy and Bill Mitchell—*Suntec*
Jim Bergmann—*Testo*
Pete Cullen—*Wöhler*
Wayne Lawrence—*Instructor and Oilheat Service Technician*
Overton "Jay" Young and Dave Levitt—*Dixon Fuel*

A big thanks goes to:
George Lanthier—*Firedragon Enterprises*
John Levey—*Oilheat Associates*
    lead writers on many chapters, editors on some.

Editor & Graphic Designer—Mike SanGiovanni, *Oilheating Journal*
Sue Carver—*Industry Publications*, layout, proofing, & production
Publisher—Don Farrell, *Oilheating Journal*

John Huber—President, National Oilheat Research Alliance

NATIONAL OILHEAT RESEARCH ALLIANCE

Oilheat Technician's Manual
2008 Edition/Silver

Copyright 2008
National Oilheat Research Alliance
600 Cameron Street
Suite 206
Alexandria, VA 22314
www.nora-oilheat.org

ISBN-13: 978-1-7335402-0-9

On being an Oilheat Technician

This manual is for anyone interested in learning to become an Oilheat Technician. Being an Oilheat Technician is a very challenging profession. Working on oil burners is tougher than plumbing, electrical, air conditioning, copiers or computers. The reasons are the sheer variety of equipment and the conditions we have to work under. There have been over 500 different oil burner manufacturers over the years, and thousands of furnace, water heater, and boiler brands and styles. Each of these unique combinations of burner and boiler, furnace, or water heater operates in a different building with a different venting system and heat distribution system. The bottom line is that there are millions of different configurations we must understand. Add to this the incredibly high degree of customer contact technicians enjoy, and all the skills that implies, and you can see why it is so difficult to learn to become an accomplished Oilheat Technician.

First, you must have pride in yourself, your company, and the Oilheat Industry. You have to have a deep personal need to do a good job, one you can be proud of. The second ingredient is to possess a strong desire to be of service. You have to enjoy helping people. The third element is insatiable curiosity. The only way to keep up with the breathtaking technological improvements and changes in our business is to be a perpetual student, always learning. Finally, it helps if you have a mentor to help you along the way. After years of experience, you should mentor someone else. We hope this manual will give you a starting point in your journey toward excellence.

Dozens of dedicated Oilheat professionals have had a hand in creating and editing it. The book is written by Oilheat Technicians for Oilheat Technicians. The first versions of the book were published in the early 1960's. This is the seventh, and probably the most ambitious revision of the book.

Disclaimer

This publication is designed to provide accurate and authoritative information in regard to the subject matter covers. It is sold with the understanding that the publisher is not engaged in rendering legal, accounting, or other technical or professional service. If specific legal advice or other technical or professional assistance is required, the services of a competent professional person should be sought.

The editors have made their best effort to be sure the material in the book is accurate. However, any book with as much detail about such a wide range of subjects, and with as many contributors as this text has enjoyed, over as many rewrites and revisions as the text has endured, is bound to have a few mistakes, omissions, and controversial opinions. We all wish to take this opportunity to apologize for any confusion or inconvenience that may result from any of these factors. However, NORA, nor those responsible for the preparation of this Manual, make any representations or guarantee, or assume or accept any responsibility or liability, with respect thereto.

This book is sold without warranty of any kind as to the accuracy of its contents. The reader accepts full responsibility for any consequence arising from the use of this book. In all cases, local codes, and equipment manufacturers' instructions take precedence over anything we have presented in this book.

Contents

Introduction

In this book, we will cover everything about oilheating, from the oil used, to exhausting the combustion gases, to distributing the heat throughout the house.

The major components of an Oil-fired Heating System are displayed on the adjacent page.

The oil tank ❶ stores the oil, the oil **lines ❷** move the oil to the burner, the oil **filter ❸** cleans the oil prior to its introduction into the burner. (Chapter Seven)

The system begins with the **thermostat ❹** and electronic controls. The thermostat senses the temperature in the house and when the house gets cold sends a signal to the **controls on the burner ❺.** These controls turn the oil burner on when heat is needed and off when the need for heat is satisfied. (Chapters Eleven and Twelve)

The **oilburner ❻** contains a **pump ❼** that moves the oil from the tank to the burner, it mixes the fuel with air and then ignites the oil. (Chapters One, Four, Five and Nine)

The **appliance ❽** is a water heater, a boiler or a furnace. A water heater heats water for use in the residence, a furnace heats air that is distributed throughout the residence, and a boiler heats water that is either distributed as steam or water to heat the residence. Within each of these appliances, there is a **combustion area ❾** where the oil burning takes place. Adjacent to the combustion area is a **heat exchanger ❿** that takes the heat from the **flame ⓫** and from the **combustion gases ⓬** in the **combustion chamber ⓭** and heats the air or water within the unit. The appliance then begins to distribute the air and water throughout the house. (Chapters Six and Thirteen)

The **heat distribution system ⓮** takes the heat from the heat exchanger and delivers it around the building. Furnaces use a fan to distribute the heat. Hot water heaters and boilers use circulators to distribute the hot water around the building. (Chapter Thirteen)

The **flue pipe ⓯** and **chimney ⓰** system remove the combustion gases from the building. (Chapter Six)

Additional chapters also cover heating oil, service procedures, energy conservation and customer service.

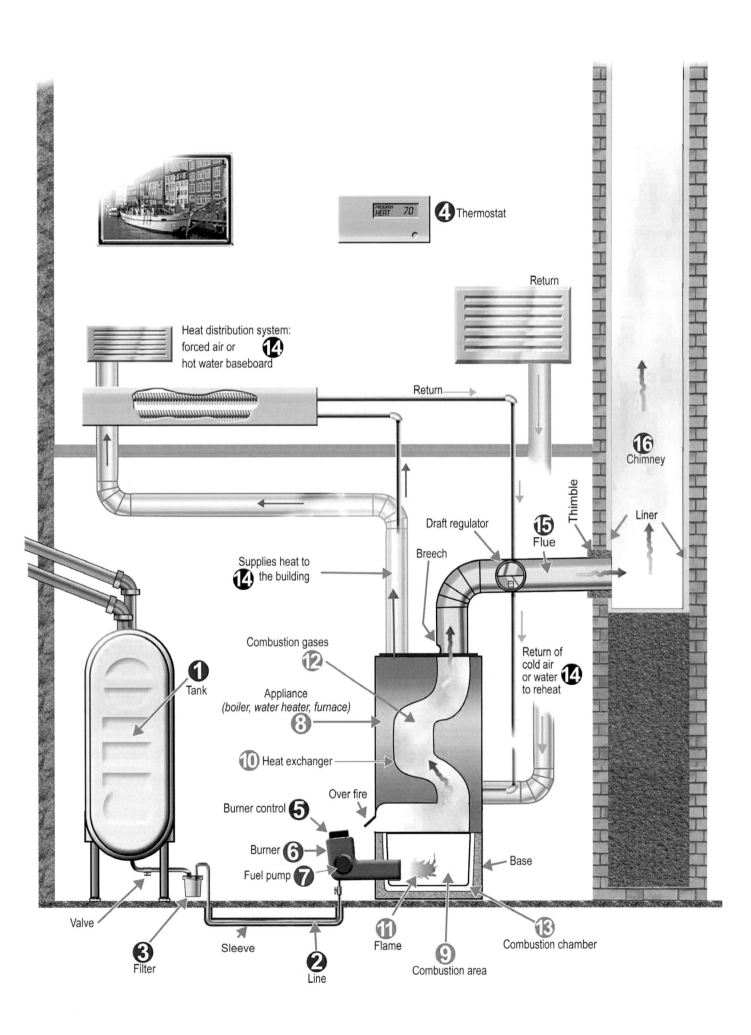

4 Thermostat

Return

14 Heat distribution system: forced air or hot water baseboard

Return

16 Chimney

Thimble

15 Flue

Liner

Draft regulator

Breech

Supplies heat to
14 the building

Return of
cold air
or water
to reheat **14**

Combustion gases
12

Appliance
(boiler, water heater, furnace)
8

10 Heat exchanger

1
Tank

Over fire

Burner control **5**

Burner **6**

Fuel pump **7**

Base

Valve

Sleeve

Filter
3

Line
2

Flame
11

Combustion area
9

Combustion chamber
13

Chapter **1**

INTRODUCTION TO OILBURNERS

IN THIS CHAPTER

- **How an oilburner works**

- **The high-pressure, atomizing, flame retention oilburner**

- **Ignition, the nozzle assembly and air adjustments**

Chapter 1

Introduction to Oilburners

Introduction

To understand oilburners, we must understand a bit about combustion. Combustion (burning) is the rapid combining of oxygen and the elements in the fuel. When the oxygen and the fuel combine, they create heat, light—and combustion gases. (We cover Combustion Theory in detail in Chapter 7.) In order for something to burn, we need three things:

1. Oxygen from the air

2. A fuel that will easily combine with the oxygen

3. Heat

Heating oil will not burn as a liquid. To burn, the liquid oil must be converted into a vapor. In today's burners, this is done by breaking the oil into tiny droplets (atomizing it). Next, each droplet is heated until it turns into a vapor. Then, to accomplish clean combustion, the oilburner must mix the oil vapor with the proper amount of air. The combined air and vapors are raised to the temperature at which they will burn. Therefore, every oilburner must atomize the oil, vaporize it, mix it with air, and heat the mixture above its ignition point.

High pressure atomizing

Today's oilburners are called high-pressure burners because they use a fuel pump to pressurize the oil to 100 pounds per square inch (PSI) or more. This pressure forces the oil through a nozzle designed to break (atomize) the oil into the

small droplets that are vaporized and burned in suspension in the combustion area. An electric spark, from electrodes installed close to the nozzle, supplies heat for ignition. A fan supplies the air required for combustion. Figure 1-1 shows how a burner operates, Figure 1-2 shows the combustion process.

Figure 1-1: Oilburner operation

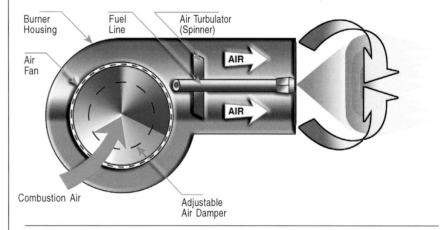

Figure 1-2: Simplified schematic of the combustion process

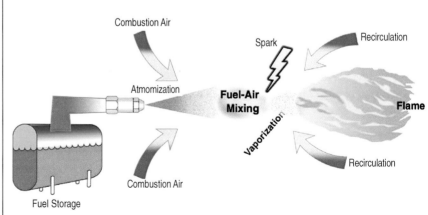

Although the high-pressure burner has been the mainstay of the industry almost from the beginning of the modern oilburner era, it has gone through many modifications. An advantage of oil is that parts are largely interchangeable, and thus it has been possible to keep many burners operating for years. In fact, some burners made in the 1930s are still operating in the field because of interchangeable parts.

Flame retention oilburners

In the 1960s, the current design for oilburners was introduced, which is called the *flame retention burner*. As the name implies, the flame is held very close to the face of the combustion head. The flame is smaller and more compact than with older burners. This design's primary characteristics are its head or end-cone, high motor operating speeds (typically 3450 RPM) and high combustion air static pressures. Figure 1-3 shows pictures of modern flame retention burners.

Figure 1-3: Flame retention burners

The flame retention head provides a modified airflow pattern for radically improved air-oil mixing. The basic idea is to produce a strongly swirling air pattern that recirculates combustion products for more complete mixing of fuel and air. This is called *recirculation*.

As the air rushes out of the end of the burner, it sucks air from the combustion

Air Pattern—Non-Flame Retention Burner

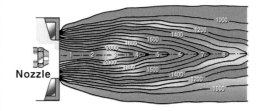

Air Pattern—Flame Retention Burner

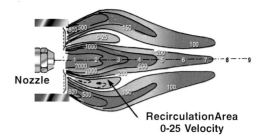

**RecirculationArea
0-25 Velocity**

area back toward it. This recirculation is what pulls the fire back toward the head, creating the flame retention effect. The flame stabilizes near the burner head, hence the name *flame retention*. The air swirling is achieved with airflow shaping heads and turbulators and by running the burner motor and fan at high speed.

The flame retention head produces more air swirl and combustion air recirculation flow, which improves fuel-air mixing. This permits operation with less excess air and with lower smoke levels. Cleaner and more stable combustion is produced and system efficiency is typically 5 to 15 percent

	Non-flame Retention (Turbulator or Choke)	Flame Retention Head Burners
Percent CO_2	7-9	11-13
Percent Excess Combustion Air	50-100	20-30
Bacharach Smoke Number	1-3	0-1
Percent Flue Heat Loss (on cycle)	30	10-20

Figure 1-4: Comparison of burner performance

higher than with older burners. See Figures 1-4 and 1-5.

Flame retention heads produce hotter flames because less excess combustion air is used than with non-flame retention head oilburners. Therefore, the combustion chamber construction materials and general condition must be checked carefully whenever a high efficiency oilburner is installed or serviced.

Construction of the high-pressure atomizing flame retention oilburners

The high-pressure retention head burners are precision-built and constructed for durability and long service. Every high-pressure burner consists of a

motor, fan (C), fuel unit (A), ignition transformer or igniter (E), nozzle assembly (B & D), and a housing to which all of these parts are attached, as illustrated in Figure 1-6 on following page.

Motor

The electric motor drives the fan and the fuel pump. The motor is manufactured in one of two designs, either a split phase type or permanent split capacitor (PSC) type motor. The motor is mounted to the housing of the burner by means of a two, three, or four bolt flange. Removing these bolts allows easy removal of the motor and access to the fan, which is attached to the motor shaft. In the event of motor failure, be sure

Figure 1-5: Difference in flame between a non-flame retention burner and a flame retention burner

Non-Flame Retention Combustion

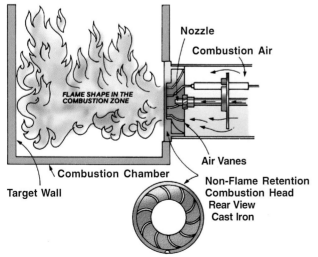

Flame Retention Combustion

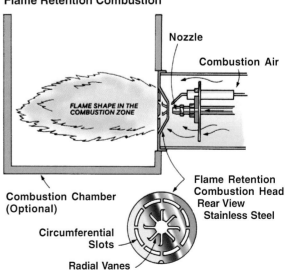

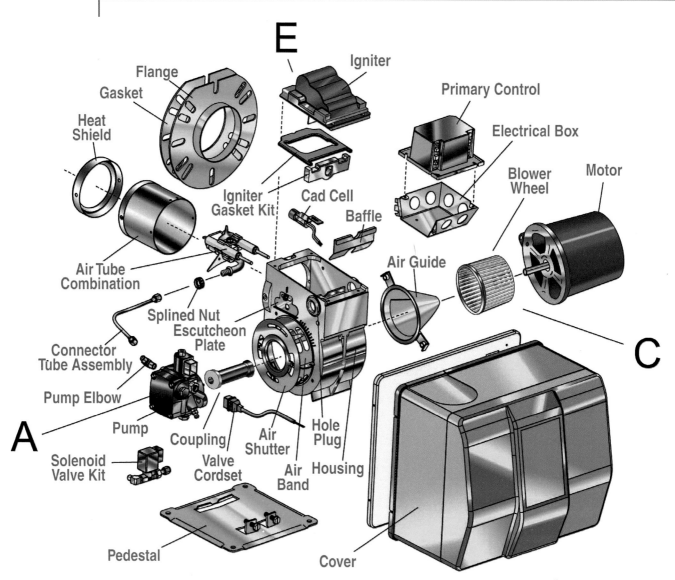

**Figure 1-6:
Components of a
flame retention
burner**

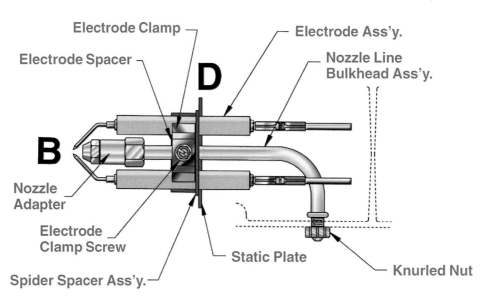

to replace the motor with a new motor of the same rotation, frame size, and revolutions per minute (RPM). Figure 1-7 shows a motor, fan and coupling. The coupling attaches to the motor shaft on one end and the pump shaft on the other, taking power from the motor and transferring it to the pump. (Motors and couplings are covered in Chapter 10.)

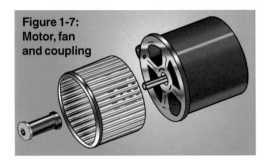

Figure 1-7: Motor, fan and coupling

Multiblade fan and air shutter

A fan wheel within the burner housing is driven directly by the motor shaft, and provides the necessary air to support combustion. An adjustable air shutter on the burner housing controls the volume of air handled by the fan.

The oilburner fan, or blower wheel as it is often called, supplies the combustion air for the flame. See Figure 1-8. They are of the squirrel cage type with beveled blades that must be kept free of dirt and lint. The slightest amount of dirt will reduce the blade bevel and reduce the amount of air delivered. They are precision balanced and every effort must be made to prevent bending the wheel at its hub.

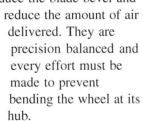

A blower wheel with a bent or broken blade will be out of balance. This

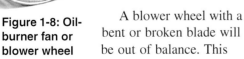

Figure 1-8: Oil-burner fan or blower wheel

can cause a vibration and put an extra strain on the motor bearings. Any fan wheel that does not slip off the motor shaft without needing to be pried off with a screwdriver must be removed with a wheel puller.

When replacing the burner fan, one must pay strict attention to the rotation as indicated by the beveled blades. Also, remember that the burner manufacturer has provided the proper fan for the proper amount of combustion air needed. Always replace it with one that has the same dimensions.

Fuel pump

The fuel pump, also referred to as the fuel unit, is driven by the motor. The pump shaft is attached to the motor shaft by the burner coupling. The pump consists of three basic parts:

1. Strainer—to remove any foreign matter from the oil before it enters the pump gears.

2. Pump—to lift the oil from the tank and deliver it to the regulating valve.

3. Regulating valve—to build up and maintain the proper operating pressure for atomizing the oil. (See Chapter 4 for more details on Fuel Units.)

Ignition transformer or solid state igniter

The ignition transformer or solid-state igniter (on new burners) provides a "step up" from the line voltage of 120 volts to over 10,000 volts. The high voltage spark produced by these components jumps across the gap between the electrode tips. This spark provides the heat necessary to vaporize the atomized oil from the nozzle and achieve ignition. (See Chapter 9 for more information on Ignition Systems.)

The nozzle assembly

The nozzle assembly also known as the "drawer" assembly, or firing assembly, consists of the oil feed pipe (called the nozzle line), the nozzle, nozzle adapter, electrodes, transformer connections, and on some burners, a flame retention ring. The entire assembly is located in the air tube of the burner. An opening at the rear, top or side of the burner housing permits access to and removal of the nozzle assembly.

Combustion heads

The combustion head (also referred to as the turbulator, fire ring, retention ring, and end cone) creates a specific pattern of air at the end of the air tube. The air is directed in such a way as to force oxygen into the oil spray so the oil can burn. In order to do so, the combustion head must have the right amount of air delivered to it down the air tube from the fan, and the fuel pump and nozzle must deliver the right amount of fuel at the proper pressure.

Elements needed for combustion

As we have discussed, the three elements we need for combustion are oil, air, and spark. If we examine these three elements one at a time we will see that:

• The amount of oil is based on the flow rate in gallons per hour (GPH) that you wish to burn. The size of the nozzle orifice (in GPH) and the pressure setting of the fuel unit determine the flow rate.

• The spark is the ignition source for the fuel oil. With new advanced control systems, the spark is only on for a short period of time (usually 25 seconds maximum) at the beginning of the running cycle of the burner. Once flame is established, the heat from the flame keeps combustion going. Continuing to have the spark on after ignition is accomplished will only detract from the performance of the burner.

• The air is the key element and the final adjustment of a burner. Air is introduced into the air tube by the fan through the air intake controlled by adjustable shutters or bands.

The flame retention head incorporates three basic air-directing elements: the center opening for primary air, the secondary slots, and the

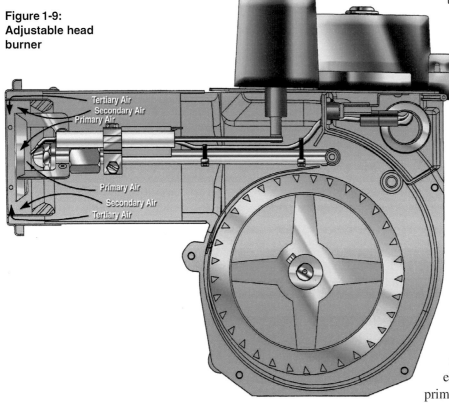

Figure 1-9: Adjustable head burner

Tertiary Air
Secondary Air
Primary Air

Primary Air
Secondary Air
Tertiary Air

tertiary opening. See Figure 1-9. The center opening is the orifice in the center of the head that allows clearance for the oil spray and the electrode spark to pass through the head without interference. The secondary slots are the slots that radiate out from the center opening towards the outside of the head. The tertiary opening is a slot that is concentric to the center opening and follows the circumference of the combustion head. All three openings affect the way air is delivered to the oil spray.

• The **primary air i**s the air that exits through the center opening hole in the flame retention ring where the oil from the nozzle is sprayed. Primary air has the least desirable effect on combustion. Air will always take the path of least resistance, so the larger the center opening, the more the air will tend to pass through this opening and push the flame out away from the face of the head. This air travels in a forward motion only. The smaller the center opening, the more air will be forced to seek its passageway through the other openings in the combustion head. (Figure 1-9).

• The **secondary air** is the air that exits through the slots cut into the flame retention ring. The secondary slots are where the most important mixing of oil and air occurs. The slot width regulates the velocity of the air passing through the slot. This is where the air acquires a spinning action. The air moves mostly in a rotary motion with little forward movement. Narrow slots will cause the air to spin faster and move forward less. This will cause the best mixing of oil and air and create a compact, intense, and efficient flame.

The secondary slots also aid in keeping the surface of the head clean and free of carbon. This air is turbulated by the flame

retention ring and it is this Secondary Air that creates the flame retention effect. By spinning this secondary air, the flame is actually pulled back toward the flame retention ring. (Figure 1-9).

• The **tertiary air** is the air that exits around the outside of the flame retention ring or through the tertiary slots. For clean oil combustion, every droplet of atomized oil MUST be completely blanketed with air in order to provide total combustion.

Tertiary Air ensures that any droplets of atomized oil escaping the oil spray pattern will contact this air and burn. Creating an envelope or curtain of air between the main swirl area of the flame and the walls of the combustion area or the chamber. The width of the slots in the outside ring control the amount of tertiary air entering the combustion area. The larger the slots the more tertiary air and less secondary air, thus the size of the slots affects the firing rate of the burner. (Figure 1-9).

Fixed and adjustable heads

Flame retention heads fall into one of two categories: fixed or adjustable (sometimes called variable heads). The difference between them is the method by which they control the tertiary opening and hence, the firing rate of the burner.

The fixed head group's tertiary opening is pre-set to a specific opening size for a specific firing rate range. There are a variety of one-piece heads available with fixed tertiary slots sized according to the firing rate for which it was designed. To change firing rates, you have to change the head.

With an adjustable head burner, the head is designed to move against or away from a ring, thus closing or opening the tertiary slot according to the firing rate requirements.

The adjustable head operation is based on the relationship between what is called the "throttle ring" and the "flame retention ring." The throttle ring is a ring at the end of the air tube that works in conjunction with the flame retention ring to create an air restriction and provide for the tertiary air effect. The adjustable head group allows the technician to move the head forward or backward in order to change the tertiary opening to accommodate different firing rate requirements, allowing fine-tuning of the burner.

The fixed head is simple and easy to use; but remember that each head is only good for a specific range of firing rates. When you are installing a new burner or changing a firing rate to optimize performance, you must be sure you have installed the proper head for the specific firing rate. The variable head burner allows an infinite ability to fine-tune the burner for hard-to-fire applications.

With the wide variety of adjustments possible, you must be careful in picking the correct adjustments. Most variable head burners come with adjustment guides to help you set the head properly.

Static pressure

Static pressure is the means of produc-

ing and maintaining flow against resistance. Oilburners on the market today create much higher static pressures than units made in the 1980s and earlier.

Some of these burners create such high static pressures that they can force the products of combustion through the heat exchanger and out of the building without the use of a chimney or power venter. See the section on direct venting in the Venting Chapter. (Chapter 6).

High static pressure burners have been developed to accommodate the modern, flow resistive appliances (boilers, furnaces, and water heaters) and to assist with low or no draft conditions. A drop in static pressure can cause problems that range from delayed ignition, rumbles, and pulsation to the inability to adjust the burner for clean operation.

The fan in a high static pressure burner starts with enough pressure to effectively push the products of combustion through the appliance without interruption. The higher static pressure also acts like a shock absorber or tightly wound spring to resist and absorb flame pulsations.

This is especially needed in most modern appliances, which are designed with tighter, more efficient heat exchanger passages and increased draft drop that results in great heat absorption by the heat exchanger, and thus, greater efficiency.

Chapter **2**

HEATING OIL & ITS PROPERTIES

IN THIS CHAPTER

- **An introduction to the petroleum industry**

- **Oil refining**

- **The properties of heating oil**

- **Fuel-related service calls**

- **Oil filtration**

Chapter 2

Heating Oil and Its Properties

Introduction to petroleum

Petroleum Fuels Our Modern Life Style

More than six thousand products are made from petroleum. It is almost impossible to get through a day without using dozens of petroleum products.

Oilheat is reliable

Oilheat has a remarkable reliability record. Despite wars, embargoes, political unrest, and natural disasters, oilheat keeps its customers warm. This reliability is partly due to the variety of places where crude oil is found, the resourcefulness of everyone from the refiners to the local oil dealer, the flexibility of the delivery system, and the stability and safety inherent in heating oil.

Refining oil

Heating Oil is a fossil fuel, as are natural gas, propane, and coal. They are called fossil fuels because they are all made from the prehistoric plants and animals that form fossils.

Fossil fuels are hydrocarbons. Hydrocarbon molecules are the building blocks of life. Everything that is or was ever alive is made of molecules composed of hydrogen and carbon atoms. Carbon is normally a solid, which, if not totally burned, becomes smoke and soot. Bonded together, hydrocarbons can be a gas like propane, a liquid like heating oil or a solid like candle wax. The hydrocarbon gases contain more hydrogen; the liquids and solids contain more carbon.

Some Petroleum Products

Gasoline, jet fuel, kerosene, diesel fuel, heating oil, propane, butane, lubricating oils, greases, waxes, asphalt, nylon, plastics, fertilizers, washing, cleaning and polishing products, medicines and drugs, photographic film, pesticides, waxed paper, food preservatives, food flavorings, beauty products, Plexiglas®, vinyl, audio and video tape, synthetic rubber, synthetic fibers, textiles, explosives, solvents, wax for candles, candy, matches, and polishes, toiletries, crayons, roofing materials, floor coverings, carbon fiber, paints, lacquers, printing inks, DVDs and CDs. Five percent of our electricity generated is oil powered.

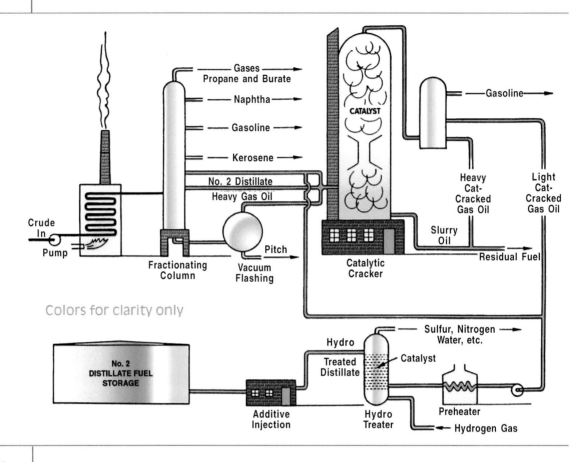

Gases
Propane and Burate

Naphtha

Gasoline

Gasoline

Kerosene

No. 2 Distillate

Heavy Gas Oil

CATALYST

Heavy Cat-Cracked Gas Oil

Light Cat-Cracked Gas Oil

Slurry Oil

Residual Fuel

Crude In

Pump

Pitch

Fractionating Column

Vacuum Flashing

Catalytic Cracker

Colors for clarity only

No. 2 DISTILLATE FUEL STORAGE

Additive Injection

Hydro Treated Distillate

Hydro Treater

Sulfur, Nitrogen Water, etc.

Catalyst

Preheater

Hydrogen Gas

Figure 2-1:
Refining oil

Petroleum comes out of the ground in the form of crude oil and wet gas. Both are a complex mix of compounds consisting mostly of the elements carbon and hydrogen. Sulfur and nitrogen are bound to some of these hydrocarbon compounds. This mixture of molecules is separated at the refinery by distillation into their various boiling ranges. Heating oil, diesel fuel, jet fuel, and kerosene are classified as middle distillates because their boiling range is in the middle of the sweep of petroleum products separated in the distillation process. Heating oil produced directly by the distillation process is called "straight run" product. Heating oil is also produced by catalytically and thermally cracking heavier, more complex molecules into the small heating oil hydrocarbon molecules. This is called "cracked" product. Blending a mixture of various middle distillate products together also creates heating oil. (Figure 2-1).

Properties of heating oil
American Society for Testing and Materials (ASTM)

ASTM publishes industry specifications for many different materials including petroleum products. The specification for Fuel Oils is ASTM D396. This standard sets the minimum specifications for the fuel.

Flash point

The *flash point* of fuel oil is the maximum temperature at which it can be safely stored and handled without serious fire hazard. The ASTM specified flash point for No.1 and No.2 oil is 100°F minimum. When oil is heated to its flash point, some of the hydrogen flashes off but the fuel will not continue to burn.

Ignition point

The *ignition* or *fire point* is lowest temperature at which rapid combustion of a fuel will take place in air. It is the temperature at which all the fuel has been sufficiently heated and vaporized to the point where it continues to burn for at least 5 seconds. For No. 2 oil, the ignition point is over 500°F.

Pour point

Pour point is the lowest temperature at which fuel will flow. Below this, it turns to waxy gel. The ASTM standard for un-treated No. 2 oil is 17°F. Additives or kerosene are added to heating oil during the winter to ensure that it flows.

Cloud point

Cloud point is the temperature at which wax crystals begin to form in the fuel—typically 10 to 20 degrees above the pour point. These crystals can clog filters and strainers, restricting fuel flow. Raising the temperature causes the crystals to go back into solution. ASTM does not list a specification for cloud point for heating oil. Both pour point and cloud point affect winter performance, and could cause problems if the fuel is not properly treated.

Viscosity

Viscosity is the thickness of the fuel and its resistance to flow. Grease has a high viscosity. Gasoline has a low viscosity—it flows easily. Heating oil's viscosity changes dramatically with temperature. As the

temperature decreases, viscosity increases. Normally the temperature of oil in a basement tank is 60°F. In the winter, you might get a delivery of 5°F oil. The colder oil will have a higher viscosity and burner

Heating Oil's Physical Properties (No. 2 oil)

ASTM Specification:	D 396
Flashpoint:	100°F minimum (37.8°C)
Ignition Point:	>500°F (260°C)
Pour Point:	17°F (8.3°C)
Cloud Point:	Pour point temp. plus 10-20° (F)
Viscosity:	Varies: increases as temp. drops
Water/Sediment:	ASTM allowable amount of H_2O: 0.1% (Water content is usually much lower in practice)
Sulfur Content:	Ranges from 0.5% to 0.05% (5000 to 500 parts per million); ASTM maximum allowable amount is 0.5%.
Color:	Colorless, but heating oil is dyed red for tax compliance reasons. Color resembles cranberry juice.
BTU Content:	139,000 (approx.)

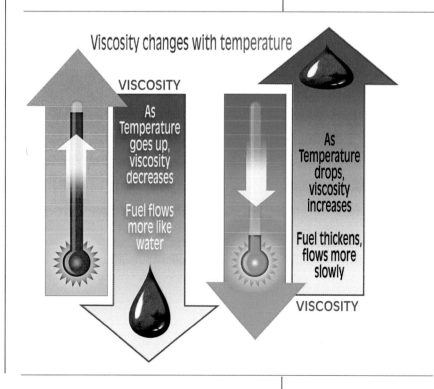

Good housekeeping, installing filters on all customers' burners, and an aggressive problem-tank replacement program can cut fuel related service calls dramatically.

performance will be affected until the fuel warms. As stated in the Nozzle Chapter (Chapter 5), cold oil causes poor atomization, delayed ignition, noisy flames, pulsation, and possible sooting.

Water and sediment

Accumulation of water in tank bottoms is undesirable, since it leads to the formation of sludge and ice. Sludge is largely oil and water. Water and oil usually do not mix, but if organic sediment is present in the fuel, it acts as a binder to stabilize the mix of fuel and water. This forms a white milky substance that will not burn. The ASTM limit for water is 0.1%, but most fuel sold has much less water. Unfortunately, water can get into the system from condensation, leaks in lines, or missing vent and fill caps.

Sulfur content

Sulfur exists in varying degrees in all fossil fuels. The sulfur content of heating oil ranges from 0.5% to 0.05%; the ASTM maximum is 0.5%.

When the sulfur burns, it mixes with oxygen and forms sulfuric dioxide. It also creates a small amount of sulfur trioxide. The sulfur trioxide reacts with the water vapor in the combustion gases to create a sulfuric acid aerosol. If the acid condenses (at 150-200°) it adheres to the heat exchanger, flue pipe and the inside of the chimney. It creates a scaly yellow to red colored crust. Scale makes up 50% of deposits on the heat exchanger. It downgrades efficiency by 1% to 4% over the year. It also blocks flue passages, restricting air flow and increasing smoke and soot.

Using low sulfur fuel all but eliminates scale and soot formation on heat exchanger surfaces. The efficiency does not degrade over the heating season, saving energy. It also results in decreased appliance service.

Color

Heating oil is dyed red to differentiate it from on-road diesel fuel for tax compliance reasons. Problems with the fuel are not indicated by the darkness of the color. A murky appearance, however, may indicate a fuel quality problem.

Fuel related service calls

The oilheat industry's top two service priorities are improved reliability and reduced heating equipment service costs. A significant number of unscheduled no-heat service calls are caused by inconsistent fuel quality, fuel degradation, and contamination.

Heating oil varies during the season. Wholesalers get their product from around the world, from Malaysia to Texas. Each of these products is slightly different; as a result, the product in the customer's tank may be a mixture of a variety of fuels. A great deal of our product is created by blending various fuels together to meet the rather loose definition for #2 heating oil laid out in the ASTM D 396 specification. Additionally, over time, fuel degrades— water may enter the system and bacteria have an opportunity to grow. Good housekeeping, installing filters on all customers' burners, and an aggressive problem-tank replacement program can cut fuel related service calls dramatically.

Potential problems in the tank

The population of oil tanks in the field is aging. As the tanks age, rust and sediments build up in the tank. Secondly, oil has a finite shelf life and breaks down over time. The third problem is the size and speed of delivery. Filling a tank kicks-up all the sediments and rust in the bottom of the tank, and that leads to plugged lines, filters and nozzles. The solutions here are not to let the level of oil in the tank get too low, to slow down the pumping speed of the truck, and to use diverters on the "blow or whistle pipes" (underground fill pipes) when filling underground tanks.

Major factors in fuel degradation

1. Chemistry of the fuel

   • *Heat causes the oxidation of organics*

   • *The presence of sulfur and nitrogen hasten degradation*

   • *Corrosion creates iron oxides (rust)*

   • *Presence of Gels caused by mercaptan sulfur*

   • *Incompatible fuels*

2. Microbiological effects

3. The tank and its environment—moisture, fuel circulation due to temperature differences

4. Lack of tank maintenance and poor design and installation that prevent adequate tank inspection, withdrawal of water and sediment, improper or no filtration, and lack of corrosion protection.

Fuel stability

Fuels degrade over time. If the fuels are contaminated, they will degrade even more quickly. The stability of heating oil depends a great deal on the crude oil sources from which it was made, the severity of the refinery process, the use of additives and any additional refinery treatment. Fuels that are stored for long periods of time and subjected to temperature extremes may form excessive amounts of sediments and gums that can plug filters, strainers, and nozzles.

Detecting "out of spec" oil

Occasionally, a bad batch of oil will be delivered. When that happens, there will be many service calls. If there is a spike in calls and they appear to be fuel related, you should alert your service manager. A fuel sample might show that the fuel can be fixed with additives, or the fuel may need to be replaced.

Water problems

The worst fuel problem is water in the oil tank. Water enters the tank in the following ways:

1. Condensation

2. Broken tank gauge (outside tank)

3. Loose fill or vent fittings and missing caps

4. Directly from delivery trucks

5. Leaking vent, fill pipes, or tank

6. Pumping old oil into a new tank

Sludge

Sludge is a combination of water, colonies of bacteria, degraded fuel, and other contaminates like sand, grit and rust. The ability of bacteria to grow almost anywhere and reproduce amazingly fast makes it an all too common problem. The bacteria live in the water and eat the fuel. They break the fuel down into hydrogen, CO_2, and carbon rich residue. The bacteria also create sticky slime or gum to protect themselves. Scientists call this slime "biofilm." This deterioration of fuel is a natural occurrence that will appear in all tanks unless proper maintenance is performed. The sludge grows at the oil-water line and when stirred up can to lead serious and recurring service problems—most notably plugged fuel lines, filters, strainers, and nozzles. Sludge is acidic and may eventually destroy the tank from the inside.

To reduce sludge formation:

• Never pump oil from one tank to another. You may be transferring tank killing sludge.

• Slow down delivery rates—high pressure filling can stir-up existing sludge causing it to be drawn into the oil line.

• Routinely check the tank for water—once you have removed the water, if possible, clean the sludge from the tank and treat the tank with a fuel conditioning additive.

• Draw the oil from the bottom of the tank—As water will condense and collect in all tanks, it is best to draw off the water as if forms. It will burn off in the combustion process. Allowing water to accumulate will create conditions favorable for the formation of sludge.

• The exception to this rule is outdoor above ground tanks. In cold weather, the water in the bottom suction line may freeze, causing a blockage and no heat. It appears that the best solution to this problem is to run the suction line into one of the top tappings on the above ground tank, use a floating suction line device, and regularly remove the water that condenses in the bottom of the tank.

Low temperature performance

As oil gets cold, several bad things happen. First, any water in the fuel freezes, plugging lines and filters. Second, the viscosity of the oil begins to increase, causing burner operation problems. Third, wax crystals begin to form in the oil. This wax or paraffin is a natural component of heating oil. Oil temperature is the main factor in changing oil viscosity. As the temperature of the oil goes down, the viscosity goes up. The oil gets thicker, which can cause a smoky fire.

How to deal with "frozen" tanks and oil lines

Cold-flow additives, called *Pour Point Depressants*, can help avoid frozen lines, but once the tank or lines have frozen or waxed, other solutions are needed.

The best solution is to top off the tank with kerosene. The agitation of the fuel in the tank caused by the kerosene delivery and the solvency of kerosene break up and

Frozen Fuel line

dissolve the wax crystals. You may also have to remove the filter temporarily, convert to a one-pipe system and heat the suction line with a hair dryer or heat lamp.

If you are unable to arrange for a delivery, some technicians report that adding as little as five gallons of kerosene can help.

Others report having success "shocking" the tank with a pour point depressant. You may have to build a temporary shelter for the tank out of plywood or cardboard, whatever is at hand, and then use a heat lamp or hair dryer to warm up the lines enough to get the oil to flow. Be very careful with heat tape. If you wrap a heat tape over itself, it can burn through its own insulation causing a short that can result in a fire. The insulation on the wires can also crack with age and exposure to the elements creating potential for a fire.

Quick tests for fuel quality:

Clear and bright test

The purpose of this test is to detect possible water or solid contaminants in the fuel by visual inspection. Using a clean glass container, take the sample at the bleed port of the fuel unit. Be sure the fuel sample tap (the bleed valve) is clean and free of loose contaminates by flushing it out at maximum flow before drawing a sample.

Let the sample settle for a minute to remove the air bubbles. Observe the sample against a light background for a clear

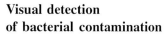

BAR CHART

Slight Haze

Ice

Base Fuel   Base Fuel with Water
Below Freezing Point

bright condition. The sample should look more like cranberry juice than red wine. Swirl the container to create a whirlpool. Free water and solids tend to collect at the bottom of the whirlpool. The term "clear and bright" does not refer to color. "Clear and bright" fuel has no floating or suspended matter, and no free water. Bright fuel tends to sparkle.

White bucket test

This is a good quick test for drivers to be sure you are filling your truck with good fuel. The purpose of this test is to visually determine the possible presence of contaminants and water in the fuel.

Fill a clean white bucket half way with fuel and let the sample stand for a minute to remove the air bubbles. Place the bucket on a level surface with good light in the bucket. Inspect the fuel, it should be clear and bright with no water, or solids. It should not be hazy or cloudy, and there should be no brown or black slime. Drop a shiny coin into the bucket. If you can easily read the date, the fuel is probably OK. The fuel should also smell "normal." Strange odors can indicate problems. With either the 'clear and bright' or 'white bucket' test, a haze caused by wax crystals may appear in the fuel if it is too cold. A haze in fuel that is not too cold may be due to contamination with water.

Visual detection of bacterial contamination

The 'clear and bright' and 'white bucket' tests can also be used for testing tank bottoms, filter cans, and fuel pump drainings for the presence of microorganisms and sludge. There will be evidence that can be seen and smelled.

Put the fuel into a clean white bucket or clear glass jar. Allow the sample to settle for two minutes. Tip or swirl the container from side to side, looking for any evidence of dark colored solids, dark colored water, substances that cling to the side of the container, or a scummy mucus like material. Hold the sample in front of a light. Check to see if the solids are rust. Move a small magnet along the outside of the container. Rust particles will collect and follow the magnet. If the sample is a dark-colored, sludge-like material and it does not respond to the magnet, then it is probably bacterial contamination.

Other indicators of these microorganisms are a matty, lumpy, or stringy consistency and a rank moldy odor.

Water detection paste

Water detection pastes determine the depth of water at the bottom of the storage tank. Apply the paste in a thin coating on a gauge stick from zero up to a couple inches above the suspected oil water interface. Carefully lower the stick into the tank until it lightly touches bottom. Hold it in this position for 30 seconds to a minute. Remove the stick— the water level will be clearly indicated by a definite color change where water contacts the paste. Water paste will not detect an oil-water emulsion. You should check customers' tanks for water once a year, and then drain off the water if detected.

Oil filtration

The installation of filters in burner fuel suction lines is strongly recommended. Filters protect the pump and nozzle by trapping contaminants before they reach these components. There are passages in the oilburner nozzle that are smaller than the diameter of a human hair. It takes very little contamination to plug up these passages in the nozzle. This is why it is critical to do everything to be sure clean oil is delivered to the burner.

There are a wide variety of filters available, but they all fall into

one of two categories: spin-on filters and cartridge type filters. The spin on filter is similar to the oil filter on your car. The filter container, or can, and filter element (resin-coated filter paper with large surface area folded into a filter housing) are all one piece. The cartridge type has a replaceable filter element cartridge that you place into a filter can that attaches to the filter head. See Figure 2-2.

Filter elements are made from a variety of materials, including: wool felt, wound yarn, sintered plastic in a continuous micro-spun fiber, resin-coated paper, and stainless steel mesh. Filters are sized by flow rate gallons per hour (GPH) and pressure drop (*inches mercury Hg*). Each filter also has a micron, or mesh rating. These ratings represent the amount of pressure drop or filtration capability. The rating means the filter will remove 95% of the particles of that size or larger. A lower micron/mesh rating indicates a tighter filter construction, able to remove finer particles.

Filter elements made from sintered plastics with pore sizes in the range 30-75 microns and large surface area or spin on filters with resin-coated paper in the 10 micron range seem to work best. Most fuel units contain a 100 micron mesh strainer.

Nozzles also have a mesh or sintered bronze filter nominally rated for filtration to 40 microns. The tangential metering slots— the things that get plugged up in the nozzle—are typically 60 to 90 microns. Grease or dirt on your fingers can plug the nozzle, so they must be carefully handled. Felt and wound yarn filters may shed fine fibers that may clog low firing rate nozzles. See Figure 2-3.

To be fully effective, a modern filter must stop particles from reaching the

Figure 2-2: Filters: Cartridge type and spin-on

Replaceable Element **Spin-on Cartridge**

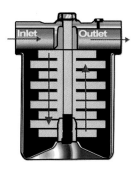 

nozzle. There are two approaches to how a filter should react when it is full. Some filters allow oil to bypass the filter when the element is full; others are designed to stop the flow of oil when they are full.

While the filters that will not allow bypass will cause a no heat call when they are full, they ensure that no particles reach the nozzle. With the bypass type filter, once the filter is full, it will allow the contaminants to flow down stream and plug the pump strainer and nozzle. This will take longer to happen, but when it does, it will require work on the burner.

Many service managers are now advocating the installation of two filters on problem installations. They install a large standard cartridge bypass filter at the tank and a 10-micron no-bypass spin-on filter at the burner.

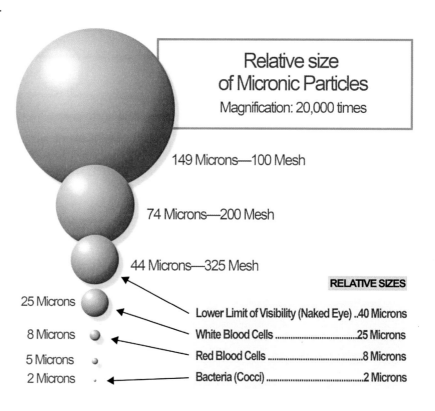

Relative size of Micronic Particles
Magnification: 20,000 times

149 Microns—100 Mesh

74 Microns—200 Mesh

44 Microns—325 Mesh

25 Microns

8 Microns

5 Microns

2 Microns

RELATIVE SIZES

Lower Limit of Visibility (Naked Eye) ..40 Microns
White Blood Cells ....25 Microns
Red Blood Cells ....8 Microns
Bacteria (Cocci) ....2 Microns

Figure 2-3: Relative size of micronic particles

Filters and sludge

Filters may fail because they have become blanketed with biologically active slime or sludge. The resulting black or gray "ball of grease" is a tough service problem. This sludge is not material that has been sucked from the tank; it is alive and actually growing in the filter.

When small particles of sludge in the oil tank are drawn into the oil line, the bacteria in these particles look for moist places to reproduce. If there is any water pocketed in the bottom of the filter canister or if there is water emulsified in the fuel, they can grow their biofilm. Contrary to popular belief, there does not have to be a layer of free water in order to support the growth of biologically active sludge. There is always some water dissolved in the fuel. This is why sludge can sometimes grow faster on filters and strainers than it can in the tank.

The rate at which sludge grows depends on the temperature and the availability of moisture and nutrients. Filters may plug, even with new tanks and lines. The "seed" sludge particles can arrive with the fuel from a contaminated tank upstream in the distribution system. They can be drawn directly into the suction line before they have a chance to settle to the bottom of the tank. If the conditions are right, a filter can plug within weeks of installation, even with

Steps to Better Fuel Performance

✓ Before removing the fill cap for a buried tank, the driver must be sure water, dirt, snow or ice cannot fall into the tank. After delivery, drivers should check gaskets and O-rings if needed on the fill cap to be sure they are in good shape, reinstall the fill cap, and make certain it is sealed tight.

✓ While making a delivery, the driver should check to be sure the vent cap is in place, there is no water around the fill, the vent pipe is solid, and there is no water in tank.

✓ On above ground outdoor tanks: are the tank legs stable on a solid foundation? Are there signs of rust, weeps, wet spots, deep scratches, or dents on the tank surface, oil leaks, or signs of spills, and does the tank need painting?

✓ Sampling of tank bottoms should be done routinely (during the tune-up) for cleanliness and lack of water.

✓ If excessive sludge and water are found, they should be removed as soon as possible.

✓ Hold up on deliveries to problem tanks until the sludge and water problem is solved.

✓ Once the sludge and water are removed from the tank: fill the tank with kerosene or specially treated fuel, tune-up the burner, hand-pump the oil lines thoroughly, then replace the filter, strainer, and nozzle. Schedule a follow-up call a month later to see to it that the tank and lines remain clean.

✓ The tank's fill boxes, fill pipes, vent caps and pipes and remote fills should be checked for cracks and leaks on every delivery and tune-up. Often the problem is a hole in the vent pipe just below ground level. Dig a few inches of soil away from the vent to check for rusting. If the fill box is in a driveway, it should be a "mushroom-type" fill box with a watertight gasket rather than a metal-to-metal fit.

✓ When additives are used, they should be added before filling the tank, if possible, to facilitate proper mixing.

an immaculately clean tank. Also, sludge is corrosive. Untreated sludge can attack the steel filter housing, causing pinhole leaks.

The answers to sludge fouling of filters is good housekeeping throughout the distribution system, keeping water out of tanks, and removing existing water. In problem jobs, the use of an effective sludge-control additive may be required. If you treat an already fouled system with an effective sludge dispersant, tiny dark particles are released from the biofilm as it breaks down. These particles are similar to those that result from fuel instability. Unstable fuel is usually dark in color—burgundy cherry to coffee colored. In both cases, the double filter system described above seems to the best answer.

Replacing the oil filter element

Cartridge type filter—shut off the oil then loosen the nut on the top of the filter head and lower the can from the head. (Use caution; the can is full of oil.) Remove the element and the gasket and clean inside the canister. Inspect the old element. Excessive sludge or evidence of water calls for action. Check the inside of the can for pitting and rust. Install the new element and new gaskets, reassemble, open the oil valve, and bleed the air out of the filter through the bleeder.

Spin-on type—shut off the oil and using a filter wrench, loosen and spin off the oil cartridge. Cut and remove the old center stud "O" ring and replace it with a new "O" ring. Remove the outside filter gasket on the new filter and apply a thin coat of petroleum jelly to both sides of the gasket. Carefully replace the filter gasket. Fill the cartridge with clean oil and spin it onto the filter head. Bleed the air from the filter.

Fuel additive treatment

Additives are designed to prevent or retard fuel deterioration. Numerous types of additives are available on the market. A successful fuel treatment program requires knowledge of the quality of the fuel in the tank and the specific service problems. Using an additive off the shelf without testing may be more harmful than doing nothing at all.

Selection of additives: The multifunctional aftermarket additives available for heating oil are proprietary products that offer a range of properties.

Guidelines:

- Define the problem and the additive that is needed.

- Make sure the fuel sample being tested represents the fuel being treated.

- Will the additive be used once, or is continuous treatment required?

- Does the additive perform more than one function?

- Does the additive supplier have technical support if there are questions or problems?

- Can the supplier provide a way to determine effectiveness in specific cases?

- Follow all safety and handling instructions on the labels and Material Safety Data Sheets that should accompany the package.

- Follow the recommended treatment rates.

- Properly dispose of the additive containers. Know and follow the local laws concerning disposal of sludge and water bottoms.

Types of additives:

Cold flow improvers: Flow improvers are designed to lower the cold temperature operability limit for the fuel, and to avoid wax plugging of the filters. Pour point reducers or anti-gels lower the temperature at which fuel gels or solidifies, and cold filter plug point reducers lowers the temperature at which wax plugs the filter. Once wax has formed in the fuel, an additive will not change the waxes present. To dissolve wax, a solvent such as kerosene, must be used.

Dispersants: Dispersants or detergents keep the little chunks of junk floating in fuel so they can slip through the fuel system and be burned, rather than letting them settle to the bottom of the tank. Initial use of dispersant may cause filter plugging as existing deposits, sludge, and dirt are broken up, suspended in the fuel and picked up by the pump.

Antioxidants and metal deactivators: Fuel degradation caused by oxidation or aging leads to gum deposits. Antioxidant additives can slow this process. Dissolved metals, such as copper, can speed aging and degradation, and produce mercaptide (sulfur containing) gels. To minimize these effects, metal deactivators combine with the metals and render them inactive. Periodic monitoring of fuel stability is recommended if these additives are being used.

Biocides: Serious problems can arise from microbial proliferation, including sludge formation, acid and surfactant formation leading to operational problems. (Translation: Critters can grow in the oil

**Figure 2-4:
Tank shed
covering an
outdoor, above
ground tank**

tank. They create a sludgy mess that will cause lots of no heat calls.) Biocides kill or prevent the growth of bacteria and other microorganisms. They must be fuel-soluble and must be able to sink to the water in the bottom of the tank where all the microbes live. Microbiological organisms in fuel are bacteria, molds, and yeast. Since biocides are poisons, you have to very careful. Read the label to determine product use, treatment rate, and human exposure hazards warnings.

Preventative maintenance

Good housekeeping means doing everything you can to minimize dirt and water from entering tanks. Water promotes the growth of microbes, which use the fuel as a food source, and accelerates the growth of sludge and internal corrosion of the tank. Water can enter the tank through cracked or leaking fill pipes and vents. They should be checked periodically and whenever water contamination is suspected. Varying air temperature and humidity can cause condensation within the tank. Dirt

and debris are generally introduced into the fuel through careless handling.

Use of rags for cleaning components
The rags used for cleaning can be a source of trouble. Using a rag contaminated with sludge or microbes can introduce these contaminates to a clean system. Also, if they are of a loose weave or have frayed edges, strings or fibers, lint from these rags can get into the system and plug the nozzle.

Tank cleaning

With massive accumulations at the bottom and on the sides of the tank, mechanical cleaning, fuel filtration, the use of additives and a preventative maintenance program are the only way to effectively remove the sludge. Portable tank cleaning/ filtration machines are available. Their effectiveness depends upon the condition of the tank, access to the interior, and the operator's skill. Before attempting to clean the tank, let the burner draw the oil down as low as possible to minimize the amount of fuel you will have to dispose. There are companies that offer tank-cleaning service. However, cleaning a residential heating oil tank is usually expensive and difficult, and a tank replacement may be more economical and effective.

Tank replacement

If the tank has gone too far, tank and fuel treatment remedies will only buy you some time. A tank's surface contains microscopic pits and craters where bacteria can 'hide." Once fresh fuel is added and a bit of water condenses, the bacteria can reproduce at an astounding rate and sludge formation begins. Often, the only solution is to replace the tank and oil lines. Never pump the oil from the old tank into the new one.

You will be transferring contaminates that caused the problem in the first place. It will take surprisingly little time to make the nice new tank as dirty as the old one.

If you are installing (or maintaining) an outdoor, above ground tank, it is recommended you paint it a light color to reflect the light. This will help keep the tank cooler and minimize moisture condensation inside the tank. Also, there are several types of tank sheds available, Figure 2-4. They minimize water build-up and frozen lines as the tank temperature is steadier.

Keep the tank full

Topping off oil tanks, especially outdoor above ground tanks in the spring, helps prevent condensation—the less air in tank, the less condensation.

Bioheat fuel®

Biofuel is a renewable, biodegradable combustible liquid fuel. Biofuel is manufactured by processing vegetable oils such as soy and rapeseed (canola). It is also made from waste cooking oils and trap grease, tallow, and animal fats such as fish

oil. Biofuel has an ASTM specification D6751 for pure biofuel (B100). It has 10-12% oxygen, so it will increase excess air to the flame. Its heating value is 125,000 Btu per gallon. It has a slightly higher density and higher cloud and pour points than #2 oil.

Bioheat fuel® is a blend of 95% or more

If you are installing (or maintaining) an outdoor, above ground tank, it is recommended you paint it a light color to reflect the light. This will help keep the tank cooler and minimize moisture condensation inside the tank. Also, there are several types of tank sheds available. They minimize water build-up and frozen lines as the tank temperature is steadier.

#2 oil and 5% or less B100 biofuel. We call a 5% blend B5. Bioheat can be used in oilburners with little or no modifications to the equipment or operating practices. While flashpoint is higher, ignition with blends of 5% or less is no problem. The viscosity is higher, yet still within ASTM limits for heating oil; but flow rate and atomization are similar. Bioheat will create slightly less deposits on the heat exchanger thanks to the reduced sulfur levels.

Bioheat fuel® has strong public appeal as a renewable fuel. It has good lubricity that will help with low sulfur fuels. It increases our fuel source diversity, reducing dependence on foreign crude and is a potentially huge market for American agriculture.

Summary

Most of our fuel problems are created in the customer's tank and heating system long after delivery. Oilheat reliability is dependent on the technicians in the field, keeping customer's systems operating at peak safety, dependability, and efficiency.

OIL TANKS & PIPING

IN THIS CHAPTER

- Oil tanks and piping

- Tank inspection procedures

Chapter 3

Oil Tanks and Piping

Introduction

The comfort, cleanliness and efficiency of today's oilheat systems rely on clean, uncontaminated fuel reaching the oilburner. To achieve this:

- Install tanks properly.

- Maintain tanks by regularly inspecting them and fixing minor defects before they lead to major problems.

- Replace aging tanks *before* they fail.

The proper installation of an oil tank is a relatively easy process, provided it is installed in accordance with the manufacturer's instructions and applicable codes and regulations are followed.

Local codes normally require you to install tanks in accordance with either their own code, the National Fire Protection Association (NFPA) or the International Code Council (ICC). It's best to check with the local authority having jurisdiction to determine which regulations you need to follow.

This chapter gives an overview of oil tanks; for more detailed information, we recommend that you read NORA's oil tank manual, *"Heating Oil Storage Tanks, Guide for Quality Installation and Maintenance."*

Why tanks fail

The most common cause of failure is corrosion—the deterioration of the tank due to reaction with its environment.

External corrosion is caused by electrical activity that occurs between different parts of the tank; between the tank and its piping; or between the tank and other metals in the area. For external corrosion to occur, there needs to be:

1. an *anode*— something to give up electrons (the tank);

2. a *cathode*— something to accept the electrical flow (piping, metals in the ground, etc.);

3. an *electrolyte*— something for the electricity to travel through (water).

There is not much you can do to prevent external corrosion in existing unprotected underground (buried) tanks. Later in this chapter, we'll show the types of tanks that can stand up to the corrosion factors that exist underground.

To reduce exterior corrosion for above-ground tanks, make sure that:

- The tank has clearance on all sides so that debris can't accumulate and hold moisture against the tank.

- There is sufficient clearance under the tank so that plant growth does not come in contact with it.

- Scratches and rust are repaired immediately.

- The tank is painted on a regular basis.

Internal corrosion is caused by sludge produced by bacteria. For internal corro-

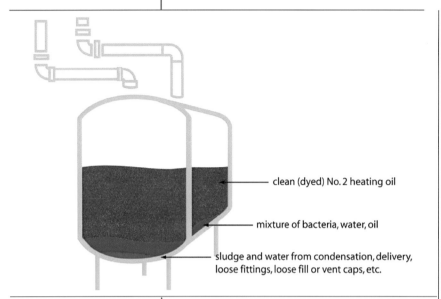

clean (dyed) No. 2 heating oil

mixture of bacteria, water, oil

sludge and water from condensation, delivery, loose fittings, loose fill or vent caps, etc.

Figure 3-1: Various layers of material in the tank

Figure 3-2: Internal corrosion with pin hole magnified

sion to occur at the tank bottom, there needs to be bacteria and water in the tank, see Figure 3-1.

The bacteria live at the oil/water interface; they "eat" the oil and create a substance that, when mixed with water, creates an acid that corrodes the metal in the tank.

The best way to reduce internal corro-

sion, Figure 3-2, is to eliminate the water at the bottom of the tank. Removing the water is just the beginning. You must also determine how the water got into the tank and take corrective steps to prevent water from building up again. Figure 3-3.

Figure 3-3: Bacterial "Bug Tracks"

The most common causes of water in tanks are:

- Condensation

- Broken tank gauges (outside tank)

- Loose or missing fill and vent caps

- Pumping oil from an old tank into a new tank

- Failing to drain water from a tank before installation.

Condensation can be greatly reduced by installing tanks indoors or in an enclosure. If a tank is located outside, you can reduce condensation by painting it a light color and protecting it from direct sunlight.

Gauges and caps should be inspected regularly and replaced when necessary.

Following manufacturer's instructions when installing new tanks and performing the inspection procedures described at the end of this Chapter, you will greatly reduce the amount of water-related problems and extend the lives of your customers' tanks.

Properly installed and maintained tanks can last for several decades—much longer than most equipment in the home. However, like everything else, tanks eventually need to be replaced.

Installation considerations

When it is time to install a new or replacement tank—answer these three questions:

- What *size* tank will be best?
- Where is the best *place* to install it?
- What *type* of tank will be best?

Size

Although large tanks are often installed for delivery efficiency, an oversized tank can cause service problems—such as:

- Poor fuel quality—fuel oil has a shelf life and deteriorates over time.
- Corrosion—larger tanks usually build up more water from condensation.

On the other hand, tanks that are too small require frequent deliveries, leading to problems during peak delivery season.

In general, the right size tank is one that holds about one-third (1/3) of the customer's annual consumption. Therefore, a customer who uses 900 gallons of oil a year should have a 275 or 330-gallon tank. (900/3 = 300)

There may be special situations that require you to install a tank that is either

larger or smaller, but in general, it is best to apply the 1/3 rule when possible.

Location

There are three possible locations for a tank installation:

1. Inside a building—usually in the basement, utility room or garage
2. Outside, above–ground
3. Outside, underground

Before selecting a tank location, be sure to consider regulations regarding setbacks from:

- Heating equipment and other ignition sources
- Property lines
- Buildings, doors, windows, vents and air intakes
- Meters

Also remember to locate the tank where:

- The delivery vehicle can safely park during filling
- It will be accessible for inspection and servicing
- An oil release will not easily enter a drain, well or waterway
- It will not be exposed to corrosion and/or damage from dripping water, falling ice, vehicles, etc.

Inside tanks

NORA recommends above ground, indoor tank installations whenever possible. These installations offer a number of advantages over outside tanks, including:

- The oil is usually warmer, which means it burns better and won't gel or have cold weather performance problems.

• There are fewer temperature changes, which means the oil will last longer.

• If a leak develops, it will cause an odor, which quickly alerts us to the problem.

• It's easier to inspect.

• Less condensation in the tank.

It is important that you follow codes and instructions regarding:

A. Distance from the tank to the burner (At least 5 feet.)

B. Size and height of the vent pipe

C. Size of the fill pipe

D. Fusible valve at the tank

E. Fusible valve at the burner

In addition:

1. The fill and vent lines must be pitched toward the tank

2. All tanks should have a vent alarm

3. All tanks should have a tank gauge

4. All systems should have an oil filter; it can be located at the tank, at the burner or at both the tank and burner.

5. The copper oil line from the tank to the burner (shown here running under the floor) should not touch concrete or soil. This can be done by sliding the copper oil lines into plastic conduit or plastic pipe or by using a coated copper line.

There should be no fittings in the copper lines below the floor. Figure 3-4.

Above-ground outside tanks

If there is no room for a tank inside the building, it must be installed outside, see Figure 3-5. In these cases, it is a good idea to install the tank in secondary containment

**Figure 3-4:
Typical indoor
installation**

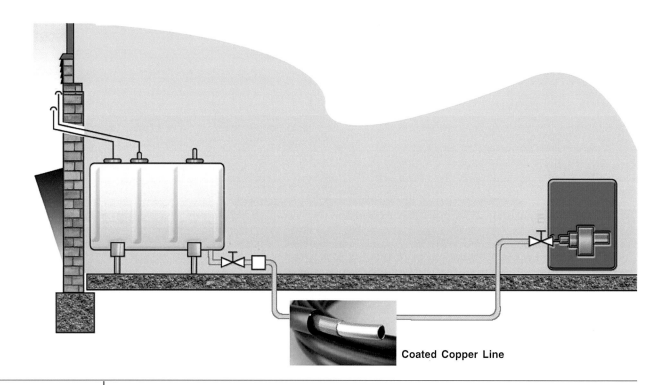

Coated Copper Line

Figure 3-5: Outside above ground tank

or in an enclosure to protect it from the elements.

The outside oil line should be connected through the top of the tank and insulated to where it enters the building. Once the line is inside, it should be connected to a

thermal shut-off valve. The oil filter should NOT be installed outside. It can be installed right after the valve where the line enters the building or at the burner.

Underground tanks

Environmental regulations and insurance concerns have greatly reduced the number of in-ground installations, Figure 3-6, and many homeowners with buried oil tanks have replaced them with above-ground tanks.

Unless there is no acceptable location available, NORA recommends that all new oil tanks be installed above ground.

Figure 3-6: Typical older underground installation

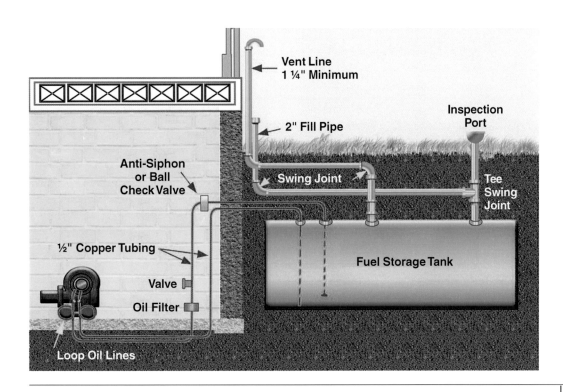

Type

Once you have determined the proper size and location to install a new tank, your customer can choose the type of tank based on price, warranty and level of spill protection. There are many choices:

Above ground tanks

Ob-round—The 275-gallon "Ob-round" steel tank, Figure 3-7, has been the standard for decades and is the most common tank. Ob-round tanks are currently available in a number of sizes from slightly over 100 gallons to 330 gallons.

Figure 3-7: Ob-round tank

Figure 3-8: Bottom tap

Newer ob-round tanks have the oil drawn from the bottom of the tank to reduce the amount of condensation and sludge build-up in the tank. Figure 3-8.

Cylindrical—These tanks are often found in mobile homes and in places where space considerations made it easier to install and service than an ob-round tank. They are typically available in sizes ranging from 160 to 320 gallons.

Figure 3-9: Externally coated tank

Externally coated ob-round—This corrosion resistant tank has a polyethylene coating on the outside of a standard ob-round tank, Figure 3-9. The coating protects the tank from external corrosion and serves as release barrier should the tank corrode internally.

Fiberglass—This corrosion proof tank is available in both single and double wall models and in 240 and 300-gallon capacities. The double wall unit is a tank within a tank— if the inner tank leaks, the outer tank prevents a release of oil, Figure 3-10.

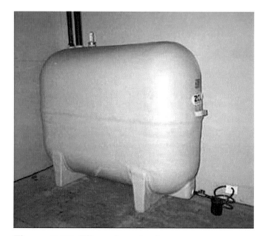

Figure 3-10: Fiberglass tank

Polyethylene/steel – These double wall tanks combine an inner tank made of polyethylene with a steel outer tank. The outer tank protects the inner tank and provides secondary containment. See Figure 3-11.

Figure 3-11: Polyethylene/steel tank

Underground tanks
Steel

Sti-P3—These tanks combine the strength of steel with a factory installed corrosion protection system, Figure 3-12. Sti-P3 tanks feature:

1. A protective coating over the steel that prevents external corrosion

Figure 3-12: Underground steel tank

2. Sacrificial anodes that protect the steel

3. Nylon isolation bushings that electrically isolate the tank from the fill pipe, vent pipe, oil lines and other attached piping

ACT-100 and ACT-100U

These tanks include a much thicker protective coating and offer protection similar to the Sti-P3 without sacrificial anodes, Figure 3-13.

Figure 3-13: ACT-100

Fiberglass (FRP)

Fiberglass reinforced plastic tanks never rust because they are made from corrosion resistant materials, Figure 3-14.

Once you've determined the right size, location and type of tank to install, you

Figure 3-14: Fiberglass (FRP) tank

must become thoroughly familiar with the current version of the manufacturer's installation instructions *before* you begin an installation.

Installation procedures

Be sure to follow the manufacturer's installation instructions and all applicable codes and regulations during the installation. This next section emphasizes some of the important steps in tank installation process.

Figure 3-14: Cover work areas

Work neat

Protect the customer's property and the components that you are installing. It is much easier to prevent a mess than to clean it up. Cover work areas with drop cloths or builder's paper or other material, Figure 3-14.

Piping connections

It is imperative that all connections are made **tight and leak proof**. All threaded connections should be joined with a pipe compound that is non-teflon, oil resistant, and remains flexible. Be careful when applying pipe compound and make sure to wipe away excess compound so it does not get into the tank or oil lines.

Fill and vent pipes

The fill and vent pipes should be made of schedule 40 steel, be pitched toward the tank and terminate outside the building at a point at least two feet from any building opening, and five feet from any air inlet or

Figure 3-15: Above ground vent pipe/fill and vent cap

flue gas outlet. All steel fittings should be malleable, not cast.

The fill pipe should be clearly marked as a fuel oil fill. The vent cap should have a screen to prevent bugs from making a nest in the vent pipe, Figure 3-15.

Vent alarms

All above ground and indoor tanks should have a vent alarm installed, Figure 3-16. The vent alarm alerts the delivery person that the tank is filled to the proper level. Vent alarms are not always required for residential buried tanks because a special filling device (vent-a fils, bazooka, deep fill, etc.) that includes a vent alarm may be used.

Figure 3-16: Vent alarm

Oil lines

For normal residential use, 1/2" O.D. oil lines are recommended. Copper oil lines should be connected with flare fittings. Compression fittings must **not** be used ("slip fittings", where the oil line enters the top of the tank, are the exception and are acceptable).

Oil lines should have as few fittings as possible and all fittings should be accessible.

Thermal shutoff valves

Indoor tanks should have a thermal safety shutoff (Firomatic®) valve in the suction line at the tank, see Figure 3-17. Outside tanks should have a shut off valve where the suction line enters the inside of the building.

Filters

An oil filter should be installed in the suction line. See Figure 3-18.

Figure 3-17: Thermal safety shutoff valve

Plug or cap

Plastic or metal plugs are used to keep water and debris out of a new tank during shipment and storage. They must be removed and discarded during installation and any unused tank openings must be plugged with threaded steel plugs.

**Figure 3-18:
Oil filter installed
in suction line**

Tank inspection procedures

Oil tanks should be inspected on a regular basis so that potential problems can be discovered and corrected before they affect tank longevity and system performance.

NORA recommends three levels of inspection—an initial inspection performed before a delivery is made to a new tank or a new customer; a routine inspection performed during routine maintenance or tune-ups; and brief, pre-delivery inspection each time the tank is filled.

1.) Initial inspections and evaluations

*NORA recommends that all tanks should be inspected and approved for delivery **before** the first delivery to a new customer or a new tank.*

An initial inspection provides the opportunity to notice flaws in the tank, not reported by the customer, which may prevent a problem in the future. It will also ensure that the fill and vent pipes are properly connected and correctly identified.

In those cases where a new tank has been installed for an existing customer, the tank inspection should include procedures to ensure that inactive fill and vent pipes have been removed.

The inspections are different for above-ground tanks and buried tanks.

2.) Routine inspections
NORA recommends that additional tank inspections be conducted as an integral part of preventative maintenance tune-ups.

While not as comprehensive as the initial inspection, routine inspections are equally important.

Routine inspections can detect problems that occur after the tank has passed the initial

inspection. For example, the tank gauge may have become defective, a tank leg may start to corrode, or another problem may have arisen long after the tank was initially approved for delivery.

In many situations, routine inspections detect minor problems that have recently started and that can be easily corrected before they cause a problem.

3.) Brief, pre-delivery inspection
NORA recommends a "no-whistle-no fill policy."

Oil delivery personnel should perform a brief visual inspection before and after each delivery. While this inspection normally isn't documented, it's important that fuel drivers understand the need to verify addresses and check tanks for obvious defects before and after delivery.

The step-by-step inspection procedures for above ground and underground tanks are on the following pages.

Figure 3-19: Inspection of above ground tank

Tank
Evaluation
Forms

Use the forms on the following pages to evaluate tank integrity and maintenance requirements.

Initial Fuel Oil Storage Tank Evaluation – Above Ground Tanks

Revised May 2006

Customer Name: ____

Address: ____

Town: ______________________ State: _____ Zip: ______________

Telephone: ____

TANK

Tank location			__________
If outside, is the tank protected by an enclosure?	☐ N/A	☐ Yes	☐ No
Is the tank installed with full secondary containment?		☐ Yes	☐ No
Tank size?			__________
Tank height?			__________
Tank type?			__________
Tank age?			__________
Tank condition satisfactory, including legs and pad or foundation?		☐ Yes	☐ No
Tank properly secured in flood prone areas?	☐ N/A	☐ Yes	☐ No
Any evidence of historic oil spills?		☐ Yes	☐ No
System checked for oil leaks?		☐ Yes	☐ No
Amount of oil in tank?			__________
Any water in tank?		☐ Yes	☐ No
If yes, how many inches?			__________
Tank gauge properly installed and accurate?		☐ Yes	☐ No
Tank bottom at least 6″ off ground?		☐ Yes	☐ No
Tank at least 5 feet from burner or other sources of fire or flame?		☐ Yes	☐ No
Evidence of excessive external corrosion?		☐ Yes	☐ No
Unused openings properly plugged?		☐ Yes	☐ No

Comments: ____

____

____

FILL PIPE

Pipe size			__________
Pitched toward tank?		☐ Yes	☐ No
Proper material?		☐ Yes	☐ No
In good condition?		☐ Yes	☐ No
Fill cap in place and in good condition?		☐ Yes	☐ No
Fill positioned to avoid buildup of water and snow?		☐ Yes	☐ No
Properly piped, outside at least 2′ from windows or openings?		☐ Yes	☐ No
Fill properly tagged?		☐ Yes	☐ No
Old fill pipe removed?	☐ N/A	☐ Yes	☐ No

Comments: ____

____

____

VENT PIPE

Pipe size		_____
Pitched toward tank?	☐ Yes	☐ No
Proper material?	☐ Yes	☐ No
In good condition?	☐ Yes	☐ No
Vent visible from fill?	☐ Yes	☐ No
Vent alarm installed?	☐ Yes	☐ No
Vent cap in place and in good condition?	☐ Yes	☐ No
Vent free of obstructions?	☐ Yes	☐ No
Positioned to avoid buildup of water and snow?	☐ Yes	☐ No
Higher than fill pipe?	☐ Yes	☐ No
Properly piped, outside at least 2' from windows or openings and 5' from appliance air inlets or flue gas outlets?	☐ Yes	☐ No

Comments: _____

OIL LINES

Line size			_____
Proper material?		☐ Yes	☐ No
Oil lines encapsulated?		☐ Yes	☐ No
Working shutoff at tank?		☐ Yes	☐ No
OSV valve installed?		☐ Yes	☐ No
All lines properly connected to tank and burner?		☐ Yes	☐ No
Outside exposed lines insulated?	☐ N/A	☐ Yes	☐ No
Any compression fittings?		☐ Yes	☐ No
Oil filter properly installed?		☐ Yes	☐ No
Fusible valves properly located?		☐ Yes	☐ No

Comments: _____

This tank is acceptable for fuel delivery.	☐ **Yes**	☐ **No**

This tank will be acceptable for delivery once the following defects are corrected:

_____

This tank is NOT acceptable and must be replaced prior to delivery.	☐ **Yes**	☐ **No**

Comments: _____

Inspected by: _____Date: _____

NORA ID: _____Date of NORA certification: _____

Company: _____

Town: _____ State: _____ Zip: _____

Telephone : _____

Page 2 of 2

PLEASE NOTE: The visual tank inspection performed by Certified Tank Inspector was limited to the items inspected on the tank as noted on this inspection form, and does not cover any other area of the house or property, or parts of the tank system not visible. The inspection conducted and the results reported on this Inspection Report represent the visible condition(s) of the tank present on the day of inspection only. This inspection should not be construed as an opinion or prediction of the condition of the tank in the future. Conditions involving the tank(s) may change in the future, and future inspections are recommended. If you notice a change in the condition of the tank, please contact your retail Oilheat company immediately.

INITIAL EVALUATION FOR ABOVE GROUND TANKS

Initial Fuel Oil Storage Tank Evaluation – In Ground Tanks
Revised May 2006

Name: _____

Address: _____

Town: _____ State: _____ Zip:_____

Telephone: _____

TANK

Tank location   _____

Tank size?   _____

Tank type?   _____

Tank age?   _____

Any evidence of historic oil spills?   ☐ Yes   ☐ No

Amount of oil in tank?   _____

Any water in tank?   ☐ Yes   ☐ No

If yes, how many inches?   _____

Comments: _____
_____
_____

FILL PIPE

Pipe Size   _____

Proper material?   ☐ Yes   ☐ No

In good condition?   ☐ Yes   ☐ No

Fill cap in place and in good condition?   ☐ Yes   ☐ No

Fill positioned to avoid buildup of water and snow?   ☐ Yes   ☐ No

Properly piped, outside at least 2' from windows or openings?   ☐ Yes   ☐ No

Fill properly tagged?   ☐ Yes   ☐ No

Old fill pipe removed?   ☐ N/A   ☐ Yes   ☐ No

Comments: _____
_____
_____

VENT PIPE

Pipe Size   _____

Proper material?   ☐ Yes   ☐ No

In good condition?   ☐ Yes   ☐ No

Vent visible from fill?   ☐ Yes   ☐ No

Vent cap in place and in good condition?   ☐ Yes   ☐ No

Positioned to avoid buildup of water and snow?   ☐ Yes   ☐ No

Higher than fill pipe?   ☐ Yes   ☐ No

Properly piped, outside at least 2' from windows or openings
and 5' from appliance air inlets or flue gas outlets?   ☐ Yes   ☐ No

Comments: _____
_____

OIL LINES

Line size   _____

Proper material?	☐ Yes	☐ No
Oil lines encapsulated?	☐ Yes	☐ No
Working shutoff at wall?	☐ Yes	☐ No
OSV valve installed?	☐ Yes	☐ No
Lines properly connected to tank and burner?	☐ Yes	☐ No
Outside exposed lines insulated? ☐ N/A	☐ Yes	☐ No
Any compression fittings?	☐ Yes	☐ No
Oil filter properly installed?	☐ Yes	☐ No
Fusible valves properly located?	☐ Yes	☐ No

Comments: _____

_____

_____

This tank is acceptable for fuel delivery.   ☐ **Yes**   ☐ **No**

This tank will be acceptable for delivery once the following defects are corrected:

_____

_____

This tank is NOT acceptable and must be replaced prior to delivery.   ☐ **Yes**   ☐ **No**

Comments: _____

_____

_____

Inspected by: _____Date: _____

NORA ID: _____Date of NORA certification: _____

Company: _____

Town: _____ State: _____ Zip:_____

Telephone :_____

PLEASE NOTE: The visual tank inspection performed by Certified Tank Inspector was limited to the items inspected on the tank as noted on this inspection form, and does not cover any other area of the house or property, or parts of the tank system not visible. The inspection conducted and the results reported on this Inspection Report represent the visible condition(s) of the tank present on the day of inspection only. This inspection should not be construed as an opinion or prediction of the condition of the tank in the future. Conditions involving the tank(s) may change in the future, and future inspections are recommended. If you notice a change in the condition of the tank, please contact your retail Oilheat company immediately.

INITIAL EVALUATION FOR IN GROUND TANKS

Routine Fuel Oil Storage Tank Evaluation – Above Ground Tanks
Revised May 2006

Name:_____ Phone:_____

Address: _____

Town: _____ State: _____ Zip:_____

TANK

Tank properly secured in flood prone areas?	☐ N/A	☐ Yes	☐ No
Any evidence of historic oil spills?		☐ Yes	☐ No
Tank checked for oil leaks?		☐ Yes	☐ No
Amount of oil in tank?			_____
Any water in tank?		☐ Yes	☐ No
If yes, how many inches?			_____
Tank gauge in good condition?		☐ Yes	☐ No
Tank at least 5 feet from burner or other sources of fire or flame?		☐ Yes	☐ No
Evidence of excessive external corrosion?		☐ Yes	☐ No
Unused openings properly plugged?		☐ Yes	☐ No

Comments: _____

FILL PIPE

In good condition?	☐ Yes	☐ No
Fill cap in place and in good condition?	☐ Yes	☐ No
Fill positioned to avoid buildup of water and snow?	☐ Yes	☐ No
Fill properly identified?	☐ Yes	☐ No

Comments: _____

VENT PIPE

In good condition?	☐ Yes	☐ No
Vent cap in place and in good condition?	☐ Yes	☐ No
Vent free of obstructions?	☐ Yes	☐ No
Positioned to avoid buildup of water and snow?	☐ Yes	☐ No

Comments: _____

OIL LINES

Working shutoff at tank?		☐ Yes	☐ No
All lines properly connected to tank and burner?		☐ Yes	☐ No
Outside exposed lines insulated?	☐ N/A	☐ Yes	☐ No

Comments: _____

This tank is still acceptable for fuel delivery   ☐ **Yes**   ☐ **No**

Inspected by: _____Date: _____

PLEASE NOTE: The visual tank inspection performed by Certified Tank Inspector was limited to the items inspected on the tank as noted on this inspection form, and does not cover any other area of the house or property, or parts of the tank system not visible. The inspection conducted and the results reported on this Inspection Report represent the visible condition(s) of the tank present on the day of inspection only. This inspection should not be construed as an opinion or prediction of the condition of the tank in the future. Conditions involving the tank(s) may change in the future, and future inspections are recommended. If you notice a change in the condition of the tank, please contact your retail Oilheat company immediately.

ROUTINE EVALUATION FOR ABOVE GROUND TANKS

Routine Fuel Oil Storage Tank Evaluation – In Ground Tanks
Revised May 2006

Name: _____ Phone: _____

Address: _____

Town: _____ State: _____ Zip: _____

TANK

Any evidence of historic oil spills?	☐ Yes	☐ No
Amount of oil in tank?		_____
Any water in tank?	☐ Yes	☐ No
If yes, how many inches?		_____

Comments: _____

FILL PIPE

In good condition?	☐ Yes	☐ No
Fill cap in place and in good condition?	☐ Yes	☐ No
Fill positioned to avoid buildup of water and snow?	☐ Yes	☐ No
Fill properly identified?	☐ Yes	☐ No

Comments: _____

VENT PIPE

In good condition?	☐ Yes	☐ No
Vent cap in place and in good condition?	☐ Yes	☐ No
Vent free of obstructions?	☐ Yes	☐ No
Positioned to avoid buildup of water and snow?	☐ Yes	☐ No

Comments: _____

_____

_____

OIL LINES

Working shutoff at wall?		☐ Yes	☐ No
All lines properly connected to burner?		☐ Yes	☐ No
Outside exposed lines insulated?	☐ N/A	☐ Yes	☐ No

Comments: _____

This tank is still acceptable for fuel delivery.   ☐ **Yes**   ☐ **No**

Comments: _____

_____

Inspected by: _____ Date: _____

PLEASE NOTE: The visual tank inspection performed by Certified Tank Inspector was limited to the items inspected on the tank as noted on this inspection form, and does not cover any other area of the house or property, or parts of the tank system not visible. The inspection conducted and the results reported on this Inspection Report represent the visible condition(s) of the tank present on the day of inspection only. This inspection should not be construed as an opinion or prediction of the condition of the tank in the future. Conditions involving the tank(s) may change in the future, and future inspections are recommended. If you notice a change in the condition of the tank, please contact your retail Oilheat company immediately.

ROUTINE EVALUATION FOR IN GROUND TANKS

Pre-Delivery Procedure/Discrepancy Report – Above Ground Tanks
Revised May 2006

Name: _____

Address: _____

Town: _____ State: _____ Zip: _____

Telephone: _____

LOCATION

Address verified?	☐ Yes	☐ No
Delivery instructions verified?	☐ Yes	☐ No
Tank location verified?	☐ Yes	☐ No

TANK: If the tank is readily accessible check the following:

Amount of oil in tank?		_____
Any water in tank?	☐ Yes	☐ No
If yes, how many inches?		_____
Tank gauge in good condition?	☐ Yes	☐ No
Any evidence of historic spills?	☐ Yes	☐ No
Tank condition satisfactory including legs and foundation?	☐ Yes	☐ No
Unused openings properly plugged?	☐ Yes	☐ No

FILL PIPE

In good condition?	☐ Yes	☐ No
Fill cap in place and in good condition?	☐ Yes	☐ No

VENT PIPE

In good condition?	☐ Yes	☐ No
Vent cap in place and in good condition?	☐ Yes	☐ No
Vent free of obstructions?	☐ Yes	☐ No
Positioned to avoid buildup of water and snow?	☐ Yes	☐ No
Vent alarm working properly?	☐ Yes	☐ No

OIL LINES

Outside exposed lines insulated?	☐ N/A	☐ Yes	☐ No

FINAL SCAN

Checked for oil leaks after delivery?	☐ Yes	☐ No

Comments: _____

_____

_____

Inspected by: _____ Date: _____

PLEASE NOTE: The visual tank inspection performed by Certified Tank Inspector was limited to the items inspected on the tank as noted on this inspection form, and does not cover any other area of the house or property, or parts of the tank system not visible. The inspection conducted and the results reported on this Inspection Report represent the visible condition(s) of the tank present on the day of inspection only. This inspection should not be construed as an opinion or prediction of the condition of the tank in the future. Conditions involving the tank(s) may change in the future, and future inspections are recommended. If you notice a change in the condition of the tank, please contact your retail Oilheat company immediately.

PRE-DELIVERY INSPECTION FOR ABOVE GROUND TANKS

Pre-Delivery Procedure/Discrepancy Report Form – In Ground Tanks
Revised May 2006

Name: _____

Address: _____

Town: _____ State: _____ Zip: _____

Telephone: _____

LOCATION

Address verified? ☐ Yes ☐ No

Delivery instructions verified? ☐ Yes ☐ No

Tank location verified? ☐ Yes ☐ No

TANK

Any evidence of historic oil spills? ☐ Yes ☐ No

Amount of oil in tank? _____

Any water in tank? ☐ Yes ☐ No

If yes, how many inches? _____

FILL PIPE

In good condition? ☐ Yes ☐ No

Positioned to avoid buildup of water and snow? ☐ Yes ☐ No

Fill cap in place and in good condition? ☐ Yes ☐ No

Fill properly identified? ☐ Yes ☐ No

VENT PIPE

In good condition? ☐ Yes ☐ No

Vent cap in place and in good condition? ☐ Yes ☐ No

Positioned to avoid buildup of water and snow? ☐ Yes ☐ No

Vent free of obstructions? ☐ Yes ☐ No

Vent alarm working properly? ☐ Yes ☐ No

FINAL SCAN

Verified that no oil spilled during delivery? ☐ Yes ☐ No

Comments:

_____

_____

_____

Inspected by: _____ Date: _____

PLEASE NOTE: The visual tank inspection performed by Certified Tank Inspector was limited to the items inspected on the tank as noted on this inspection form, and does not cover any other area of the house or property, or parts of the tank system not visible. The inspection conducted and the results reported on this Inspection Report represent the visible condition(s) of the tank present on the day of inspection only. This inspection should not be construed as an opinion or prediction of the condition of the tank in the future. Conditions involving the tank(s) may change in the future, and future inspections are recommended. If you notice a change in the condition of the tank, please contact your retail Oilheat company immediately.

PRE-DELIVERY INSPECTION FOR IN GROUND TANKS

FUEL UNITS
& OIL VALVES

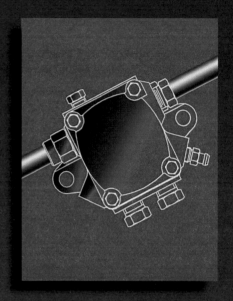

IN THIS CHAPTER

- **Fuel units and oil valves**

- **Troubleshooting oil storage and supply systems**

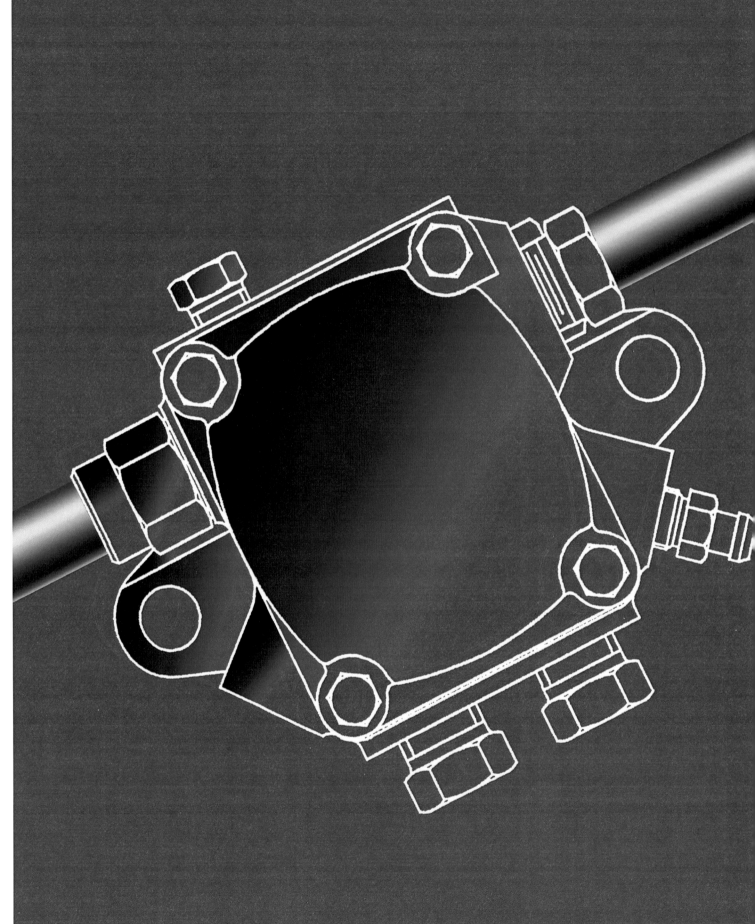

Chapter 4

Fuel Units and Oil Valves

Figure 4-2:
Cutaway of oil
valve

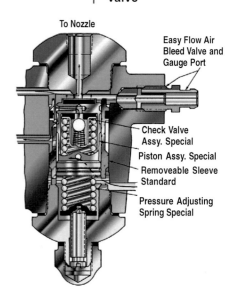

Introduction

Function of fuel units: These components lift the oil from the tank to the burner, deliver oil at a constant and regulated pressure to the nozzle, and provide clean cutoff of fuel.

Component parts of the fuel unit

• The fuel unit contains a set of machined gears, which provide both vacuum and pressure. The single stage fuel unit, Figure 4-1, contains one set of fuel pump gears.

• The pressure-regulating valve controls the pressure of the oil discharged to the nozzle. A cutaway of this valve is shown in Figure 4-2. This assembly consists of a valve body and matching piston. In the closed position, the piston is held against the nozzle discharge port by a

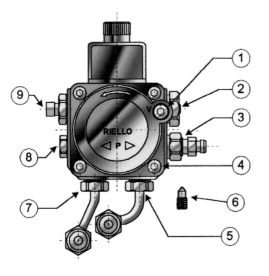

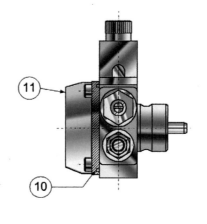

Figure 4-1: Single stage fuel unit

No.	Description
1	Vacuum Gauge Connection Port
2	Pressure Regulator Adjustment Screw
3	Pressure Gauge Connection Port and Bleeder
4	Pump Cover Screws
5	Return Fuel Line Port
6	By-pass Plug
7	Supply Fuel Line Port
8	Capillary Tube Connection Port
9	Oil Delivery Port
10	Pump Cover O-ring
11	Pump Cover

spring located behind the piston. When the fuel pump gears develop sufficient pressure to overcome the spring tension, the piston is forced back, allowing oil to flow through the nozzle discharge port. The pressure adjusting screw regulates the spring tension controlling the pressure of the oil discharged to the nozzle.

- The strainer screen, see Figure 4-3, within the fuel unit reservoir, filters the incoming oil and helps to prevent any contamination from entering the nozzle.

    - A solid shaft extending through the pump housing seal drives the gear pump. The end of this shaft is connected to the burner motor by a flexible coupling. (Note that the

R.P.M. rating of the gear pump must be the same as the burner motor.)

- A shaft seal is provided to prevent oil from leaking out of the fuel pump housing around the rotating shaft. Lubrication is provided to this seal through internal porting.

Operation of the single stage fuel unit

The single stage fuel pump, Figure 4-4, produces both pressure and vacuum. Pressure is the force created by the meshing of the pump gears, and is expressed in pounds per square inch (PSI). Pressure moves the oil away from the pump. Vacuum is expressed in inches of mercury, and is abbreviated as *in. Hg*. Normally we simply show the numerical value of the

Figure 4-3: Strainer screen and gasket.

Figure 4-4: Suntec Industries; Cutaway example single stage fuel unit

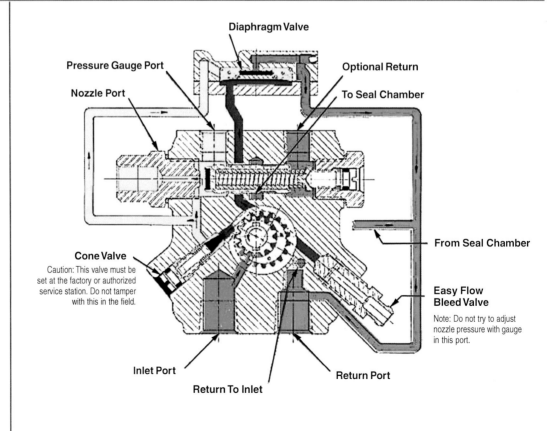

vacuum with an inch (") mark. Example: 10" of vacuum. Vacuum brings oil to the pump. We need about .75" to 1" Hg of vacuum for each foot we lift the oil, 1" of vacuum for each 10 feet of horizontal run, and ½" for a clean oil filter. For example, if we have 4 feet of lift from an underground tank, plus 10 feet of oil line run to the burner, and add the oil filter, the calculated vacuum reading should be 5.5". A vacuum gauge reading of from 5" to 6" is acceptable.

When the motor turns the pump shaft, oil enters the strainer chamber through the intake port, either by gravity or by the vacuum developed on the intake side of the gear pump. As the gears rotate, the teeth squeeze the oil and discharge it on the pressure side to the pressure regulating valve. The pressure adjusting screw on the regulating valve controls spring tension, which determines the pressure at which the oil will force the piston open and be discharged through the nozzle port. This pressure is about 80% to 95% of the operating pressure. The minimum factory set operating pressure is 100 PSI.

The pump can deliver 5 to 20 times the amount of oil required by the nozzle. This excess oil is bypassed by the pressure regulating system and returned to the strainer chamber. The total oil capacity of a gearset is referred to as TGSC or Total Gear Set Capacity. The bypassed oil returns through internal porting in the pressure regulating valve and pump body. As the excess return oil is no longer at pressure, some of this oil is used for the lubrication of the shaft pump seal.

In order for the excess oil to return to the strainer chamber, the bypass plug located between the pump and the strainer chamber must not be installed. If this plug were in place, the excess oil could not

return to the strainer chamber and would require a return line from the pump back to the tank. If there were no return line, the high-pressure oil would be forced into the front seal chamber, which would rupture this seal. In most pressure fuel units, this seal can only withstand 10 PSI of pressure. You should always check to be sure that the bypass plug has not been installed when using the unit on a one pipe installation. The bypass plug is only installed when using a two pipe system.

For acceptable vacuum, figure 1" Hg per foot of lift plus 1" per ten feet horizontal run and add 1/2" for the oil filter

Pressure regulating valve operation

The discharge oil pressure of the fuel unit can be adjusted between 100 and 200 PSI. Normal pressure setting on a high-pressure burner is 100 PSI, but some burners are designed for higher oil pressure. For variations in this pressure setting and its resulting effect on nozzle performance, see the Nozzle Chapter # 5, of this manual. Also refer to manufacturers' specifications for recommended pump pressure on flame retention burners.

On burner shutdown, spring tension against the pressure regulating piston will cause the piston to close, shutting off oil discharge to the nozzle at a pressure approximately 20 percent below operating pressure. Therefore, if the pump pressure is adjusted to its normal operating 100 PSI, the shutoff pressure will be about 80 PSI. For pumps with high-speed cut off, the cut off pressure may be different than 20 percent. What is important is that the pressure should drop and hold.

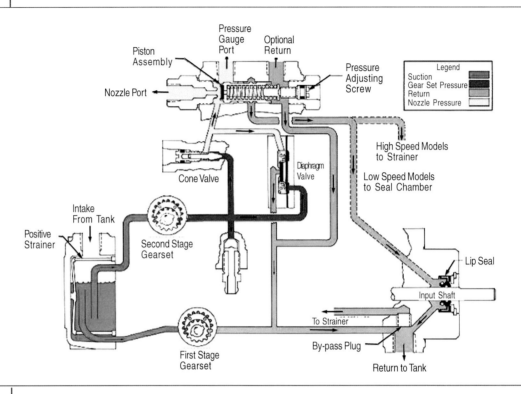

Figure 4-5:
Suntec Industries;
cutaway example
two-stage
fuel unit

One pipe system

Most of today's Oilheat systems require only a suction line to bring the oil from the tank to the burner. We call these *one pipe systems*. Older single stage fuel units should be piped only as one pipe where oil can flow to the unit under gravity conditions; that is, the burner is located level with or lower than the bottom of the oil tank.

Newer single stage pumps operate at a maximum of 6" of vacuum on a one pipe system. They can create much more, but the oil will begin to give us trouble over 6". If your calculated vacuum is less than 6" and you are using a new fuel unit, it should be installed one pipe.

Two pipe system

If more than 6" of vacuum is required, a single stage fuel unit should be piped with a return line to the tank or fuel de-aerator. This is called a *two pipe system*. An example of such an installation would be an abnormally long run from the oil tank to the unit. If a single stage fuel unit two pipe system has an operating intake vacuum over 10", unstable flame conditions, carboned-up firing assembly, after fire, and noisy flame may result. High vacuum may also shorten the life of the fuel unit.

Two stage fuel unit, two pipe system

If more than 10" of vacuum is required, you should install a two stage pump or booster pump. The two-stage fuel unit has two sets of fuel pump gears. The first set purges the pump of air and supplies an

uninterrupted flow of oil to the second
stage that pressurizes the oil to the nozzle.
Figure 4-5 shows the oil flow in a two
stage pump. The first gear set provides the
vacuum to fill the strainer chamber as well
as the low pressure oil supply to lubricate
the shaft seal. From the shaft seal chamber,
the oil flows to the low-pressure side of the
pressure regulating valve and then back to
the tank. The second set of gears provides
the pressure for the oil taken from the
strainer chamber, with the surplus oil being
bypassed through the porting in the
pressure regulating valve and back to the
strainer chamber.

Note that the bypass plug is installed in
this unit because two stage pumps must
always be two pipe. If a two-stage pump is
connected to one pipe, it becomes a single
stage pump. The first stage will only take
oil from the cover and return it to the
cover. Installing two stage pumps on one-
line systems is a waste of money. Not only
does the pump cost more, it also uses more
electricity to turn the second set of gears.

Even though single stage pumps are
capable of creating 20" of vacuum, we
need two stage pumps because fuel oil
starts to break up or "vaporize" at vacuum
levels as low as 6.7" (Figure 4-6). When
this happens, foamy oil collects in the
pump and the pump begins to cavitate. The
pump sends this foam directly to the
nozzle, causing unstable atomization,
smoke, and soot. Also when the burner
shuts down, the air bubbles in the nozzle
expand, pushing oil out of the orifice,
creating after drip. The two stage pump
may correct the foaming oil problem. The
first set of gears brings the oil into the
pump, and returns any foam back to the
tank via the return line. It is important to
use the lower intake port so even at 17" of

Figure 4-6

Figure 4-7

vacuum, only foam free oil is picked up
and delivered to the nozzle. It is recommended that all two-stage pumps be
mounted right side up so the air will collect
in the top of the pump and can be sent back
to the tank.

In a two pipe system with a two stage
fuel unit, it is not advisable to exceed 17"
of intake vacuum. Figure 4-7 shows the
effect that 20" of vacuum has on a pump.
With long oil line runs where excess
vacuum is required, or for overhead

Figure 4-8: Booster pump

burners, the use of a booster pump is required, Figure 4-8. The installation and associated piping of a system using a booster fuel pump is fully described later in this section.

Avoid two pipe systems

Two pipe oil systems should be avoided if possible. With a two-pipe system you are filtering way too much oil. The average oil pump, pumps over 15 gallons of oil an hour. The average burner fires at 1 gallon per hour. This means you are filtering over 15 gallons of oil for every one burned. You are using up the filter 15 times faster than needed. You are cleaning the oil tank through the filter. This is very expensive and inconvenient.

The second problem is that the average return line is under about two pounds of pressure. A lot of oil can leak out of a small pinhole under two pounds pressure in the hundreds of hours a year a burner runs. The burner will not be affected by a return line leak. The only way you know you have a leak is when the customer runs out of oil or the oil shows up in the sump pump pit. This is way too late!

If these were not reasons enough, it appears that two pipe systems are sludge machines. Copper is a catalyst that can affect hydrocarbons. Prolonged exposure to copper causes little hydrocarbon molecules to clump together into big, long hydrocarbon strings. They can plug up nozzles, strainers, and filters. Since we pump over 15 gallons an hour and burn only one, think of how many times each little hydrocarbon molecule has to travel back and forth to the burner through all that copper pipe before it is finally burned. On each trip the fuel gets a bit less stable and a few more hydrocarbon strings show up in the tank.

Most fuel pump manufacturers say that the maximum vacuum for a one pipe system is 6"; therefore to convert from two pipe to one pipe, your calculated vacuum must be less than 6". If you need over 6", consider installing a de-aerator in the oil line, especially if the line comes out of the top of the tank, so the pump will not get air bound.

Fuel de-aerators

Fuel de-aerators shown in Figure 4-9 have been developed to eliminate air problems caused by excessive vacuum. Here is how the system works:

1. Oil is drawn from the tank to the de-aerators through a single pipe. A dual-pipe system, operating between the unit and the oil pump allows the device to remove the air. Only the amount of oil that is burned is replaced from the oil tank. The single pipe system eliminates the need to circulate unnecessary oil and its impurities throughout the system.

Figure 4-9: Fuel de-aerator

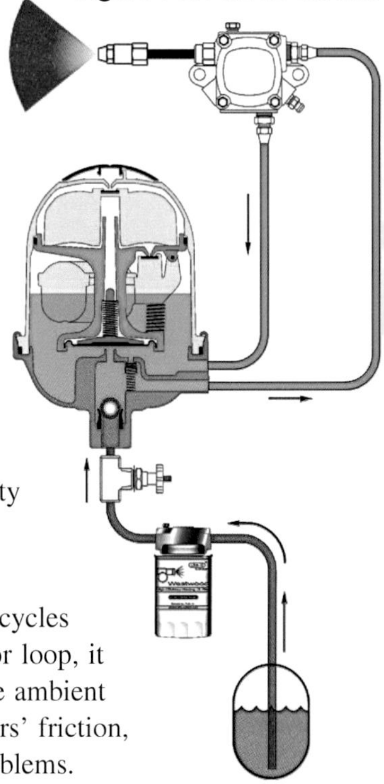

2. The surplus oil is pumped back to the de-aerator, instead of back to the tank.

3. De-aeration increases the pump's suction capacity while reducing its sensitivity to minor leaks in the suction line.

4. As surplus oil cycles through the de-aerator loop, it absorbs heat from the ambient air and the pump gears' friction, reducing cold oil problems.

Booster fuel units

Booster fuel units are normally used to assure an adequate supply of oil to one or more overhead furnaces. They are usually capable of lifting oil 15 feet and supplying the oil up to 35 feet above the pump. They can be used as continuous or intermittent duty transfer units for filling a small overhead feeder tank or for other similar purposes. Booster pumps are a fuel unit and motor. Figure 4-10 shows a Booster Fuel Unit.

Figure 4-10: Booster fuel unit

The pressure regulating valve assembly functions as a relief valve. A vacuum breaker is recommended as a protection to insure an instantaneous supply of oil when more than one burner is being supplied.

Piping: Suction and return lines should be sized to the specific model boost pump and lift location. Follow manufacturers' instructions. All fittings should be of the flare type. A return line from the fuel pump bypass connection to the tank is required in all installations. Extend the return line to the same depth in the tank as the suction line. Also check local code before making the installation. Figure 4-11 shows the input or low pressure side of the installation. The Auxiliary Tank Installation shown in Figure 4-12 is another way of hooking up multiple suspended furnaces.

Figure 4-13 on following page shows a Pressurized System installation.

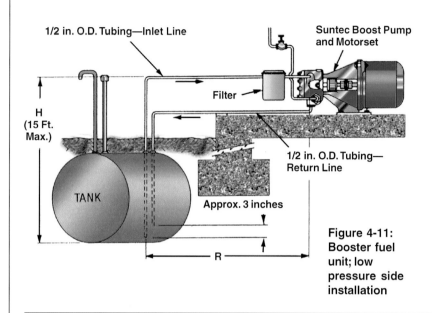

Figure 4-11: Booster fuel unit; low pressure side installation

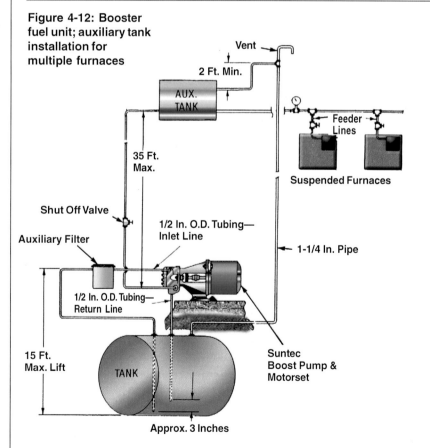

Figure 4-12: Booster fuel unit; auxiliary tank installation for multiple furnaces

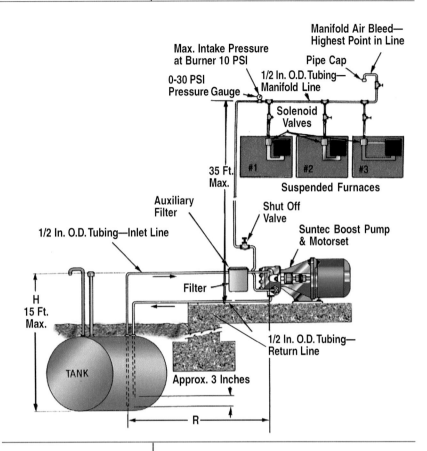

Figure 4-13:
Booster fuel unit;
pressurized
system
installation

Pumps with integral solenoid valves

There are two types of pumps with built in electronic shut off valves called integral solenoid valves. One is the blocking valve pump and the other is the by-pass valve pump.

The blocking valve stops the flow of oil to the nozzle just like an externally mounted solenoid valve does. With this pump, the oil is shut off two ways: with the electric valve, and the pressure regulating valve.

The by-pass valve pump has a valve that controls the flow of oil to the nozzle indirectly by diverting oil flow inside the pump. When it is time to shut off the oil flow the dumping valve opens, causing the pressure to drop quickly and the pressure regulating valve to close sooner. This is opposite the blocking valve operation. When the blocking valve opens, oil flows; when the dumping valve opens, oil stops.

Either type of valve will give you quick cutoff, but to get delayed cut-in, and cleaner starts, you need either a valve-on delay primary control, a hydro-mechanical pump delay, or an electric delay device.

Servicing and testing the fuel unit

Primary venting and bleeding

In a one pipe system, when a pump runs out of oil or picks up air due to high vacuum or a leak or break in the oil supply line, the air must be bled from the fuel unit and line after the tank is filled or the supply line is repaired. Failure to do this properly can cause pulsation, changes in flame condition, or excessive dripping at the nozzle after the burner shuts off. There are two methods for air elimination in a one pipe system. If the system is a gravity feed and

Fuel unit limitations

1. NFPA31, the National oilburner code, limits the shaft seal pressure to 3 PSI, although most pumps can take up to 10 PSI.

2. Single-stage pumps should not be operated beyond 6" of vacuum when hooked up one pipe. Single stage, two pipe installations should not be operated above 10" of vacuum.

3. Two-stage pumps should generally operate below 12" of vacuum because at very high vacuums, oil foams within the pump.

the unit is mounted so that the oil supply line enters at the bottom of the unit, the inlet port plug in the cover may be loosened and removed. This will allow the oil to flow by gravity into the unit and fill the strainer chamber. Then the intake port plug should be replaced and the burner fired.

If it is not possible to fill the strainer chamber in this manner, then the bleeder plug on the side of the regulating valve chamber should be loosened, the burner operated, and sufficient oil allowed to flow from this plug to purge the entire system of air until there is a steady stream of oil. If the pump has been completely drained of oil it may be necessary to remove the supply line and fill the unit with oil before adequate suction can be obtained. In the newer units, an Allen screw, or easy bleed plug, Figure 4-14, has been provided in this port to allow for bleeding. Continue to bleed the pump for 15 seconds after the last air bubble can be detected. After bleeding the unit, always check the flame for stability and burner shutdown to be sure all

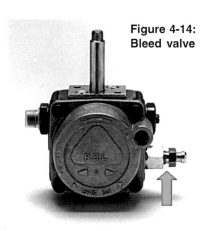

**Figure 4-14:
Bleed valve**

air has been purged from the system. Venting of air is normally not necessary in a two pipe system with a two stage pump,

but may be done faster if the bleeder plug is opened to expel air.

Vacuum power bleed

If the oil lines run above the oil tank and back down to the burner (a siphon system) proper bleeding of the pump is crucial. To bleed a pump line and everything else all the way back to the tank, do the following: First fill the pump with oil. Place a hose over the bleeder. A device like the one shown in Figure 4-15 works well for this purpose. Open the bleeder one-half turn. Make sure that the open end of the bleed hose is immersed in oil in your pail or

**Figure 4-15:
Bleeder
wrench**

bucket. Close the inlet valve at the tank and start the burner. Wait until the pump starts to whine. If you have a vacuum gauge inserted, it will show 20" to 25" of vacuum. (If white smoke starts coming out of the hose, you didn't fill the pump and the oil is burning.) Open the inlet valve and bleed for several minutes. After a tune-up, you would see some oil, then lots of bubbles and then air free oil. Once it's bled out, close the bleeder with the pump running.

Field pressure and cutoff checks

Two of the most important service checks for a fuel unit are the output pressure check and the cutoff pressure

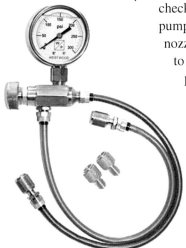

**Figure 4-16:
Pressure
tester**

check. These checks can be made on some pumps by inserting a pressure gauge into a nozzle port, with others a tester may have to be used, Figure 4-16. You will need a pressure gauge capable of reading at least 300 PSI.

First operate the burner to determine fuel unit pressure, which should normally be adjusted to 100 PSI or more depending on the burner manufacturer's recommendations. Turn the pressure regulator adjusting screw (normally clockwise) until the pressure increases 40 to 50 pounds (but not above 200). If the pump cannot achieve at least 150 pounds, the pump gears or regulating valve are worn out and you should replace the pump. Then back off the pressure adjusting screw (counterclockwise) to the desired operating pressure.

Uneven or fluctuating pressure can cause severe flame pulsation. A pulsating pressure reading (gauge needle jumps about from high to low) may indicate:

1. A partially clogged filter or pump strainer.

2. Air may be present in the pump caused by:

   a. Loose strainer chamber cover or defective strainer chamber gasket.

   b. Air leak in the suction line.

   c. Excessive intake vacuum.

3. Slipping pump coupling.

Note: Slight regular vibrations of the needle are considered normal as the resonance frequency of gauges is very close to gearset frequency. Liquid filled gauges can help dampen or eliminate frequency vibrations and are preferred.

If a fuel unit operating pressure of at least 100 PSI cannot be obtained, the problem may be, in addition to the above items, one of the following:

1. Worn pump gears.

2. Nozzle capacity beyond pump capacity.

3. Motor not up to speed.

4. Loose shaft coupling.

5. Defective pressure regulating valve.

Pressure check at cutoff

Once you are finished with the operating pressure check, shut off the burner. Insert a pressure gauge directly into the pump pressure port, Figure 4-17, and run the burner until the pump reaches its pressure setting and then shut the burner off.

(Note that cutoff pressure cannot be measured at the bleeder port as the pressure-regulating valve has an internal bypass system which does not hold pressure at the bleeder port on shutdown.) As soon as the burner shuts off, the pressure should drop very quickly about 10 to 25%, and then hold that pressure. The pressure cutoff reading should hold for at least five minutes without change.

Figure 4-17: Pressure test

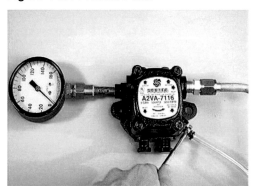

Any decrease from the cutoff pressure indicates a defective or dirty pressure regulating valve (piston or piston seat) that will result in oil dribbling from the nozzle and an after fire. The fuel pump should be replaced in this case.

Field vacuum check

While there are many reasons for the following problems, one of the leading possibilities is a leaking suction line, fittings or gaskets. If there is no other obvious cause for these problems, you should take an operating vacuum test to determine if you have a leak.

1. Pulsating pump pressure
2. Oil pump noise
3. Hard starting (ignition)
4. Poor flame retention
5. Noisy fire
6. Loss of flame during running cycle
7. Burner flame will not establish after long shutdown
8. After fire

Checking system vacuum

The first step is calculate what the vacuum should be, then test to see what it actually is and compare the two.

To calculate the vacuum, figure about 1" of vacuum for each foot of oil lift, 1" of vacuum for each 10 feet of horizontal run, and ½" for a clean oil filter. If the actual operating vacuum is significantly less than the calculated vacuum, you probably have a leak either in the pump or somewhere in the line.

To do this test, a vacuum gauge capable of reading 30" of vacuum should be screwed into the unused intake port. It is important that the vacuum gauge be securely tightened so that vacuum leaks will not develop around the threaded fittings.

If the unit to be tested is set up for a one-pipe system, a return oil line from the unit nozzle port should be provided to catch the oil removed from the strainer chamber during the vacuum check. Then run the burner, bleed the pump, and read the vacuum. The vacuum reading should approximate the calculated vacuum.

If the gauge reading is substantially above the calculated vacuum, there is a restriction in the oil supply that may be caused by of one of the following:

1. Plugged fuel filter
2. Kinked oil supply line
3. Partially closed oil supply valve
4. Check or foot valve inoperative or sticking

> *Note:* The excess vacuum caused by a partially clogged pump strainer cannot be read on the gauge. Be sure to look at the strainer through the inlet port before installing the gauge. If it appears dirty, remove the strainer and clean or replace it.

If vacuum reading is below the calculated operating vacuum, the probable causes are:

1. Clogged pump strainer
2. Air leak in the suction line or suction line fittings
3. A suction leak around strainer chamber cover plate and gasket
4. Worn pump gears

Vacuum test

If the operating vacuum is less than the calculated figure, you have a leak to find. First determine if the pump or fittings up to the pump shut off valve are leaking by performing a Vacuum Test.

1. Fill the fuel unit with oil.

2. Shut off the valve closest to the pump. If there is no valve, disconnect the supply line at the fuel unit.

3. On a two pipe system, disconnect the return line and place an open container below the return port of the fuel unit.

4. If the system is single pipe, connect a bleed hose to the bleeder port and the opposite end in an open container.

5. Install your vacuum gauge in the alternate inlet port on the pump. (If there was no shut off and you have disconnected the suction line, install the gauge in the inlet port.)

6. Start the burner and open the bleed port. Run it until a vacuum of 15" is reached. On a single pipe system you must open the bleed port while the burner is running to raise the vacuum.

7. Once the vacuum is reached, close the bleed port. (You may need to jumper the F-F terminals on the primary control after burner start up to get the burner running long enough to reach the vacuum reading.)

8. While the burner is running and you have reached the required vacuum, on the two pipe system, plug the return port and turn the burner off. On a single pipe, close the bleed port and turn the burner off.

9. Check the vacuum reading after shut down. The vacuum should hold for at least five minutes. If the vacuum does not hold steady, you could have a leak in the pump, a leak in strainer chamber gasket, loosened strainer

chamber bolts, pump seal leak, or the pump leaking at ports, or it could be the fittings up to the shut off valve. Recheck the gasket, plugs and fittings and try again. If you are sure everything is tight, the leak may be in the unit itself, and you will have to replace it.

10. If the vacuum holds, you know that the fuel unit and all the piping up to the shut off valve are OK. Now it is time to open the shut off valve near the pump, and if there is one, shut off the valve at the tank, or at the wall where the suction line enters the building. Do the test again. If the vacuum holds, you know the leak is between the valve and the tank.

> **Warning: We used to check for leaks using the pressure test method. The problem with pressurizing oil lines is it usually creates more leaks than it finds. We strongly urge you to never pressurize oil lines or tanks. This includes blowing out the lines with a CO_2 cartridge; instead use a hand pump to suck the line clear, Figure 4-18.**

Visual test or sight glass test for air in oil lines

When you detect air in oil lines, you must find the source of the leak. The first step is to tighten all fittings in the suction line and tighten unused inlet port plugs in the pump. Be sure there are no compression fittings in the oil lines. Then check the filter cover and gaskets, making sure there is a good gasket on the pump cover. If none of this eliminates the air, you must start searching for the source of the leak. To confirm that there is a leak and to pinpoint the source, use the Visual Test or Sight Glass Method.

**Figure 4-18:
Hand pump**

To do a visual test, use of a vacuum gauge and plastic tubing with fittings such as the Oil Watcher or Clearview, see Figure 4-19. Install the device between the pump, shut off valve and the suction line. Bleed all the air out of the lines, then run the unit and look for bubbles. One at a time, heading toward the tank, coat the fittings with lithium grease. The grease temporarily seals the leak. When the leaking fitting is covered, the air bubbles will disappear. Repair the leaking fittings and clean the grease off everything you have coated.

An easier way to find leaks is by using an electronic sight glass. The electronic sight glass is a tool used by many air conditioning technicians. It is a hand held meter that has two transducers which you can easily mount at any point in your

Figure 4-19: Oil leak test kit

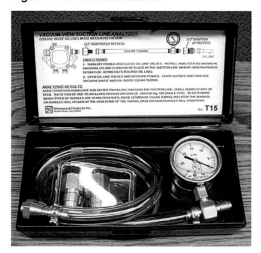

suction line. When operating, one transducer transmits and the other receives an ultrasonic signal. The pulse the signal receives tells the unit if there is air in the pipe. If it detects air, it makes a noise. When using the electronic sight glass, attach the sensors just prior to the first fitting in the line. If no air is detected, attach the sensors just past the same fitting

and test again. Proceed in this manner until you arrive at a fitting with no air coming into it, but air after the fitting. You know that fitting is leaking. Continue on until all the leaks have been found.

To check for leaks in the return line:

More difficult to find is a leak in the return line. Over time, these can be the most troublesome leaks, because they can go for so long before being detected. When the burner is running, return lines can have up to five pounds pressure. This can add up to a lot of lost oil in a short time.

The best way to check for a leaking return line is to hook the return line up to the suction side of the fuel unit and perform the operating vacuum test. The operating vacuum on the return line, when it is hooked to the pump as the suction line, should be about the same as the operating vacuum reading for the original suction line. If the vacuum is less than the return line, it is either leaking or the orginal suction line is partially plugged. The potential problem with this method is that the installer may not have run the return line all the way to the bottom of the tank.

If you cannot draw oil up the return line you will not know if it is a big leak, or the line terminates at the top of the tank. Either way your next tool will be a shovel to dig up the top of the tank. (Do not hook up the suction line as a return, it could plug it up, or if there is a foot valve or other check valve in the line, it will blow the pump seal. Just vent the return oil into a bucket).

If the operating vacuum is much less than the calculated vacuum or the operating vacuum of the suction line, look for air in the oil. If air is present, there is a good chance that you have a leak. Check all fittings and joints, as well as the optional inlet plug on the fuel unit. Be sure all flare fittings are done properly and there are no compression fittings. Be sure all oil lines that go through a wall or under concrete are sheathed in plastic tubing. Be sure to use non-hardening oil pipe dope on threads. Do not use Teflon® tape on fittings; it will void the pump warranty.

Selection of replacement fuel units

It is good general practice to replace a fuel unit with one of a similar type, unless you have determined that there is a mismatch between the fuel unit capacities and the operating requirements of the burner. Fuel unit manufacturers attach identification plates to their units. These plates contain serial numbers that identify the units and their operational characteristics. Reference material for these identifying serial numbers is available from the manufacturers and should be included in your burner service data, as it will make selection of proper replacement units easier. When replacing fuel units, consider the following.

Shaft rotation

Pumps are designed for either clockwise (CW) or counterclockwise (CCW) rotation and proper rotational direction is shown on the unit identification plate. With the unit shaft held toward you, clockwise rotation will be to the right, often shown by an arrow pointing to the right. Counterclockwise to the left, with an arrow pointing left. This rotation must be matched to the burner motor.

Rotational speed

The great majority of older domestic oilburner motors operate at a speed of 1725 RPM, while most flame retention burners operate at 3450 RPM. Pump speed should be matched to motor speeds.

Nozzle discharge port location

For ease of installation, fuel units are built with both right and left-hand nozzle or discharge ports. Again, a right or left hand port location is determined by holding the unit with the shaft pointing toward you.

Shaft sizes

Most oil pumps have either a 5/16" shaft or a 7/16" shaft. The smaller shaft may be bushed up for substitute replacement.

Installation requirements

Be sure that the replacement unit is properly mounted and in line with the motor coupling. The Allen screws or flange mounting bolts, which hold the fuel unit to the burner housing, must be securely tightened. If the coupling between the motor and the fuel unit has Allen set screws, these should be securely tightened against the motor shaft, after tightening unit-mounting bolts. To do otherwise may result in a jammed coupling and damage to the pump or the motor may occur.

Pump strainers

It is necessary to periodically clean the fuel unit strainer, Figure 4-20. To clean or replace the strainer, loosen the strainer

Figure 4-20: Dirty strainer

chamber cover bolts and remove the cover and slide out the strainer. Whenever you take the cover off the strainer, be sure to scrape off the old gasket between the cover and unit body and replace it with the proper replacement gasket. Some Webster pumps have no strainers, but they do contain chopper gears that clean the oil and the cover should be removed on a routine basis and cleaned out. Make sure you have the proper gasket before you do this.

Clean the pump strainer screen in heating oil or kerosene and reassemble, making sure to tighten all cover bolts evenly to prevent distortion of the cover. When putting the burner back into service, be sure to bleed the air from the system and check for proper flame cutoff. Remember that the strainer is a secondary filter and that a proper installation also has an external or primary filter.

Pump gaskets

It is also important that the correct gasket be used. Using incorrect gaskets can damage the pump.

Noise problems in fuel units, oil lines or tanks

Noise generated as a result of pump operation, or noise transmitted by oil lines, is annoying to the customer and should be eliminated.

Pump noise: In addition to noise created by worn internal parts in the pump, misalignment of the fuel unit and motor coupling shaft or loose installation bolts may be the source of noise problems. All fittings and bolts should be tightened securely.

Oil line noise is the result of improperly fastened oil lines which are allowed to

vibrate against surrounding objects such as sheet metal furnace covers, duct work, etc. If oil line noise is a result of noise transmitted from the fuel unit, check the anti-hum device in the pump. The return line on two pipe systems may occasionally provide line noises. If the suction and return lines touch each other they can create line noise.

Tank noise: This is not a common source of noise complaints. If such a complaint should develop, the cause can normally be traced back to transmission of noise by the oil lines. Tank noise can also be eliminated in many cases by a hum eliminator. A commonly overlooked source of tank noise is improper installation of the return line. The end of the return line of a two pipe system should be located approximately 3" above the bottom of the tank. This will permit discharge of return oil to be at a point beneath the surface of the oil, thereby eliminating the noise of return oil falling into the tank.

Potential leaks in oil lines

Leaking suction and return lines can cause serious problems. We all must be ever vigilant for possible pipe leaks.

• Treat every out of oil/automatic delivery as a potential leak that should be further investigated.

• Study oil deliveries; further investigate each tank that takes more oil than projected.

• Respond quickly to any calls from customers for oil smells and concerns about increased consumption. These can be early warning signs of trouble.

• Treat every water-in-the-tank call as a potential tank leak that must be investigated.

• Operating problems with the burner can signify a leak, and any air in the oil pump call, poor pump cut-off, noisy operation, and erratic fire calls, loss of flame retention (flame pulsates on the end cone), loss of oil prime, rough starts or shut downs, pump whine and pressure fluctuation, and after drip could all indicate a leak.

In order to check for leaks in the suction pipe and fittings you must first run an operating vacuum test, covered earlier in the chapter.

Valves

Solenoid oil valves

Not allowing oil to flow until the burner is up to full speed and air flow into the heat exchanger has been established can make for cleaner start up. The use of a solenoid oil valve can delay fuel delivery to the nozzle for anywhere from 4 to 15 seconds after burner startup. Figure 4-21 shows an oil valve. To achieve a longer delay. a primary control with a valve-on delay feature and a non-delay valve should be used. On burner shutdown, the oil valve closes immediately, providing a much more rapid shutdown than is obtainable with the pressure control valve on the fuel unit. Figure 4-22 shows how the valve works.

In operation, this valve can solve many problems associated with poor startup and shutdown conditions such as:

1. Pulsating starts

2. Puff back

3. After fire as a result of a malfunctioning pressure regulating valve

4. Long term soot buildup in heat exchanger resulting from incomplete combustion on burner startup and shutdown

Figure 4-21: Delayed oil valve

Figure 4-22: Construction detail with valve closed

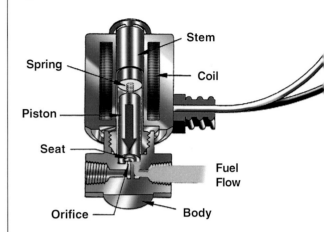

Figure 4-22: Construction detail with valve open

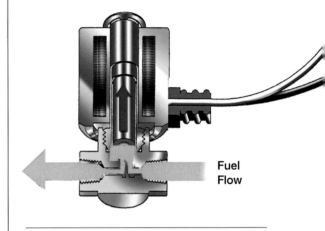

Operation of the delayed action solenoid valve

The delayed oil valve may also help in preventing a puff back as a result of poor ignition. During startup, the burner motor requires a substantial starting current. This current requirement may rob voltage from the ignition system, resulting in a weak spark at the electrodes. When the motor reaches operating speed, the current requirement of the motor drops appreciably and the full supply voltage is available to the transformer. This results in maximum ignition voltage at the time the delayed oil valve opens and oil is supplied to the nozzle.

On burner shutdown, the delayed oil valve closes immediately, shutting off the fuel supply and providing a clean cutoff of the flame. Without the delayed oil valve, the motor speed must decrease before the pressure regulating valve closes, which again causes smoke because of a lack of air.

Note: The delayed oil valve will only produce a clean shutdown if the oil supply system is free of entrapped air. The delayed oil valve will not control nozzle after drip that results from air in the oil supply system between the valve and the oil nozzle. This air is caused by an air leak in the suction line or pump fittings or high vacuum.

Installation: The delayed oil valve is installed on the output side of the fuel unit. Standard 1/8" (I.D.) black iron pipe can be used to connect the inlet port of the delayed oil valve to the nozzle discharge port on the fuel pump. Use of the 1/8" pipe provides a rigid mounting for the valve.

The coil is electrically connected in parallel with the burner motor. See Figure 4-23 for a wiring diagram. If the burner has interrupted ignition, be sure that the solenoid valve is connected to the motor leads and not to the ignition leads. If the valve is inadvertently wired to the interrupted ignition circuit, the valve will close when ignition is cut off and burner will go off on safety lockout.

It is code in most jurisdictions, and good practice in all cases, to run the electrical leads from the delayed oil valve through Greenfield tubing to protect electrical leads from the valve to the burner junction box. The oil valve housing cover is threaded to accept Greenfield connectors or the tubing itself. Use anti-short bushings on the ends of the Greenfield. A handy device to have for the installation is a double Greenfield (BX) connector that allows two pieces of Greenfield to be connected to a single hole. This will make the electrical installation much easier in cases where the burner junction box does not have an extra outlet hole.

Figure: 4-23: Delayed oil valve installation for interrupted ignition

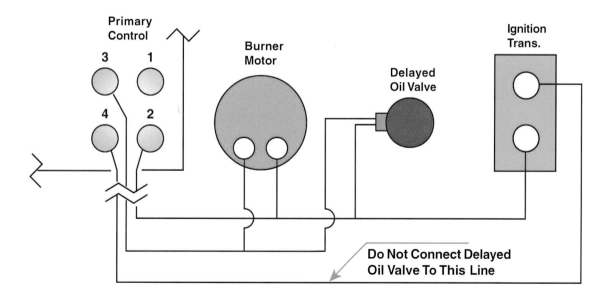

A conventional fuel line flared fitting is installed in the outlet port of the delayed valve (in most cases this will be the same fitting you have removed from the nozzle discharge port) and the fuel line to the drawer assembly fuel pipe should be

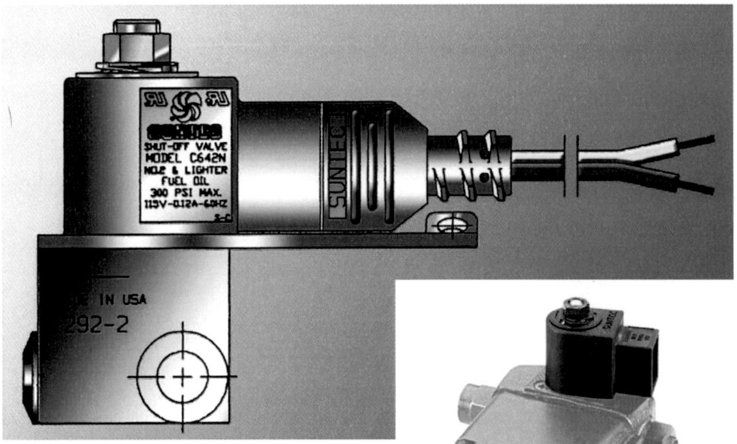

Figure: 4-24: Drawing of a solenoid valve

Figure: 4-25: Fuel pump with solenoid

reinstalled. With some small amount of reworking, it should be possible to use the same fuel line that was on the burner before installation of the delayed valve.

Servicing: The most sensitive part of the delayed valve system is the thermal delay switch that is taped to the valve coil. Should the valve at any time fail to operate due to a defective time delay switch, it is possible to temporarily remove this switch from the circuit by removing the tape bindings and twisting

the two leads of the switch together. As this field fix removes the delay feature of the valve, a new coil should be installed at the earliest possible time.

The delayed oil valve is needed on burners with older pumps. Most of the new burners utilize non-delay instant opening solenoid valves because of the relative unreliability of the thermal delay switch. Figure 4-24 shows a solenoid valve.

Manufacturers have gone to microprocessor based primary controls with Valve-Delay-On and Motor-Delay-Off, commonly known as pre- and post purge technology. The delay is built into the primary so the delay timing can be more precisely controlled. It is becoming increasingly popular for manufacturers to attach the solenoid valve, controlled by the primary, directly to the fuel unit. See Figure 4-25.

Anti-siphon valve and oil safety valve

If the oil tank is higher than the burner, some codes require an overhead suction line and an automatic valve that will break the siphon should an oil line leak develop. Two popular anti-siphon valves are the Webster Oil Safety Valve (OSV), and the Suntec PRV.

Figure 4-26 shows a Suntec PRV. Its job is to protect against line leaks and tank

Figure 4-26: Suntec PRV

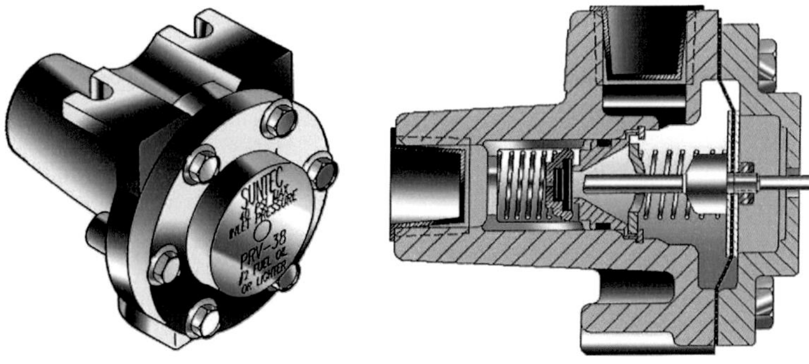

siphoning as well protect the pump from excess head pressure. When the burner comes on the pump creates a vacuum that pulls the valve stem down and opens the valve. When the burner shuts off, if there are no leaks the valve stem will stay down and remain in this position. If there is a leak between the PRV and the burner, the siphon created by the leak will close the valve, shutting off the oil supply to the line. If the red stem sticks out of the top of the valve, you know a loss of vacuum (siphon) has occurred.

If the top of the oil supply source is more than 8 feet above the fuel unit you need to install a PRV. The NFPA rating for the head pressure on a fuel unit is only 3 PSI, about 8 feet. If the tank head (height of oil supply above the unit) is greater than 8 feet, the supply oil pressure may exceed 3 PSI and thereby shorten shaft seal life. If it is necessary to locate the tank at a greater height, a pressure reducing valve or an oil safety valve should be used in the oil supply line.

Thermal safety valve

A thermal safety shut off (Firomatic) valve should be installed in the suction line at the tank. The shut off valve should be UL listed and should be equipped with a fusible type handle that melts at 165°F.

Also install a shut off valve before the filter and at the fuel pump for ease of service. If the tank is outside of the building, there should be a shutoff valve at the wall where the suction line enters the building.

Foot valves

Foot valves are check valves installed on the end of the suction line in underground tanks. They are no longer needed and not recommended; however, they were common on older installations and some are still in the field. It is not unusual for them to get stuck closed and not allow oil to flow.

There are two options in this case:
1. Run new oil lines from the tank to the burner.
2. If the return line extends to the bottom of the oil tank, you can convert the system to a one-pipe system by capping the suction line and using the original return line as the new suction line. (Remember to remove the bypass plug in the fuel pump).

Suntec has provided a very helpful Technical Bulletin and System Trouble Shooting Flow Chart which reviews the service procedures for both old and new style pumps, shown on pages 4-23 thru 4-25.

Troubleshooting Fuel Units

No Oil Flow at Nozzle	Oil level below intake line in supply tank. Fill tank with oil.
Clogged strainer or filter	Remove and clean strainer. Replace filter element.
Clogged nozzle	Replace nozzle.
Air leak in intake line	Tighten all fittings in intake line. Tighten unused intake port plug. Tighten in-line valve stem packing gland. Look for leaks in piping.
Restricted intake line	Replace any kinked tubing and check any valves in intake line.
A two-pipe system that becomes air bound	Check for bypass plug.
A one-pipe system that becomes air bound	Loosen gauge port plug, or open the bleed valve, start the burner, and drain oil until foam is gone. Check for high vacuum (over 6" vacuum). Check for air leaks in pump or oil line.
Slipping or broken coupling	Tighten or replace coupling.
Air Leak	Loose plugs or fittings. Dope with good quality thread sealer or pipe joint compound.
Leak at pressure adjusting cap nut	Fiber washer may have been left out after adjustment of pump pressure. Replace the washer.
Blown seal—One-pipe system	Check to see if bypass plug has been left in unit. Replace fuel unit.
Blown seal—Two-pipe system	Check for kinked tubing, rust in pump, or other obstructions in return line. Replace fuel unit. Check tank for water.
Noisy Operation	Bad coupling alignment, loosen fuel unit mounting screws slightly and shift unit in different positions until noise is eliminated. Retighten mounting screws or replace coupling.
Pulsating Pressure	Partially clogged strainer or filter. Remove and clean strainer. Replace filter element.
Air leak in intake line	Tighten all fittings and valve packing in intake line.
Air leaking around cover	Be sure strainer cover screws are tightened securely. Install a new gasket.
Improper Nozzle Cut-Off	To determine the cause of improper cut-off, insert a pressure gauge in the nozzle port of the pressure fuel unit. After a minute of operation, shut the burner down. If the pressure drops approximately 20% from normal operating pressure and holds at that pressure, the pump is operating properly and air is the cause of improper cut-off. If, however, the pressure drops more than 20% in 5 minutes, fuel unit should be replaced.
Air pocket remaining in nozzle line after disassembly	Run burner, bled pump, stopping and starting unit, until smoke and after-fire disappear.
Air leak in intake line	Tighten intake fittings and packing nut on shutoff valve. Tighten unused intake port plug.
Partially clogged nozzle strainer	Replace nozzle. Clean and flush out oil line and pump.

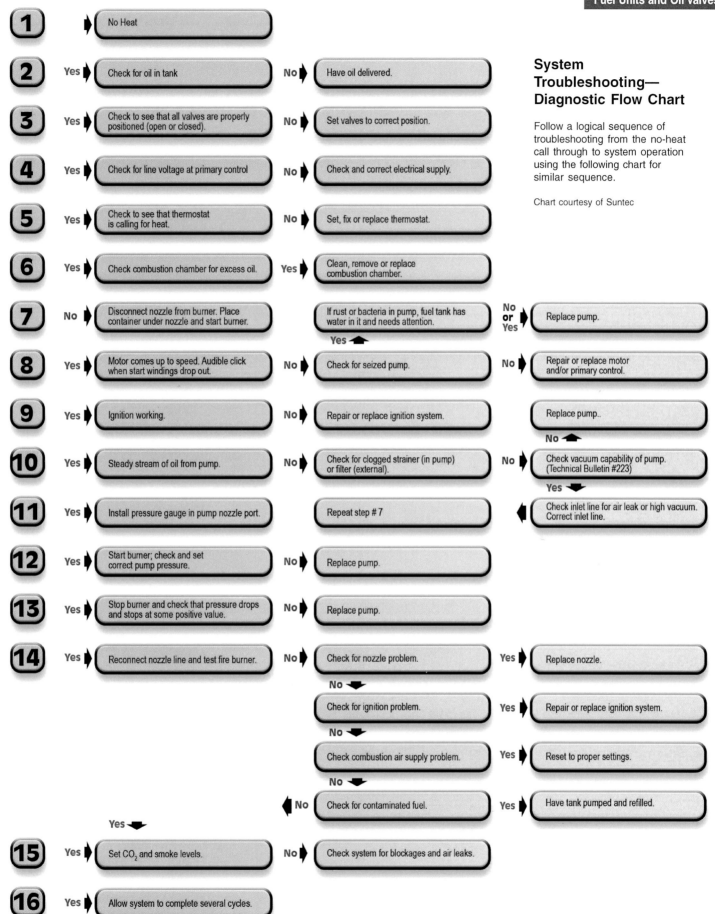

1 No Heat

2 Yes ➤ Check for oil in tank | No ➤ Have oil delivered.

3 Yes ➤ Check to see that all valves are properly positioned (open or closed). | No ➤ Set valves to correct position.

4 Yes ➤ Check for line voltage at primary control | No ➤ Check and correct electrical supply.

5 Yes ➤ Check to see that thermostat is calling for heat. | No ➤ Set, fix or replace thermostat.

6 Yes ➤ Check combustion chamber for excess oil. | Yes ➤ Clean, remove or replace combustion chamber.

7 No ➤ Disconnect nozzle from burner. Place container under nozzle and start burner. | If rust or bacteria in pump, fuel tank has water in it and needs attention. Yes ➤ | No or Yes ➤ Replace pump.

8 Yes ➤ Motor comes up to speed. Audible click when start windings drop out. | No ➤ Check for seized pump. | No ➤ Repair or replace motor and/or primary control.

9 Yes ➤ Ignition working. | No ➤ Repair or replace ignition system. | Replace pump.. No ➤

10 Yes ➤ Steady stream of oil from pump. | No ➤ Check for clogged strainer (in pump) or filter (external). | No ➤ Check vacuum capability of pump. (Technical Bulletin #223) Yes ➤

11 Yes ➤ Install pressure gauge in pump nozzle port. | Repeat step #7 | ◄ Check inlet line for air leak or high vacuum. Correct inlet line.

12 Yes ➤ Start burner; check and set correct pump pressure. | No ➤ Replace pump.

13 Yes ➤ Stop burner and check that pressure drops and stops at some positive value. | No ➤ Replace pump.

14 Yes ➤ Reconnect nozzle line and test fire burner. | No ➤ Check for nozzle problem. | Yes ➤ Replace nozzle.
No ➤ Check for ignition problem. | Yes ➤ Repair or replace ignition system.
No ➤ Check combustion air supply problem. | Yes ➤ Reset to proper settings.
No ➤ ◄ No Check for contaminated fuel. | Yes ➤ Have tank pumped and refilled.

Yes ➤

15 Yes ➤ Set CO_2 and smoke levels. | No ➤ Check system for blockages and air leaks.

16 Yes ➤ Allow system to complete several cycles.

System Troubleshooting— Diagnostic Flow Chart

Follow a logical sequence of troubleshooting from the no-heat call through to system operation using the following chart for similar sequence.

Chart courtesy of Suntec

GAGES AND FIELD SERVICE

William J. Mitchell, Manager of Field Service

Fuel pumps have pressure, vacuum, and flow ratings for proper sizing to the application. Today's high efficiency furnaces and boilers require these parameters be checked on initial installation and service calls to insure that high efficiency is maintained. During trouble calls it is necessary to take pressure and vacuum readings to isolate pump problems from system problems.

VACUUM TEST FOR PUMPS AND INLET LINES

1. Single Pipe Installation

A. Establish Vacuum With Bleeder
   Valve Open
B. Close Bleeder Valve
C. Shut Off Burner

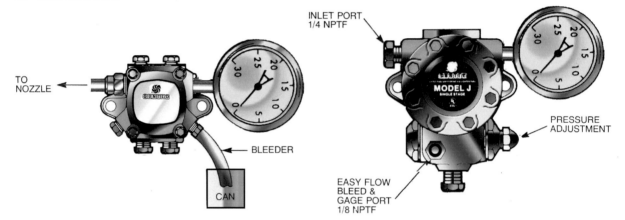

2. Two Pipe Installation

A. Establish Vacuum With Return
   Port Open
B. Plug Return Port
C. Shut Off Burner

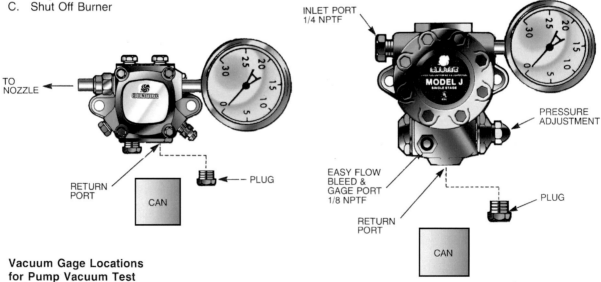

**Vacuum Gage Locations
for Pump Vacuum Test**

TO CHECK PUMP VACUUM:

Single Pipe

1) Remove inlet line and install vacuum gage in the inlet port.
2) Turn on burner, open bleed port. When pump reaches 15 in.Hg., close bleed port.
3) Pump should hold vacuum for five minutes.

Two Pipe

1) Remove inlet line and install vacuum gage in the inlet port.
2) Remove return line.
3) Start burner.
4) When 15 in.Hg. vacuum is established, block return port and turn off burner.
5) Vacuum should hold for five minutes.

If pump cannot attain 15 in. Hg. or hold for five minutes, the pump should be repaired or replaced.

TO CHECK SYSTEM VACUUM

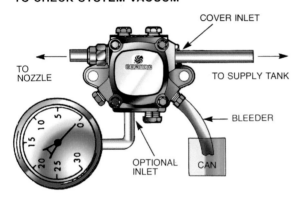

1) Install vacuum gage in optional inlet or tee into supply line at pump. (If optional inlet used for line, install gage in cover inlet.)
2) Turn burner on.
3) Bleed pump if on one pipe system.
4) Close bleed valve and observe gage.

If vacuum reading exceeds the following specifications:

1) 6 in.Hg. if single pipe single stage (A or J) or two stage (B or H)
2) 10 in.Hg. if two pipe single stage (A or J)
3) 15 in.Hg. if two pipe two stage (B or H)

If there is a problem with the piping or application:

1) Check the installation bulletin for the pump:

   a) Form #440100 for A's and B's.
   b) Form #400245 for two step and high pressure B's
   c) Form #1011 for E's and F's
   d) Form #440041 for J's and H's

2) If the lift and run is not excessive for the pump model, the problem is being caused by one of the following:

   a) Number and types of bends in the piping (includes kinks and flattening)
   b) Number and types of fittings in the piping
   c) Number, types, and condition of filters and strainers
   d) Number and types of valves in the system
   e) Level of contaminate buildup on inside walls of the piping.

If the vacuum level is not excessive, and there is air in the oil, it is usually indicative of a leak in the piping. This can be checked by closing the tank valve and pulling a vacuum on the system by the pump. Shut the burner off and the vacuum should hold five minutes.

PRESSURE TEST OF PUMPS AND SYSTEMS

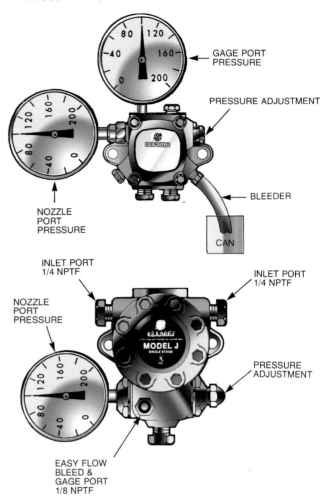

Pressure Gage Locations for Operating Pressure Test

TO CHECK PRESSURE WHILE OPERATING SYSTEM

1) Install gage in gage port
   a) If pump is on a positive head system, shut off tank valve before installing gage.
   b) If pump is on a lift system, single pipe, bleed pump at bleed valve following gage installation.

2) Turn on burner and observe gage.
   a) Disregard slight jiggling of gage as the mechanical resonance of small gages is close to gearset frequency.
   b) If setting is high or low, readjust pressure adjustment screw.
      — On J's and H's there can be some leakage with the acorn nut removed. This stops when the nut is replaced.

3) Turn off burner. The pressure should fall to zero or the amount of head on the pump.

TO CHECK OPERATING AND CUTOFF PRESSURE

1) Install gage into nozzle port of the pump.
2) Turn on burner and observe gage. Readjust pressure if necessary.
3) Turn off burner and observe gage. It should fall to 80% or higher and stop.
   a) If it continues to fall, the pump has a cutoff problem and should be repaired or replaced.

Chapter **5**

NOZZLES & COMBUSTION CHAMBERS

IN THIS CHAPTER

- **Nozzle construction and operation**

- **Air-oil mixing and flame patterns**

- **Solving after-drip problems**

- **Combustion chambers**

Chapter 5

Nozzles and Combustion Chambers

Part 1: Nozzles

Proper nozzle selection is the key to efficient, clean combustion. By knowing how to determine the proper firing rate, the right spray angle, and the appropriate spray pattern, you can ensure good reliable combustion.

Construction of the nozzle

The oilburner nozzle is a precisely engineered product, manufactured to the very close tolerances necessary to atomize and meter fuel in the spray patterns and angles required of today's oilheating equipment.

Nozzles are made of either stainless steel or a combination of stainless steel and brass, allowing them to withstand the temperatures, pressures, and variety of fuels found in combustion environments.

Nozzle function

The nozzle performs three vital functions for an oilburner:

1. Atomizing: Heating oil must be vaporized to burn. Although the vaporization is actually accomplished with heat, the oil must be 'broken down' into tiny droplets first. This is called 'atomization' and allows the oil to vaporize quickly and evenly for fast and quiet ignition. See Figure 5-1.

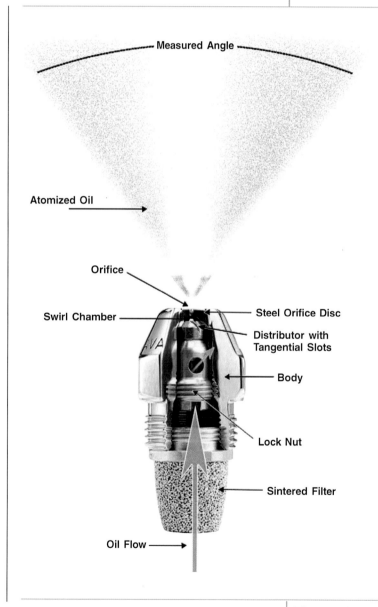

Figure 5-1: Nozzle; cutaway view

before atomization,
one gallon of fuel oil
has a surface area of

180 sq. in.

After nozzle atomization

one gallon of fuel oil
has been broken into

55,000,000,000 droplets!

and its surface area is

670,000 sq. in.

pattern and angle best suited to the requirements of each specific burner and combustion area.

Effects of pressure on nozzle performance

Historically, 100 PSI was considered satisfactory for the fixed oil pressure supplied to the nozzle, and all nozzle manufacturers calibrate their nozzles at that pressure. Many burner and appliance (boilers, furnaces, and water heater) manufacturers are recommending higher pressures for their products. Higher pressures create better atomization, i.e. smaller droplets. See Figure 5-2.

2. Metering: A nozzle delivers a fixed amount of atomized fuel to the combustion chamber. The amount of fuel is measured in gallons-per-hour (GPH) at 100 pounds pressure. For burning rates below five GPH, there are more that 25 different flow rates each in 6 different spray angles and six or more spray patterns.

3. Patterning: A nozzle is expected to deliver the fuel to the combustion area in a uniform spray

Figure 5-2: Fuel pressure vs. droplet size

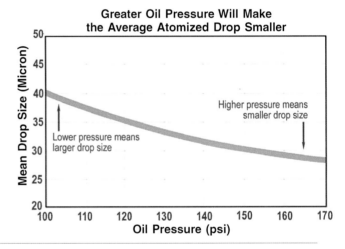

How a nozzle works

Heating oil, under pressure (100 psi) passes through the strainer to remove contamination, then through a set of slots, cut at an angle into the swirl chamber. The angle of the ejected oil creates a high velocity swirl, like a tornado. As the oil swirls against the swirl chamber walls it creates an area of low pressure in the center. This pressure differential moves the oil out through the orifice in a hollow tube shape where it spreads into a film that stretches until is ruptures into billions of tiny droplets.

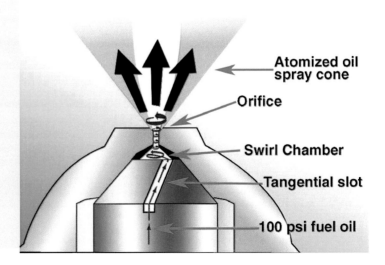

In Figure 5-3 we can see how the spray from a nozzle changes as the pressure increases. At low pressure, the cone shaped film is long and the droplets are large and irregular. As the pressure increases, the spray angle becomes better defined. Once a stable pattern is formed, any increase in pressure does not affect the spray angle directly in front of the orifice. However, at higher pressure, the angle of spray further away from the orifice does start to narrow by one to two degrees. This is because the droplets are starting to slow down due to air resistance and the air the spray draws in moves the droplets inward. This is the same effect that causes a shower curtain to be drawn into the shower spray.

As you might expect, pressure increases cause a corresponding increase in the amount of oil flowing through the nozzle. A nozzle rated at one gallon-per-hour at 100 PSI will deliver about 1.23 gallons-per-hour at 150 PSI. Increasing pressure also reduces the size of the droplets in the spray. For example, an increase from 100 to

10 PSI   100 PSI   300 PSI

Figure 5-3: Nozzle spray droplets

300 PSI reduces the droplet diameter by about 28%. Lower pressure means larger droplets that are much harder to vaporize and burn. While pressures greater than 100 PSI are sometimes desirable, never operate at less than 100 PSI. See Table 5-1 on following page.

Spray pattern

There are many different spray patterns offered by manufacturers. Although all spray patterns are hollow to some degree, nozzles are grouped into three general classifications—solid, hollow, and semi-solid. See Figure 5-4.

Hollow cone: As the name implies, the greatest concentration of droplets is at the outer edge of the spray, with little or no distribution in the center. Generally, hollow cone nozzles are used on low firing rate burners, particularly those firing less than 1 GPH. This is an important advantage in fractional gallonage nozzles, such as those used in mobile home furnaces, where cold, high viscosity oil may cause a reduction in spray angle and increases in droplet size. Hollow flames also tend to be quieter.

Solid cone: Here the distribution of droplets is more uniform throughout the pattern. These nozzles work best when the air pattern of the burner is heavy in the center or where long fires are required. They provide smoother ignition for burners

**Oil Nozzle Type A
Ordering Table**

Semi-Solid

Solid

Hollow Cone

Figure 5-4: Nozzle spray patterns

Table 5-1:
Nozzle capacities
US gph

Nozzle Flow Rate vs. Pressure (Approx.)

Flow Rating
USGPH @ 100 PSI

Flow Rates in US GPH
Pressure PSI

GPH	125	145	175	200	250	300
0.40	0.45	0.48	0.53	0.57	0.63	0.69
0.50	0.56	0.60	0.66	0.71	0.79	0.87
0.60	0.67	0.72	0.79	0.85	0.95	1.04
0.65	0.73	0.78	0.88	0.92	1.03	1.13
0.75	0.84	0.90	0.99	1.06	1.19	1.30
0.85	0.95	1.02	1.12	1.20	1.34	1.47
1.00	1.12	1.20	1.32	1.41	1.58	1.73
1.10	1.23	1.32	1.48	1.56	1.74	1.91
1.20	1.34	1.44	1.59	1.70	1.90	2.08
1.25	1.40	1.51	1.65	1.77	1.98	2.17
1.35	1.51	1.63	1.79	1.91	2.13	2.34
1.50	1.68	1.81	1.98	2.12	2.37	2.60
1.65	1.84	1.99	2.18	2.33	2.81	2.86
1.75	1.96	2.11	2.32	2.47	2.77	3.03
2.00	2.24	2.41	2.65	2.83	3.16	3.46
2.25	2.52	2.71	2.98	3.18	3.56	3.90
2.50	2.80	3.01	3.31	3.54	3.95	4.33
2.75	3.07	3.31	3.84	3.89	4.35	4.76
3.00	3.35	3.61	3.97	4.24	4.74	5.20
3.25	3.63	3.91	4.30	4.60	5.14	5.63
3.50	3.91	4.21	4.63	4.95	5.53	6.06
3.75	4.19	4.52	4.96	5.30	5.93	6.50
4.00	4.47	4.82	5.29	5.66	6.32	6.93
4.50	5.03	5.42	5.95	6.36	7.12	7.79
5.00	5.60	6.00	6.60	7.10	7.91	8.66
5.50	6.10	6.60	7.30	7.80	8.70	9.53
6.00	6.70	7.20	7.90	8.50	9.49	10.39
6.50	7.30	7.80	8.60	9.20	10.28	11.26
7.00	7.80	8.40	9.30	9.90	11.07	12.12
7.50	8.40	9.00	9.90	10.80	11.86	12.99
8.00	8.90	9.60	10.60	11.30	12.65	13.88
8.50	9.50	10.20	11.20	12.00	13.44	14.72
9.00	10.10	10.80	11.90	12.70	14.23	15.59
10.00	11.20	12.00	13.20	14.10	15.81	17.32
11.00	12.30	13.20	14.80	15.60	17.39	19.05
12.00	13.40	14.40	15.90	17.00	18.97	20.78
13.00	14.50	15.70	17.20	18.40	20.55	22.52
14.00	15.70	16.90	18.50	19.80	22.14	24.25

NOZZLE MANUFACTURERS AND SPRAY PATTERNS

DANFOSS	DELAVAN	HAGO	MONARCH	STEINEN
AS-SOLID	A-HOLLOW	ES-SOLID	R-SOLID	S-SOLID
AH-HOLLOW	B-SOLID	P-SOLID	NS-HOLLOW	SS-SEMI-SOLID
AB-SEMI-SOLID	W-ALL PURPOSE	SS-SEMI-SOLID	AR-SPECIAL SOLID	H-HOLLOW
	SS-SEMI-SOLID	H-HOLLOW	PLP-SEMI-SOLID	
		B-SOLID	PL-HOLLOW	

Figure 5-5:
Manufacturers use
different
designations for
their spray
patterns

firing over 2 GPH. An interesting characteristic of solid cone patterns is that they become more and more hollow as flow rates increase, particularly above 8 GPH. In addition, increased pump pressure tends to make both hollow and solid patterns more hollow.

Semi-solid: Many burners perform well with solid or hollow spray patterns. To accommodate these designs, nozzle manufacturers have developed patterns that are a compromise between solid and hollow. We call these semi-solid patterns.

Your job as a technician is to select the nozzle that puts the oil spray where the air velocity delivered by the burner is greatest. In most modern equipment, the appliance manufacturer designates the nozzle to use. Figure 5-5 describes the manufacturers' different designations for their spray patterns.

Spray angle

Spray angle refers to the angle of the cone of spray from the nozzle. Spray angles are available from a 30-degree angle to a 90-degree angle to meet the wide variety of burner air patterns and chamber shapes. Generally, round or square chambers are fired with 70 to 90-degree nozzles. Short wide chambers need a short fat flame. Long narrow chambers usually require 30-degree to 70-degree solid cone nozzles. The spray pattern and angle must be such that all the droplets burn completely in suspension in the combustion area. Unburned oil must not strike (impinge) on any cold surface such as the chamber walls or floor, the crown sheet of the heat exchanger, or the burner end cone. Impingement of unburned drops will cause high smoke and will lead to future service calls. The correct spray pattern and angle depends on the air-oil mixing design of the burner and the shape of the combustion chamber. See Figures 5-6 and 5-7.

Figure 5-6: Spray angles

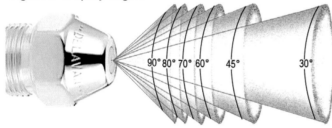

90° 80° 70° 60° 45° 30°

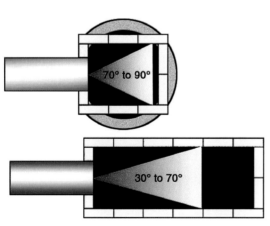

70° to 90°

30° to 70°

Figure 5-7:
Spray angles based on chamber design

Flow rate

Atomizing nozzles are available in a wide range of flow rates. Generally, with hydronic and warm air heating systems, the smallest firing rate that will adequately heat the building on the coldest day of the year is the proper size to use. Another guideline is to select a flow rate that provides a reasonable net stack temperature regardless of the connected load. This avoids acid condensing in the stack, which occurs at about 150 to 200°F. If the appliance is undersized for the load (highly unlikely), it may be necessary to fire to the load and ignore the efficiency. A nozzle that is too small will not produce adequate heat and hot water. A nozzle that is too large will cause the unit to short cycle, reducing efficiency and wasting fuel. Whenever it is possible, determine the manufacturer's recommendations on nozzle selection and *never overfire the rating* of a heating appliance.

Dual filtration

Double filtration nozzles are available for mobile home installations and other units with very low firing rates. In addition to the standard nozzle filter, these nozzles have a secondary internal filter located immediately before the metering slots. This extra filter gives the nozzle 35% more nozzle filtration. The internal filter does not change the nozzle's performance; it just increases its longevity.

There is also a nozzle available from Delavan Spray Technologies for low firing rates that uses two swirl chambers and short metering slots, keeping the oil contaminants in suspension and flushing them from the orifice. Particles are not allowed to collect or stick together, limiting buildup and plugging.

> Whenever it is possible, determine the manufacturer's recommendations on nozzle selection and never overfire the rating of a heating appliance.

Burner air patterns

Burner air patterns are much like nozzle spray patterns in that they fall into solid and hollow classifications.

Burners with solid air patterns are often referred to as open-end burners. There is no restrictive air cone in the end of the air tube to direct the air effectively in any desired pattern. This produces high velocity air down the middle of the air pattern and works best with a solid nozzle and narrow spray angles. This situation does not apply to flame retention burners.

Flame retention burners are equipped with air handling devices in the air tube that afford better mixing of air and oil vapor in the combustion area. Many flame retention burners can fire both solid and hollow nozzles with good results because of the strong recirculation air pattern they produce. This recirculation of air and oil in the chamber also affects the fire box pressure.

In the flame retention burner, the flame front is held very near the burner head. It creates a flame that is less likely to pulsate or produce soot. Nozzle selection for these burners should follow manufacturer's recommendations and the following general guidelines:

• **Burners with flow rates up to 2 GPH:** Hollow nozzles can be used successfully for most applications, even on burners with most of the air down the middle. Hollow nozzles in lower firing rates produce the quietest operation. It is often better, especially in furnaces, to sacrifice 1 or 2 points in efficiency for quiet operation.

• **Burners with flow rates between 2 and 3 GPH:** You may use hollow or solid nozzles depending upon the burner air pattern. At this higher firing rate, spray patterns are not as critical.

• **Burners with firing rates above 3 GPH:** Here it is advisable to standardize on solid nozzles which produce smoother ignition in most burners. Burners with hollow air patterns are the exception. Check the manufacturers' recommendations.

Nozzle brand interchange

Replacing nozzles of one brand with those of another can sometimes present problems. There are subtle differences between manufacturers because they use different methods of production and evaluation.

The burner manufacturers test their burners in different appliances and determine what type nozzle, from which nozzle manufacturer, works best in that particular application. Burner manufacturers publish nozzle recommendations called OEM Specification Guides. Be sure to have this information at hand.

If you are working on a unit not listed in the Specification Guide, you will find that generally, all hollow nozzles have similar spray patterns and may be interchangeable. The variation shows up mainly in the solid nozzles, and if you must change brands, you will have to do some testing to determine the best nozzle for that application. Check with your supply house to secure a nozzle interchange chart to help you in your testing.

Nozzle care and service suggestions

Never, under any conditions, interchange the inner parts of a nozzle with those of another nozzle. Each nozzle component is matched exactly to all the other components of that nozzle. In fact, you should leave a nozzle in its original container until you install it. You should store all your nozzles

in a proper nozzle box. They are available from the nozzle manufacturers.

Handle nozzles carefully. Pick them up by the hex flats only. Do not touch the strainer or orifice. Even clean hands have enough dirt on them to plug up the tiny slots inside the nozzle. Obviously, you should never disassemble a nozzle you plan to use.

Only install nozzles with clean tools to reduce the possibility of contamination. If possible, use a nozzle changer or nozzle wrench when changing a nozzle. Most open-end wrench handles are too long and increase the possibility of stripping the nozzle adapter threads. Before installing a new nozzle, flush out the nozzle line and adapter with clean oil, kerosene, or a solvent.

Before you install the nozzle in the adapter, be sure the inside of the adapter is clean and free of carbon or contamination. Carefully examine the sealing surface of the adapter to be sure there are no scratches or nicks. These can be caused by careless handling, or just wear and tear. If it is scratched or nicked, then replace the adapter. Do not take a chance here. A leak between the nozzle and the adapter can cause serious problems. Do not put anything on the nozzle threads! Screw the nozzle into the adapter one-eighth to one-quarter turn past hand tight (about 88 to 138 pounds of torque).

The nozzle orifice face is polished to a mirror finish. Do not ruin it with a wire or pin, or by bumping it with a wrench. This will ruin the spray. If a nozzle is dirty, or plugged, change it. It is impossible to clean it out properly. It is tempting, especially in the middle of the night to try to clean out the orifice with a pin or tooth pick. It will not work. Replace it!

A good quality nozzle should last at least two heating seasons. Contamination

Figure 5-8

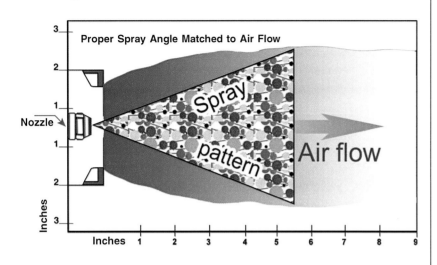

Figure 5-9

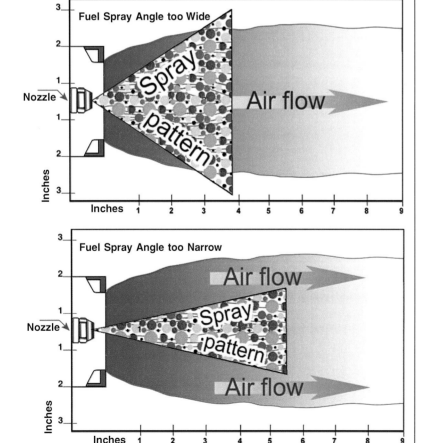

and excessive heat are the main causes of nozzle failure. Contamination can be limited by installing a good oil filter in the supply line. If there are excessive tank bottom sediments in the tank, you may need to clean the tank and adopt a fuel additive program. For severe cases, replace the tank.

Nozzles should not be very hot when operating because of the amount of air and fuel traveling past them. Nozzles overheat from poor or no over-fire draft. Over-fire draft should be at least -.01" to keep nozzles cool. There are some exceptions to this rule. As usual, manufacturer's instructions take precedence. Be sure the end of the burner air tube does not extend into the chamber. The face of the end tube should be flush with the face of the chamber, or recessed about one quarter inch.

Air-oil mixing and flame patterns

What constitutes a perfect oilburner flame? Theoretically, each droplet of oil that leaves the nozzle orifice should be completely surrounded by air. It should be vaporized and then burst into flame—totally burning all the hydrogen and carbon atoms in the fuel. This air volume, generated by the burner fan, and, in most applications, aided by the draft-over-the-fire, should be adjusted to deliver the exact amount of air required by the fuel being fed through the nozzle, see Figure 5-8.

It is impossible to reach this perfect state in the field, but it is a good target to shoot for. The closer you come to this perfect air-oil match, the cleaner, quieter, more efficient and odor free the flame will be.

There are six elements for the perfect air-oil match. They are: air volume, oil volume, oil pressure, oil spray pattern, oil spray angle, and the air pattern of the burner. The air pattern of the burner is the most important factor. This is unfortunate, because you cannot control or adjust air pattern; it is fixed by the burner design. Also, you cannot see the burner air pattern; you must rely on trial and error in our quest for perfection. See Figure 5-9.

Your tools in your search for the perfect flame are: the smoke tester, stack thermometer, draft gauge, pressure gauge, CO_2 or O_2 tester, the manufacturer's recommendations and the experience of the person who was there before you. Always use the condition of the unit as you found it as your best guide to what needs to be done. If you find the unit running well and reasonably clean, the nozzle installed in the unit is probably pretty close to being the right one. However, if the unit is not running well, it may be time for some changes. The single greatest factor in combustion inefficiency is excess air. It absorbs large quantities of heat and carries it wastefully up the chimney. It also reduces the flame temperature, decreasing the rate of heat transfer to the heat exchanger. Both of these raise stack temperatures, which lower efficiency.

The best burner adjustment is one that allows a smokeless, sootless operation with a minimum of excess air. We determine excess air by measuring the percentage of oxygen (O_2) in the flue gases. You will learn more about this in the combustion chapter.

Nozzle application procedure

If the manufacturer's recommendations are not available, or if you are upgrading an old unit with a new burner, the following is a step-by-step procedure you may use for selecting the best nozzle.

1. Set the over-the-fire draft to -.02", check the oil pressure, and install a nozzle that does not exceed the rating of the appliance.

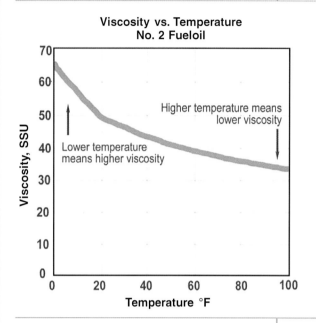

2. Start with an 80-degree hollow nozzle, and adjust for a 1 smoke and mark the air band opening.

3. Try an 80-degree solid nozzle and take another smoke test. If it is lighter, you have a solid air pattern; if the smoke is heavier, it is hollow.

4. Try a 60-degree hollow or solid nozzle as indicated by the previous two tests.

5. Select the nozzle that creates the lowest smoke and highest efficiency.

6. Once the tests are completed, record the results. Post the results near the burner and report them to the office where they should become a permanent part of the customer's service history.

Effects of viscosity on nozzle performance

One of the important factors affecting nozzle performance is the viscosity of the fuel. Viscosity is the resistance to flow—the thickness of the fuel. Thus, gasoline is "thin", having a lower viscosity, while *grease* is "thick", having a higher viscosity.

Figure 5-10: Viscosity vs. temperature change

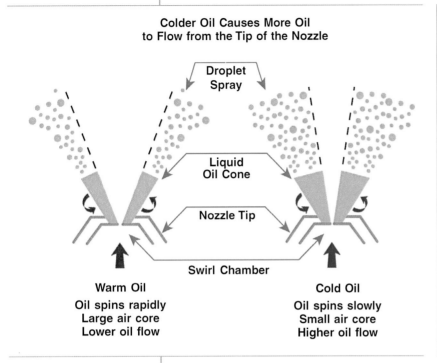

Colder Oil Causes More Oil
to Flow from the Tip of the Nozzle

Droplet Spray

Liquid
Oil Cone

Nozzle Tip

Swirl Chamber

Warm Oil
Oil spins rapidly
Large air core
Lower oil flow

Cold Oil
Oil spins slowly
Small air core
Higher oil flow

Figure 5-11:
Comparison of
warm vs. cold oil
on nozzle flow
rates

spray becomes narrower. The flame is longer, thinner, bigger, and less stable. This creates incomplete combustion that means increased smoke and soot. It is also harder to light cold oil, so ignition is delayed, and if the viscosity is very high, flame out and no heat result. See Figure 5-11.

Outside, above-ground storage tanks suffer most dramatically from the problems of cold oil. Let's say you do a tune up on a sunny hot summer day. The temperature of the oil in the tank is 80°F. You adjust the burner to run clean at that viscosity. As the temperature drops, the oil becomes much thicker and the amount of oil flowing out of the nozzle increases, causing the burner to over-fire. Not enough air is delivered and smoke increases. The angle of the spray decreases and the fire gets longer and

What makes the viscosity of oil increase? Temperature is the main factor in changing oil viscosity. As the temperature of the oil goes down, the viscosity goes up. The viscosity of No.2 oil is 35 SSU (seconds saybolt universal) at 100°F. When the temperature drops to 20°F, the viscosity goes to 65 SSU. See Figure 5-10 on previous page.

The effects of increased viscosity can be confusing. As the viscosity of the fuel flowing through a nozzle increases, so does the flow rate. Here is how it happens. As higher viscosity oil passes into the nozzle through the tangential slots and into the swirl chamber, the rotational velocity slows down. As a result, the walls of the tube of oil leaving the nozzle orifice are thicker—more oil enters the chamber and the oil droplets are bigger. The result is that the flame front moves out into the chamber and the angle of the

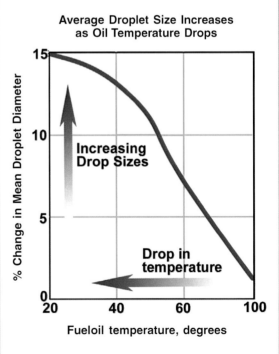

Figure 5-12:
Nozzle droplet size in relation to temperature

hits the back wall, which also increases smoke. The thick stream of oil makes for larger droplets that result in delayed ignition and smoke. Suddenly, the appliance is full of soot. Fortunately, as the oil gets colder, so does the air. This increases draft. The stronger draft draws in more combustion air and helps accommodate the increased volume of combustion gases.

This can happen to a lesser degree to underground tanks that are normally at about 50 to 55° F, and even to indoor tanks that are at room temperature. As oil trucks are not heated, it takes several days for a fresh load of cold oil to warm up in an underground or indoor storage tank. Until the oil warms, you can have viscosity problems. See Figure 5-12.

The easiest way to cut down on the effects of cold oil is to increase pump pressures. This decreases droplet size and better defines the spray angle, which makes burners less susceptible to high viscosity

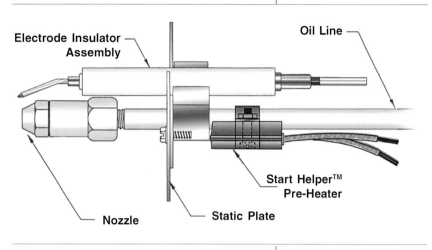

Figure 5-13: Nozzle line pre-heater

oil. Remember, it also increases the flow rate, so size the nozzle correctly. Another solution to cold oil is to install a nozzle line pre-heater. This simple, strap-on device increases the temperature of the oil arriving at the nozzle to about 100 to 120° F. See Figures 5-13 and 5-14.

The nozzle line heater is wired in parallel with the limit control so it is energized whenever there is power to the heating system. It works on electrical resistance. When the resistance gets too high, it stops heating. As the unit cools, the resistance drops and it heats up again. Pre-heaters draw about one amp and only heat the fuel to about 80 degrees above the ambient temperature—between 120 and 130°F—during stand-by. When the burner is running, the cold oil brings the temperature well below

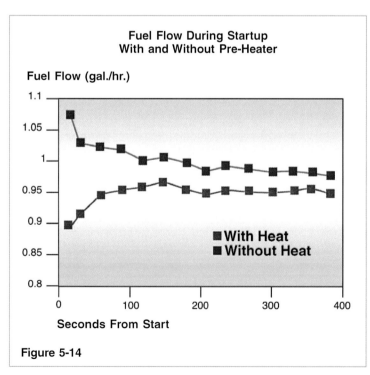

Figure 5-14

120°. Yet another way to help with this problem is to blend kerosene or additives with heating oil.

Thermal stability

If you find a fuel failure but the filter and strainer are clean and the nozzle is plugged with coke (a dull black substance), the problem is probably thermal stability. Oil can become unstable in the prolonged presence of heat, particularly when in contact with copper and other "yellow" metals. As the oil sits in the nozzle and drawer assembly and its temperature rises, it can form coke. This is more of an installation issue than a fuel issue.

Nozzles should not get hot. If the nozzle is hot enough to overheat the oil, you probably have either a bad draft situation, an old hard brick chamber reflecting excessive heat back on the nozzle after shut down, an after-drip problem, or a draw assembly and end cone sticking into the chamber. There are good mechanical fixes for these problems—i.e. post purge, draft inducers, interrupted ignition, ceramic chamber liners, and end cone amulets, to name a few.

If you encounter a thermal stability problem, find out what is causing the nozzle to get hot. The problem is most likely to occur after burner shutdown. Check the over-fire draft after shut-down. Check to see if the draft regulator closes after shutdown. If it stays open, it will reduce draft over-the-fire needed to cool the nozzle. Check electrode settings and the type of chamber. Check to be sure that the end-cone is flush or slightly recessed from the chamber face. Check for after-drip. Any of these problems could be the cause of your thermal instability.

Another cause of overheating is a hard brick chamber. When replacing an old non-flame retention burner with a new flame retention burner, it is tempting to leave the old chamber in place. The problem is, new burners have much higher flame temperatures than the old burners. It did not matter with the old burner's cool flame that the hard brick chamber held its heat for hours. The white-hot flame from the new burners, however, heats the chamber to very high temperatures. When the burner shuts off, the old chamber reflects all this heat back and overheats the nozzle.

The solution is to replace the old chamber or line it with a ceramic liner. In some cases, with big old dry base boilers, you can fill in the old chamber and install the new burner in the clean-out door, firing against a target wall—essentially creating a wet base boiler.

Many units are very tight or operate without a chimney and offer little or no over-fire draft. The best way to avoid nozzle overheating in these situations is motor-off-delay (commonly called post-purge.) Using a solenoid valve, the primary control shuts off the flow of oil but keeps the burner running for a few minutes, blowing air from the burner air intake through the air tube and past the nozzle—keeping it cool.

Nozzle after-drip

The quickest way to soot up a heat exchanger is nozzle after-drip. This happens when oil drips from the nozzle orifice after the burner shuts down. If the combustion

> There are three basic causes of after-drip—a defective pump shut off valve, air entrapped in the nozzle line, and oil expansion in the nozzle line caused by excessive radiated heat at shut down.

area is still hot, this oil burns with a smoky fire. If the combustion area is not hot enough, the oil drips out and collects in the bottom of the chamber. When the burner comes back on, all this extra oil lights and results in smoke, soot and rumbles.

There are three basic causes of after-drip—a defective pump shut off valve, air entrapped in the nozzle line, and oil expansion in the nozzle line caused by excessive radiated heat at shut down. The first is easy to check. Install a reliable pressure gauge in the nozzle discharge port of the fuel unit. Start the burner and let it run for the duration of the safety timing cycle. When it locks out, the pressure should drop about 20% and hold indefinitely. If it fails to stabilize and slowly descends to zero, you know the pressure-regulating valve in the pump is no good and the pump should be replaced.

If air is trapped in the nozzle line or adapter, it will cause an after-drip. See Figure 5-15. A bubble of trapped air will be compressed to $1/7^{th}$ its original volume by the 100 PSI pressure of the oil. When the burner shuts off, the pressure eases back to normal and the air bubble expands back to its original volume. This rapid expansion pushes oil out of the nozzle, causing an after-drip for several seconds. This can lead to delayed ignition, sooted heat exchangers and the smell of fumes.

This condition is diagnosed by looking into the combustion chamber at burner shut down. If there is no view port, you can perform the same check by tilting the transformer back and looking through the combustion head. If air is present, check for air leaks using the procedure described in the Chapter on Fuel Units.

Expansion of oil in lines can also cause after-drip. For every degree F of temperature rise, there is a .04% expansion of volume. After-drip occurs when the burner shuts down and the temperature of the oil in the nozzle line and adapter rise because of the heat from the appliance. Hard refracto-

**Figure 5-15:
Air trapped in
nozzle line**

**(1) Air bubbles trapped in oil line are compressed
while oil is under pressure during firing period.**

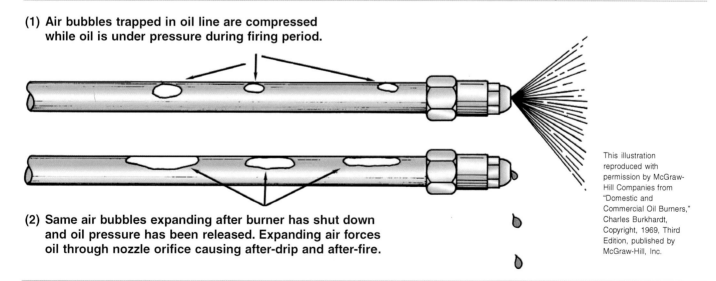

**(2) Same air bubbles expanding after burner has shut down
and oil pressure has been released. Expanding air forces
oil through nozzle orifice causing after-drip and after-fire.**

Figure 5-16:
Hago Ecovalve

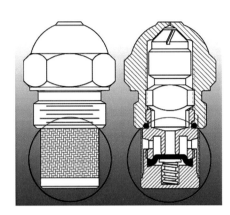

Figure 5-17:
Delavan
ProTek valve

ries, such as firebrick, tend to radiate more heat after shut down and thus are more likely to have this type of after-drip. To prevent this, line old refractory with ceramic.

Oilburner nozzle anti-drip valves

Another solution is the use of nozzles with check valves. These nozzles are designed to cut-off fuel flow from the nozzle quickly. See Figures 5-16 and 5-17.

Nozzle check valves also eliminate the incomplete atomization that can occur on start up and shut down of

the oilburner. They also eliminate after-drip associated with air bubbles in the nozzle line or expansion of the oil caused by reflected heat from the combustion chamber. Figure 5-18 shows how these valves reduce hydrocarbon (smoke) emissions.

These check valves are built into the nozzle strainer assembly and must be installed or changed at the time the nozzle is changed. The check valve is calibrated to open and close within a very tight tolerance of the burner operating pressure. For this reason, different nozzle check valves are manufactured to match different operating pressures. If you are about to change the operating pressure of a burner, you should first check to see if it has a check valve installed. If it does, be sure to install the right check valve for the new operating pressure.

Figure 5-18: Standard vs. anti-drip valve; emissions chart.
Dark tint area is a standard nozzle,
light shaded area is with a nozzle check valve.

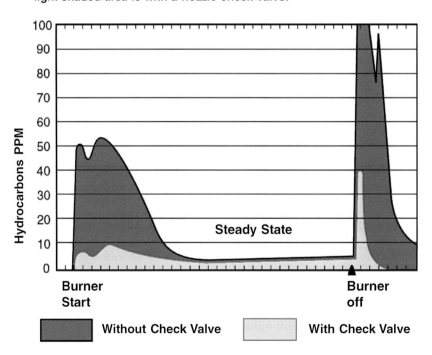

Part II: Combustion Chambers

Introduction

The flame from the oilburner is contained in the combustion chamber. A chamber must be made of the proper material to handle the high flame temperatures. It must be properly sized for the nozzle-firing rate and it must be the correct shape and the proper height. Combustion chambers have a profound effect on the first three of the four rules for good heating oil combustion:

1. The oil must be completely atomized and vaporized.

2. The oil must burn in complete suspension.

3. The mixture of air and oil vapors will burn best in the presence of hot refractory.

4. A minimum amount of air must be supplied for complete, efficient combustion.

To burn the oil in suspension means that the fire must never touch *any* surface— especially a cold one. The cold surface will reduce the temperature of the gases turning the vaporized carbon in the fuel into smoke and soot before it has a chance to burn. For combustion to be self-sustaining, the heat produced by the flame must be sufficient to ignite the fresh mixture of oil vapor and air coming into the combustion zone from the burner. The hotter the area around the burning zone, the easier and more completely the oil will burn.

The combustion chamber provides the necessary room for all the oil to burn before contacting or impinging on cold surfaces. It also reflects heat back into the burning zone, ensuring clean, quick combustion. If the chamber is too small or the wrong shape for the burner air pattern, or the nozzle is too close to the floor, there will be flame impingement, causing smoke and soot. With non-flame retention burners, an oversized chamber refractory will not reflect enough heat back into the burning zone to burn the carbon—smoke will be created. If the chamber sides are too low, combustibles will spill over the top and burn incompletely. It is your job to be able to diagnose an incorrectly built chamber as well as to build and design a correct one.

Chamber materials

Chambers should heat up quickly, reflect as much heat back into the burning zone as possible, and cool off quickly when the burner shuts down. There are five common types of materials used in combustion chamber construction.

Insulating fire brick: The porous nature and lightness of this brick makes it highly resistant to the penetration of heat. The side of the brick facing the fire glows red hot in about 15 seconds while the rear surface remains relatively cool. (The bricks come in a variety of sizes and are available in pre-cast chambers). For fires up to 3 GPH, you can use 2000°F firebrick. It will take up to 3000-degree temperatures, but structurally it cannot take the starting violence of a large fire. Proper refractory cement should be used with the insulating brick so the expansion of the brick and cement will be equal.

Common fire brick or hard brick: This weighs more than insulating brick and it absorbs much more heat before it begins reflecting any back into the burning zone. It is unsatisfactory for residential purposes, but is used in commercial units because it stands up better to the shock loads of high firing rates. The brick comes in the standard size of 9" long by 4.5" high, and 2.5" deep. It is also made in runners and pre-cast chambers.

Metal fire chambers: Metal chambers are used primarily in factory-built "packaged units" because they can be shipped in place without damage or breakage and do not require bracing. Metal chambers are much better than common fire brick. However, they are sensitive to improper nozzle selection and overfiring. A nozzle-firing rate that is too high, or a lopsided fire can distort or even burn a hole through the wall of the chamber. Direct flame impingement on the chamber must be avoided. Metal chambers must have free flowing air behind them to keep them from burning through. Do not put any kind of insulating material, including soot, around the chamber. The higher flame temperatures of flame retention burners is tough on metal chambers; it is usually a good idea to replace a burned out metal chamber with a pre-cast ceramic one.

Ceramic chambers: Ceramic material is excellent for chambers. It reflects heat quickly while absorbing very little and it is easy to install. If the old chamber is still in good condition, you may use ceramic blanket material to line the old chamber. Be sure to seal any air leaks in the old

chamber first. If the old chamber is deteriorated, wrap the material with a stainless steel binder. If the old chamber was too small or the wrong shape, lining it will not help. Ceramic chambers become brittle after firing. Do not touch it with a vacuum cleaner hose or flame mirror after it has been used. The material is intended for firing rates below 3 GPH, and will withstand about 2,300°F. It can be purchased by the foot or is available in pre-shaped sizes. The material gives quieter operation, less smoke and fuel savings.

Molded chamber: Many manufacturers install their own molded chambers in their packaged units. They are usually made of semi-insulating refractory material.

Chamber shapes

The best shape for a chamber is round or oval so the hot gases can sweep back smoothly. In a square or rectangular chamber, eddy currents develop in the corners requiring more excess air to burn completely. The correct height is most important. All combustion should take place in the chamber. There should be little if any flame above the chamber. The top of the chamber should be about as far above the nozzle as the floor is below it. See Figure 5-19.

Sizing the chamber

The gallons-per-hour firing rate determines the size of the chamber. A firing rate of .75 to 3 GPH requires 80 square inches of chamber floor space per gallon of fuel. A firing rate from 3.5 to 5 GPH requires 90 square inches, and over 5.5 GPH requires 100 square inches per gallon. See Table 5-2 and Figure 5-20.

Installing a low firing rate chamber

There are many very good pre-cast

Figure 5-19: Combustion chamber design

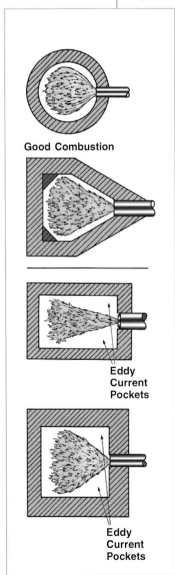

Good Combustion

Eddy Current Pockets

Eddy Current Pockets

Table 5-2: Combustion chamber sizing data (preferred)

Oil Consumption gph	Square Inch Area Combustion Chamber	Square Combustion Chamber Inches	Dia. Round Combustion Chamber Inches	Rectangular Combustion Chamber Inches	HEIGHT FROM NOZZLE TO FLOOR IN INCHES			
					Conventional Burner Width x Length	Conventional Burner Single Nozzle	Sunflower Flame Burner Single Nozzle	Sunflower Flame Burner Twin Nozzle
.75	60	8 x 8	9	—	5.0	x	5.0	x
.85	68	8.5 x 8.5	9	—	5.0	x	5.0	x
1.00	80	9 x 9	10-1/8	—	5.0	x	5.0	x
1.25	100	10 x 10	11-1/4	—	5.0	x	5.0	x
1.35	108	10-1/2 x 10-1/2	11-3/4	—	5.0	x	5.0	x
1.50	120	11 x 11	12-3/8	10 x 12	5.0	x	6.0	x
1.65	132	11-1/2 x 11-1/2	13	10 x 13	5.0	x	6.0	x
2.00	160	12-5/8 x 12-5/8	14-1/4	6	x	7.0	x	
2.50	200	14-1/4 x 14-1/4	16	12 x 16-1/2	6.5	x	7.5	x
3.00	240	15-1/2 x 15-1/2	17-1/2	13 x 18-1/2	7.0	5.0	8.0	6.5
3.50	315	17-3/4 x 17-3/4	20	15 x 21	7.5	6.0	8.5	7.0
4.00	360	19 x 19	21-1/2	16 x 22-1/2	8.0	6.0	9.0	7.0
4.50	405	20 x 20		17 x 23-1/2	8.5	6.5	9.5	7.5
5.00	450	21-1/4 x 21-1/4		18 x 25	9.0	6.5	10.0	8.0
5.50	550	23-1/2 x 23-1/2		20 x 27-1/2	9.5	7.0	10.5	8.0
6.00	600	24-1/2 x 24-1/2		21 x 28-1/2	10.0	7.0	11.0	8.5
6.50	650	25-1/2 x 25-1/2		22 x 29-1/2	10.5	7.5	11.5	9.0
7.00	700	26-1/2 x 26-1/2		23 x 30-1/2	11.0	7.5	12.0	9.5
7.50	750	27-1/4 x 27-1/4	Round Combustion Chambers Usually Not Used In These Sizes	24 x 31	11.5	7.5	12.5	10.0
8.0	800	28-1/4 x 28-1/4		25 x 32	12.0	8.0	13.0	10.0
8.50	850	29-1/4 x 29-1/4		25 x 34	12.5	8.5	13.5	10.5
9.00	900	30 x 30		25 x 36	13.0	8.5	14.0	11.0
9.50	950	31 x 31		26 x 36-1/2	13.5	9.0	14.5	11.5
10.00	1000	31-3/4 x 31-3/4		26 x 38-1/2	14.0	9.0	15.0	12.0
11.00	1100	33-1/4 x 33-1/4		28 x 29-1/2	14.5	9.5	15.5	12.5
12.00	1200	34-1/2 x 34-1/2		28 x 43	15.0	10.0	16.0	13.0
13.00	1300	36 x 36		29 x 45	15.5	10.5	16.5	14.0
14.00	1400	37-1/2 x 37-1/2		31 x 45	16.0	11.0	17.0	14.5
15.00	1500	38-3/4 x 38-3/4		32 x 47	16.5	11.5	17.5	15.0
16.00	1600	40 x 40		33 x 48-1/2	17.0	12.0	18.0	15.0
17.00	1700	41-1/4 x 41-1/4		34 x 50	17.5	12.5	18.5	15.5
18.00	1800	42-1/2 x 42-1/2		35 x 51-1/2	18.0	13.0	19.0	16.0

Row group labels (left margin):
- .75 through 3.00: 80 Square Inches per Gallon
- 3.50 through 5.00: 90 Square Inches per Gallon
- 5.50 through 18.00: 100 Square Inches per Gallon

1 Firing Rate (gph)	2 Length (L)	3 Width (W)	4 Dimension (C)	5 Suggested Height (H)	6 Minimum Dia. Vertical Cyl.
0.50	8	7	4.0	8	8
0.65	8	7	4.5	9	8
0.75	9	8	4.5	9	9
0.85	9	8	4.5	9	9
1.00	10	9	5.0	10	10
1.10	10	9	5.0	10	10
1.25	11	10	5.0	10	11
1.35	12	10	5.0	10	11
1.50	12	11	5.5	11	12
1.65	12	11	5.5	11	13
1.75	14	11	5.5	11	13
2.00	15	12	5.5	11	14
2.25	16	12	6.0	12	15
2.50	17	13	6.0	12	16
2.75	18	14	6.0	12	18

Figure 5-20: Recommended minimum inside dimensions of refractory-type combustion chambers

NOTES:

1. Flame lengths are approximately as shown in column 2. Tested boilers or furnaces will often operate well with chambers shorter than the lengths shown in column 2.

2. As a general practice, any of these dimensions can be exceeded without much effect on combustion.

3. Chambers in the form of horizontal cylinders should be at least as large in diameter as the dimension in column 3. Horizontal stainless steel cylindrical chambers should be 1 to 4 inches larger in diameter than the figures in column 3 and should be used only on wet base boilers with non-retention burners.

4. Wing walls are not recommended. Corbels are not necessary, though they might be of benefit to good heat distribution in certain boiler or furnace designs, especially with non-retention burners.

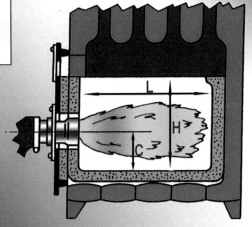

chambers available. If the existing chamber is in reasonable condition, ceramic liners are an option. If you find yourself in a situation where the chamber must be replaced and there is no pre-cast one available for that furnace or boiler, you may have to build a chamber. If so, the following step-by-step procedure may be helpful—especially for dry base boilers.

1. Remove the old chamber.

2. Seal up any leaks in the unit base.

3. Lay down a 1" layer of powdered insulating material on the unit floor. This will reduce sound transmission and level uneven surfaces.

4. If you are building the chamber on non-combustible material, lay down a 1" floor of insulating fire brick.

5. Using insulating firebrick, build the bottom half of the chamber in a shape suitable to the burner's fuel and air patterns.

6. Pack rockwool or vermiculite around the outside of the chamber.

7. Take a piece of smoke pipe slightly larger than the burner air tube, and use it to form the burner air tube opening. Then build up the chamber around it, making sure to observe the proper floor to nozzle center line, and making the end of the smoke pipe recess one quarter inch for the inside face of the chamber.

8. Install the top half of the chamber and pack, making sure that on a dry base boiler the bricks extend at least one course above the dry base.

9. Build up the front of the chamber and finish off the outside with a 50-50 mix of Portland cement and insulating material.

10. Use the same material to cap off the top of the chamber over the packed vermiculite. Form the cap so it is pitched from the chamber up to the boiler.

11. Install the burner with the face of the end cone one-quarter inch back from the chamber face. See Figure 5-21.

12. Snugly stuff the space around the air tube with fireproof rope.

13. Cap off the inside and outside around the air tube with the 50-50 mix.

14. Fire the chamber in short bursts for 10 to 20 minutes to dry the chamber materials.

Unlike dry base boilers and furnaces, wet base boilers may be fired without a chamber. The water jacket surrounds the fire zone. The flame from modern burners are self-propagating, they do not need hot refractory reflecting heat back into the flame to burn cleanly. Although a chamber wall is not needed, a target wall with little wing walls is still a good idea. As with chambers, the nozzle must be properly sized so the flame does not impinge on any cold surfaces.

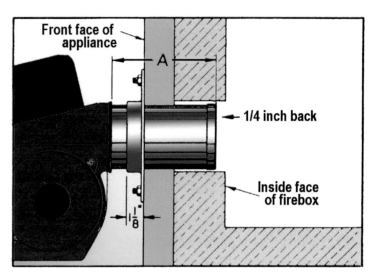

"A" = Usable air tube length.

Air Tube Insertion
The burner head should be 1/4" back from the inside wall of the combustion chamber. Under no circumstances should the burner head extend into the combustion chamber. If chamber opening is in excess of 4 3/8", additional set back may be required.

**Figure 5-21:
Burner
installation,
chamber guide**

There are advantages to chamberless firing:

• Target walls are less expensive than chambers.

• Heat transfer to the water improves because there is no insulating chamber material between the cast iron and the fire.

• Nitrogen oxide emissions are reduced.

• Flame temperatures are lowered since there is no chamber to reflect heat back into the fire and the iron absorbs all that heat. Lower flame temperatures produce lower NOx emissions.

Finally, when in doubt about nozzles, chamber, chamber design or chamber materials refer to the manufacturer's instructions, ask your supplier, or call the manufacturer's technical service hot line.

Chapter **6**

DRAFT
& VENTING

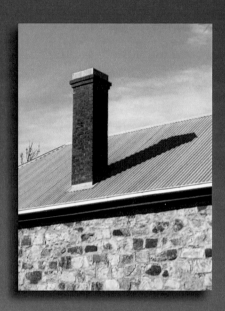

IN THIS
CHAPTER

- **Draft—Why it is needed and how it is measured**

- **Why we regulate draft, and the effects of draft upon burner operation and efficiency**

- **Alternative venting systems: power-venting and direct-venting**

Chapter 6

Draft and Venting

Introduction

Air is needed to burn oil cleanly and efficiently. We must understand how to supply air to the burner and how to ensure that all of the gases created in burning the fuel are vented to the outside. Additionally, for non-condensing appliances, we must make sure the water vapor created during combustion is vented to the outside prior to condensing.

What is draft?

Draft is a current of air in an enclosed area that is created by a difference in pressure. In practical terms, draft is a force that "pulls" or "sucks" the exhaust gases out of the heating unit and sends them up the chimney.

During the combustion process hot gases rise through the heating appliance to the flue pipe and travel up the chimney, creating negative pressure or suction, also known as "negative draft" at the bottom of the chimney.

The pressure difference is created because:

• When the burner is off and the chimney is cold, the air inside the combustion area, heat exchanger, flue pipe, and chimney is at atmospheric pressure.

• When the burner starts, the burner fan creates "static pressure" as it pushes air into the combustion area where it combines with the fuel to create a fire.

• When the air and fuel burn, the temperature rises dramatically and the combustion gases expand to more than double their volume. This expansive pressure adds to the pressure created by the burner fan and pushes the combustion gases through the heat exchanger.

• As the hot combustion gases travel up the chimney they create a pressure drop behind them that sucks the combustion gases out of the heat exchanger, Figure 6-1.

Draft is the total effect of the positive pressures of the burner fan, the expansive pressure of the flame, and the negative pressure of the hot gases escaping the top of the chimney.

Figure 6-1:
Chimney draft

Hot Air Causes Lower Weight (Pressure) at Bottom of Chimney than Cold Air

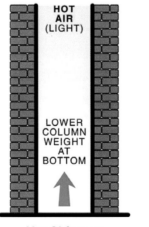

Hot Chimney   **Cold Chimney**

Oilburners need steady draft for proper operation. Insufficient or variable draft can cause operational problems. For example, a fire that pulsates or a rumble in the appliance may result from insufficient draft.

Chimney venting creates natural draft

There are two types of natural draft created in the chimney— thermal and currential.

Thermal draft is created when the air in the chimney is hotter, and therefore lighter (less dense), than the air outside. As the lighter air moves up the chimney, (See Figure 6-2), more air moves in from the surrounding room to replace it.

Currential draft is caused by the suction created as wind rushes over the chimney top, creating a negative pressure in the chimney. Because wind is variable, currential draft is unpredictable and must be controlled. Occasionally wind will blow down the chimney causing a 'down draft.' A variable draft is created by a pressure difference between the top and bottom of the chimney.

What affects draft

Draft is created by a pressure difference between the top and bottom of the chimney. The draft produced by a chimney is variable, not constant. The temperature of the outside air, the temperature of the flue gases, the barometric pressure, and humidity of the air all affect draft.

When the burner is first fired, the chimney is full of cool air and there is little

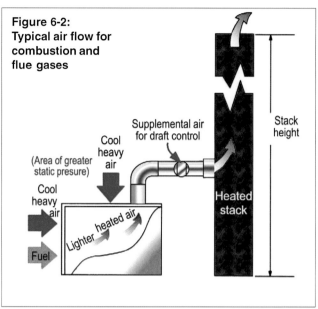

Figure 6-2:
Typical air flow for combustion and flue gases

or no thermal draft. As the chimney and gases warm, the draft will strengthen. As the outside air cools, the temperature difference increases, and draft increases.

Other conditions that affect draft include wind velocity across or into the top of the chimney and flow restrictions in the chimney, flue pipe, or heat exchanger. It is important that the chimney be properly constructed, clean, and have no air leaks through cracks and gaps.

The placement of the chimney and its construction can also affect draft. A chimney operates best when it is warm and dry. Therefore, a chimney with one or more of its walls outside the building does not work as well as an inside chimney.

The outside chimney heats up slowly and cools off rapidly. Additionally, the chimney must extend at least two feet above nearby objects, such as the roof peak, trees, and other buildings within 10 feet. Overhanging trees or high buildings can affect the draft and can cause wind

Table 6-1
Theoretical Chimney Draft for Various Conditions

Case 1   OUTSIDE AIR = 60°F

AVG CHIMNEY TEMP. °F	CHIMNEY HEIGHT IN FEET				
	10	15	20	25	30
100	0.01	0.02	0.02	0.03	0.03
200	0.03	0.05	0.06	0.08	0.09
300	0.05	0.07	0.09	0.12	0.14
400	0.06	0.09	0.12	0.14	0.17
500	0.07	0.10	0.13	0.17	0.20
600	0.07	0.11	0.15	0.19	0.22
700	0.08	0.12	0.16	0.20	0.24
800	0.09	0.13	0.17	0.22	0.26
900	0.09	0.14	0.18	0.23	0.27

Case 2   OUTSIDE AIR = 0°F

AVG CHIMNEY TEMP. °F	CHIMNEY HEIGHT IN FEET				
	10	15	20	25	30
100	0.03	0.04	0.05	0.07	0.08
200	0.04	0.05	0.09	0.11	0.13
300	0.06	0.09	0.12	0.14	0.17
400	0.07	0.10	0.14	0.17	0.20
500	0.08	0.11	0.15	0.19	0.23
600	0.07	0.12	0.17	0.21	0.25
700	0.09	0.13	0.18	0.22	0.27
800	0.09	0.14	0.19	0.23	0.28
900	0.10	0.15	0.19	0.24	0.29

$$\text{Draft} = 0.01467 \times \text{Height} \times \left(1 - \left([\,OAT + 460\,] / [\,TEMP + 460\,] \right) \right)$$

Where:

Draft = Inches Water Column

OAT = Outdoor Air Temperature

TEMP = Average Chimney Temperature = (Tin - Tout)/2

Based on information in the North American Combustion Handbook, Second Edition, 1978.

currents to tumble, causing down draft. (Figure 6-3).

Improper or variable draft can cause problems

Variations in chimney draft can change the amount of combustion air entering the burner. Low draft will cause the burner fan to push against higher air pressure resulting in less air for combustion and a smoky fire. High draft will cause too much air to rush into the combustion zone resulting in reduced efficiency. Excessive draft will also cause excess air to leak into the unit, further increasing stack temperatures. Table 6-1 (previous page) shows how draft is affected by outdoor temperature, chimney height and chimney temperature.

Changes in draft can cause severe problems with older units. Variations in draft have a strong effect on non-flame retention burners. These older burner fans produced very little static pressure and relied on the pressure drop created by the chimney to help draw in their combustion air. Because thermal draft is very weak during a cold start up with these burners, they tend to rumble and smoke until the chimney warms up.

Effects of draft on air leakage

High draft will draw air into the appliance through leaks. This air will cool the combustion products while increasing their volume, reducing the efficiency of the heating system.

Ensuring the draft is proper (See Draft Regulators) will help improve efficiency. Additionally, sealing all air leaks with furnace cement or high temperature silicone wherever possible

will reduce the amount of air drawn through the appliance. Air flowing up the chimney is replaced by air being drawn into the building through windows, doors or other gaps in the building envelope.

The most common locations for these air leaks are around the burner mounting flange, between the base and the floor, between the base and the heat exchanger, between the sections of a boiler, and around clean-out and inspection doors and plates. Figure 6-4 shows outdoor air infiltration caused by the heating system and chimney.

Effects of draft on stand-by losses

Whenever the air inside the chimney is warmer than the air outdoors, the chimney will create thermal draft. This is good when the burner is running, but not when the burner shuts off. Most pre-1970s heat exchangers have very large, open passages that offer very little restriction to air flow.

It is very easy for the draft from the still warm chimney to draw warmed air from the

Figure 6-3: Down draft

building into the burner air intake and up through the heat exchanger. As it does so, it also takes heat from the heat exchanger as it goes up the chimney. This new hot air keeps the chimney warm, which, in turn, keeps producing draft that cools the building.

Old equipment, especially boilers, have very high stand-by losses. New burner air intakes, air handling parts and combustion heads are not as wide open as the old ones, and new heat exchangers are much more restricted than the older types. The result is much higher efficiencies, less off-cycle heat loss and much lower oil consumption.

Draft regulators

It is necessary to regulate draft because natural draft is so variable. The most common draft regulator is the by-pass or air-bleed type. Since it responds to changes in barometric (atmospheric) pressure, it is also called a barometric draft regulator or damper (Figure 6-5).

The regulator consists of a counter weighted swinging door that opens to allow room air to flow into the flue and mix with the exhaust gases. The room air dilutes and cools the exhaust gas which reduces the temperature difference between the gases leaving the chimney and the outside air. This reduces the draft. When the draft

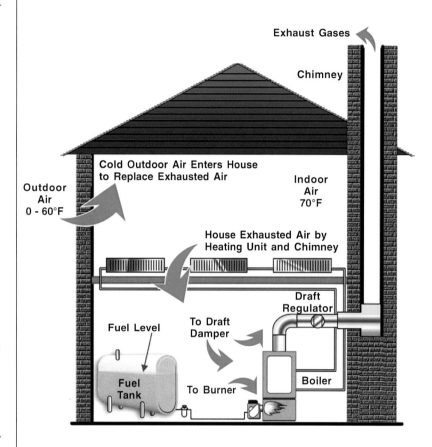

Exhaust Gases

Chimney

Cold Outdoor Air Enters House to Replace Exhausted Air

Outdoor Air 0 - 60°F

Indoor Air 70°F

House Exhausted Air by Heating Unit and Chimney

Draft Regulator

Fuel Level

To Draft Damper

To Burner

Boiler

Fuel Tank

Figure 6-4: Outdoor air infiltration caused by the heating system and chimney

drops below the draft regulator setting, the counterweight closes the draft regulator door.

It is important to understand that no draft regulator can cause an increase in draft, it can only decrease draft over-the-fire. It also cannot prevent down drafts caused by wind currents blowing down the chimney.

Figure 6-5: Draft regulators

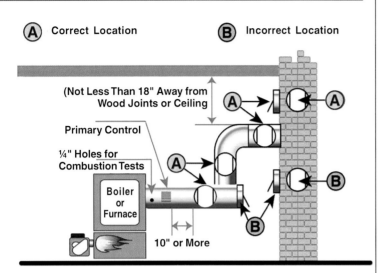

(A) Correct Location   (B) Incorrect Location

(Not Less Than 18" Away from Wood Joints or Ceiling

Primary Control

¼" Holes for Combustion Tests

Boiler or Furnace

10" or More

Figure 6-6:
Draft regulator
locations:
Correct and
incorrect

The draft regulator should be installed in the flue pipe between the chimney and the stack mounted primary control, if there is one. It should be at least 10 inches to 12 inches from the control and 18 inches is preferred. If installed closer to the control, the cool air from the regulator can cause the unit to shut off on safety even when the system is operating properly. See Figure 6-6 for draft regulator locations.

Some newer heating appliances are designed to operate without a draft regulator. The burners create enough static pressure to move the combustion products up the chimney and the heat exchangers are tight enough to resist the effects of strong and variable negative draft.

As with all Oilheat appliances, always follow the manufacturers' instructions regarding draft.

Measuring chimney draft

We measure draft in 'inches of water column.' One inch of water column is the pressure difference required to lift a column of water one inch up a tube. Typically, chimney drafts required for oil-fired heating units are close to -.05 inches. Draft is checked at two places: over-the-fire (draft at the top of the combustion area) and in the flue pipe, as close to the breech as possible.

Before any measurements or adjustments are made, the condition of the draft regulator should be checked. The pivot shaft should be horizontal, not cocked, and the door should swing freely. Have burner run long enough to be sure that the chimney is warm.

Draft over-the-fire

Draft over-the-fire is the most important draft measurement and should always be measured first. The over-the-fire draft must be constant so burner air delivery will also be constant. The setting must be high enough to ensure that combustion products do not leak into the building, but are drawn through the heat exchanger. Normally, an over-the-fire draft of -.01" to -.02" will be sufficient.

If the over-the-fire draft is higher than manufacturers recommendations (typically -.02"), the draft regulator weight should be adjusted to allow the door to open more. If the draft is below manufacturer's recommendations, the weight should be adjusted to close the regulator door. However, some equipment is able to operate under very low or zero draft. In fact, some appliances operate under positive pressure, so that when an over the fire reading is taken, the draft is positive.

If the draft regulator door is already wide open, you may need to install a larger or second regulator.

Draft at the breech

After setting the over-the-fire draft, the draft at the breech should be measured. The draft in the flue pipe will be slightly higher than the over-fire draft due to the restric-

Draft over-the-fire is the most important draft measurement and should always be checked first

tion caused by the heat exchanger. This restriction, or the lack of it, is a clue to the design and condition of the heat exchanger. A clean heat exchanger of good design will normally cause the breech draft to be in the range of -.03" to -.07" when the over-the-fire draft is from -.01" to -.02". The difference between the breech draft and the over-the fire draft is often called the 'draft drop' or 'pressure drop' across the heat exchanger. If the breech draft is -.07" and the over-the-fire draft is -.02", the draft drop is .05".

Excessive draft drop may indicate heavy soot and scale deposits in the unit. It is important to understand that over-the-fire draft is indirectly controlled. It is a function, not only of the draft created by the chimney, but also of restrictions in the heat exchanger.

A burner operating at more than zero smoke will cause soot deposits to build in the heat exchanger. These deposits increase the draft drop, lowering over-the-fire draft, reducing combustion air, and creating more smoke. The increased smoke causes even more soot to build up, increasing draft drop even further. The result is a quickly plugged heat exchanger.

Sometimes there is little difference between the breech draft and the over-the-fire draft, usually with older units originally built for coal. If a boiler measures a low efficiency with a high stack temperature (600°F or more), it may be possible to install baffles in the heat exchanger passages. However, as with most older equipment, the best alternative is to recommend a new boiler or furnace of higher efficiency.

Chimney sizing

Proper chimney sizing is important for the safe and efficient operation of all heating appliances. As the requirement can vary depending upon the size and design of

How draft controls work

Static pressure of the cool air exerts pressure on the outside of the furnace or boiler, the breeching, and flue. The pressure difference between the room air and heated gas (air) causes products of combustion to flow (draft) through the unit and rise through the breeching and chimney. Room temperature air enters through the barometric draft control in the precise amount needed to overcome the excess drafts caused by temperature variations, wind fluctuations and barometric pressure changes. Combustion of fuel is complete and the process is stabilized. The velocity of combustion gases through the heat exchanger is slowed so more heat is extracted.

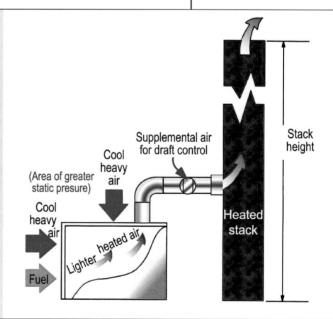

the appliance, the manufacturer's instructions must be followed.

Installing flue pipe

Be sure to check the condition of the flue pipe during each service call. If it looks questionable—replace it. The stack temperatures on new high efficiency units are much lower and are more likely to cause condensation and rusting of the flue pipe. This is extremely important because combustion gases can enter the building if the flue pipe is porous or disconnected.

The flue pipe must be at least 18 inches from a combustible wall or ceiling as a fire prevention measure. It should never be smaller than the flue pipe collar at the breech of the boiler or furnace. The flue pipe should be as short as possible and should not exceed 10 feet of horizontal run unless a draft fan is used. It should have a minimum of ¼" per foot pitch from the appliance up to the chimney and be run with minimum number of elbows. Use 45-degree elbows instead of 90's when possible.

The flue pipe should be firmly joined with sheet metal screws and supported with straps or wire. It should be tightly fitted to the breeching and installed into a clay or metal thimble that is securely cemented into the chimney. Be sure the thimble and pipe do not protrude beyond the inside wall of the chimney tile.

No sort of dampers, except for the barometric damper (draft regulator) should be installed in the flue pipe or breeching. They are not needed and could cause problems if they close accidentally.

Chimney and draft problems

Insufficient draft can occur with too many appliances connected to a chimney. Whenever connecting two or more fuel burning appliances to a single chimney, verify that there is sufficient draft for safe operation of all units. Insufficient draft also occurs when obstructions such as soot, loose bricks, birds' nests or other foreign objects build up in the chimney and restrict flow. See Figure 6-7 for common chimney troubles and their corrections.

Lack of air in the furnace room

Insulation, tight windows and doors, and tight construction can prevent outside air from entering the building. As a result, the building cannot 'breathe.' Oilburner

Diameter of Flue or Breeching	If Chimney Height Is	Use This Size Control	If Chimney Height Is	Use This Size Control	If Chimney Height Is	Use This Size Control
4	15' or less	4"	16' or more	5"		
5	15' or less	5"	16' or more	6"		
6	15' or less	6"	16' or more	7"		
7	15' or less	7"	16' or more	8"		
8	15' or less	8"	16' or more	9"		
9	15' or less	9"	16'-30'	10"	31' or more	12"
10	20' or less	10"	21'-40'	12"	41' or more	14"
11	20' or less	12"	21'-40'	12"	41' or more	14"
12	20' or less	12"	21'-40'	14"	41' or more	16"
13	22' or less	14"	23'-45'	16"	46' or more	18"
14	22' or less	14"	23'-45'	16"	46' or more	18"
15	22' or less	16"	23'-45'	16"	46' or more	18"
16	30' or less	16"	31'-50'	18"	51' or more	20"
17	30' or less	18"	31'-50'	20"	51' or more	20"
18	30' or less	18"	31'-50'	20"	51' or more	20"
19	30' or less	20"	31'-50'	20"	51' or more	24"
20	30' or less	20"	31'-50'	20"	51' or more	24"
21	30' or less	20"	31'-50'	24"	51' or more	24"
22	30' or less	24"	31'-50'	24"	51' or more	24"
23	35' or less	24"	36'-60'	24"	61' or more	28"
24	35' or less	24"	36'-60'	24"	61' or more	28"
25	35' or less	28"	36'-60'	28"	61' or more	28"
26	40' or less	28"	41'-70'	28"	71' or more	28"
27	40' or less	28"	41'-70'	28"	71'-100'	28"
28	50' or less	32"	51'-100'	28"	100' or more	32"
29	50' or less	32"	51'-100'	32"	100' or more	32"
30	50' or less	32"	51'-100'	32"	100' or more	32"
31	50' or less	32"	51'-100'	32"	100' or more	Two 24"
32	50' or less	32"	51'-100'	32"	100' or more	One 24" One 28"
33	50' or less	32"	51'-100'	One 32" One 20"	100' or more	One 32" One 24"
34	50' or less	32"	51'-100'	One 32" One 24"	100' or more	One 32" One 24"

Figure 6-7: Combustion chimney troubles

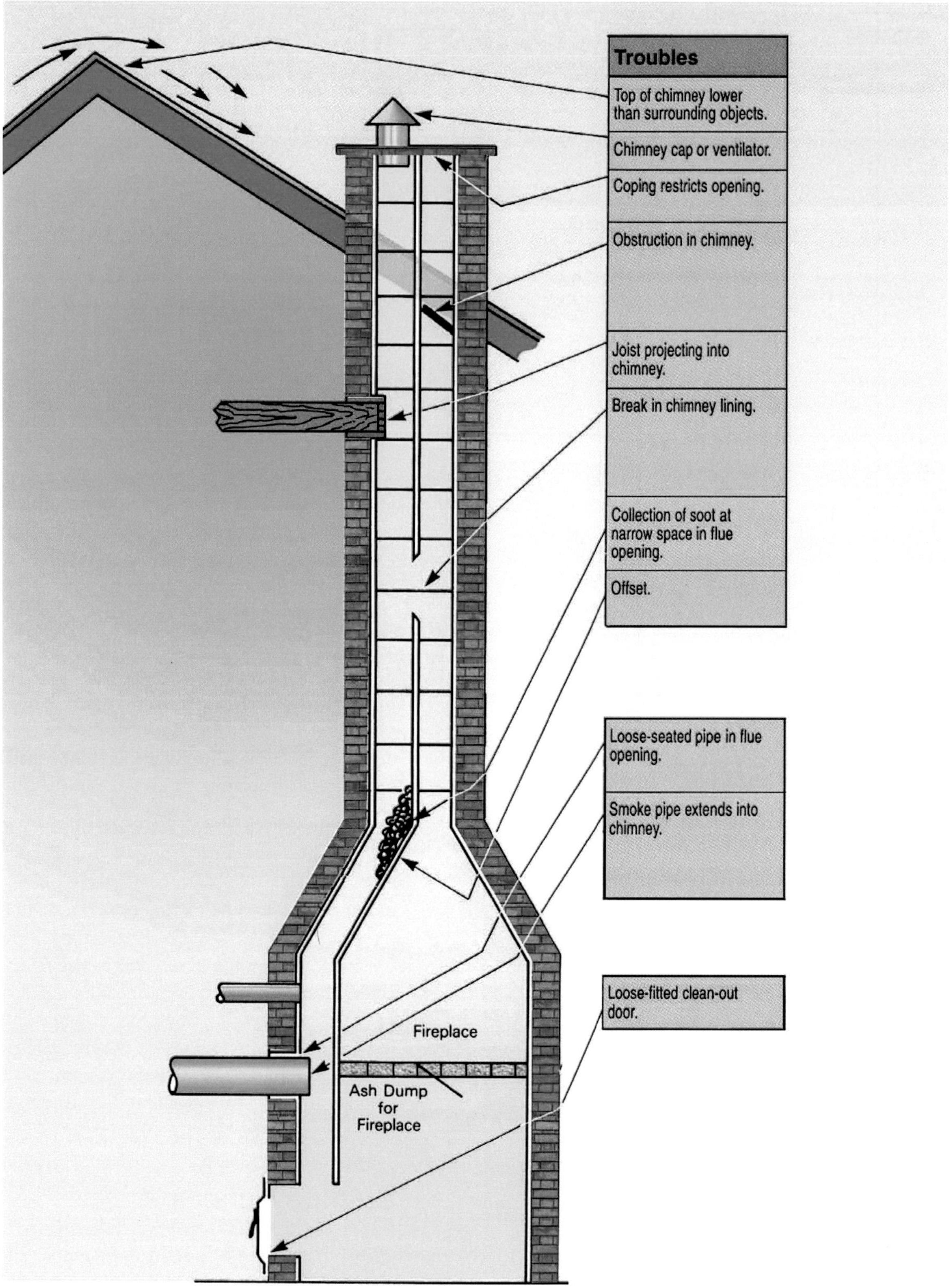

Troubles

Top of chimney lower than surrounding objects.

Chimney cap or ventilator.

Coping restricts opening.

Obstruction in chimney.

Joist projecting into chimney.

Break in chimney lining.

Collection of soot at narrow space in flue opening.

Offset.

Loose-seated pipe in flue opening.

Smoke pipe extends into chimney.

Loose-fitted clean-out door.

Fireplace

Ash Dump for Fireplace

combustion requires a great deal of air to operate properly. It competes with the fireplace, exhaust fans and the clothes dryer for air. All of these appliances drawing on the air in a tight house make it difficult for the oilburner to draw in enough combustion air.

With the building so tight, the indoor air pressure drops below the outdoor air pressure and the appliance becomes back-vented. Odors, soot, smoke and carbon monoxide may be drawn into the building. 'Isolated combustion' (ducting outside air directly to the burner) is the best solution to this problem and there are many effective isolated combustion air options available. (See Figure 6-8)

Water heater and furnace stack connections

When an oil-fired water heater is installed, it is usually necessary to connect the flue to the same chimney as the furnace or boiler. This can be done in two ways:

1. The two flue pipes can be joined together with a Y connector, as shown in Figure 6-9. ('T' connectors should NOT be used as they often cause venting problems for both appliances.) The exit, or chimney side of the Y should be at least one size larger than the largest flue pipe.

2. If you do not use the Y fitting, you can make a second opening in the chimney.

If two or more openings are provided into one chimney flue, they must be at different levels. The flue pipe from the unit with the lower firing rate should enter at the highest level consistent with available headroom and clearances to combustible material (see Figure 6-10). A separate draft regulator should be installed for each appliance.

Developments affecting chimneys and exhaust

High efficiency equipment has brought about changes that can affect chimney draft. Some of these developments, such as lower flue gas temperatures, reduced firing rates, and cold start boilers, will reduce the draft produced by chimneys, and can cause operational problems.

The most serious consequence of lowered flue gas temperatures is condensation. The water vapor in the combustion products can drop below the dew point, and turn into water. Because of the sulfuric oxides present in the gases, this water is acidic. It creates scale in the heat exchanger, corrodes the flue pipe and attacks the cement in the chimney. A net flue gas temperature of at least 350°F is recommended to avoid this problem. Corrosion resistant chimney liners also help.

Chimney check

The objective of a chimney check is to identify obvious and serious chimney problems. It is not intended to be a detailed

Figure 6-8: Typical installation of an outside air kit

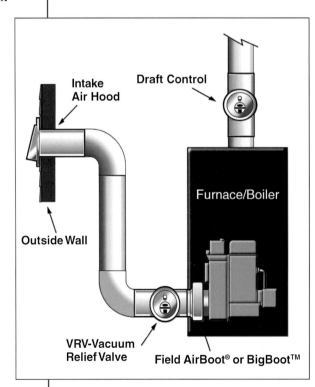

inspection. If any chimney damage or deterioration that would inhibit the safe operation of the heating appliance is found, the owner of the building should be notified immediately. A qualified chimney professional should be called-in for a follow-up inspection. See Figure 6-11 on following page.

The chimney check should include the following:

• If there is one, visually inspect the clean-out at the base of the chimney for excessive or abnormal debris. Be sure the clean out door is shut tight and sealed when you are finished.

• Remove the flue pipe from the chimney breech and inspect the inside of the chimney with a light and a flame mirror for signs of damage or deterioration. Debris, mortar, brick, and pieces of liner material at the base of the chimney are signs of trouble.

• Go outside, walk around the building, and observe the exterior of the chimney. If you observe damage, deterioration, or that the chimney is leaning to one side; further inspection by a chimney professional is required.

Chimney caps and draft inducers

Chimneys may suffer variable draft due to changes in wind or air turbulence A simple and inexpensive solution to this problem is to install a cap (Figure 6-12) or hood over the top of the chimney. However, these caps can rust and discolor roofs, so ensure that a high grade stainless steel is used.

Figure 6-12: Chimney cap

Figure 6-9: Water heater stack connections

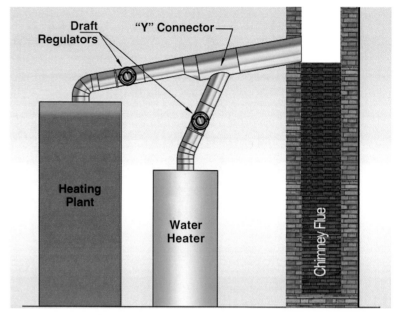

Each section sized to handle combination of all appliances attached

Figure 6-10: Water heater stack connections

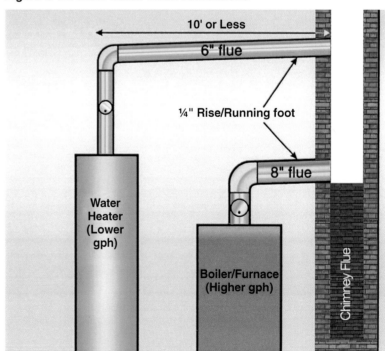

The larger appliance firing rate enters the chimney below the smaller appliance firing rate

Figure 6-11: Chimney check

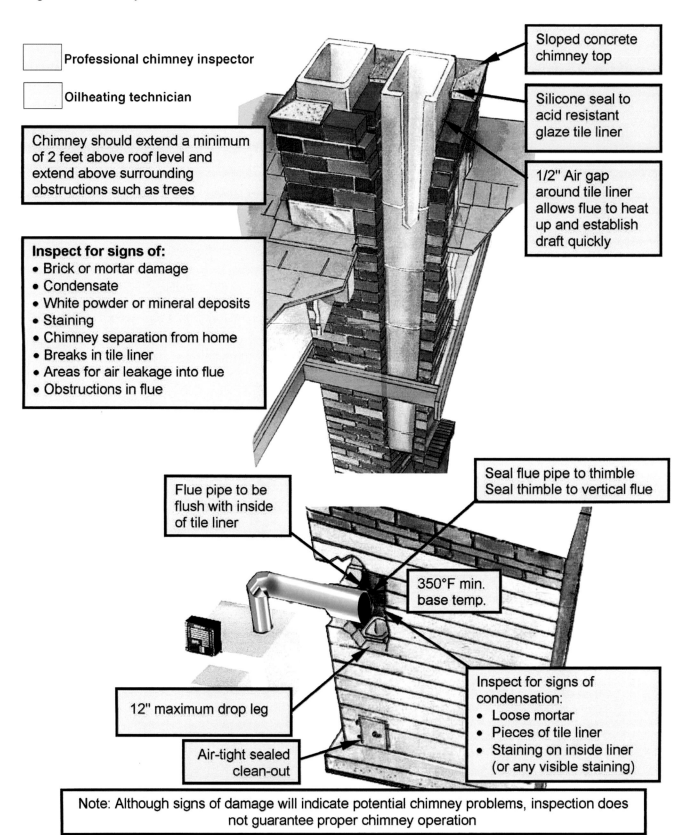

Professional chimney inspector

Oilheating technician

Chimney should extend a minimum of 2 feet above roof level and extend above surrounding obstructions such as trees

Inspect for signs of:
- Brick or mortar damage
- Condensate
- White powder or mineral deposits
- Staining
- Chimney separation from home
- Breaks in tile liner
- Areas for air leakage into flue
- Obstructions in flue

Sloped concrete chimney top

Silicone seal to acid resistant glaze tile liner

1/2" Air gap around tile liner allows flue to heat up and establish draft quickly

Flue pipe to be flush with inside of tile liner

Seal flue pipe to thimble
Seal thimble to vertical flue

350°F min. base temp.

12" maximum drop leg

Air-tight sealed clean-out

Inspect for signs of condensation:
- Loose mortar
- Pieces of tile liner
- Staining on inside liner (or any visible staining)

Note: Although signs of damage will indicate potential chimney problems, inspection does not guarantee proper chimney operation

Another alternative is to use a draft inducer, Figure 6-13. Draft inducers are electrically powered fans installed in the flue pipe. They help to pull the air from

Figure 6-13: Draft inducer

the unit and push it up the chimney. They can also be used to boost the draft if the natural chimney draft is too weak. A draft inducer can also solve the loss of draft from the rapid cooling of combustion products in the chimney.

Poorly insulated metal flues and over-sized or unlined chimneys can cause a rapid cooling of combustion products and lead to a loss of draft. A draft inducer can offer a reasonable temporary solution but the ideal solution is to line and insulate the chimney.

Induced draft has the advantage of developing controlled draft under most conditions. It can help to provide a clean start with no rumbles and it can provide adequate draft in a chimney that is too small, too low, or too large. Installation of a pressure or draft-proving switch is required by codes and is strongly recommended with an induced draft installation. See Figure 6-14, the draft proving switch is DIP-1.

Alternative venting systems

In recent years, manufacturers have created alternative forced draft venting systems that do not use a chimney for oil-fired heating systems. The technology takes two different approaches: power- venting and direct-venting.

Power-venting: a fan is attached to the flue pipe at the exit terminal from the building to pull the products of combustion out of the heating unit. Power-venters do not need a chimney and are usually sidewall vented.

Direct vent: the static pressure created by the burner fan pushes the combustion gases through the heat exchanger and out of the building. A direct-vented system is a positive pressure system. No chimney is needed with a direct vent system.

The advantages of alternative venting systems are:
- More positive control of draft
- No chimney warm-up problems
- Lowered cost in new building con struction and electric to oilheat conversions (eliminates the chimney)
- There is a significant reduction in burner noise with direct venting

Figure 6-14: Draft inducer with draft proving switch, typical installation

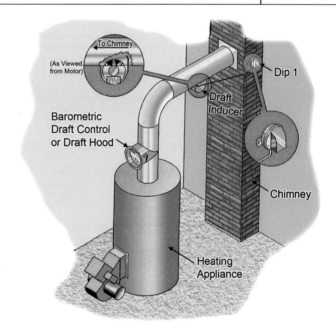

• Eliminate back drafts caused when a nearby structure is above the top of the chimney

• Reduction in system standby losses by eliminating off-cycle chimney draft

When installing or servicing either of these systems, it is very important that you read and understand the manufacturer's instructions. When you are finished, be sure to leave the instructions in an obvious place for the next technician.

The installation and use of any alternative venting system must not only follow the manufacturers' instructions, but also comply with all local and state building codes. Most of the instructions and codes conform to the following guidelines for the location of the exit terminal of the system. See Figure 6-15.

Figure 6-15: Vent hood location

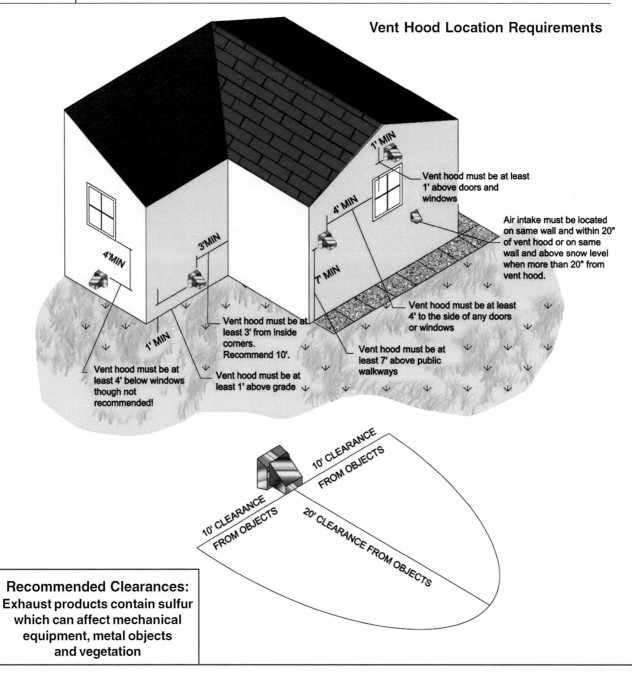

Vent Hood Location Requirements

1' MIN

Vent hood must be at least 1' above doors and windows

4' MIN

Air intake must be located on same wall and within 20" of vent hood or on same wall and above snow level when more than 20" from vent hood.

3'MIN

4'MIN

7' MIN

1' MIN

Vent hood must be at least 3' from inside corners. Recommend 10'.

Vent hood must be at least 4' to the side of any doors or windows

Vent hood must be at least 4' below windows though not recommended!

Vent hood must be at least 1' above grade

Vent hood must be at least 7' above public walkways

10' CLEARANCE FROM OBJECTS

10' CLEARANCE FROM OBJECTS

10' CLEARANCE FROM OBJECTS

20' CLEARANCE FROM OBJECTS

Recommended Clearances:
Exhaust products contain sulfur which can affect mechanical equipment, metal objects and vegetation

**The following guidelines
are often required by code:**

• Direct vent systems can be placed on any wall, but if possible they should not be located on the wall facing the prevailing wind (the prevailing wind generally comes from the north and the west; if possible, locate on the south or east side of the building).

• The vent terminal must be at least one foot above grade level, and three feet away from any inside corner. It may need to be higher in areas with snowfall.

• The vent terminal shall not be less than three feet above any forced air inlet into the building that is located within 10 feet of the terminal.

• The vent terminal shall not be less than four feet below, four feet horizontally, or one foot above any door, window, or gravity inlet into any building. The vent shall not be installed in a window well.

• The vent terminal shall not be less than two feet from an adjacent building.

• The vent terminal shall not be less than seven feet above grade when located adjacent to public walkways.

• The vent terminal shall be located so that flue gases are not directed to jeopardize people, overheat combustible structures or materials, or enter buildings.

• All positive pressure joints in the vent system (all joints in direct-vent, all joints on the exhaust side of the power-venter) are to be sealed with Permatex #81164 high temperature sealer or equivalent to prevent leakage of the products of combustion into the building. We are referring here to both the joints between pieces of pipe and the slip joints on elbows.

• The minimum distance to combustible materials from any single wall, vent system component is 18 inches.

• The vent termination should not be mounted directly above or within three feet horizontally from a gas meter, electric meter or air conditioning condenser.

Power-venting

Power-venting is an economical alternative to conventional chimney venting. Power-venters use a motor and fan to vent the products of combustion from the appliance to the outdoors.

Power-venters are designed with the fan located either outdoors or indoors just before the outside wall, as in Figure 6-16. This insures that combustion gases in the flue pipe are always under negative pressure, so if there are any leaks, air will leak into the pipe and the combustion gases will not spill into the building.

The flue gases are discharged through a double wall vent termination piece and an

Figure 6-16: Power venter, indoor fan

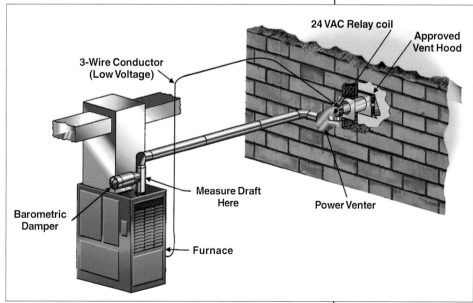

outside vent hood (Figure 6-17). Although these models have operated successfully for years, they often cause noise and vibrations in the building. They should be fastened securely to the outside wall or hung from the floor joists to reduce the transmission of noise.

Some power-vented systems use a double wall exhaust connection that draws cooler outside air into the outer pipe, and the hot exhaust gases are contained in the inner pipe (concentric venting). This provides a layer of safety between the hot exhaust gases and the combustible wall and floor joist materials and pre-heats the combustion air.

System operation: Power-venting requires that the oilburner primary control has delayed valve-on and burner motor-off delay features, similar to pre-purge and post-purge. When the thermostat or aquastat calls for heat, the power-venter motor starts. After the power-venter motor has come up to speed, the pressure switch closes (in one to two seconds). This closes the circuit to the burner primary, allowing the burner to operate. After the heating requirement is satisfied, the thermostat or aquastat circuit opens, activating the burner motor off delay (post-purge) cycle. During this cycle, the oil valve closes shutting off the flame, but the power-venter and the burner motor continue to run for a period of time, venting the last of the combustion products and cooling the burner components.

Inspection and maintenance: The power-venter should be inspected once a year.

• Check to be sure the motor and fan rotate freely.

• To prolong the life of the motor, lubricate it as directed by the manufacturer.

• Inspect the power-venter wheel to clear out any soot, ash, or coating that inhibits either rotation or air flow.

• Remove and clean the air sensing tube.

• Remove all foreign materials before operating. Inspect all vent connections for looseness, for evidence of corrosion, and for flue gas leakage.

• Replace, seal, or tighten all of the pipe connections as necessary.

• Check the choke plate to insure it is secured in place.

• Check the barometric draft control to insure the gate swings freely.

• Check the safety system devices—start the heating system, and then disconnect the pressure sensing tube from the pressure switch. This should stop the burner. Reconnecting the tube should restart the burner.

For proper system installation, set-up and testing, you must follow the manufacturer's instructions exactly. It is

Figure 6-17: Outside vent hood

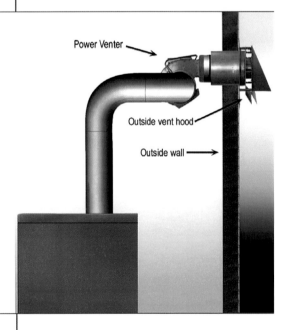

Power Venter

Outside vent hood

Outside wall

also a good idea when installing a power-venter, that you also install a fresh air kit to bring combustion air to the burner from outdoors. Many power-venters integrate a fresh combustion air intake into their system. If they do not, you should ensure that the pipes are spaced so that they do not interfere with each other—at least 12 inches apart. Fresh air should be brought in from the same wall as the power-venter exhaust to equalize air pressure within the vent and intake system.

Direct venting

Direct-vent systems use the power of the burner fan to push the products of combustion out of the building. Direct-vent provides sidewall venting without the use of a power-venter, extra motors, fans, or wiring. Direct-vent systems feature sealed combustion, utilizing clean outside air for combustion. The direct vent system normally uses a stainless steel combination vent hood. Figure 6-18 shows an example of a sealed combustion system.

Unlike chimney venting and power-venting, with direct-vent the air pressure inside the boiler or furnace and flue pipe is greater than the pressure in the building. If there is a leak in the heat exchanger or the flue pipe, products of combustion will leak into the building. Direct-vent systems are sold as a complete package. You should only use components that are supplied with the manufacturer's direct-vent system. Mixing and matching, or do-it-yourself engineering may void the manufacturer's warranty and may create a hazardous condition.

**Other drawbacks
to a direct-vent system are:**
• Surface discoloration of the building may occur due to improper burner and control adjustment.

• The residential units can only push the exhaust gases and pull combustion air from about 20 feet maximum. This means that you must locate the boiler, furnace, or water heater as close to an outside wall as possible.

Things to consider when installing direct-vent systems are:
• Seal all joints on the venting system with a high temperature sealant.

• Combustion efficiency tests should be taken at the port provided on the unit by the manufacturer. Do not puncture the stainless steel vent tubing. Adjust the burner combustion with a 'window of tolerance.' Set the air to produce a trace of smoke. Take the CO_2 reading at a trace of smoke and reduce the CO_2 by 1.5% to 2%. For instance, if the CO_2 reading with a trace is 13%, reduce it to 11% to 11.5% CO_2. This will compensate for variations in fuel and outdoor temperatures, and other variables over the year. See Chapter 7 on combustion for more details.

**Figure 6-18:
Direct side-wall venting and outside combustion air**

Sealed Combustion Furnace   Sealed Combustion Boiler

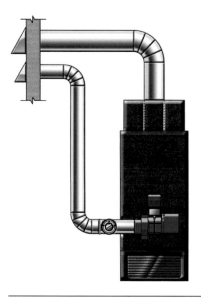
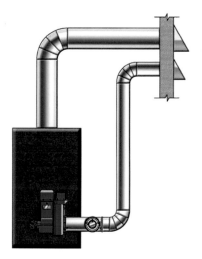

Chapter **7**

COMBUSTION

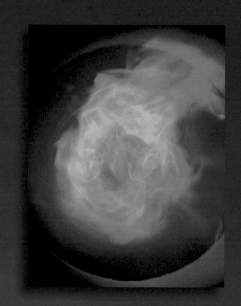

IN THIS CHAPTER

- **Combustion theory**

- **Common causes of smoke, soot and low efficiency**

- **Carbon monoxide**

- **Combustion efficiency testing and troubleshooting**

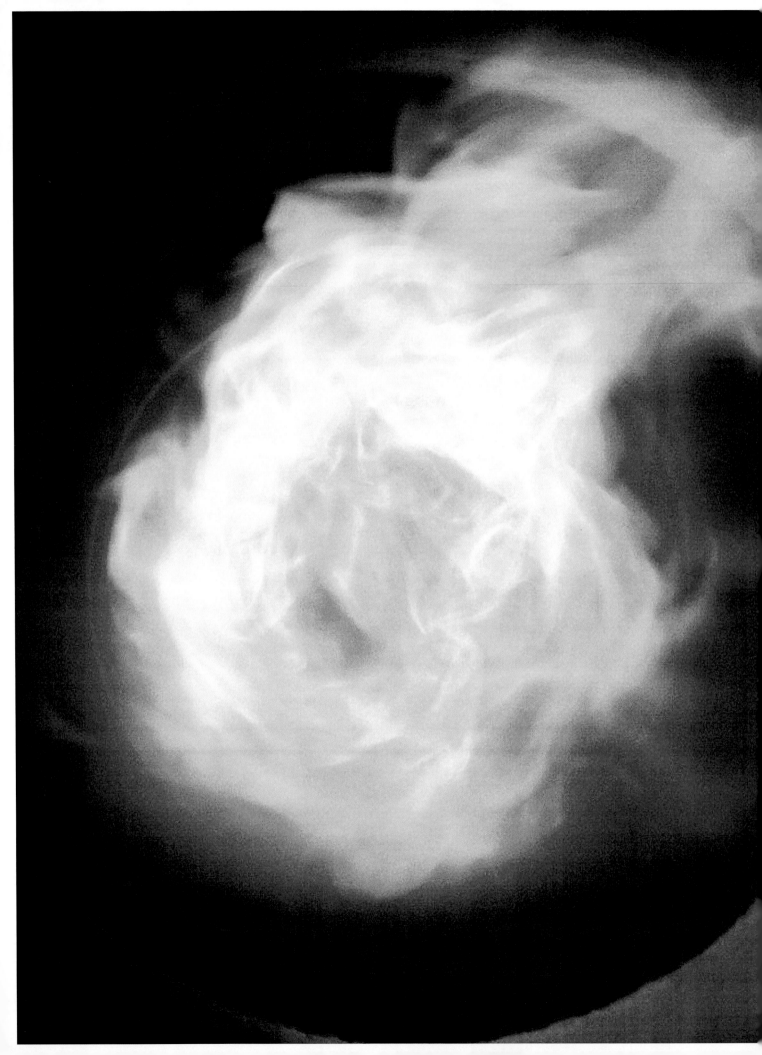

Chapter 7

Combustion

Combustion theory

As a technician, you have an obligation to assure the equipment you are working on is operating at peak performance levels. Understanding combustion theory is the basis for adjusting oilburners for safe, clean, reliable, and economical operation.

Combustion is a controlled chemical reaction

Three things are needed to make a fire: oxygen, ignition, and fuel. When heating oil is burned, the chemical energy in the fuel is converted to heat.

The oxygen required for combustion comes from the air that is delivered by the oilburner fan. The spark delivered by the electrodes provides the heat needed to start the combustion process.

The heat from the spark vaporizes the oil droplets delivered by the nozzle then lights the vapor on fire. If the conditions for combustion are right, this process continues until all the droplets vaporize and burn completely and cleanly within the combustion zone.

Combustion is the rapid oxidation of any material that will combine readily with oxygen.

The resulting flame contains the hot gases produced when the hydrogen and carbon in the fuel react and combine with the oxygen in the air. This reaction creates light, and releases large quantities of heat. This heat from the combustion gases is extracted by the heat exchanger in the furnace, boiler, or water heater, and heats the air, water, or steam we use for space and domestic water heating.

Every gallon of oil contains about 140,000 Btus per gallon. A Btu is the energy required to raise one pound of water one degree Fahrenheit—about the amount of energy contained in a birthday candle flame. In a typical oil-fired appliance, every gallon of oil burned puts about 119,000 Btus into the building and about 21,000 Btus go up the chimney. Figure 7-1.

Heating oil is 85% carbon and 15% hydrogen. These fixed ratios of hydrogen and carbon in the fuel combine with a specific quantity of oxygen to form combustion gases. Therefore a precise

Figure 7-1: Heat loads, heat loss

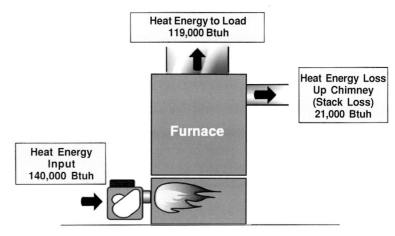

Heat to Load = Heat Energy Input - Stack Loss

quantity of combustion air is needed so all the fuel will burn completely. Too much air will lower efficiency, and too little air causes incomplete combustion and smoke.

During combustion, new chemical substances are created from the fuel and the air. These substances are called combustion gases. Most come from chemical combinations of the fuel and oxygen, but the gases can also include chemical combinations from the air alone.

When a hydrocarbon-based fuel (oil) burns, the exhaust gases include water (hydrogen + oxygen) and carbon dioxide (carbon + oxygen). Combustion gases can also include carbon monoxide (CO), oxides of nitrogen (NOx, nitrogen + oxygen) and since sulfur is present in the fuel, sulfuric oxide (sulfur + oxygen).

As the fuel and air are turned into combustion gases, heat is generated. Heat is required to start combustion and is itself a

product of combustion. Once combustion gets started, we don't have to continue to provide the heat source, because the heat produced by the combustion process will keep things going.

What is air?

Air is 20.9% oxygen, 78% nitrogen, and 1.1% other gases. For every one part of oxygen, we get four parts nitrogen, see Figure 7-2. Nitrogen is an inert gas and most of it goes through the combustion process unchanged. It cools the chemical reaction (burning temperature) and lowers the maximum heat content deliverable by the fuel. Therefore, it is impossible to achieve combustion efficiencies above 95% for most fuels, including natural gas, when air is used as the source of oxygen for the combustion process.

With flame retention burners, some of the nitrogen combines with the oxygen to form nitrogen oxide or NOx.

**Figure 7-2:
Combustion
process in a burner**

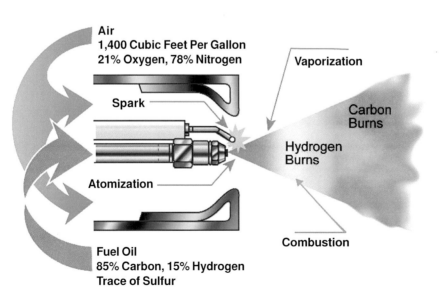

Combustion

Air
1,400 Cubic Feet Per Gallon
21% Oxygen, 78% Nitrogen

Vaporization

Spark

Carbon
Burns

Hydrogen
Burns

Atomization

Combustion

Fuel Oil
85% Carbon, 15% Hydrogen
Trace of Sulfur

Heat
138,690

Hot Nitrogen
Carbon Dioxide
CO_2

Water Vapor
H_2O

Nitrogen Oxides
NOx

Excess Oxygen
O_2

Sulfur Oxides
SOx

Free Carbon
Smoke

Carbon Monoxide
CO

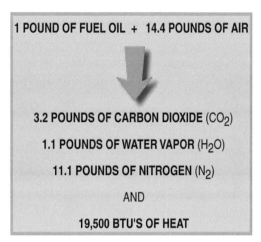

1 POUND OF FUEL OIL + 14.4 POUNDS OF AIR

3.2 POUNDS OF CARBON DIOXIDE (CO_2)

1.1 POUNDS OF WATER VAPOR (H_2O)

11.1 POUNDS OF NITROGEN (N_2)

AND

19,500 BTU'S OF HEAT

Figure 7-3: Fueloil combustion in air

Heating oil flames

Combustion is a series of exact chemical reactions that create exact quantities of combustion gases. It takes 14.4 pounds of air to burn each pound of heating oil and we produce 15.4 pounds of combustion gases, Figure 7-3.

If we could achieve stoichiometric, or perfect combustion, each gallon of oil consumed would need 1,360 cubic feet of combustion air. The actual amount of air required will vary by the heat value of the fuel and the design of the burner. Heating oil contains about 19,500 Btus per pound. Non-flame retention burners need at least 1,700 cubic feet of air to burn clean. Current burners need about 1,500 cubic feet.

Buildings today are so well insulated and weather-stripped that getting adequate combustion air to the burner is becoming a problem. When troubleshooting combustion problems, get into the habit of asking yourself, "Where is my combustion air coming from?" and "Do I have enough to burn all of my fuel?"

Oilburner flames produce various combustion gases in fixed quantities. With perfect combustion, every pound of oil burned will produce 3.2 pounds of carbon dioxide, 1.1 pound of water vapor, and 11.1 pounds of hot nitrogen. This constant ratio of combustion gases allows us to test the quality of a flame against this perfect standard to determine optimum adjustment.

Heating oil atomization and vaporization

Heating oil will not burn as a liquid. It must be converted to a vapor before the rapid reaction between the fuel and the air can produce a flame. The oilburner's job is to convert the liquid fuel into a vapor so it can be burned.

The oil is pumped to the nozzle at high pressure (100 psi or more) where it is broken up into a mist of small droplets (atomized). The droplets evaporate quickly when exposed to the heat of the spark or flame, producing vapors that burn easily with the air supplied by the burner fan.

Combustion air supply and air-oil mixing

The better the air and the oil vapor are mixed, the better our combustion. Burner air parts, (including turbulators, spinners, end cones, and flame retention heads), are designed to give good mixing of the atomized fuel droplets and the combustion air. Good fuel and air mixing assures that all the fuel vapors contact enough oxygen for complete burning.

In high pressure atomizing burners, several factors control the quality of air-oil mixing. The spray pattern of the oil droplets must be similar to the air pattern created by the burner.

Flame retention burners have much better air/oil mixing capabilities than older burners. They use high speed burner motors (3,450 RPM) and air pattern shaping to create the high static air pressure needed to make the high velocity air swirl and the internal recirculation needed for clean, efficient combustion.

This recirculation is created by the drop in pressure in the center of the air swirl, like the eye of a tornado. This pulls some of the hot flame gases toward the burner head, the way the spray from a showerhead pulls in the shower curtain.

These hot gases add heat to the fuel droplets coming out of the nozzle speeding up their vaporization and burning rates, which gives us a nice clean, stable fire close to the burner head.

New oilburners should not produce smoke

Smoke and soot, which are nothing more than unburned carbon, are created by outdated burner designs and incorrect burner service and adjustment. Smoke production is unnecessary and must be

Figure 7-4:
Soot affects fuel consumption

eliminated, because it reduces efficiency, increases service calls, and is a nuisance to homeowners. It can be prevented using modern burners and by careful adjustment of burners using combustion test equipment.

Excessive smoke wastes fuel because it deposits soot on the heat exchanger surfaces, Figure 7-4. This insulates the heat exchanger, limiting its ability to extract the heat from the combustion gases. A layer of soot only 1/8" thick can reduce heat absorption by over 8%.

Efficiency loss caused by a smoky burner occurs as the soot slowly builds up. Soot also affects the reliable operation of the burner. If it builds up on the cad cell or the bimetal of the stack relay, it can act like a flame failure and cause the control to lock out on safety, creating an unnecessary service call.

Overfiring can cause smoke: If a unit is overfired, the burner will create heat faster than the heating system can distribute to the building. When this happens, the burner short cycles (goes on and off frequently for short periods of time). The problem is that older oilburners create smoke when they start and stop.

Up to two thirds of all the smoke produced by burners made before the year 2000 is produced on start up and shut down. Therefore, properly sized nozzles will produce less frequent burner cycling and less smoke.

Sulfur

Sulfur exists in varying degrees in all fossil fuels. The sulfur content of heating oil ranges from 0.5% to 0.05% by weight.

When burned, the sulfur mixes with oxygen to form sulfuric oxide (SOx). It reacts with the water vapor in the combustion gases to create sulfuric acid aerosol.

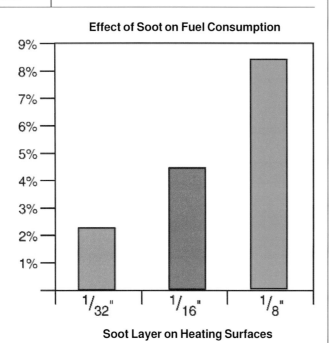

Effect of Soot on Fuel Consumption

Soot Layer on Heating Surfaces

When the acid condenses (at about 150 to 200°F), it adheres to the flue pipe and heat exchanger surfaces in a film and reacts with the iron in the pipe and heat exchanger wall. This creates iron sulfates, the light yellow to rust colored crusty scale you find clinging to the heat exchanger.

Scale buildup downgrades efficiency by 1% to 4% over the year. It also blocks flue passages, restricting air flow and increasing smoke and soot. Sulfur levels in heating oil are gradually being reduced, so this will be less of a problem in the future.

Carbon monoxide

Carbon monoxide, or CO, is a toxic gas that can occur in homes and buildings where combustion by-products are generated, not properly vented and allowed to accumulate. CO is a colorless, odorless, tasteless poison. Carbon monoxide is readily absorbed in the body and can impair the oxygen-carrying capacity of the blood (hemoglobin).

Impairment of the body's hemoglobin results in less oxygen to the brain, heart, and tissues. Even short-term over exposure to carbon monoxide can be critical or fatal to people with heart and lung diseases, and to the young or the elderly. It may also cause headaches and dizziness and other significant medical problems in healthy people. At low concentrations, CO can go undetected and contribute to nagging illnesses, and can compound pre-existing health problems. Figure 7-5.

Carbon Monoxide is a result of incomplete combustion due to unburned fuel. During combustion, carbon in the fuel oxidizes through a series of reactions to form carbon dioxide (CO_2). However, 100% conversion of carbon to CO_2 is rarely achieved under field conditions and some carbon only oxidizes to the intermediate step, carbon monoxide or CO. Carbon Monoxide is usually produced by insufficient combustion air. However, excess air and mismatched oil to air patterns and ratios can also reduce flame temperature to a point where CO is produced. So, adding too much air to clean up a smoky fire can create CO. When any part of the flame is reduced below 1,128°F, CO will be produced. Flame impingement also results in lower flame temperature and CO production.

Ambient CO limits (Recommended)

0 ppm. This level is most desirable, but cannot always be achieved due to cigarettes, candles, and appliances such as gas stoves.

1-9 ppm. Normal levels within the home.

10-35 ppm. Advise occupants, check for symptoms (slight headache, tiredness, dizziness, and nausea or flu like symptoms), check all appliances, including the furnace, water heater and boiler, check for other sources including internal combustion engine operation in attached garages.

36-99 ppm. Recommend fresh air, check for symptoms, ventilate the space, recommend medical attention.

Figure 7-5:
Carbon
monoxide levels
of concern

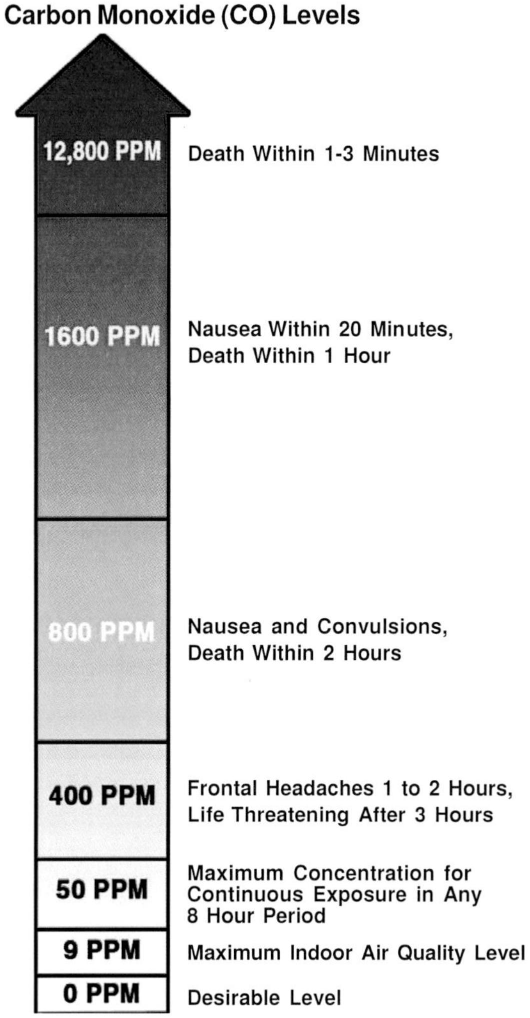

Carbon Monoxide (CO) Levels

12,800 PPM	Death Within 1-3 Minutes
1600 PPM	Nausea Within 20 Minutes, Death Within 1 Hour
800 PPM	Nausea and Convulsions, Death Within 2 Hours
400 PPM	Frontal Headaches 1 to 2 Hours, Life Threatening After 3 Hours
50 PPM	Maximum Concentration for Continuous Exposure in Any 8 Hour Period
9 PPM	Maximum Indoor Air Quality Level
0 PPM	Desirable Level

100+ ppm. Evacuate the home (including yourself!) and contact emergency medical services (911). Do not attempt to ventilate the space. Short-term exposure to these levels can cause permanent physical damage.

Carbon monoxide is released into homes by vent blockage, flue pipe damage, heat exchanger cracks, and restricted air supply into the house. This last problem is progressively getting worse as new homes become tighter in their construction, and many homeowners are weather stripping and insulating their older homes.

Most homes have a number of devices such as exhaust fans, clothes dryers, and fireplaces, that remove air from the home. This suction is often stronger than the suction of the heating system's chimney or power vent. This back drafting causes the emissions from the heating system, the water heater, gas ovens, gas stoves, gas dryers, and wood stoves or fireplaces to enter the living area and elevate CO levels.

Oilheat's CO warning signs

If you see smoke near the burner, dark smoke coming from the chimney, or smell a sharp raw oil smell, the burner is probably producing unacceptable levels of carbon monoxide. With insufficient combustion air, oilburners usually produce elevated smoke levels before high CO levels are reached. This smoke is a warning signal.

The result is that the danger from high CO levels is much lower from oilburners than any other hydrocarbon burner. However, if oilburners are operated with too much combustion air, it chills the flame and creates CO with no smoke! Improper nozzle to air patterning can also produce CO.

What to watch out for

CO is odorless and tasteless, therefore in order to detect its presence, we perform combustion tests and look for other clues for combustion or ventilation problems such as:

- Sharp gas or oil smell
- Stale or stuffy air
- Soot, rust, or scale build-up on or around appliances and vents
- Loose or disconnected chimney or vent connections
- Debris or soot falling from chimney, fireplace, or appliance
- Excessive moisture on the inside of windows or walls
- Chalky white powder forming on the chimney or vent
- Visible smoke in the living space

Light off CO levels: High CO levels at light off may be an indication of rough or delayed ignition, warranting further investigation. The CO readings will peak on startup, then dramatically drop. CO readings should stabilize within 10 minutes of operation and should never be rising during operation.

Mechanical problems and CO: If the appliance being tested has sufficient combustion air and is still producing higher than acceptable CO air-free levels, it could be a mechanical problem.

Inspect the burner for cleanliness, proper alignment, fuel pressures, and evidence of impingement. Impingement occurs when the flame hits an object that has sufficient mass to transfer enough heat from the flame to cause low flame temperatures and incomplete combustion. This can be as simple as a screw poking into the heat exchanger or as major as a collapsed refractory.

Missing burner covers, improper air band adjustment or oil pressures can also contribute to higher than normal CO levels.

CO ambient air testing
(Combustion air zone & living space)

Ambient CO levels should be checked and the equipment should be run through a complete cycle if you suspect any combustion problems.

If at any time ambient CO levels exceed 100 ppm, evacuate occupants and call emergency services.

The most common sources of CO are exhaust from a vehicle in an attached garage, and depressurization of the home resulting in insufficient air for combustion. If CO is detected, all possible sources of CO should be checked, including—but not limited to—water heaters, gas ovens and stoves, the furnace, (non-electric) space heaters, and vented or unvented appliances such as gas logs.

Combustion efficiency testing

Combustion efficiency testing is one of the most important things we do when servicing oilburners, Figure 7-6. The tests determine the quality of the combustion

Figure 7-6: Combustion efficiency test

process and tell us if we have set up the burner correctly. In this section, we will explore how to use instruments to measure and improve efficiency, cleanliness, and safety of the unit. We will also cover the reasons for high and low efficiency, and how testing can pinpoint current and future problems.

It is imperative to perform a combustion analysis during routine service, or any time changes are made that will affect combustion. Combustion testing provides numerous benefits to the customer and service technician including:

- Saving money
- Saving time
- Avoiding callbacks
- Limiting liability
- Maintaining equipment warranty
- Providing confidence
- Providing increased comfort
- Providing increased safety
- Increasing energy efficiency
- Lowering environmental emissions

Modern burners require proper setup, making the use of instruments necessary. Using instruments assures low smoke and soot, improves your image, and increases customer comfort and satisfaction. Today's burners are superior to the older models when set up correctly—but can be troublesome when setup incorrectly. You cannot see a #2 smoke, you also cannot feel a 350° stack, smell a 6% CO_2, or 100 ppm of carbon monoxide, yet if you leave the unit operating in *any* of these conditions, you will not be doing your job.

With the older units, you could observe the flame, see its shape and color, and determine to some extent how the burner was performing. However, even with the older units, there is no way you can accurately determine whether the chemical reaction is complete by just observing the fire.

The most important setting you make on the burner is excess air. You cannot really do this without instruments. If you give testing a fair trial, you will find it will reduce the time required to accurately service, troubleshoot, and adjust a heating system.

Principles of combustion testing

Combustion test instruments measure the composition and temperature of flue gases as they leave the boiler or furnace. We use this information to calculate the amount of excess air and the combustion efficiency. We also measure the amount of smoke and draft produced in order to properly adjust the flame and identify problems.

Combustion testing measurements:

- Temperature of the flue gases

- Draft produced by the chimney, power-venter or venting system

- Smoke concentrations in the flue gases

- Composition of the flue gases (excess air, CO_2, O_2, and NOx)

- Carbon Monoxide concentrations in the flue gases

The three things we adjust that affect the combustion process are: fuel pressure, combustion air, and draft. Other factors can affect the combustion process, including impingement, excess air leaks into the heat exchanger, insufficient combustion air due to tight construction or improper ventilation, or an improperly installed venting system.

If you perform combustion testing prior to and after a tune up, you can calculate how much improvement you have made in the combustion efficiency, and how much money you have saved your customer.

Combustion test equipment

Combustion testing equipment can be separated into two groups: the manual instruments (Figure 7-7), and the continuous sampling digital electronic instruments, Figure 7-8. The manual equipment has been

Figure 7-7: Manual instruments

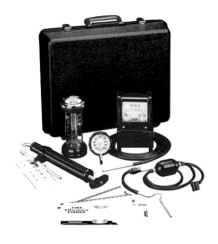

Figure 7-8: Continuous sampling digital electronic instruments

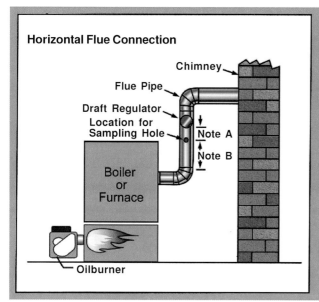
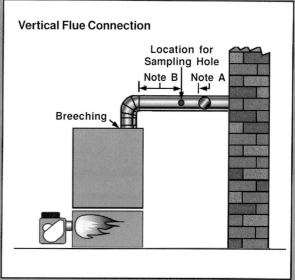

Horizontal Flue Connection

Chimney
Flue Pipe
Draft Regulator
Location for
Sampling Hole
Note A
Note B
Boiler
or
Furnace
Oilburner

Vertical Flue Connection

Location for
Sampling Hole
Note B   Note A
Breeching

A. Locate hole at least one flue pipe diameter on the furnace or boiler side of draft control.

B. Ideally, hole should be at least two flue pipe diameters from breeching or elbow.

**Figure 7-9:
Measuring for
combustion
efficiency**

used for many years and can produce reliable results if used and maintained properly.

The problem is, testing with the older manual equipment is time-consuming and only gives you a fuzzy snapshot of the burner performance. (Each squeeze of a wet kit bulb represents a different snapshot of the flue gas. A manual test blends all those snapshots together into one reading.)

The digital equipment is much quicker, and does efficiency calculations automatically. The best feature of the digital equipment is that they sample continuously, like using a video camera, so you can see the results change as you make the adjustments. It gives you a much better idea of what is going on.

Holes for testing

Measurements are taken through a three-eighths (3/8) inch hole drilled in the flue

pipe near the boiler or furnace outlet (the breech), see Figure 7-9.

With electronic testers, the hole may have to be larger to accommodate the probe. The hole should not be in an elbow.

With the older test equipment, you will want to drill two holes to speed up the process. They should both be as close to the breeching (the place where the flue pipe connects to the furnace, boiler or water heater) as possible.

The holes should be at least 6" from the draft regulator on the furnace or boiler side of the regulator. There is no need to plug the holes in the stack, but we do suggest that you insert self-threading screws or snap caps in the holes.

You will also need a hole in the fire or observation door over the burner. Some new units do not have a door over the burner. If this is the case, check to see if the manufacturer has provided a special port for you to do your over-fire test. See Figure 7-6.

**Figure 7-10:
Draft gauge**

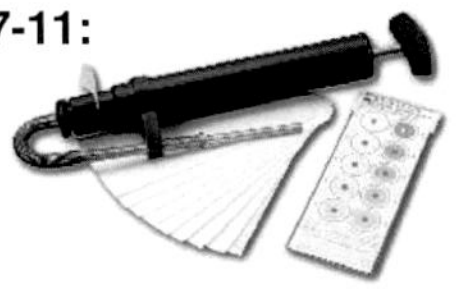

**Figure 7-11:
Smoke
tester**

**Figure 7-12:
Orsat tester**

**Figure 7-13:
Stack
thermometer**

Manual combustion test equipment

To successfully adjust oilburners with the manual equipment, we need the following:

1. To test for draft, we need a draft gauge. (Figure 7-10).

2. To test for smoke, we need a smoke tester and a smoke scale. (Figure 7-11).

3. To test carbon dioxide (CO_2) we need an Orsat tester. (Figure 7-12).

4. A stack thermometer is used to measure the temperature of the flue gases. (Figure 7-13).

5. We need the combustion efficiency slide ruler to calculate efficiency.

While not needed to calculate efficiency, it is important to know if the oil pressure to the nozzle is correct, and to measure this we need a pressure gauge capable of reading up to at least 300 pounds pressure.

We also need a vacuum gauge to determine the condition of the oil delivery system. (See Chapter 4.)

Steady state

For accurate test results, measurements should be made after the unit has achieved steady state. Steady state is the point at which the stack temperature stops rising. At steady state there are no changes in the combustion gases, the unit has thoroughly warmed-up and will maintain constant conditions as long as the burner runs. This will require you to run the unit for 5 to 10 minutes, until the stack temperature reaches its highest point and levels off.

Stack temperature

The stack (flue gas) temperature is the temperature of the combustion gases leaving the appliance, and reflects the energy that did not transfer from the fuel to the heat exchanger. The lower the stack temperature,

Step-by-step testing procedure

The traditional order for taking these tests is:

Stack Temperature: With manual equipment, two holes will speed up testing and the thermometer should be placed into the unit on start and the rest of the testing done in the other hole when the temperature reading stabilizes.

Draft: Do draft second because the other tests will be affected by any increase or decrease of draft.

Smoke: To adjust for zero smoke number, you start by opening the burner air shutter or adjusting the head. Then

fine-tune the air to reach a zero smoke.

CO_2 or O_2 : This is done last because if draft or smoke are wrong, it does not matter what CO_2 is—you cannot leave the unit that way.

Calculate Efficiency: Once the air is adjusted properly, take a final temperature reading, then compare the CO_2 reading and the net stack temperature using the slide ruler to get the combustion efficiency of the unit.

Important: Make a record of the results of each test on a Combustion Survey Form, which should show all before and after readings. Then you will know just how much improvement you are achieving.

the more effective the heat exchanger design and heat transfer. Stack temperature is a measurement of the heat exchanger's ability to draw the heat from the combustion gases.

As the excess air goes up, so does the stack temperature, Figure 7-14. To understand why this happens, we must look at the heat exchanger. The longer the combustion gases are in the heat exchanger, the more the heat the exchanger can pull from them, and the lower the stack temperature will be. As the excess air increases so does the volume of combustion gases.

The volume of gases traveling through the heat exchanger determines how fast the gases must travel. The more air we put in, the faster it goes, and the less time the exchanger has to suck the heat out of the gases.

Therefore, as the excess air goes up, the stack temperature does too, even though the flame temperature is reduced. As stack temperatures go up, efficiency comes down, and our customers' heating costs increase, see Figure 7-15.

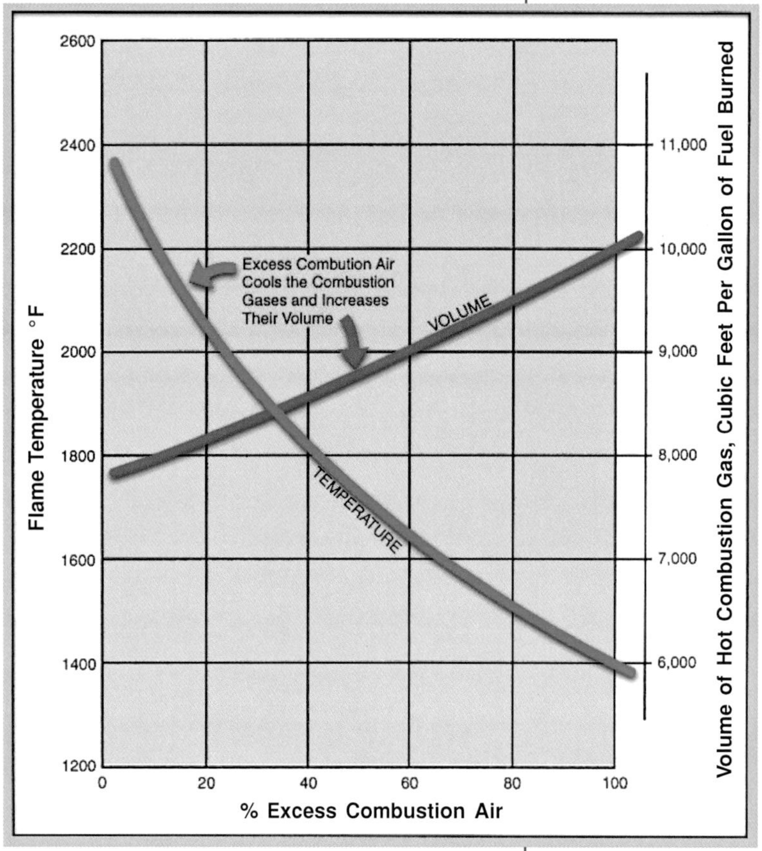

Figure 7-14: Relationship of excess air, flame temperature, and volume of combustion gases

Figure 7-15: Efficiency vs. net stack temperature

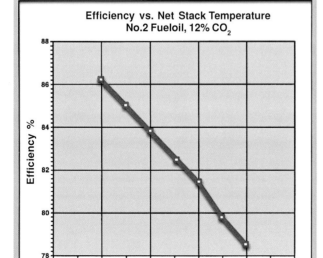

The flue gas temperature and all other tests should be measured in the flue gas hot spot. This is the point in the center of the flue where the stack temperature and the CO_2 are at the highest level and the O_2 is at its lowest level.

The primary importance of stack temperature is to provide enough heat in the flue to prevent water formation. If the temperature is not high enough, water in the combustion gases can condense in the flue pipe or chimney. Condensing in non-condensing appliances can cause chimney deterioration, liner failure, and rusting of the appliance.

Take a gross stack temperature reading, subtract the temperature of air entering the burner (ambient air temperature) from the gross stack temperature to get the net stack temperature needed for calculating efficiency. The relationship between the percentage of excess air in the flue gases (CO_2 or O_2) and the net stack temperature is the combustion efficiency.

Causes of high stack temperature

• Soot Deposits: The insulating effect of soot deposits prevents good heat transfer through the heat exchanger. Inspect the heat exchanger, clean if necessary, and adjust the burner to a zero to trace smoke.

• Excess Air: Excess air cools the combustion gases and increases their volume. This results in lower heat exchanger efficiency. Excess air can be due to poor air-fuel mixing, poor burner adjustment (more air than needed to stop smoke), and air leaks into the heat exchanger.

• Overfiring: Firing a heating system at a higher GPH (gallons per hour) than it was designed for causes high rates of gas flow through the heat exchanger and results in high stack temperature.

Dew point temperature

The dew point temperature is the temperature below which the water vapor contained in the flue gas turns into a liquid. This change is often referred to as condensation. Below the dew point temperature, moisture exists; above the dew point temperature, vapor exists. If the chimney or venting material falls below the dew point temperature, condensation in the flue will occur.

To prevent condensation, the stack temperature should range from 270°F to 370°F above the ambient air temperature for non-condensing appliances. (With new high efficiency equipment that does not have a draft regulator, combustion gases can be on the low end of this range; if there is a draft regulator, they should be closer to the high end.)

With the new condensing appliances, the stack temperature will be close to the return air or water temperature from the heating system and usually below 125°F. The lower the heating system return air or water temperature, the higher the efficiency will be on a condensing appliance.

Using the dial type stack thermometer

Slide the holding clip out to the end of the thermometer stem. Insert the small tab into the top of sampling hole in the stack and push the thermometer in far enough so the tip is in the center of the flue pipe. Operate the burner until the thermometer reading is rising no faster than 3 degrees per minute and record the reading. If the stack temperature begins to approach 1,000 degrees, remove the thermometer, because readings above this temperature will damage it.

Draft

Draft is the flow of air and combustion gases through the burner, heating unit, and venting system. Draft is required to remove the flue gases from the heat exchanger.

If draft is too low, then the combustion

> **Draft is the flow of air and combustion gases through the burner, heating unit, and venting system. Draft is required to remove the flue gases from the heat exchanger.**

air flow will be reduced, causing excessive smoke. If the draft is too high, then too much excess air will be drawn into the unit and the combustion gases will be pulled through the heat exchanger too fast, lowering efficiency.

During steady state operating conditions, the draft should be stable. Over-fire drafts of -.01" to -.02"wc [water column, see below] are generally recommended for residential units. Measurement and adjustment of draft are important because draft affects all other burner adjustments.

Draft measurement

To measure draft, we use a manometer, a U-tube or a gauge. The U-tube is a glass tube bent into the shape of a U. The tube is filled with water up to a zero mark on a scale etched on the tube. A sampling tube is attached to the right leg of the tube, and it is inserted into the unit to be tested. The left leg is left open to atmospheric pressure.

The draft on the right leg causes a pressure drop on that side and pulls the water up in the tube, and the atmospheric pressure on the open side pushes the water down in the left leg.

The difference between the water levels in the two legs is the draft in inches of water column. The suction from draft is so slight the difference is only a few hundredths of an inch. One one-hundredth of an inch of draft is expressed as -.01"wc.

Since it is a vacuum and not a pressure, we call it negative draft. If the right leg measured a pressure higher than atmospheric the water would go up in the left leg and we would call it positive draft.

Our modern draft gauges (manometers) are the mechanical equivalent of the U-tube. An important thing to remember when using the draft gauge is you must "zero it out" before using it. Atmospheric pressure changes all the time, so we take this variable pressure out of the equation by adjusting the gauge reading to zero before we take each test.

To zero out the draft gauge place it on a level surface near where you are going to test and slide the lever on the side of the unit until the arrow points to zero. You should also be sure the gauge is functioning properly by spinning the rubber sample tube or blowing gently across the end of it to be sure the needle is not stuck. It should move smoothly and return to zero.

> An important thing to remember when using a draft gauge is to "zero it out" before using it

---

The most important draft reading on residential equipment is the over-the-fire draft. On most residential and light commercial negative draft units, this reading should be -.01" to -.02"wc. If upon reaching steady state you cannot obtain this reading, you should next check the draft at the breech, and adjust the draft regulator. If you still cannot achieve sufficient over-fire-draft, then you probably have one of the following problems.

Common causes of poor draft

- Chimney is too small for the load of the attached appliances

- Chimney is too large in diameter or cross-section

- Chimney too short or improperly constructed

- Leakage of air into chimney, thimble, stack, or breeching

- Obstruction in chimney or at top of chimney

- Top of chimney is lower than the peak of the house

- Flue pipe diameter is too small. It should never be smaller than the breeching size

- Too many 90 degree elbows in the stack

**Figure 7-16:
Effects of
leaving a unit
operating with
a 5 smoke**

- Flue pipe does not have sufficient pitch upward from breeching to thimble; it should be at least ¼" per running foot

- Flue pipe extends too far into the chimney flue

- Heat exchanger passages are clogged with soot and scale, too restricted, or too baffled

- Appliance is overfired; the volume of flame and combustion gases is too great for the heat exchanger design and are creating back pressure or a positive draft over the fire

- Unit is underfired, so that the chimney gases never get hot enough to create normal draft conditions

- Insufficient ventilation or combustion air in the appliance room, starving the flame for air and draft flow

- Improper adjustment of the draft regulator

- Differences between breeching and over-fire draft (draft drop): More than .05" difference between the two draft readings usually means trouble. Check for heavy soot deposits in the heat exchanger, particularly if the burner was found with a heavy smoke

- Little or no difference between the breeching and over-fire draft: If the stack temperature is high, baffling or heating unit replacement should be considered

- Over-fire CO_2 higher than breeching CO_2: Check for air leaks between top of combustion chamber and heat exchanger outlet (Breeching)

- Visible openings for air leakage: Study how the heating unit is put

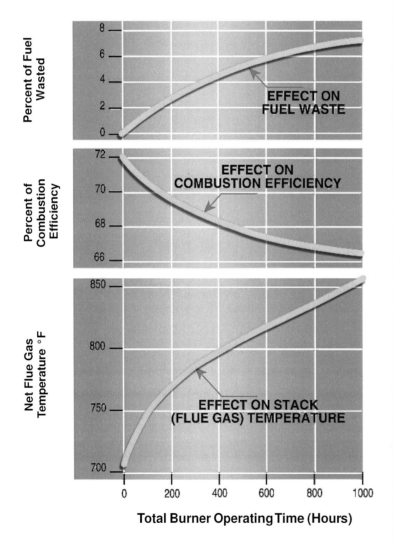

Total Burner Operating Time (Hours)

together and check all joints for possible leaks. If you suspect air leaks, but cannot find them, temporarily set the draft regulator to give maximum draft and run a candle or lighted match around the joints to see where the smoke is drawn in. Repair the leaks and set the over-fire draft to -.01" to -.02". Also, look for locations where light from the flame can be observed through cracks.

Smoke

After you have determined that draft conditions are correct, the next step is to adjust the burner to create a flame that will not produce smoke.

Keeping smoke to a minimum is a must if the heating system is to operate at peak efficiency without further attention during the entire heating season.

We measure smoke concentrations by taking a sample of the flue gases with a smoke tester and smoke scale, which identify smoke numbers from zero (no

smoke) to a number 9 (heavy smoke). Any smoke numbers above a number 2 cause rapid soot accumulations on heat exchanger surfaces. This causes flue gas temperatures to rise and efficiency to drop, Figure 7-16.

Excess combustion air is needed to reduce smoke concentrations to a minimum acceptable number (less than a number 1).

As we have discussed, this excess air must be held to a minimum in order to reach peak efficiency. Thus, correct burner adjustment is the proper balance between smoke and combustion air.

To reach high efficiency, we must adjust burners for Zero Smoke and low excess air while maintaining a high level of CO_2 or a low level of O_2, Figure 7-17.

The typical smoke tester draws a total of 2,200 cubic centimeters (ten full strokes of the sampling pump illustrated) of flue products through a standard grade filter paper. The color of the resulting smoke stain on the filter paper is matched to the closest shaded spot on the

Figure 7-17: Smoke vs. percent CO_2 curve

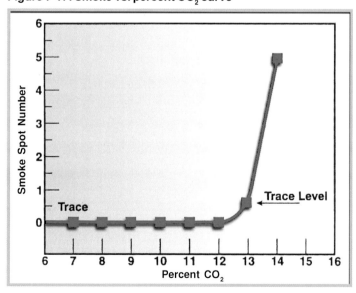

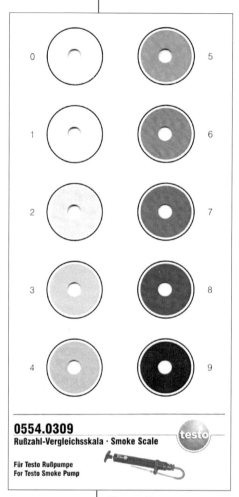

0554.0309
Rußzahl-Vergleichsskala · Smoke Scale

Für Testo Rußpumpe
For Testo Smoke Pump

Figure 7-18: Smoke scale

standard graduated smoke scale, Figure 7-18. This scale has ten shaded spots with an equal difference between successive spots. Spot Number 0 is white, and represents smoke-free combustion. Spot Number 9 (darkest) represents the maximum smoke that typically will be produced.

When pumping ten full strokes of the smoke tester pump, do not pump too fast. Hold the handle at its most extended position a second or two between strokes. If you take more than one sample from a burner, use the same uniform method of pumping each sample. If you fail to follow this method, you could get two different smoke numbers, even though you have made no adjustments to the burner.

An oily or yellow smoke spot on the filter paper is a sign of unburned fuel, indicating very poor combustion (and likely high emissions of carbon monoxide and unburned hydrocarbons). If too much excess combustion air is supplied, the combustion process will be chilled so much that some of the fuel cannot burn. The flame is actually being blown out. Further evidence is liquid fuel in the heat exchanger, white smoke (fuel vapor) and strong odors outside the home.

To adjust for a zero smoke, first adjust the burner for a trace smoke then open the air gate just a bit farther to go to zero

smoke. By initially adjusting to a zero smoke you will be introducing an unknown amount of excess air which can lead to: lower CO_2, cooler flame temperatures, higher stack temperatures, and possible elevated carbon monoxide production.

Remember that excess air cools the combustion products and increases their volume so that it is difficult for the heat exchanger to absorb the heat before it escapes to the breeching and up the chimney. Most new burners are designed to operate at zero smoke.

Common causes of smoke and soot:
Poor fuel atomization: small fuel droplets vaporize quicker than large ones. Large droplets are caused by:

- Damaged or worn nozzles
- Low fuel pump pressure
- Cold oil

Inadequate combustion air is caused by:
- The burner air control is not open far enough
- Poor chimney draft
- Build up of soot and scale in the heat exchanger
- Accumulation of lint, hair, sawdust, and dirt on the air shutter and the burner fan
- Restrictions of the air flow to the room the burner is in, and the operation of exhaust fans that de-pressurize the building

Effects of insufficient combustion air

For the proper operation and venting of gas or oilheating appliances, sufficient outside air must be supplied to the structure to make up for the air lost from venting heating appliances, fireplaces, clothes dryers, exhaust fans and other building air losses.

Insufficient combustion air can cause major problems for proper draft and operation of both gas and oilheating systems.

For years it has been assumed that when a heating appliance was located in an unconfined area, there was sufficient air for both ventilation and combustion. Today, in most cases, that is not true! New construction standards, insulation, weather stripping, and energy efficient windows and doors have reduced the amount of air changes per hour.

The combustion and make up air requirements in the codes are based on 1/2 air changes per hour.

For newer homes and conversion of electrically heated homes, the air changes could be reduced to 1/3 or less air changes per hour. Air problems are most notable on the coldest days when heat loss is the greatest and there is a chance that windows or doors are closed for an extended period of time.

When installing new equipment or troubleshooting problem equipment, the first determination that needs to be made is whether the equipment is located in a confined or unconfined space. In accordance with NFPA 31 and NFPA 54, an unconfined space is defined as follows: Any space whose volume is equal to or greater than 50 cubic feet per 1,000 Btu (or 20 Btu/Cubic Foot). This is calculated on the sum of the total input ratings of all fuel burning appliances installed in that space. Only areas connected to the space that have

no doors or with fully louvered doors can be considered part of the unconfined space.

Note: If the actual free area of the louvers is not known, wood louvers are assumed to have a 20% to 25% free opening. Metal louvers or grills are assumed to have 60% to 70% free opening.

Calculating confined space

Example:
A room 20' by 30' with an 8' ceiling height and the heating appliance is 140,000 Btu. See Figure 7-19.

Determine the maximum total input firing rate allowable in a room without modification.

Example: Boiler room 20x30x8 =
    4,800 cu ft.
4800 cu. ft. x 1000 Btu/50 cu. ft. =
    96,000 Btu
96,000 Btu x 1 gph #2 fuel/140,000 Btu =
    0.69 GPH
Result: If you fire greater than 0.69 GPH or 96,000 Btus, you will need additional combustion air.

**Figure 7-19:
Calculating
confined space**

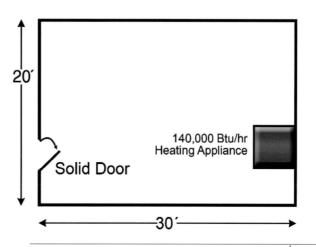

To add air from an adjacent room, two openings between the room could be made 12 inches above the floor and 12 inches below the ceiling. The size of these openings is based on 1 square inch per 1,000 Btu input.

To add air directly from the outside of the structure, two openings could be made. The size of these openings is based on 1 square inch per 4,000 Btu input. The above requirements are based on guidelines in NFPA 31 or NFPA 54.

Alternately, if operating in a confined space, additional air may be added by a duct to the outside, sized on 1 square inch per 5,000 Btu input.

Incomplete air-oil mixing

Improper mixing creates fuel rich and fuel lean pockets in the combustion area and prevents complete burning. Some of the causes are:

- Mismatch of the fuel droplet spray and the burner air pattern

- Inadequate air swirl and turbulence caused by outdated burner design

- Improper burner head size

- Improper adjustment of air handling parts of the burner

- Irregular or unbalanced fuel spray caused by a partially plugged nozzle

- Off center installation of the nozzle

- Dirt or soot accumulation on burner air forming parts or air fan blades

- Defective or damaged burner parts such as the end cone, air tube, fan, and motor coupling

- Using a nozzle that is either too small or too large for the burner head and combustion area

- Fuel pump pressure set too low or too high

- Cold oil producing larger fuel droplets, and increasing the firing rate beyond the air setting

Figure 7-20: Relationship between excess air and CO_2

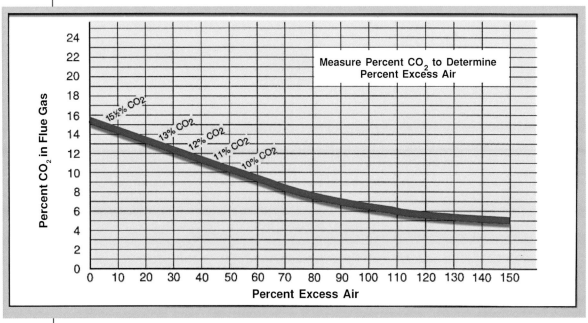

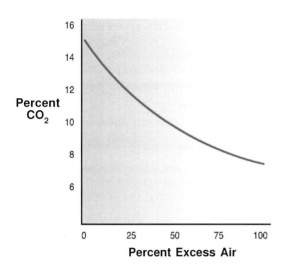

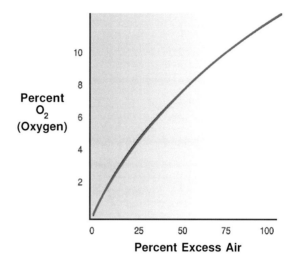

**Figure 7-21:
Relationship of
CO_2, O_2 and
excess air**

Flame impingement

The flame must not touch any solid surfaces of the burner, the end cone, the combustion chamber, or the heat exchanger. If this happens, the flame will be cooled and the unburned carbon atoms will turn to smoke and soot. Possible causes:

- Overfiring, too large a nozzle or excessive oil pump pressure

- Incorrect oil and/or air pattern

- Burner installed too high, too low, or off center

- Incorrect combustion chamber size or shape, or base of the chamber full of soot

- Partially plugged nozzle

- Cold oil

Smoky shut down

Check the cut-off valve by using a pressure gauge in the fuel pump nozzle port. See the nozzle and fuel unit chapters for causes of after drip. (Chapters 4 and 5).

Correlation of Percent of CO_2, O_2 and Excess Air		
Carbon Dioxide	Oxygen	Excess Air (Approx.)
15.4	0.0	0.0
15.0	0.6	3.0
14.5	1.2	6.0
14.0	2.0	10.0
13.5	2.6	15.0
13.0	**3.3**	**20.0**
12.5	**4.0**	**25.0**
12.0	**4.6**	**30.0**
11.5	**5.3**	**35.0**
11.0	**6.0**	**40.0**
10.5	6.7	45.0
10.0	7.4	50.0

The ranges that you will use most frequently are bold-faced and in color.

Excess air: CO_2 and O_2

As we add excess combustion air, the amount of nitrogen and unburned oxygen increase. The amount of water and carbon dioxide remain the same because we have already burned all the fuel; therefore the percentage of CO_2 drops and the percentage of oxygen starts to increase. (Figure 7-20). By measuring either the percentage of CO_2 or the percentage of unused oxygen (O_2) we can determine the quantity of excess air. They are the opposite of each other. As the percent of O_2 increases the CO_2% decreases. (Figure 7-21).

Why we must control excess air

Properly adjusting the burner air shutter is a compromise between too little air, which produces smoke, and too much air, which lowers efficiency. See Figures 7-22 and 7-23.

Earlier we found that a fixed quantity of combustion air is required to burn each pound of oil. We call this the theoretical fuel-air ratio.

Oilburners require a controlled amount of excess air above the theoretical value to assure complete combustion and smoke free operation. This excess combustion air serves as a safety margin to prevent incomplete combustion and smoke.

The air pressure in the building is always changing, the temperature of the fuel changes, and the draft produced by the chimney is not constant. Excess air gives us the safety factor we need for all these variations.

While excess air is needed for reliable clean operation, it also reduces efficiency. When increasing air for more oxygen, excess nitrogen comes along for the ride. This dramatically increases the amount of combustion gases that must be vented. Heat exchangers need time to absorb the heat from the combustion gases. The more gases forced into a heat exchanger, the faster they travel through the heat exchanger. This gives the heat exchanger less time to pull out the heat so the stack temperature goes up, and the efficiency goes down.

Limiting the amount of excess air can increase efficiency and save our customers money.

We measure excess air by determining

Figure 7-22: 0% Excess air

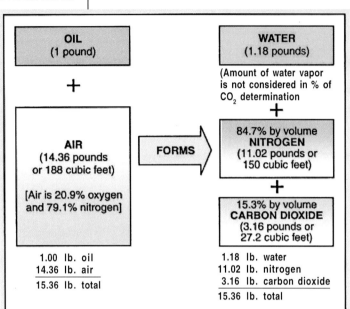

Figure 7-23: 50% Excess air

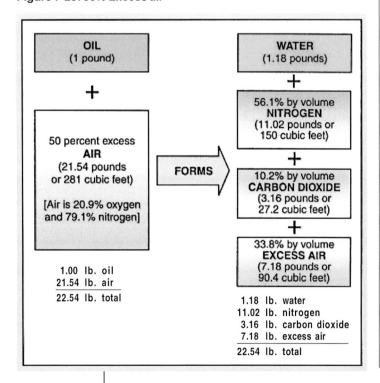

the percentage of oxygen (O₂) in the combustion gases. For each 1% decrease in oxygen levels introduced into the combustion process, efficiency increases by up to 1%. While some excess air is needed for complete combustion, we must set the air to the manufacturer's specifications to ensure maximum efficiency.

Another problem with excess air is that it cools the flame. This creates incomplete burning in the combustion area and carbon monoxide levels can rise. Therefore we must exactly control the amount of excess air we allow into the burner. The only way we can achieve this delicate compromise between smoke and efficiency is by using combustion test equipment. You cannot see flue gases; the only way you can be sure you are right is testing.

CO₂ measurement

The Orsat CO₂ analyzer, named for its inventor, uses chemicals that absorb CO₂ from a mixture of gases without absorbing any other gas. The chemical usually used is potassium hydroxide (KOH) because it has the capacity to absorb large amounts of CO₂. When it does so, it expands. By measuring how much it expands we can determine the amount of CO₂ in the gases.

There are two main parts to this analyzer:

1. The sampling pump:

A. The sample tube that is inserted into the stack gases, or replaced by a longer tube for over-fire sampling.

B. The yarn filter and water trap, which stops soot and water from entering the analyzer.

C. The sample pump, a rubber bulb with rubber flapper suction and discharge check valves that allow flow in only one direction into the analyzer.

D. The rubber connector, which seals the

sampling pump system to the analyzer.

2. The analyzer:

A. A body, which has two cavities or "cups" at the top and the bottom, connected by a narrow tube with an adjustable scale alongside. (Figure 7-24).

B. A valve system that either seals the gases and liquid inside the analyzer, or else lets a sample be pumped into the top cavity while the narrow tube and the lower cavity are sealed off.

C. A diaphragm, or flexible disc in the bottom cavity, which prevents a vacuum from forming inside the analyzer and lets the liquid in the bottom cavity be drawn up into the narrow tube after CO₂ is absorbed.

Using a CO₂ analyzer

A. Prime and "wet" the instrument by tipping it over and then back once, and allow the fluid to drain from the upper cavity while holding the instrument at a 45-degree angle. Next, hold upright and depress valve on top several times and release the valve. Loosen the lock nut on the sliding scale on the right side. Slide the scale until "0" lines up with top of fluid in the center tube. Tighten the locknut.

B. Insert the sampling tube into the stack to draw the gases to be sampled through the sampling hole in the stack. This gives you a stack CO₂ reading.

However, under certain conditions, it is desirable to determine the over-fire CO₂. To do this you must replace the short metal sampling tube with a ¼" metal tube about 30" long. This must extend through the sampling hole in the fire door to a point above

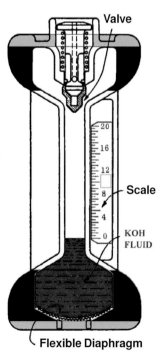

Figure 7-24: An analyzer

Valve

Scale

KOH FLUID

Flexible Diaphragm

Study the instruction manual and take the time to learn how your analyzer works before you expect it to perform for you. Be sure to follow the manufacturer's recommended maintenance and service procedures.

the center of the flame in the combustion chamber.

Place the rubber connector end of sample pump on top of valve and push it down to open the valve. Squeeze and release the rubber bulb 18 times to pump combustion gases into the analyzer. Release the valve while the bulb is still collapsed on the 18th stroke, and remove the rubber connector from the instrument.

C. Tip the analyzer completely over and back twice, allowing gas to bubble completely through the fluid. Hold at 45 degree angle for 5 seconds to complete draining of fluid. The fluid has now absorbed the CO_2 from the gas sample, and has been pulled up in the center tube. Hold the analyzer upright and read the CO_2 on the scale opposite the top of the fluid.

D. Depress the valve on top of analyzer several times, release, and check to see that the zero setting has not changed. If it has, repeat the above steps.

E. If the CO_2 analyzer is cold, run one or two tests to warm it up before using the reading.

NOTE: **The CO_2 test fluid is hazardous. Do not invert analyzer while the plunger valve is depressed. If fluid gets on your hands, wash them immediately.**

Combustion efficiency calculations

Since it is not possible in the field to measure the temperature of the flame due to dilution of the gases and absorption of the heat by radiation to the surrounding areas, we use a combustion equation to determine the quality of the combustion process. The efficiency calculation is based upon the theoretical heat value of the fuel being burned minus the stack losses.

To calculate the combustion efficiency with older test equipment, you need to know:

1. The Net Stack Temperature: This is the measured or gross temperature as indicated by the stack thermometer, minus the ambient or intake air temperature.

2. The % CO_2 in the Stack Gases: Do not use the % CO_2 measured over the fire. This is for air leak checks only. Test the CO_2 at the breech.

To calculate the steady state efficiency, use combustion efficiency tables or the combustion efficiency slide ruler. Adjust the large slide to the right so that the net stack temperature appears in the small window in the upper right corner marked *"Net Stack Temperature"*; then move the small vertical slide until the arrow points to the CO_2 reading. Through the window in the arrow on this slide you now read the figures: combustion efficiency in black and on-cycle heat loss in red.

Electronic combustion test equipment

One drawback of manual combustion test instruments is the time required to use them properly. This is especially true when the tests must be repeated during oilburner fine-tuning. New digital electronic testing instruments have been developed in recent years that can reduce the time needed for oilburner testing and adjustment.

Digital instruments are faster, more accurate, more reliable, and have a higher repeatability. Digital instruments stay in calibration, allow trending, allow more complex functions and save time.

Digital instruments allow data to be recorded and reported without human error, and provide reliable and accurate results for you and your customers. Data can be recorded much faster than any technician could ever do the calculations.

With the optional printer, the data can be recorded as an un-editable record, so the print out is what was measured at the jobsite. Permanent records allow the user to track system changes and determine if the system is operating within the design parameters or if changes have taken place.

Only digital analyzers allow you to take real time tests.

Study the instruction manual and take the time to learn how your analyzer works before you expect it to perform for you. Be sure to follow the manufacturer's recommended maintenance and service procedures. Most manufacturers ask that you not expose the analyzer for extended periods of time to freezing temperatures, as this has an impact on sensor life. In the winter, do not leave the tester in a cold truck over night.

The electronic combustion analyzers use advanced methods of measuring flue gas composition and temperature through a single probe.

A pump within the electronic analyzer draws a flue gas sample through a series of sensors. These electronic analyzers are capable of measuring oxygen percentage (O_2), carbon monoxide (CO), carbon dioxide (CO_2- calculated), excess air, draft, stack and ambient temperatures and many can even determine other gases like oxides of nitrogen (NO, NO_2, NOx) for advanced flue gas emissions level readings. The only thing they cannot measure is smoke.

Since the electronic analyzers are sensitive to carbon build-up, to extend the life of the sensors and instrument, take smoke tests with a smoke tester, and adjust for a low smoke reading before using the electronic analyzers.

The electronic analyzers eliminate the cumbersome work required by the manual test equipment and more importantly, they eliminate human error caused by varying interpretation of results we have with manual equipment. With the electronic analyzers, any two technicians will get identical results.

The use of these electronic instruments also indicates to customers that you are a professional equipped with the most up-to-date testing equipment. It adds to your image as an energy expert. This can assist with customer acceptance of energy conservation options, such as flame retention burners and new boilers and furnaces.

Some of the electronic instruments compute efficiency and display the results on a printed readout. This can be used to demonstrate to the homeowner the actual efficiency of their boiler or furnace. This information can serve as a sales tool to identify the fuel savings that are available by installing new equipment and can also provide a written record that everything was as you say it was when you left the job.

Measurement procedure

Connect the flue gas sampling probe assembly to analyzer per manufacturer's instructions. Verify the condensate trap plug is properly seated in combustion analyzer, and that water trap and thermocouple are not touching the side of the probe assembly. Before inserting the probe into the unit, start the analyzer and allow it to do its start up procedure. This is called the zeroing process. Never allow the

analyzer to zero in the stack unless manufacturer's design allows this.

As with older test equipment, measurements must be made in the stack between the barometric damper (if equipped) and the breech. Allow burner to operate until stack temperature stabilizes before testing.

Observations to make before testing

With experience, you will be able to quickly pinpoint the likely problems in the heating unit by looking at the instrument results, and making a few quick observations.

• **Look at the flame.** Is it normally shaped? Is it lopsided? Is it striking the sides or floor of the combustion chamber? (Be sure the flame observation door is closed when you do your tests. The air flowing into the open door will lower the CO_2 readings and raise the stack temperature.)

• **Check the burner-operating period.** Burning periods of less than 5 minutes do not usually produce enough heat to give good results. Short burner operating periods can be caused by overfiring of unit, or by improper functioning of automatic electrical controls.

• **Watch the flame while the burner shuts down.** A flame that lasts more than two seconds after the burner shuts off may be due to a poor cut-off. The primary two causes are air in the oil or the cut off in the fuel unit is defective. Refer to the Fuel Units Chapter for testing pump cut off. (Chapter 4).

• **Test for air leaks** around the burner air tube, the combustion chamber and all access doors on the furnace. A common cause of low CO_2 readings is air leaks into the unit. To see if the problem is air leaks, take a CO_2 test over the fire. If it is higher

Heating System Evaluation

Name

Street

City _____ Acct No.

COMBUSTION TEST	HEATING SYSTEM
Date:	Boiler/Furnace
	Manuf.
Gross Stk Temp	Model
	☐ F Warm Air ☐ G. Warm Air
	☐ F Hot Water ☐ G. Hot Water
Net Stk Temp	☐ Steam ☐ Coal Converted
	No of Zones
☐ CO2% ☐ O2%	Aquastat Setting
	Burner
Smoke	Manuf.
	Model Info
Breech Draft	Nozzle
	Size__ Angle__ Spray__
Overfire Draft	Winter K-Factor
	Combustion Chamber
	☐Replace ☐Repair ☐OK
EFFICIENCY %	Domestic Hot Water
☐ Excellent	☐ Oil ☐ Gas ☐ Electric
☐ Good	☐ Separate ☐ Tankless
☐ Fair	☐ Tankless with Booster Tank
☐ Poor	Tankless Size ____gpm
Technician	Temperature Setting
Certificate No.	Oil Tank
	Size _____ Gals.

Chapter 7
Combustion

than the reading at the breech, you have air leaks into the heat exchanger. Because of leakage, air has been pulled into the heat exchanger passages by the negative draft within the unit, lowering system efficiency.

Keep a record of efficiency tests

They have a saying in the nursing profession, "If you didn't write it, you didn't do it." Why go to all the trouble of taking these tests if you don't brag about it? Create or buy an efficiency test report form, and use it to record the results of your efficiency tests. These reports are important for three reasons:

1. They serve as a starting point for diagnosis and service.

2. Efficiency test results can be valuable sales tools when trying to convince customers to upgrade their equipment.

3. Having a written record can help protect you if there is ever a future problem.

With most of the electronic combustion test equipment available today, a printer option is available. This gives you proof that you performed the test. Additionally, it provides time, date, and exact information as to burner performance when you left the unit. This can be invaluable when having to prove the burner operation at the time you made the adjustments.

Typical Combustion Test Readings

Non-flame retention burners:
Oxygen: 5 - 9%

Flame Retention Oxygen:
3 - 6%

Carbon Dioxide:
10–12.5%

Stack Temp:
60–79% Efficiency 400°F to 600°F

Stack Temp:
80+ Efficiency 330°F to 450°F

Stack Temp:
90+ Efficiency less than 125°F

Draft:
-0.02"wc Over fire

Draft (Stack):
-.04"wc to -.06"wc

Carbon Monoxide:
Less than 50 ppm (diluted)

Smoke spot:
Zero to #1

Always Follow Manufacturer's Specifications

Report to the customer

Your report to the customer can be written or oral. A properly written report, including a conservative estimate of savings you anticipate from any changes you have made or suggested, can build customer good will and increase equipment sales.

Combustion air test

Modern buildings are much tighter than the old buildings; some do not allow enough air to leak into the building from the outdoors to replace the air going up the chimney. Winterization practices on older homes have sealed many of the openings that formerly provided combustion air.

If the building does not allow enough infiltration air in, provisions must be made to bring in the outdoor air to replace the air used in the combustion process. The following test will tell you if you have enough infiltration.

1. Visually inspect the venting system

Chapter 7—Combustion   7-27

for proper size and horizontal pitch and be sure there is no blockage, restriction, leakage, corrosion, or other deficiencies that could cause an unsafe condition.

2. Shut off the unit and any other fuel-gas-burning appliance within the same room.

3. Inspect burners for blockage and corrosion.

4. Furnaces: Inspect the heat exchanger for cracks, openings, or excessive corrosion.

5. Boilers: Inspect for evidence of water or combustion product leaks.

6. Insofar as is practical, close all building doors and windows and all doors between the space in which the appliance is located and other spaces of the building. Turn on the clothes dryer. Turn on any exhaust fans, such as range hoods and bathroom exhausts, so they will operate at maximum speed. Close fireplace dampers.

7. Place the appliance being inspected in operation.

8. Determine that the burner ignition and operation is satisfactory.

9. Turn on all other fuel and gas-burning appliances within the same room.

10. Determine that all units are burning properly.

11. Use a monometer to test if the pressure in the room that the unit is in is less than the pressure outdoors.

12. Return doors, windows, exhaust fans, fireplace dampers, and any other fuel-gas-burning appliance to their previous conditions of use.

Testing for a leaking furnace heat exchanger

A combustion analyzer can be used for finding leaking cracks or holes in a furnace

heat exchanger. The static pressure created by the system blower can overcome any positive pressure in the heat exchanger causing air to leak into the fire side of the exchanger rather than out.

Readings that change when the blower comes on after stabilization has taken place are indicative of a combustion air, venting, or mechanical problem such as a cracked heat exchanger. Furnaces can have cleanout doors leaking that will test positive for leakage. This is not a heat exchanger failure. Inspection door gaskets should be replaced and doors should be properly sealed.

Procedure:

1. Follow the manufacturer's instructions to properly zero the combustion analyzer. Insert the combustion analyzer probe in the flue pipe.

2. Start the furnace and observe the oxygen reading for stability (1-3 minutes).

3. When the blower starts, watch for a change in the O_2 reading. If the O_2 reading goes up, there is a leak.

Corrective action: Attempt to visually find the crack or hole.

A. If you can find the defect, show it to the customer.

B. On the service invoice, write that your testing indicates a leak in the heat exchanger. (Do this even if you cannot find the leak.)

C. Inform the customer, in writing, that the heat exchanger has a defect and that the furnace should be replaced. You should not attempt to repair a heat exchanger.

Checking and caring for the instruments
1. Smoke tester
    A. Clamp a piece of filter paper in the

smoke tester. Place a finger over the end of sample tube and try to pull the plunger handle out and then release. The handle should return by itself to approximately the original position. If it does not, the hose, paper holder, and plunger should be checked for leaks. If leakage is indicated, the hose in the sampling line may need replacement. Leakage may also occur if the surfaces of the filter paper holder are damaged. These areas (on the nylon inserts) should be inspected. The plunger can be removed for inspection if leakage is occurring across the plunger.

B. A clean piece of filter paper should be clamped in the smoke tester and a 10 stroke sample of fresh air taken after very dark smoke readings have been observed. If the air sample does not give a clean spot, repeat until it does. In extreme cases, the tube, and possibly the pump, may have to be cleaned with soap and water.

C. Sticky action of the plunger can be

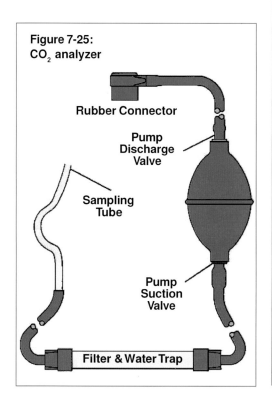

**Figure 7-25:
CO$_2$ analyzer**

Rubber Connector

Pump
Discharge
Valve

Sampling
Tube

Pump
Suction
Valve

Filter & Water Trap

helped by coating the plunger cup with petroleum jelly (Vaseline) after wiping the cup and the bore of the body clean.

2. CO$_2$ analyzer

A. After about 200 samples have been measured with the analyzer, the fluid will begin to lose its strength. This can be checked by measuring a sample in the normal manner, after the height of the fluid is measured on the % CO$_2$ scale, invert the instrument two more times, let it drain, and reread. If the % CO$_2$ reading changes more than ½ a number, the fluid is becoming weak and should be replaced.

B. The sampling pump should be checked for leaks in the following manner:

1. Place a finger over the end of the sampling tube and squeeze the rubber bulb. The bulb should stay collapsed. If it does not, an air leak exists between the bulb and the sampling tube, or the discharge valve in the rubber bulb is leaking, Figure 7-25.

2. Place a finger over the rubber connector at the other end of the pump and seal off the hole tightly. Apply moderate pressure to the rubber bulb. If the bulb cannot hold pressure, a leak exists between the bulb and the rubber connector or the suction valve in the rubber bulb is leaking.

C. Any evidence of fluid leakage from the analyzer should be checked. Such leakage is an indication of possible air leaks in the analyzer, which will give inaccurate CO$_2$ readings.

D. If the CO$_2$ scale will not slide low enough to adjust the zero setting, it may be necessary to add water or more KOH fluid to bring up the fluid level. Add 2 or 3 drops of tap water into the space around the valve in the top of the analyzer. Depress the valve and release it several times, allow the water to drain down, and then check fluid level. If the level is still too low, add 2 or 3 more drops and repeat. This should be used only as a stopgap procedure until you can obtain new potassium hydroxide (KOH) fluid.

E. If the fluid must be changed, refill kits are available and a spare should always be kept on hand. This kit includes fluid, gasket, screws, and filter yarn for the pump. To change the fluid:

(1) Remove four screws in top of analyzer.

(2) Remove top and discard fluid and rubber gasket (do not spill fluid, it is harmful to hands, paint, etc.)

(3) Clean unit using soap and water.

(4) Pour in full bottle of new fluid.

(5) Install new rubber gasket cover, and new screws. Tighten screws evenly. The filter yarn in the sampling pump must also be changed. This filter yarn may be changed more often than the fluid to provide easy sampling pump operation.

F. The analyzer should be stored in an upright position with the valve on top to prevent any possible fluid leakage. When placing the analyzer in the carrying case, it should be placed with its valve toward the handle side of the case. Extensive storage in warm places such as car trunks during summer should be avoided. The fluid should be checked for strength following long storage periods.

3. Oxygen (O_2 analyzers)

Measuring the oxygen content of the surrounding air can check the accuracy of oxygen sensors. When fresh air is drawn through the instrument, a reading of 20.9 percent O_2 should be observed. The instrument should be adjusted to this value. If you cannot get a 20.9% reading, replace the oxygen sensor.

4. Stack temperature gauge

A. Other than checking for obvious damage, the only problem that might occur with a temperature gauge is a bent stem. The gauge will not read accurately with a bent stem.

B. Many manual and electronic temperature instruments can be checked in boiling water (212°F), and readjusted if needed.

5. Draft gauge

A. Check to be sure the indicator needle moves freely. This can be done by blowing lightly across, and then toward, the end of the sampling tube. The needle should move smoothly and return accurately to the zero setting position.

B. The draft gauge should be checked against an accurate manometer at least once a year.

6. Electronic analyzer calibration

All manufacturer instructions concerning equipment care and maintenance must be followed carefully. Oxygen cells, batteries, and calibration of the instrument must be done as needed to assure accurate readings. Electronic analyzers should be sent back to the manufacturer for calibration as required by the manufacturer. This will insure accuracy of the sensors in the analyzer.

Problem	Possible Cause	Remedy
Insufficient O2 and/or excess carbon monoxide production	Insufficient combustion air	Adjust air band settings(s) Check for adequate combustion air into the furnace zone
	Burner over firing	Adjust fuel input
	Low stack draft	Adjust/install barometric control Check for restricted heat exchanger or vent system Check for improperly sized or improperly constructed chimney or vent system
High O2 reading	Excess combustion air	Adjust air band settings(s)
	Burner under firing	Adjust fuel input
	Loose cleanout ports, access doors, gasket missing in boiler sections, etc.	Repair
	Excess stack draft	Adjust/install barometric control
Fluctuation in O2 and/or carbon monoxide readings	Changing atmospheric conditions (i.e. wind speed)	Evaluate for barometric control
	Cracked Heat Exchanger	Replace
	Loose cleanout ports or gasket missing in boiler sections	Repair
Excess stack temperature	Inadequate air flow across the heat exchanger	Check for dirty filter, blower and/or air conditioning coil Increase blower speed. Don't over amp motor! Increase return or supply ducting if needed
Insufficient stack temperature	Burner underfired	Adjust fuel input
	Excess air flow past heat exchanger	Check temperature rise per manufacturer
Low temperature rise	High fan speed	Decrease fan speed or baffle blower to reduce air flow
	Burner underfired	Adjust fuel input
Low stack draft •Less than -.02 WC" in flue (gas) •Less than -.04 WC" in flue (oil) •Less than -.02 WC" over fire with gas or oil power burners	Improperly sized vent connector or chimney	Properly size system
	Blocked vent system	Remove blockage
	Excess elbows or long horizontal runs	Re-vent or move appliance to better location for venting
	Leakage in chimney or vent connections	Seal
	Improper vent termination	Re-vent
	Inadequate combustion air	Add combustion air
	Improperly adjusted barometric control	Adjust
High stack draft •Greater than .04 WC" in flue (gas) •Greater than .06 WC: in flue (oil) •Greater than .02 WC" over fire with gas or oil power burners	Improper vent system sizing	Properly size system
	Absence of or improperly adjusted barometric control	Install or adjust barometric control

Courtesy of Bacharach

Chapter **8**

BASIC ELECTRICITY

IN THIS CHAPTER

- **General overview**

- **Understanding electrical circuits**

- **Measuring electricity**

- **Electrical safety**

OIL

BURN

ON

↑

ON

↓

OFF

EMERGENCY

SWITCH

Chapter 8

Basic Electricity

Introduction

Our objective for this Chapter is to make you feel more comfortable with electricity and to give you the information you need to service and troubleshoot electrical devices.

The easiest way to learn about electricity is to define the words used to describe electricity and its properties. Let's start with the word *electricity*. Electricity is an almost magical way to take the potential energy locked up in coal, natural gas, oil, waterfalls, and even inside atoms—move that energy great distances—and ultimately have it do useful work for us.

Any source of electricity must get the energy from somewhere. The battery gets energy from a chemical reaction. The generator gets energy from the work done turning the shaft. The work it does for

Electrical safety

Electricity can be dangerous. It can create three hazards: fire, skin burns, and shock. Shock can cause muscle spasms, unconsciousness and even death.

Proper installation of all electrical equipment is essential. The National Electrical Code® sets the standards. Local communities can make this code law, and in addition, they can make their own codes even more restrictive.

A common and dangerous practice is testing the ignition transformer with a screwdriver. The transformer is putting out 10,000 volts and can give you a dangerous and serious shock.

Electric energy needs a pathway from the source and back to the source. If you do your job, this pathway is our electric circuit.

But any wet object has enough minerals in the water to provide an alternate pathway. The human body is over 50% water, and when the skin is damp it will provide a good pathway back to the source if there is not an easier one. Never allow your body to be that pathway! Always consider all electrical components to be energized until you test and prove they are not.

When you are working on electricity, remove all metal objects such as watches and jewelry from your hands and wrists. Until you are absolutely sure a circuit is shut off, only use one hand—keep the other in your pocket. This prevents the electric pathway from going from one hand to the other hand through your heart. Be sure to replace any damaged or frayed wires, protect wires from touching moving equipment, and keep them clear of walkways.

Oilheat is to power our motors that pump oil and water, make the spark needed for ignition; and automatically control the entire heating process.

Electrical current flows through wires, switches, and transformers to our heating appliances.

The force that pushes the current through the wire is called *Voltage*, which is measured in *Volts*. The amount of current flowing through the wire is called *Amperage* or *Current*, which is measured in *Amps*. The *Resistance* to this flow is measured in *Ohms*. The power used to run our motors and create spark is measured in *Watts*.

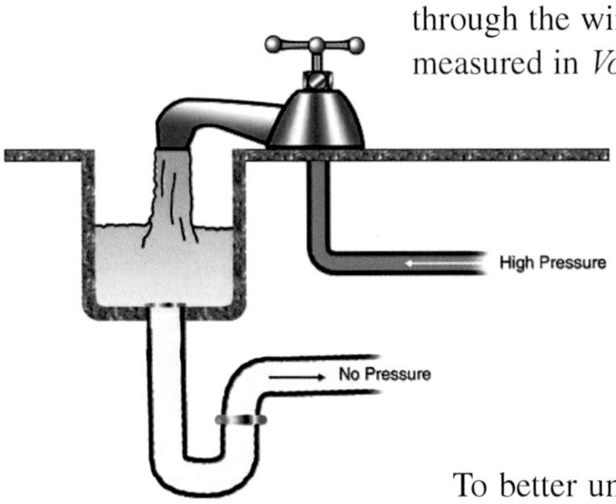

To better understand these important words, it might be helpful to compare electricity to the flow of water in a pipe.

Volts

Voltage is like water pressure (pounds per square inch), and like water pressure, does not need an actual flow. Regardless of the faucet being open or closed, there is still water pressure in the pipe. Likewise, there are volts at an electrical outlet even though nothing is plugged into that outlet and there is no flow. Of course, the potential for flow is there and that is why volts are referred to as electric potential; it could flow if the conditions were right even though it is not flowing now.

Voltage is the force created by the power source (the battery, transformer, or generator). This is called the electromotive force (EMF).

When water comes out of a faucet, it flows under pressure. But when that water drains out of the sink, it has no pressure except gravity. Voltage is the same. As

voltage pushes the electricity through the wires, it keeps it under pressure.

Once the electricity has finished doing its work (turning a motor, making a spark), it returns to where it came from under no pressure. The voltage is all "used up". Therefore, voltage supplied to the circuit is voltage *used by* the circuit.

Amps = water flow

Amperes, or amps for short, are a way of expressing the amount of electricity flowing through the wire, the rate of flow (current). They are like the gallons per hour flow of water through a pipe. Figure 8-1.

The voltage is like the force of the water in the pipe and the amps are like the amount of water flowing out of the faucet.

Ohms = resistance to flow

As water flows through a pipe, it encounters *resistance* to the flow depending upon the physical characteristics of the pipe. How much water flows through the pipe, at any given amount of water pressure, is affected by the size of the pipe and even the smoothness of the inner walls.

Amps also meet resistance from insulation, motors, circuits or anything that restricts the free flow of electricity. This resistance to the flow of Amps is called *Ohms*.

Resistance to flow makes friction and friction makes heat

Resistance to flow, whether it is water or electricity, creates friction, and friction converts energy to heat. Electricity faces much resistance trying to fight its way through wiring, and it creates a lot of heat doing it. The greater the resistance to flow in the wire, the more heat is produced. This isn't all bad. The heat can be used to make

**Figure 8-1:
Water analogy**

High Pressure

No Pressure

electric heaters for toasters, electric water heaters, and electric baseboard heat. This heat can also be used to make heat anticipators in thermostats and safety timers in primary controls.

What's a watt?

Watts are the power consumed by an electrical circuit. One amp (remember, that's the amount of flow) driven by one volt (the amount of pressure) through a circuit equals one watt of power, see Figure 8-2. This work can also be called *horsepower*. One horsepower equals 746 watts.

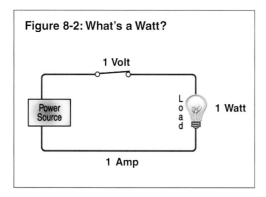

Figure 8-2: What's a Watt?

1 Volt

Power Source

Load

1 Watt

1 Amp

If a circuit using one watt operates for an hour, this called a *watt-hour*. Sometimes, AC power is called *volt-amps* (VA) or *apparent power*. As current or voltage increases in a circuit, the power consumption and work done also increases. Every electrical device needs a certain amount of power, so it is given a power rating based on it being supplied with a specific number of volts and amps. If the right amount is not supplied, it changes the device's power consumption and performance.

> **Did you know?**
> Electric company bills are based upon kilowatts per hour, kwh.
> A kilowatt is 1,000 watts.

> **The math**
> Volts, amps, ohms and watts are all related to each other. If you change one, you change the others, too. These relationships are described by two math formulas:
>
> volts = amps times ohms
>
> and watts = volts times amps
>
> **Remember, if one changes, it affects the others.**

Conductors

Some materials offer very little resistance to the flow of electricity; these materials are called conductors. Most metals are good conductors. Gold, silver, copper, and aluminum are very good conductors. That's why wires are made out of metal. Also, some switches are made out of mercury (a liquid metal).

Wires are the conductors; they are very much like pipes for water. In a water pipe, not only does the pipe material affect the resistance to flow, the size of the pipe or wire also determines how much resistance to the flow there is. A fat wire, like a fat pipe, offers less resistance than a skinny one, and a short wire offers less resistance than a long one. In electricity, temperature is important, too. Cold conductors offer less resistance than hot ones. Force is needed to overcome this resistance. Remember, in water, the force is called pressure (pounds per square inch), and in electricity, the force is measured in volts.

Insulators

Many materials offer a lot of resistance to the flow of electricity, these materials are called *insulators*. Air, glass, porcelain, plastic, and rubber are all good insulators. They stop the flow of electricity. These

**Figure 8-3:
Water circuit**

Current (flow)
is the same in
all parts of the
circuit

High
Pressure

No Pressure

Pump

Valve

materials are used to contain or control the flow of electricity along a conductor, such as a copper wire. Because air is a good insulator, the resistance of the air stops the electricity at the end of a wire like a wooden plug stuck in the end of a pipe. If enough water pressure is put on that plug it will pop out and the water will flow. If enough electric pressure (volts) are put against the insulating air it, becomes a conductor and lets the electricity flow in the form of a spark. A ten thousand volt transformer can make electricity jump across the air space between the ignition electrodes in an oilburner. This creates the "spark" that ignites the oil.

Loads

A *load* is a device that converts electrical energy to some other form of energy in order to do work. A load also creates resistance that opposes electrical flow. Here is an example: a light bulb converts electric energy to heat and light because the filament resists the flow of electricity, getting so hot it actually glows. Another example: a motor changes electric energy into mechanical energy.

Some of the loads found in oil burner circuits are:

- *Motors*—in the burner, circulator, fan, power venter, humidifier

- *Electromagnetic coils*—in relays, solenoid valves

- *Transformers*—in ignition and control

- *Heaters*—in the primary control safety switch, thermostat heat anticipator

Electrical circuits

The most important thing to understand about electricity is the electric circuit. Electricity has to flow from a source out into the circuit and back to the source. Figure 8-3.

A typical circuit, then, has a conductor that carries the electric current from the source, through a switch, to a load—and back to the source. Current flows only in a complete circuit. However, the energy it gains in the electromotive force (measured in volts) from the power source is lost in the resistances (ohms) it encounters in the circuit. The switch is a device that interrupts the circuit. When it is open, electricity can't flow. When closed, the circuit is complete and the flow continues. See Figure 8-4.

**Figure 8-4:
Open and closed switches**

Close the switch and the light comes on

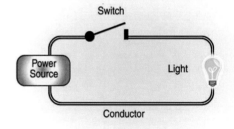

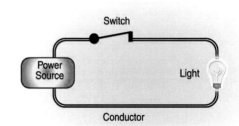

A complete circuit should always include a load of some sort. If you just run a conductor from the source back to the source without going through a load, you have a *short circuit*. Since there is no resistance to slow up the electrical current, the amps just keep going higher and higher. This increases the heat build-up from the resistance in the conductor until it gets so hot it starts a fire.

Fuses or circuit breakers are installed in the circuit to prevent this from happening. Circuit breakers are automatic switches that cut off the current if it starts to reach dangerous levels. Figure 8-5.

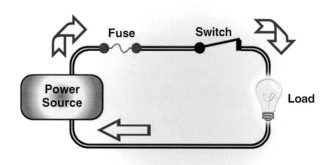

The primary resistance to flow in a circuit is the thing doing the work, the "load". It converts the electrical energy into another from of energy. However, the conductor can also restrict the flow, especially if it is undersized, too hot, or too long.

Resistance (ohms) opposes flow. Voltage overcomes resistance to create flow. Any change in ohms will cause the opposite change in amps because volts from the power source are relatively constant. An increase in ohms reduces amps. A decrease in ohms increases amps. Increasing volts increases amps, this is called *Ohms Law*, Figure 8-6. It states: *"It takes 1 volt to push 1 amp through 1 ohm."*

Figure 8-5: Fuse or circut breaker protects the circut

Figure 8-6

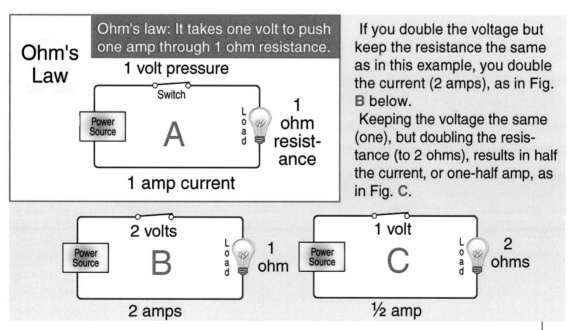

Series Circuit

A series circuit is one where there is only one path for the electric current through the loads. Remember the old Christmas tree lights (each light is a load) where, if one burned out, they all went out? That was a classic series circuit. Aside from the problem of losing one load and shutting off all the rest, the other drawback to a series circuit is that each load steals electricity from the other loads.

In a series circuit, the power is delivered in the greatest quantity to the point of

largest resistance. This is why poor connections in a circuit, where the resistance is high, tend to overheat.

Since voltage applied to a circuit is voltage used by that circuit, more than one load in the same pathway will share the supply voltage. Loads in the same pathway reduce the voltage to each load as well as the current through the entire circuit. The volts drop as they go from load to load. The current flow (amps) is affected by both the volts and the total ohms of the circuit, and is the same in all parts of the circuit.

To review, in a series circuit the total resistance (ohms) is equal to the ohms of all the individual conductors, switches, and loads present in the circuit. The current flowing (amps) in all parts of the circuit is the same. By adding all the voltage drops of all the loads together it equals the applied voltage (volts from the source). Figures 8-7 and 8-8.

Parallel circuit

A parallel circuit has separate branches for each load. This way, if one load burns out, it will not affect the other loads. Also, all the loads receive the same voltage.

The loads are parallel to each other. In a parallel circuit, some of the loads and not others can be turned on. For example, the burner motor and the ignition can run separately, so the spark can be shut off once flame is established.

In a house circuit, all the lamps and appliances are wired in parallel. This way each can be turned on and off separately. See Figures 8-9B and 8-10B.

The resistance of the load in each branch circuit determines the current (amps) delivered to that branch. The current in the common lines is equal to the current flowing in the branch circuits served by

Figure 8-7:
Volts, amps and ohms in a circuit

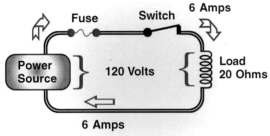

Figure 8-8:
Multiple loads in series

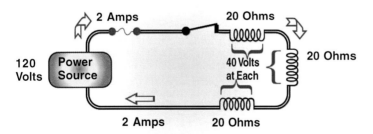

that section of the common line. Unlike in a series circuit, the current may vary in different parts of a parallel circuit.

As the number of branch circuits increases, the total current draw increases. If you plug too many appliances into an extension cord the amp rating of the wire might be exceeded. The wire will get hot. The overloaded circuit could cause a fire.

Overloaded circuits also decrease the voltage to all the loads. As the wire heats up, its resistance increases. The wire starts acting like a load in series with the other loads, and starts stealing electricity from all the loads in the circuit. This is why the oilburner should be wired with its own individual circuits, not sharing the circuit with any other loads.

Combination circuit

Oilheating systems use what is called a combination circuit. The switches and limit controls are in series with the primary control. If any one of them opens, the electric current to all the loads stops. All loads are wired parallel to each other to allow individual component control and to ensure full voltage is supplied to each load.

Safe capacity for 120 volt circuits

To be sure you will not overload a circuit, check the amps needed for each of the loads connected to the circuit. This information is on the label of the load. Add up all the watts to be sure they are within the safe capacity. The rated *ampacity* of controls, switches, and conductors must be followed.

AC/DC

Electric current is either direct current (DC) or alternating current (AC). Direct current typically comes from a battery. It

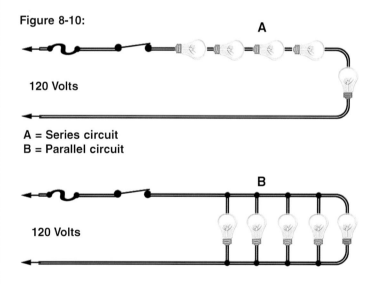

Figure 8-9:
Series and parallel circuits

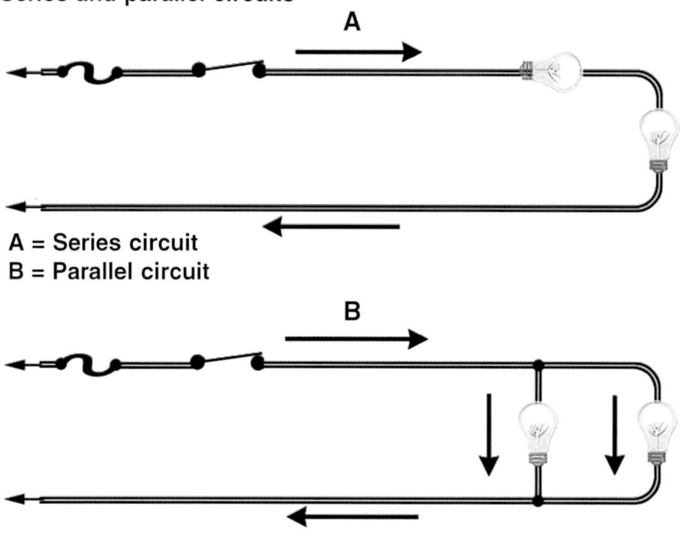

A

A = Series circuit
B = Parallel circuit

B

Figure 8-10:

A

120 Volts

A = Series circuit
B = Parallel circuit

B

120 Volts

only flows in one direction, from the negative side of the battery through the circuit to the positive side. Alternating current is what the electric company supplies. It changes direction, flowing back and forth in the wire. Each back and forth change is called a cycle. In North America, the electricity cycles 60 times a second, 120 changes of direction.

The current delivers power to the load no matter which way it is flowing. The voltage goes from and returns to zero 120 times a second. A light bulb in an AC circuit glows dim and bright in just this rhythm.

In a DC system, there are two kinds of electrical charges—positive and negative. Positive is also referred to as "hot" and negative as "neutral". In an AC system, the switched line is referred to as "hot" (H) or L1 and the unswitched side is referred to as "neutral" (N) or L2. (Be careful: L2 is also labeled as the second hot leg in most electric distribution panels. The L2 referred to here is the neutral wire.)

Separating electricity into two wires is called polarization. It is a way of making sure the electricity goes where it is wanted. You have probably noticed that most small appliances have a wide blade and a thin blade on their plug. There is only one way you can plug these things in. This way the appliance's switch will control the hot wire, not the neutral wire allowing for a safe shut-off of current. If polarization is reversed in heating systems, some controls will appear to function normally, but the limit control will be interrupting the neutral. This is dangerous.

Wiring diagrams

Wiring diagrams are sort of like road maps or blueprints that show us how a circuit is designed. To install or service electrical equipment, you must be able to read the wiring diagram.

One of the confusing things about wiring diagrams is that a complete circuit is always needed, and then the diagram starts right out with a big space between the two wires feeding the circuit. These two wires are labeled + (positive or hot) and - (negative or neutral), or as mentioned previously, they are now called L1 and L2 (line 1 and 2). All three names mean the same thing. When you see these labels, it means there is a complete circuit—without actually drawing it.

If you follow L1 and L2 off to the left off the page, they go back to the circuit breaker, the main breaker, and all the way to the big transformer hanging on the pole in front of the building. From there they go all the way back to the power plant. Just remember, the arrows on L1 and L2 are pointing at the power plant, and they represent a complete circuit. Figure 8-11.

L1 is the electrically charged line that causes electrical flow and L2 is the return line home. The direction of flow is from L1 to L2—from charged to uncharged—pressurized to unpressurized.

Wires

Wire comes in many different sizes. Wire sizes run from 0000 (4 naught, the largest) to 40 (the smallest); the lower the number, the fatter the wire. To size a wire, consider the maximum voltage rating of the wire and the amperage draw of all the loads in the circuit.

The number of wires bundled together in the wire sheathing (insulating jacket) is printed on the sheathing after the wire

**Figure 8-11:
L1 and L2
point to the
power source**

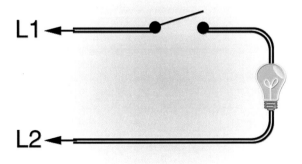

gauge number (14/2 and 14/3). Only insulated wires are counted, so 14/2 has a black, white, and a bare ground wire which is not insulated and therefore not in the count. 14/3 has an added red wire. Thermostat cables can have from two to seven wires in them, depending on the added functions of the thermostat (air conditioning, humidifier, and fan functions.)

To make identification easier, the color-coding of the wire insulation is standardized.

The spot where wires are joined together or hooked to a control is the weakest link in a circuit. Be very careful when making these connections. All connections must be in a junction box or protected control box with clamps at the entrance and exit to be sure stress is not placed on connections if the wires are pulled.

If exposed to high heat or humidity, connections may become dirty or corroded. Always check exposed connectors (like the terminal block on primary controls), and always seal hidden connections with electrical tape. Copper wire is recommended for all oilburner wiring and is required in some cases.

Armored cable

Any wiring around an oil-powered appliance should be protected by either flexible metal conduit or armored cable. There are two kinds of armored cable: BX and MC.

BX has no ground wire. Its metal sheathing serves as the ground. Some people mistake the thin metal bonding strip in the cable for a ground wire. The strip is easily broken and is used only to make a conductive connection to a metal junction box. Older BX used heavy steel sheathing. Aluminum is now used because it is lighter, easier to cut, and is a better conductor.

MC cable is like BX, but with a green insulated grounding wire. Most codes require MC instead of BX for a sure ground.

Flexible metal conduit has no conductors installed in it. The National Electrical Code® specifies how it can be used and how many conductors may be installed in the conduit.

Switches

Switches are used to stop the flow of electricity. It is a simple idea; just cut the conductor and put an insulator (air) between the two cut pieces of the conductor.

A switch is like a drawbridge installed in the middle of a race course. Imagine what would happen if during a race, you suddenly opened the drawbridge, leaving a big hole in the track. All the cars would stop; there would be no more current flow. Thanks to the car brakes, the resistance would be very high but there would still be voltage. The cars would still have all that

---

Did You Know?

When the switch is open, the electricity flows out of the power source to the open switch. It can go no farther. In a fraction of a second, the potential on the power side of the switch reaches the same as the potential from the power source, and there is no further flow of electricity. At the same time, the potential on the other side of the switch reaches the level from the other side of the power source, and there is no current. When we close the switch, the negative charge instantly goes to the positive potential on the other side and electricity flows through the circuit.

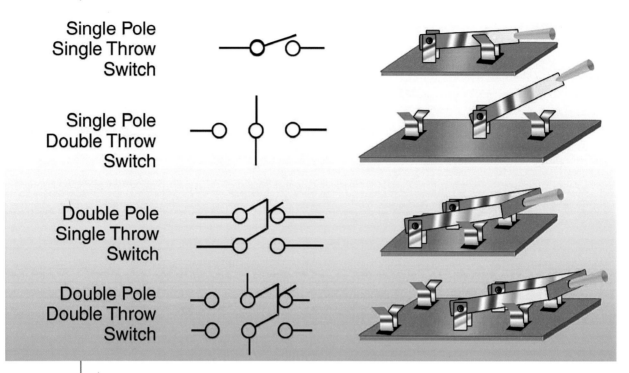

**Figure 8-12:
Switching
arrangements
(various setups)**

power available from the engines even if they were not using it.

Electric switches open to stop the flow of electricity just like the drawbridge opens to stop the flow of traffic. Switches can be manually or automatically operated.

For a switch to safely control a load on a typical oilheat system, it must be located in the source or hot line (L1), never in the neutral line! Switches in the neutral line can turn the load on and off but will not allow work to be done on the load without the risk of electric shock.

There are many different kinds of switches. The most common switch is a single pole, single throw switch, or SPST for short. They are either on or off. This is a swinging gate (or drawbridge) that can make an air break in a conductor when it is open and connect the break when it is closed. A SPST switch turns everything in a single circuit on and off. There can be many SPST switches in one hot line.

Another type of switch is a single pole double throw switch, or SPDT. This switch is used to turn the electricity on or off in one or the other of two separate circuits. This would be like a Y intersection. You can decide to drive on one road or the other. Some heat/cool thermostats have SPDT switches.

Double pole single throw (DPST) switches can make or break two separate circuits at the same time. The two circuits being switched can be off the same voltage or different voltages. This would be like a drawbridge that had a street and a railroad track on it. The main breaker at the electric panel is a DPST.

Double Pole Double Throw (DPDT) switches re-direct the power of two separate supply lines to two different circuits. See Figures 8-12.

The contacts of automatically operated switches in wiring diagrams are shown in their normal (at rest) position when the unit is not operating. Contacts on automatically operated switches are classified as normally open (NO) or normally closed (NC). The determination is made by the position of the contacts when the device is either not energized or not sensing the condition it is designed to sense.

Manual switches are operated by hand. Examples of manual switches in oilburner circuits are the stair switch, the on/off switch at the burner, the manual/auto fan and thermostat switches and the reset button on the primary control and motor. The reset button is an example of a manual switch that also is switched automatically.

Automatic sensing switches respond to a change in conditions such as: temperature, pressure, flow, liquid level, light and humidity.

Some switches open when the temperature, pressure, light, or liquid level rises and some open when one of these things falls. If the switch "makes" (closes) on fall, this is called "makes on fall" or "breaks (opens) on rise." If a switch opens as a result of a rise in the sensed condition, this is called a direct acting (DA) switch. If it opens on fall in the sensed condition, it is a reverse acting (RA) switch.

Heat-only thermostats and high limits are direct acting switches since they open on the rise in temperature. Cooling thermostats, fan off switches in fan-limit controls, low-water cutoffs, and reverse acting aquastats are reverse acting because they open on the fall of the sensed condition.

Timers–bimetals & warp switches

As you will learn in the primary control chapter, one of the things an oilburner circuit must do is shut itself off on "safety" in case flame is not established after the burner has been energized.

In many of these controls, there is a timer switch that uses small electrical heaters in combination with bimetals. Figures 8-13 and 8-14 shows how it works.

A bimetal is composed of two different strips of metal fused together. One end of the strip is secured and a small electric heater is placed under it. As it heats up, the two metals expand at different speeds. The

Figure 8-13: Warp switch, often used as a safety switch in controls

Firgure 8-14: Warp switch locking burner out on safety

Figure 8-13

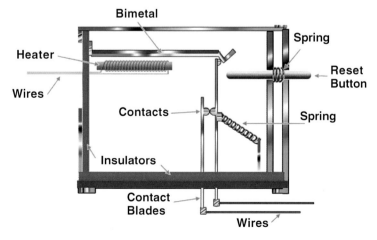

Figure 8-14

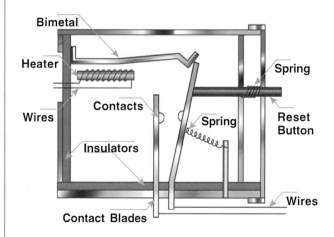

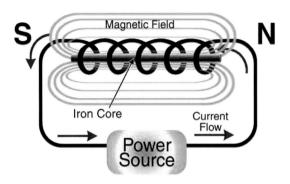

Figure 8-15:
Electromagnet

through the wire. As electric current flows through the wire, it creates a magnetic field around the wire. A coil of wire creates a stronger magnetic field than a straight wire. The coil is called a solenoid. If an iron core were placed inside the coils of a solenoid and the solonoid is energized, the magnetic field created magnetizes the iron core while the current flows. This is an electromagnet. See Figure 8-15.

Two factors affect the strength of an electromagnet:

1. The intensity of the current in the coil.

2. The number of turns of wire in the coil.

Electromagnets are rated in amp-turns.

Solenoid valves

To make a solenoid valve, an iron bar is placed into the center of a coil of wire and electricity is sent through the wire. The electromagnetic force will pull and hold the bar in the center of the coil. If a spring is attached to the iron bar (or valve stem), it returns to its original position when the electricity is shut off. If a valve seat is put on the end of the valve stem you have an electrically operated valve. Figure 8-16.

one closer to the heater expands faster. Since the two pieces of metal are fused together and they are secured on one end, the quickly expanding piece of metal bends away from the heat and makes the strip warp. This is why it is called a warp switch.

As you can see in the illustration, as the bimetal warps, it releases the movable contact and the spring on the movable contact opens the circuit. This puts the oilburner on 'safe' and stops the flow of electricity to the heater, see Figure 8-15. The only way to close this switch again is to wait for the bimetal to cool and warp back and then someone must push the 'reset' button to reset the moveable contact under the lip of the bimetal.

Electricity and magnetism

Electromagnetism describes the relationship between electricity and magnetism. If you move a wire in a magnetic field, you generate voltage if that wire is part of a complete electrical circuit. The generated voltage will cause electric current to flow

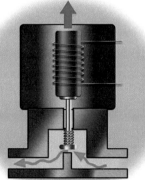

Figure 8-16:
Solenoid valve

Relay switches

Relays are electromagnetic switches found in primary controls, operating controls, and switching relays that use electromagnets to open and close. To create a magnetic field, wrap a coil of wire around a metal core. The magnetic field magnetizes the core and this electric

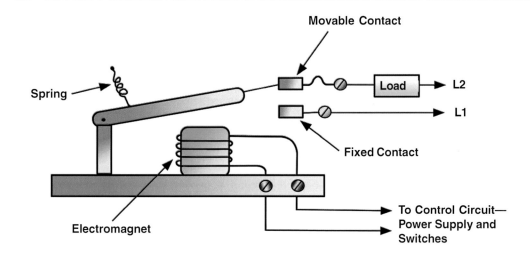

Figure 8-17:
Simple relay

magnet is used to open or close a switch that is held in its normal position by a spring, see Figure 8-17.

The nice thing about this kind of automatic switch is that low voltage wiring can be used for the electric magnet and the switch that sends electricity through the coil that can make or break a line voltage switch. When the low voltage remote switch (thermostat) opens, the magnetism immediately stops and the spring quickly returns the switch to its normal position. This snap action reduces arcing as the switch opens or closes.

The biggest problem with relays is the contacts. Dirty or corroded contacts add resistance to the circuit, resulting in reduced voltage to the load, which can create arcing that shortens the life of the contacts. The good news is that most new relays are enclosed in plastic to keep them clean. A properly working relay will not cause any voltage drop when closed.

Relays are represented in wiring diagrams as the coil of wire and the switch.

The coil is usually energized by low voltage. The switch can control either a high or low voltage circuit. The working limit of the switch is determined by the amperage draw of the circuit it is controlling. Many relays are single pole double throw switches, so you might have a low voltage switch and a line voltage switch. The way to keep track of all this is to label the coil with a number and a letter like 1K. Then label the switch contacts controlled by that coil 1K1 and 1K2.

Transformers

Transformers use electric power at one voltage to produce an almost equal power at another voltage. In our industry transformers operate on alternating current (AC); they are made of an iron core with two separate wire coils wrapped around two sides. The coil where the electricity goes in is the primary coil, and the coil where the electricity comes out is the secondary coil. Figure 8-18.

Thanks to AC, the electric field in the primary coil pulses back and forth, causing the magnetic field it creates to pulse back and forth in the iron core causing the north and south poles to switch back and forth. This pulsating magnet field creates a pulsing electric field in the secondary coil.

Step-down transformers have more primary coils than secondary and reduce voltage. Step up transformers have more coils in the secondary coil and increase voltage. There is no electrical connection between the primary and secondary coils. The only connection between the two is the magnetic field.

When voltage is applied to the primary coil, a magnetic field is generated which creates voltage in the secondary coil. The amount of voltage generated in the secondary coil is determined by the ratio of coils between the primary and secondary coils.

Transformers are very efficient and can provide as much as 90% of the energy put into the primary side to the secondary side. The small energy loss is due to the heating of the wires in the coils.

Why are transformers and solenoids loads?

The greater the current, the greater the magnetic field around the conductor. The magnetic field limits current flow by pushing back against the source voltage.

Remember, current is not only caused by voltage from the power source, it is caused by any electromotive force that acts upon the conductor. As the electricity goes through the coil of wire in the transformer or solenoid, it creates a magnetic field that resists the flow of electricity. It becomes a load. This is called this "back emf" because it counteracts the voltage (electromotive force) from the power source.

Motors

Motors turn electrical energy into mechanical energy.

If a permanent magnet is mounted on an axle and placed between the opposite poles of two fixed magnets, the magnet on the axle will spin until its north pole faces the south pole of the fixed magnet, and its south faces north. (Like poles repel each other, opposites attract.)

If you could reverse the poles of the fixed magnets just as the rotating magnet was coming to a stop, it would force it to turn another half circle until the opposite poles lined up again. Figure 8-19.

If you make the fixed magnets electromagnets every time the alternating current in the electromagnet changes direction the poles in the magnet flip (north becomes south and south becomes north) driving the rotating magnet around again. It will keep turning as long as the current in the fixed magnets keep flipping. The fixed (stationary) electromagnets are called the stator, and the rotating magnet the rotor.

Measuring electricity

Since electricity can not be seen (except for sparks), testing and measuring devices are needed in order to properly troubleshoot heating and air conditioning systems.

**Figure 8-18:
Basic design used
in an iron core
transformer**

Primary   Secondary

To measure voltage (volts), amps (current), and ohms (resistance), you can buy a device called a multimeter that lets you test all three. Your meter will come with directions on how to use it. Read and follow those directions.

Using a multimeter

The handiest device for electric testing is the multimeter mentioned above. It can measure voltage, current and resistance. You can buy analog meters that use a swinging needle to give you continuously varying readings, or a digital meter that gives readings with discrete numbers on a screen. Digital meters are easier to read and don't need to be "zeroed out" before use.

If you are reading a stable DC or AC voltage or current, a digital meter is a good thing. If you are measuring a slowly, varying current or voltage, a digital meter could be constantly refreshing itself, making the display very hard to follow.

Before you can use your meter, you must decide what you want to measure (i.e. voltage, current or resistance) and what

reading (range of value) you expect to get. This way, you can pick which function to use and which scale setting within that function. To prevent damage to the meter, do this before connecting the meter. Switching the function selection dial while attached to a live circuit could damage your meter. Always disconnect the test leads or shut off the circuit before changing the selection dial.

Each function has a maximum and minimum range. Exceeding the maximum is dangerous to you and the meter. The closer you are to the middle range, the more accurate your reading will be. Pick the range on the multi-position rotary switch that gives you the most accurate reading while not exceeding the maximum for the range. If you are not sure, always start with the highest range and work your way down.

Read your meter's instructions to determine what the symbols on the dial mean. The black lead should always be connected to the COM (common plug) jack. The position of the red lead varies

Figure 8-19: Arrangements of magnets to create motion

with the different functions based on the symbols marked on your meter.

- Be careful how you treat your meter

- Protect it from moisture and high temperatures

- Replace worn or cracked test leads

- When not in use store it in its case

- Check the battery for corrosion

- Remove the batteries for long storage periods

- Do calibration checks against known volts, amps, and ohms regularly

Measuring voltage

A voltmeter is used to measure the difference in electric pressure between two points. Since a load creates a difference in electric pressure (or force) as it does work,

Figure 8-20

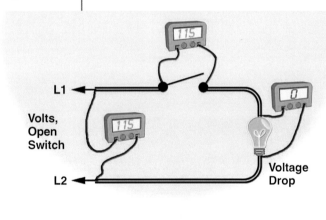

Volts,
Open
Switch

L1

L2

Voltage
Drop

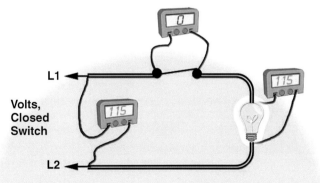

Volts,
Closed
Switch

L1

L2

the pressure is relative; that is, one point must be measured against another.

Electrical charge flowing from any power source is at a high energy level; when it returns from the circuit, its energy is low. The power source's job is to boost the energy level of the charge. The voltmeter measures this change in charge (the difference in energy level) through the circuit.

Somewhere in the circuit, the energy of the flowing charge is converted into other forms by the load. When a light bulb is lit, the electric energy becomes heat and light. To measure this conversion of energy (change in charge), use a voltmeter. Figure 8-20.

Remember, "Voltage applied is voltage used." Whatever voltage is applied to a circuit will be used up by that circuit. This is why measuring voltage is the best way to find out if a circuit is working properly.

A voltmeter allows very little current to go through it. It has very high resistance, so it has almost no effect on the circuit being measured. When you connect the leads from the voltmeter to two different points in the circuit, it measures the difference in potential (volts) between those points. It tells you how much energy is being used between the points where the two leads are touching the circuit.

To measure voltage, touch the one of the voltmeter's leads to each of the two wires on either side of the load. This will measure the voltage drop of that load. Voltage drop is the amount of electrical energy that is being converted by that load. If you touched the meter leads to L1 and L2, you would measure the voltage step-up from the energy source.

There will be no voltage drop across a closed switch. The pressure drop across an open switch will be the applied pressure of the power source.

A voltmeter measures the difference in electrical pressure or the potential difference in emf between two points in contact with the test leads. Voltmeters are used in parallel to whatever is being tested.

The two things to remember when testing for voltage on a live circuit are: There has to be resistance between the two points being measured and there must be a complete circuit to make a zero reading mean something.

Measuring current

An ammeter measures the rate at which the electric current flows from the power source, through the wire and load, and back to the source.

There are two kinds of ammeters; in-line and clamp-on. In-line ammeters are not commonly used by service technicians in our industry. They are primarily used during bench testing.

The clamp-on ammeter is easy to use. It uses electromagnetic induction. Whenever electricity flows through a wire, it creates a magnetic field around that wire. The clamp-on ammeter converts the strength of the magnetic field into a current reading.

To use a clamp-on ammeter, first pick the correct scale (when in doubt start high) then open the jaws of the meter, insert one line between the jaws, close the jaws and take a reading. This meter can be used safely on a live circuit without disconnecting the power since the magnetic field is not affected by the wire's insulation. See Figures 8-21 and 8-22.

Clamp over one line at a time because the magnetic fields from each wire cancel each other out. If you placed both the hot

Figure 8-21: Clamp-on ammeter

and neutral lines between the jaws you would get a zero reading even if there was current flowing in the wires. You can test either the hot or neutral line, but not both at the same time. Since AC and DC currents create different magnetic fields, be sure to set your meter for the current you are measuring.

If the current you are measuring is too low for your meter to read accurately, you can loop the wire around the jaws several times to increase sensitivity. Just divide the reading by the number of loops. Ten loops is an easy number to use.

Figure 8-22

**Clamp-on Ammeters
(Each Load is 100 ohms)**

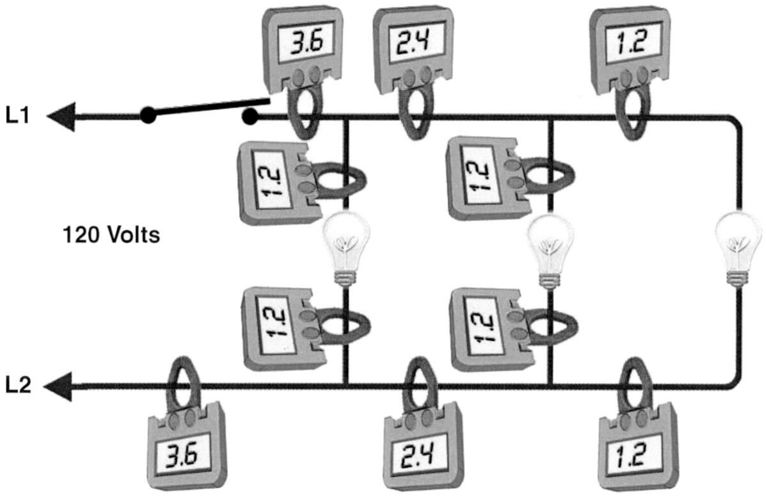

L1

120 Volts

L2

3.6   2.4   1.2

1.2   1.2

1.2   1.2

3.6   2.4   1.2

To understand what your ammeter is measuring, you should know:

- The type of circuit

- The design ampacity (current carrying capacity) of the components

- The design current draw of the loads.

The design ampacity is usually marked on each component and must be higher than the amp rating of the fuse protecting that component. For example, a 15-amp fuse should protect components exposed to 120 VAC.

The design current draw of a load is usually listed on the rating plate. The listed design current draw, in amps, is for steady-state normal operation. On start-up and under increased motor load, there is a higher required torque and a slower operating speed, the motor current will be higher.

The surge current draw on initial start-up of a motor may be four or five times its normal current draw. Sometimes the surge current draw is also listed on the rating plate.

If a burner motor bearings are dry, or the oil pump has rust in its gear set, the motor will not be able to function normally and the current draw might be less than the listed rating.

Measuring resistance

The ohmmeter is used to measure resistance. It measures the resistance between two points. It can measure just one load or a whole circuit.

The ohmmeter has its own electric source (a battery). Since it provides its own power, disconnect the circuit or device to be tested from the power source. It measures the resistance between two points by applying a steady voltage from the meter's battery to a de-energized circuit or device. Figure 8-23.

You can use the ohmmeter to see if theres is a complete circuit. This measurement is called *continuity*. If you touch one ohmmeter lead to a wire disconnected from the power source going into a circuit and, at the same time, touch one of the leads to the wire coming out of the circuit and there is no current returning to the meter, it means the pathway between the two wires is broken.

The ohmmeter will read infinite resistance and there is no continuity. If, on the other hand, 1 amp of current returns for every volt applied to the circuit, there is no resistance. The ohmmeter will read zero. This is a short circuit. Any reading between zero and infinite is the resistance to flow for the circuit measured.

Unlike the voltmeter and ammeter, the ohmmeter must never be connected to a live circuit. It supplies its own power from its battery, and it will be damaged if outside current goes through it.

To use the ohmmeter, disconnect the power supply and isolate the line or device

Figure 8-23:
Ohmmeter
readings

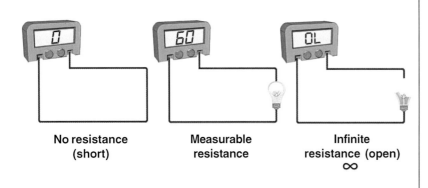

| No resistance (short) | Measurable resistance | Infinite resistance (open) ∞ |

being tested from other paths back to the source. Do this in case there is a capacitor (a device that stores electricity) in the circuit.

The ohmmeter must be zero adjusted before every test. Just touch the two test leads together creating a short circuit with zero resistance and use the zero adjustment dial. Most digital meters automatically zero adjust. If your meter will not read zero, the battery is too weak and must be replaced.

To test for resistance, disconnect L1 and L2 (H and N wires) from the power source and touch the two leads on either side of the component to be tested. If there is no resistance the reading will be zero. If there is no connection between the two points the resistance will be infinity. The digital meter will read OL (overload). A reading between zero and the maximum scale setting is the resistance between the connected points.

Not only must you isolate the circuit to be tested from the source, it must also be isolated from the rest of the circuit. Otherwise, you will get a false reading from the resistance of another load in a branch parallel circuit. Figure 8-24.

Electrical safety

Electricity can be dangerous. It can create three hazards: fire, skin burns, and shock. Shock can cause muscle spasms, unconsciousness and even death.

Proper installation of all electrical equipment is essential. The National Electric Code® sets the standards. Local communities can make this code law, and in addition, they can make their own codes even more restrictive.

A common, but dangerous practice, is testing the oilburner ignition transformer with a screwdriver. The transformer is

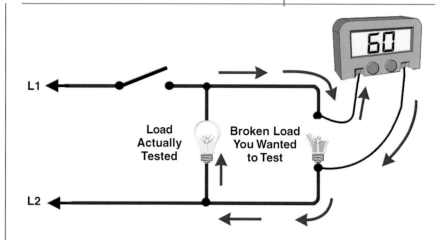

putting out 10,000 volts and that can give you a dangerous and serious shock. Always use proper test equipment.

Be sure to verify that all capacitors are fully discharged before touching or working on them. To safely discharge a capacitor you will need a 20,000 ohm 5 watt resistor, two insulated screwdrivers and two jumper wires with alligator clips on both ends. Figure 8-25. Connect one jumper wire clip to one wire of the resistor and clip the other jumper wire to the other resistor wire. Connect the clips on the

Figure 8-24: Common ohmmeter reading error, isolate the load to be tested

Figure 8-25: Safely discharging a capacitor

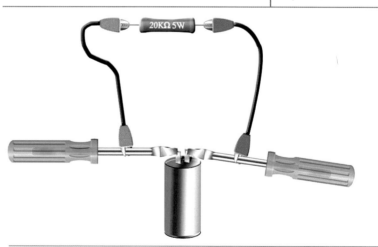

The lower the wire number, the bigger the wire and the more amps it can carry.

opposite ends of both jumper wires to different screwdrivers, hold the handles of the screwdrivers and touch the blades to opposite terminals of the capacitor.

Electric energy needs a pathway from the source and back to the source. If you do your job, this pathway is our electric circuit.

Any wet object has enough minerals in the water to provide an alternate pathway. The human body is over 50% water, and when the skin is damp it will provide a good pathway back to the source if there is not an easier one. Never allow your body to be that pathway! Always consider all electrical components to be energized until you test and prove they are not.

When you are working on electricity, remove all metal objects such as watches and jewelry from your hands and wrists. Until you are absolutely sure a circuit is shut off, only use one hand—keep the other in your pocket. This prevents the electric pathway from going from one hand to the other hand through your heart. Be sure to replace any damaged or frayed wires, protect wires from touching moving equipment, and keep them clear of walkways.

Fire

Every wire has resistance and converts some electrical energy into heat. When current flows, the wire warms up and keeps getting hotter until it reaches steady state where the heat it loses to its surroundings equals the heat being created. If there is too much current being drawn by the loads in a circuit, the steady state temperature of the

Multimeter Tips

Voltmeter:
   Touch one lead from the meter to one side of the load or circuit to be tested and one to the other so the meter is parallel to what you are testing. This test is done on a live circuit. The reading is the difference in voltage from the spot where one lead is touching to the spot where the other is touching.

Ammeter:
   Now, energize the circuit and the meter will tell you the amps traveling to that load or circuit. The clamp on ammeter is much easier and less intrusive to use. Close the clamp around the single wire you wish to test while the circuit is energized and it will tell you the amps flowing through that wire. The meter will read the amps through the wire cover, so this test need not be done on bare wire.

Ohmmeter:
   Disconnect the hot and neutral wires from the power source and discharge any capacitors that may be in the circuit to be tested. The ohmmeter supplies its own power. Touch the leads from the meter to the wires you have disconnected from the power source and the meter will show the resistance of that circuit or load.

wire may be dangerously hot, creating a fire. This is called an overloaded circuit.

Common causes of overloads are:

- Too many devices on the circuit

- Devices working harder than they are supposed to

- Damaged or worn out devices

- Current surge when a motor starts

A short circuit causes a sudden excessive draw well beyond the capacity of the circuit. It happens if the resistance of the loads is removed, or there is a direct unrestricted current flow to ground, conductors touching grounded metal, or the source conductor is touching neutral.

Fuses and circuit breakers

To protect against any circuit carrying too much current, every circuit needs a fuse or circuit breaker. It is wired in series so all the current in the circuit goes through it. These are automatic switches that open if the current goes higher than their rating.

Fuses are one time only devices. When they blow, they must be replaced. Circuit breakers can be reset and used repeatedly. Never used an oversized fuse or circuit breaker; this defeats the purpose of the fuse or breaker and may create a dangerous situation. You should find out *why* the circuit is drawing too many amps, causing the fuse or breaker to open.

Shock protection

The electric shock from a 120-volt circuit is dangerous and can be fatal. A shock occurs when a person becomes part of an electric circuit. The severity of shock depends upon:

- Amount of current

- Type of voltage (AC or DC)

- The path the electricity takes through the body

- Amount of voltage

- Time duration of the shock

- Condition of the skin

To protect from shock, electricity must be kept in the wire. Install the circuits so that in case the electricity escapes, it does no harm.

A shock is when an electric current passes through the body, causing spastic contraction of muscles. If it goes through the heart, it may kill.

Shocks happen when you touch a wire carrying lots of volts and some other part of your body is touching something at ground potential. Bare feet, especially when wet, are very dangerous. A dry human body is pretty resistant to electric flow, but a sweaty or otherwise wet one is a very good conductor. Rubber soled shoes insulate your body from ground and prevent the formation of a complete circuit.

Good insulation keeps the electricity inside the wire, but insulation may crack with age or high temperature and may also wear off if it is touching a moving part. So even if it was wired right at first, with age it may go bad and let electricity leak out, presenting a shock hazard.

To be sure that the electricity has an easy way to get home without going through you, install a ground fault protection system (GFI- Ground Fault Interrupter). Grounding provides a direct low resistance path from the circuit to ground.

For example, suppose the insulation on the wire inside a burner motor cracks and the wire is touching the motor case. If you kneel down on a damp floor to work on the burner and you touch the motor with your hand, the current could flow through your body into the floor, and over to the ground rod from the house service—a complete circuit. This is a dangerous situation. To stop this from happening, run a ground (bare copper or green) wire from the burner back to the ground rod.

This pathway will offer much less resistance to the electricity than your body and the cellar floor and the current will go that way. Electricity is lazy; it will always go the easiest way, the path of least resistance. Figure 8-26.

All electric codes including the NEC—National Electrical Code®—call for careful grounding. Connections from one wire to another must be enclosed in insulation. Every switch, outlet, and appliance must be protected. All these devices should be connected to each other by grounding wires connected to a rod driven 10 feet into the earth. The ground wire is the third prong on plug-in devices.

To protect us, the ground wire must go from the load back to the panel without any breaks. The best way to check this is to touch one lead from your voltmeter to the either the hot or neutral wire and one to the ground wire. If the ground is good you will get the same reading as you would from hot to neutral.

Stay on the lookout for potential problems
When troubleshooting a circuit, electric junction boxes often must be opened. This can be dangerous. Sometimes wires from more than one circuit might be hiding in a

box. If you can, try to trace all the wires going into the box to see if more than one goes back to the service panel. The goal is to shut off all the electric wires going to that box before removing the cover.

If this is not possible then treat the wires in the box as if they were hot. While holding the cover plate, use an insulated screwdriver to carefully loosen the screws and ease off the plate. To test for power, use only one hand to gently pull out the wires so all connections are at least an inch apart. Unscrew the wire nuts and use your meter to test for voltage.

Watch out for overcrowded junction boxes
Too many wires jammed into too small a box can cause shorts.

• Check for old and cracked insulation.

• Confirm polarization. White wires go to silver terminals. Black goes to brass. Be sure there is only one wire hooked to each terminal.

• Check armored cable connectors. The cut end of the metal cable can be sharp. To prevent the wire insulation from being cut be sure protective plastic bushings are installed at the cable ends.

Safety tips
The Occupational Safety and Health Administration's (OSHA) electric safety regulations require that anyone doing electrical repairs must receive safety training. They also require that employers must adopt safe electrical work practices and that a lock out tag out must be used for hard-wired equipment that is de-energized.

The key to safety is to know the dangers of electricity and how to avoid hazards.

Figure 8-26

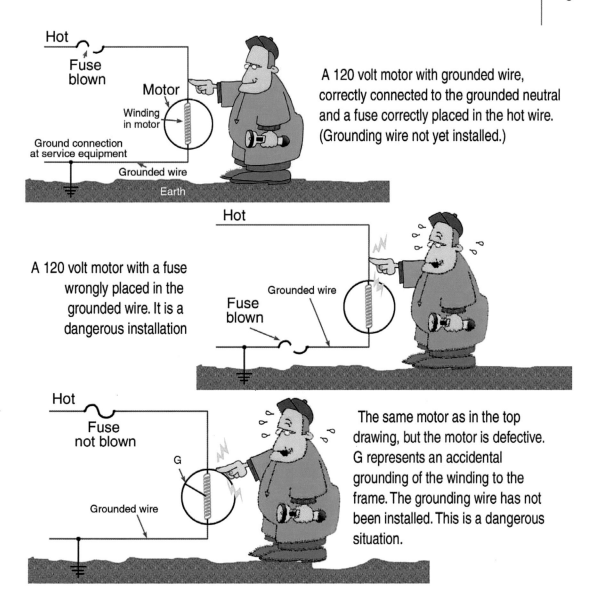

A 120 volt motor with grounded wire, correctly connected to the grounded neutral and a fuse correctly placed in the hot wire. (Grounding wire not yet installed.)

A 120 volt motor with a fuse wrongly placed in the grounded wire. It is a dangerous installation

The same motor as in the top drawing, but the motor is defective. G represents an accidental grounding of the winding to the frame. The grounding wire has not been installed. This is a dangerous situation.

The same defective motor as in the figure above, but now a grounding wire has been installed from the frame of the motor to ground. Even though the winding is accidentally grounded to the frame, as prepresented by G, there is no shock hazard.

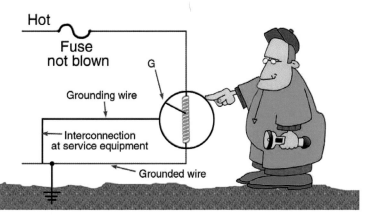

The following are some safety tips:

• Shut off the power!

• Stay focused! Even after turning off the power, work as if the wires are live.

• Post a sign on the electric panel and remote switch so no one will turn on the power while you are working on the circuit.

• Always check to be sure that the equipment being used is grounded.

• Always use insulated tools and be sure the insulation is in good condition. Use electrical tape on wire nuts and connections for added protection.

• Water on the floor is a good conductor—when working in wet areas, be sure to use protective equipment like rubber-soled shoes.

• Do not overload electrical circuits.

• Use extra caution with extension cords. Their insulation can be cut, and they can be overloaded leading to increased danger.

• Inspect heating equipment before starting repair to be sure it is de-energized.

• When inspecting a circuit, keep one hand in your pocket to prevent hand-to-hand shock.

Lock out tag out

This procedure is used to be sure that no one turns on a switch and energizes electrical equipment while you are working on it. Use a tag or lock connected to the switch or circuit breaker to let other people know you turned it off on purpose and you want it to stay off. The only person who

should remove locks and tags is the person who put them there.

To do a lock out tag to OSHA's satisfaction, a lockout device and tag stating not to remove the lock should be placed over the circuit breaker, fuse box, or switch that will prevent a person from energizing the circuit.

It is difficult to put a lock on a stair switch. As an alternative to locking out a piece of equipment, tag outs can be used if it will provide an equivalent level of safety.

OSHA indicates that shutting off the equipment in two places will provide such equivalence. For example, if you shut off the circuit breaker and emergency switch at the top of the stairs and stick a note on both of them you have met the requirement.

Obviously this procedure is very important if the circuit breaker and remote switch are in different rooms than the equipment you are working on. You do not want some helpful person thinking they found the problem with the heater and turning on the breaker in the other room while you are hooking the black wire from the primary control to the L1 wire.

Practical tips

Splicing wires

To splice wires first strip the wires with a wire-stripping tool. (Don't use a knife; it might nick the wire, reducing its electric carrying capacity.) Slip the wire into the correct hole in the stripper, squeeze, twist, and pull off the insulation.

Next hold the stripped wires together and grab the ends with lineman's pliers. Twist clockwise, making sure all wires turn. Twist them together like a candy cane into a neat looking spiral. Now snip off the end leaving enough exposed metal so the wire nut will just cover it. (About a half inch is good.) Now slip on an appropriately rated wire nut as far as it will go and turn it clockwise until tight, Figure 8-27. Finally wrap electrical tape around the bottom of the nut and wires.

Figure 8-27: Wire nut

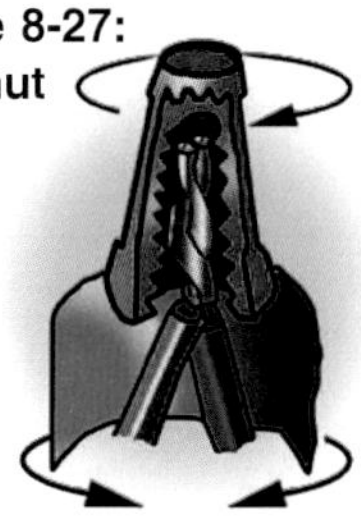

Hooking wires to a terminal

Before you start, many devices come with the terminal screws unscrewed. Screw in any terminal screws for terminals you are not going to use. Now you are ready to hook up your wires.

Strip about three quarters of an inch of insulation from the wire end. Then using long nose pliers grab the wire just above the insulation and bend it back at about a 45-degree angle. Move the pliers up about a quarter inch from the insulation and bend again in the opposite direction about 90 degrees to start a loop. Now move the pliers another quarter inch and bend the wire into a question mark"?". Leave an opening in the end just big enough for the terminal screw. (You can buy a wire-bending screwdriver to make this job easier.) Figure 8-28.

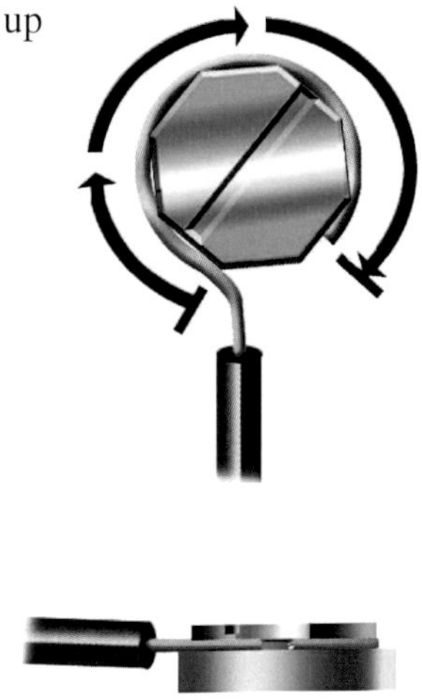

Figure 8-28: Strap and wrap wire

Make sure the terminal screw is unscrewed far enough, and then slip the loop over the screw threads, with the loop running clockwise. Use the long nose pliers to squeeze the loop around the terminal, and then tighten the screw.

You should never attach two or more wires to one terminal screw. To make a multiple connection, make a "pigtail" wire by cutting a six-inch length of wire, strip both ends, splice the multiple wires to one end, and then attach the other end to the terminal screw.

Armored cable

To cut armored cable, bend it about one foot from the end and squeeze the bend until the armor breaks apart slightly. If you have trouble, use a pair of channellocks to squeeze the wire. Figure 8-29.

Grasp the cable firmly on each side of the break and twist the waste end clockwise until the armor comes apart enough for you to slip in cutters. If you have trouble doing this with your hands, use two pairs of pliers.

Cut through one rib of the armor with a pair of side-cutting pliers. Slide the waste armor off the wires. Remove the paper wrapping and plastic strips. Leave the thin metal bonding strip alone. Use side-cut pliers to trim away pointed ends of the sheathing that could nick a wire.

The next step is to slip the plastic bushing over the wires. Slide it down into the armor so it protects the wires from the sharp edges of the armor. If there is a bonding strip, cut it to about two inches and wrap it over the bushing and around the armor to ensure conductive contact between the armor and the box.

Option: If you plan to do a great deal of wiring, you might want to buy an armored wire cutter to speed up this job.

Now attach the clamp (connector) to the cable. Remove the lock nut from the armor cable clamp and slide the clamp down over the bushing as far as it will go. Then tighten the screw.

Finally remove the knockout from the junction box, and poke the wire and connector into the hole. Slide the locknut over the wires, and thread it onto the cable clamp. Use a hammer and screwdriver to tap the locknut tight.

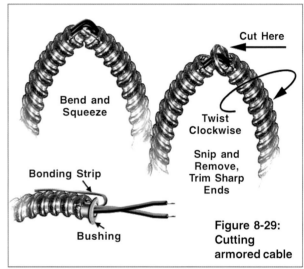

Figure 8-29: Cutting armored cable

Basic Concepts about Electric Circuits

- Electricity must have a complete path from an electrical source through a load and back to the source.

- Conductors offer less resistance to electric current than insulators.

- Voltage is the electrical pressure difference between two points in a circuit that causes electricity to flow.

- Current is the rate of flow as measured in amps.

- Resistance is the opposition to flow measured in ohms or pressure drop.

- A load offers resistance to an electrical current. It determines the current draw for any voltage applied.

- The load will only draw enough current to overcome that resistance.

- Voltage applied is voltage consumed.

- It takes one volt to push one amp through one ohm.

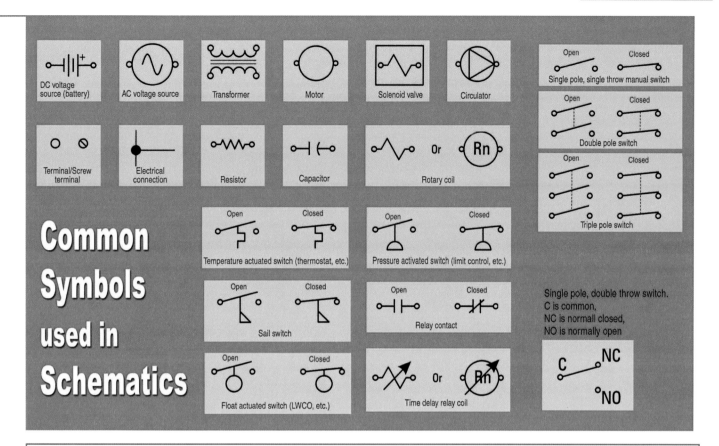

Common Symbols used in Schematics

In the image:

DC voltage source (battery)

AC voltage source

Transformer

Motor

Solenoid valve

Circulator

Open / Closed — Single pole, single throw manual switch

Terminal/Screw terminal

Electrical connection

Resistor

Capacitor

Or Rn — Rotary coil

Open / Closed — Double pole switch

Open / Closed — Temperature actuated switch (thermostat, etc.)

Open / Closed — Pressure activated switch (limit control, etc.)

Open / Closed — Triple pole switch

Open / Closed — Sail switch

Open / Closed — Relay contact

Single pole, double throw switch. C is common, NC is normall closed, NO is normally open

Open / Closed — Float actuated switch (LWCO, etc.)

Or Rn — Time delay relay coil

C NC NO

In case you are interested

In this chapter we have talked about what electricity does. We have not really covered what it is. That is because electricity can be confusing. However, some of you might be wondering what electricity actually is. So for those brave souls who want to know more, read on. If you are already hopelessly confused, you can stop reading now.

Everything contains electrically charged particles, both positive and negative. These particles make up the atoms that are the building blocks for everything in the universe. Atoms are really, really small. It would take several million of them, lined up, to reach across the dot at the end of this sentence. Each atom is electrically neutral because it contains equal amounts of positive and negative charge.

The positive charge of an atom is in the center, called the nucleus. The nucleus is made of protons that have a positive charge and neutrons that have no charge. The number of protons determines what kind of material the atom is. For example, hydrogen has one proton, and oxygen has eight.

Circling around the outside of the nucleus are electrons. They are sort of like planets circling around the sun. As in the solar system, there is a lot of empty space. The nucleus is like a marble sitting in the middle of a football field. Some of the electrons are at the back of the end zone. The electrons have almost no mass, but they carry a negative charge equal to the positive charge of the proton. So a neutral atom has as many electrons in the space surrounding the nucleus as it has protons inside it. The electrons are held close to the nucleus by the electric force of attraction between opposite charges.

In different kinds of atoms, the electrons farthest from the nucleus may be bound strongly or weakly. The ones that allow their electrons to escape easily are called conductors. The atoms that hang on tight to their electrons are insulators.

The flow of free electrons in a conductor is what we call electric current. If you throw a switch to turn on a lamp five feet away, it takes 40 minutes for the little electrons to fight their way through the conductor from the switch to the lamp. What turns on the lamp right away is a pulse, each electron pushing those ahead of it until the pulse reaches the lamp. The pulse travels almost at the speed of light.

If you are feeding the lamp with AC, it is not a pulse that travels but a wave. Each electron vibrates back and forth, passing its energy along to the next, just like molecules of air passing a sound wave or water in the ocean passing a wave.

Chapter **9**

IGNITION SYSTEMS

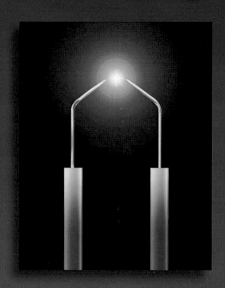

IN THIS CHAPTER

Chapter 9

Ignition Systems

Introduction

The completely automatic electric ignition system is an important part of oilburner technology. There are two different main components used for ignition systems on oilburners: the ignition transformer and the solid state ignitor.

The **ignition transformer** is a step-up transformer using copper windings around an iron core. It steps up the incoming voltage of 120 volts to an output voltage of 10,000 volts. This is accomplished by a 90 to 1 primary to secondary winding ratio around the iron core.

The **solid state ignitor** utilizes electronics to produce an output voltage of anywhere from 14,000 to 20,000 volts peak.

Both components supply this high voltage electricity to the electrodes. A spark jumps from the tip of one electrode to the tip of the other. The electrical arc then ignites the atomized oil.

Let's examine the various components of the ignition system shown in Figure 9-1.

The voltage travels from the transformer or ignitor through the ignition cables, buss bars, or spring clips to the electrodes which are held in place by the ceramic insulators (porcelains). When it reaches the tips of the electrodes it jumps the gap between them, creating our spark.

**Figure 9-1:
Ignition system
components**

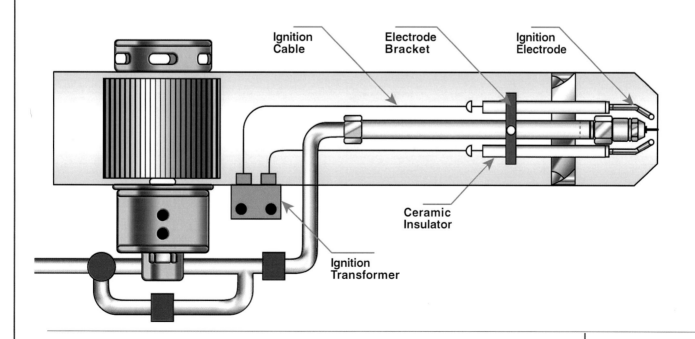

Ignition
Cable

Electrode
Bracket

Ignition
Electrode

Ceramic
Insulator

Ignition
Transformer

Oilburners use one of two types of electric ignition control systems:

Interrupted ignition: the ignition spark remains on for only a short time at the beginning of each burner operating cycle, and is turned off once flame is established.

Intermittent ignition: the spark that ignites the oil vapors remains on as long as the burner runs. Intermittent ignition used to be called "constant ignition," and some manufacturers call intermittent ignition "constant duty ignition."

Interrupted ignition is better

Over time, the industry has switched between interrupted and intermittent ignition. Interrupted ignition has proven superior because having the spark on during the entire burn cycle *detracts* from performance for several reasons:

• Electrode life is significantly reduced.

• Ignitor or ignition transformer life is significantly reduced.

• Electrical consumption is increased dramatically.

• Operational noise in increased dramatically.

• Intermittent ignition may hide combustion problems that can cause soot-plugged boilers and oil running saturation. The constant arc keeps the flame burning even if it is belching smoke, soot, and unburned oil. With interrupted ignition, a poor flame goes out and the unit would go on safety.

• NOx (nitrogen oxide) emissions are higher with intermittent ignition because the spark burns nitrogen, creating NOx.

A strong spark

The spark across the electrode gap at the tips of the electrodes must be strong enough to withstand the velocity of the air being blown through the air tube by the burner fan. The air being blown through the air tube forces the ignition spark to form an arc toward the oil spray. This arc extends into the spray causing the oil vapors to ignite, and the flame to establish. The ignition voltage must be high enough to create a spark that is hot enough to ignite the oil. In some cases, widening the spark will produce better ignition.

The transformer

The AC transformer is a device that receives electricity at one voltage and delivers it at another voltage, either higher or lower.

Essentially, the transformer consists of two separate coils of wire wound on an iron core. One winding receives the electrical energy from the power source and is called the primary; and the other delivers electrical energy and is called the secondary. If the secondary winding delivers a voltage that is higher than the primary, then it is known as a step-up transformer. On the other hand, if the secondary voltage is lower than the primary voltage, then it is known as a step-down transformer.

The factor that determines whether a transformer is of the step-up or step-down variety is the relative number of turns in the primary and in the secondary windings.

Step-up transformers are used for ignition purposes on oilburners.

Generally, it will be found that ignition transformers are made up of 90 to 100 turns of fine wire in the secondary coil to one turn of stout wire in the primary coil. In the example, you will note there are 60,000 turns in the secondary and 690 turns in the primary coil, a ratio of about 90 to 1. In Figure 9-3 on following page, we can see what the ignition transformer looks like with its outer case removed.

As voltage increases, amps decrease

This is a good time to explain a most important characteristic of transformers, see Figure 9-2. The rule: If the voltage (E) flowing out of a transformer is increased, the current, or amperage (I), is always decreased proportionately. For instance, if the voltage is doubled, the current will be cut in half. In the case of the transformer in our example, the primary voltage of 115 volts is increased 90 times to 10,000 volts in the secondary coil, where the current flow (I_2) is 23 milliamperes, which is 23/1000ths of one ampere. Although not shown in the example, the current flowing in the primary coil can be determined by multiplying .023 x 90, or about 2 amperes, which is average for ignition transformers. This can be proven in the field by checking amperage in the primary circuit with an amperage meter.

Moisture proofing

It is important that both the primary and secondary coils of the ignition transformer

Figure 9-2:
Transformer wiring

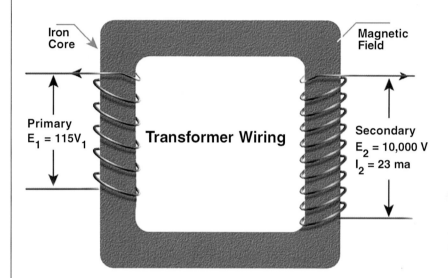

$$\frac{E_2}{E_1} = \frac{N_2}{N_1}$$

$$\frac{10,000}{115} = \frac{60,000}{N_1}$$

$$10,000\, N_1 = (115)\,(60,000)$$

$$N_1 = \frac{(115)\,(60,000)}{10,000}$$

$$10,000\, N_1 = 690 \text{ TURNS}$$

Warning! All high voltage circuits, especially AC circuits, are potentially hazardous. Depending on the size of the person, contact area and time, and voltage characteristics (magnitude, frequency, and path), electric shock can occur and cause bodily damage, burns, or death. Use extreme caution at the input or output end of an ignition transformer!

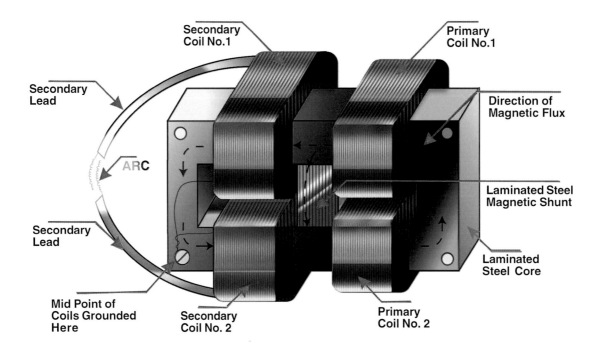

Secondary Coil No.1
Primary Coil No.1
Secondary Lead
Direction of Magnetic Flux
ARC
Laminated Steel Magnetic Shunt
Secondary Lead
Laminated Steel Core
Mid Point of Coils Grounded Here
Secondary Coil No. 2
Primary Coil No. 2

Figure 9-3: Construction of an ignition transformer

are covered with a tar-like compound, whereas solid state ignitors feature epoxies which serve the purpose of moisture proofing the device. Epoxy, by its very nature, is somewhat more resistant to moisture and acts as an excellent corrosion inhibitor and heat conductor.

If you must replace a transformer

When ordering replacement transformers, several facts must be known:

1. The size of the mounting base and location of mounting holes

2. The position of high tension terminals

3. The style of transformer high tension clips

4. Secondary coil voltage

5. Primary coil voltage

6. Transformer body size

Wiring ignition transformers

Wire the ignition transformer into the burner circuit as follows:

For intermittent ignition, attach a wire from the transformer or ignitor to the neutral wire, and the other wire to the orange motor wire from the primary control. See Figure 9-4 for wiring a

Chapter 9
Ignition Systems

Figure 9-4:
Wiring a primary
intermittent
igntion

primary intermittent ignition
(the spark is on whenever the
motor is on).

**For interrupted
ignition**, you need a primary
control built for this purpose.

Attach one wire from the
transformer or ignitor to the
neutral wire and the other wire
to the ignition wire or terminal
on the primary control.

See Figure 9-5 for wiring a
primary control interrupted
ignition (the spark shuts off once
flame is established).

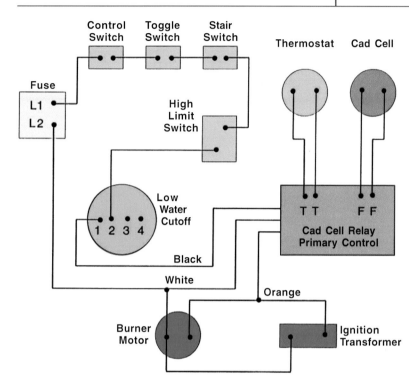

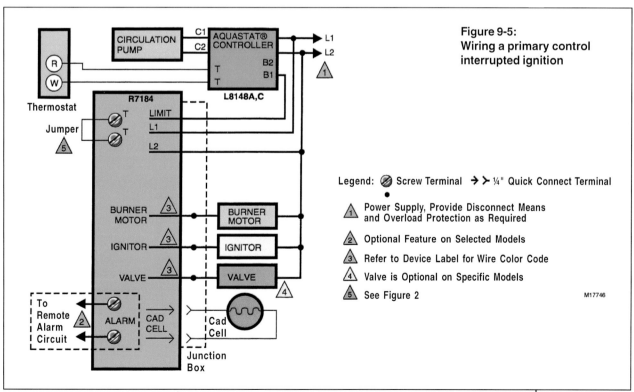

Figure 9-5:
Wiring a primary control
interrupted ignition

Drawbacks to iron core ignition transformers

An ignition transformer does just what it claims to do—it transforms voltage. There is a single copper winding on the primary side for every 90 to 100 windings on the secondary side and that is how it transforms voltage. This becomes a problem when input voltage drops. For every one volt you remove from the primary side, you remove ninety volts from the secondary side. The ignition of the atomized oil is not a result of the spark, but rather the result of the heat generated from the spark.

Remember, the ability of an ignitor to ignite oil depends on more than just high voltage; it depends on arc output as well! Spark heat energy = voltage times current. You must provide between 600-700° Fahrenheit to ignite atomized No.2 fuel oil.

> Note: 9,000 volts by itself is not what is required to ignite oil; 9,000 volts is considered sufficient to create an arc across the air gaps between the electrode tips normally used in oil-burners. The secondary current flowing through the arc heats the air and lights the oil. The important factor in creating an arc is voltage; the important factor in igniting the oil is current. This is why Underwriters Laboratory (UL) requires 10,000 V ignition transformers to have a short circuit current of at least 19.5 MA (11.6 MA across a 1/8" air gap). Most 10,000 V ignition transformers our industry uses are rated for 23 MA.

This translates to approximately 9,000 volts and about 19 MA short circuit current. A 10,000 volt 23 MA transformer only has a small margin of error built into it, and can be a problem.

A few facts

• Ignition transformers are insulated with tar. Tar can melt with heat and the tar oozes from the transformer and typically deposits on the combustion head assembly, making for a nasty clean-up.

• An ignition transformer's tar-covered windings are susceptible to moisture infiltration. Moisture infiltration will cause an immediate shorting of the component.

• Electrical consumption with an ignition transformer is typically 80 to 100 watts of electricity. This is the approximate equivalent to a 100 watt light bulb turned on over the burner when the transformer is running.

• Finally, ignition transformers deteriorate over time. During this deterioration, they cause delayed ignition problems that worsen until, finally, the transformer can no longer light the atomized oil.

Transformer testing

Over the years, there have been many and various methods of testing transformers. Regardless of the method used, one thing must be kept in mind and that is to be sure the transformer has the correct input voltage to the primary coil. This is very important because the output of the transformer is relative to the input voltage. In other words, if the input is down by 10%, the output will also be 10% lower.

Figure 9-6: One of several transformer testers available

Several types of transformer testers are available, Figure 9-6. These testers are dependable and usually come in their own carrying case with all the instructions. The one shown will also act as a backup transformer and can be left on the job as a temporary solution and this can be especially helpful with older obsolete burners. When using any one of these testers, read the instructions for that particular tester because competitive units will operate differently.

Resistance testing

Another test for iron-core transformers is to check the quality of the windings using an ohmmeter. The following procedure is used:

1. Turn the power to the unit off. Disconnect the primary leads from the circuit.

2. Test the resistance across the primary winding. Attach the test leads from your ohmmeter to the primary leads of the transformer. You should get a reading of 3 ohms, plus or minus 10% (2.7 through 3.3 ohms). If your reading is higher or lower, you should replace the transformer.

3. Test the secondary side of the transformer. Touch one of your ohmmeter leads to a secondary terminal and the other to a mounting screw or ground. You should get a reading of 12,000 ohms plus or minus 10% (10,800 through 13,200).

Then perform the same test from the other secondary terminal to a mounting screw or ground; you should read approximately the same. If you get a higher or lower reading that varies widely, you should replace the transformer.

The following table is used with this procedure for specific brands:

Trade Brand	Primary Leads	Secondary Posts (each post to ground)
Allanson	2.4 ohms	9,200 ohms
Dongan	3 ohms	12,000 ohms
France	3 ohms	12,000 ohms

Solid state oilburner ignition systems, electronic ignitors

Manufacturers are now mostly using solid-state electronic ignitors. These units are known for their small size, light weight, and starting power. They may be for dedicated use on a particular type of burner and are also available in generic versions for retrofit applications, depending on the mounting plate used. Output voltages of between 14,000 volts and 20,000 volts peak with amperages between 16 MA to 45 MA respectively, on the secondary coil, are considered normal, Figure 9-7.

Figure 9-7: Ignitors

A solid state ignitor is a radical departure from the traditional ignition transformers commonly used on oilburners. Solid state ignitors eliminate transformer design shortcomings. Ignitors utilize a solid state printed circuit board with what is called a 'tank mechanism.' This technology allows the ignitor to have a more constant output if the input voltage decreases. Therefore, we have fewer problems with voltage drops.

Ignitors are insulated with epoxy, not tar. Epoxy is virtually resistant to heat and will not melt on the combustion head assembly. This same epoxy makes the ignitor virtually impervious to moisture. Electrical consumption from an ignitor is 30 to 50 watts, much less than the transformer. Ignitors are made from solid state electronic components and are truly ignition control systems.

Testing electronic ignitor systems

Since these units contain solid-state devices such as transistors, their troubleshooting and servicing should be done to manufacturers' recommendations. Do not use a transformer tester to test electronic ignitors. Doing so will give you an inaccu-

rate measurement and may harm the ignitor and tester. Testing electronic ignitor systems is different from testing ignition transformers because ignitors utilize a high frequency output. The cycling operations of a solid state ignition system are 20,000 times per second. Standard AC transformers cycle at 60 times per second. This is the reason you cannot test a solid state ignitor with a standard ignition transformer tester.

The testing of electronic ignitors is more complicated than testing the iron-core transformer. Before you perform any of these tests, make sure the manufacturer approves of the test, and be extra careful not to directly short the terminals without a spark between them. In many cases, it will short out the ignitor and destroy its internal circuitry. Keep in mind that ignitors are not merely a pair of coils, but rather a complex electronic device made up of several electronic circuits and components.

The first basic test for ignitors is to place an ohmmeter across the ignitor output terminals with the power off and measure the resistance from each ignitor post to ground, Figure 9-8. Normally, the ignitor is considered good if the resistance from each post to ground has no more than a 10% difference between posts. Each manufacturer is different and they should

Figure 9-8: Ohmmeter test

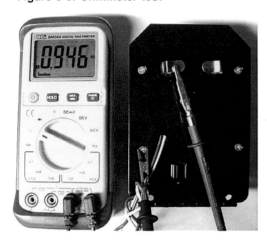

be consulted for the proper output range and differential. It's also important that you verify continuity between the ignitor case ground and true ground.

Another test that is approved by most manufacturers is to bring the ignitor output terminals to within ½ to ¾ of an inch apart and turn on the power, Figure 9-9. A strong blue spark should be generated. Another trick is to let it spark for a few minutes, five to ten in most cases, and see if the spark changes from blue to orange; if it does change, replace it.

Finally, you can check both electronic ignitors and iron-core transformers with a common test. Bring the ignitor or trans-

former output terminals to within ½ to ¾ of an inch apart. Place a milliammeter in series with the hot line going to the ignitor and turn it on, Figure 9-10. Again, the reading should stay steady and not vary for at least five minutes with a strong blue spark throughout the test while staying within 10% of the rated amperage draw for the device.

Cables, buss bars, spring clips

In order to transport the high voltage from the secondary terminals of the ignition transformer, an effective and efficient path must be provided to the ignition electrodes. This path may be an ignition cable, buss bars, or spring type conductors.

Ignition cables are normally constructed of heavy stranded copper wire covered with special heavy insulation to insulate against dampness, and ensure transmission around, over, or under any other conducting surface between the transformer location and the electrodes. The outstanding feature of ignition cables is flexibility, permitting easy handling, bending and installation in any burner. Some nozzle assemblies are equipped with clips to hold the flexible cable off the bottom of the burner air

Figure 9-9: Spark test

Figure 9-10: Milliammeter

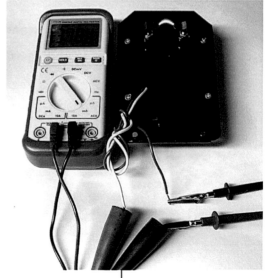

tube, especially when the air tube is long; if they are provided, use them.

Buss bars are non-insulated heavy gauge strips of metal that are made by the oilburner manufacturer to the length and shape to fit a certain model of burner; they are not interchangeable with other models.

Spring clips are similar to buss bars, except that contact with the transformer is maintained by spring tension. After some time, these clips can lose their tension and prevent proper and desired contact. They should be checked whenever the burner is serviced.

Electrodes

Electrodes are metal rods made of specialized steels, and partially covered with a ceramic (porcelain) insulator, Figure 9-11. These insulators are usually made in two major external diameters (7/16" and 9/16"). As we can see in Figure 9-13, these porcelains come in various lengths. They may be ordered in individual lengths 4" to 30", or they may be sized on the job through the use of a special tool for cutting the porcelain insulator.

The porcelains serve two purposes: They securely position the electrode rods and they serve as insulators, protecting the metal rod against shorting out to the nozzle assembly. These insulators are center bored to fit the metal electrode rods, either 1/8" or 3/32" in diameter.

Electrode holders permit secure and correct mounting

of the porcelains and electrodes so that, after adjustment, they cannot shift from vibration or other causes and alter their position. In many cases, the electrode holder is incorporated with the air spinner or turbulator.

Electrode testing and setting

Figure 9-12 shows one method for testing the porcelain insulator of an electrode for spark leakage. A neon test lamp, with one probe touching the ceramic insulator, the other end of the test lamp free, is shown. By moving the one end of the test lamp over the surface of the porcelain, it can be easily determined whether or not the ceramic insulator is

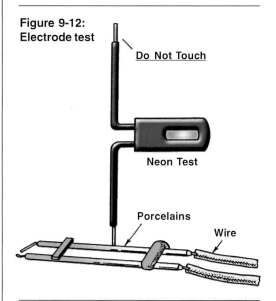

Figure 9-12:
Electrode test

Do Not Touch

Neon Test

Porcelains

Wire

cracked. If the insulator is defective, the neon test lamp will glow when the probe reaches the defect.

Figure 9-13 is a setting for electrodes when one is not available from the manu-

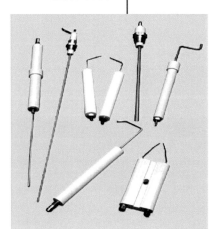

Figure 9-11:
Electrodes

facturer. The recommendations
of the burner manufacturer
should be followed whenever
they are available. Electrode tips
should never be permitted to
touch or extend into the oil
spray, because a carbon bridge
will build up between them,
ultimately causing ignition
failure.

Ceramic insulators should
always be treated gently. They
should never be dropped or
packed loosely in service kits.
In field servicing, they should always be
wiped clean with a cloth, or cleaned with a
solvent. If they show signs of aging or
cracking, they should be replaced immediately.

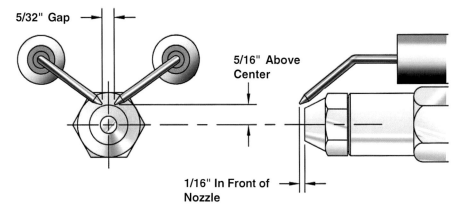

Ignition service problems

Correcting faulty ignition is important.
Delayed or faulty ignition is the prime
cause of puffback. Puffback is the most
disagreeable of all burner problems. It
occurs when ignition is delayed. Due to
some fault in the ignition system, the oil
vapor does not ignite until after the burner
has run for some time. Then the accumulated vapors all ignite at once, creating
more combustion products than the venting
system can handle. Delayed ignition can
cause soot to blow out of the draft regulator, and in severe cases—called puff
backs—it can knock down the flue pipe.

Ignition problems are usually the easiest
to recognize and solve. In most cases, we
find it necessary to merely clean the
electrodes and cables, and be certain that all
connections are tight and that the spark gap
is in proper adjustment. We must make
certain that the electrode porcelains and the

transformer terminal porcelain insulators
are not crazed (small cracks on surface),
cracked, or oil soaked.

It is important that all exposed metallic
components of the ignition system be a safe
distance away from any other metallic part
of the burner, since it is grounded. The
shortest metal-to-metal distance throughout
the entire ignition system should be that
distance between the two electrode tips.
Common sense tells us that any other
arrangement would cause the spark to short
out before the spark bridges the electrode
tips. The best way to avoid this problem is
to strictly adhere to the recommended
electrode tip settings as shown in the
manufacturer's recommendations.

Troubleshooting ignition problems

1. **Connections at transformer
junction box loose.** Always check line
voltage connections from the neutral wire
of the primary control and the orange wire
of the primary control (for intermittent
ignition) and the ignition wire of the
primary (interrupted ignition) to determine
if there are loose connections at this

**Figure 9-13:
Typical generic
setting**

Label text in figure: 5/32" Gap, 5/16" Above Center, 1/16" In Front of Nozzle

Correcting faulty ignition is important. Delayed or faulty ignition is the prime cause of puffback.

junction box. If they are loose, tighten them securely. Also check for loose connections at all terminals and make sure that wire nuts are tight.

2. **Test the transformer.** If the transformer is defective, replace it.

3. **Loose connections at either the secondary terminals of the transformer, or loose connections where the high tension leads or buss bars are fastened to the electrodes.** If these connections are found to be loose, attempt to tighten them. If this fails to solve the problem, replace the connectors. Also clean out any dust or dirt that may have accumulated in or around the secondary terminals of the transformer. As previously outlined, check the high voltage leads to determine if the insulation has become defective.

4. **Remove the porcelain insulators from the electrode holder to determine whether they are cracked.** In many cases the porcelains will crack beneath the clamp of the electrode holder. Replace cracked or crazed porcelains, even though they are still functioning properly.

5. **Carbonized insulator.** Carbon accumulations on the ceramic insulators will conduct electricity, thus causing the spark to short out against either the nozzle adapter, nozzle line, or the electrode holder. The carbon must be removed with a solvent or cleaner. Then the insulators must be dried and checked for cracks and/or spark leakage. The procedure for checking for spark leakage has been outlined.

6. **Electrodes in oil spray.** If the electrode tips are permitted to operate while extending into the oil spray, it will promote a carbon bridge between the electrode tips, thus shorting out the spark and ultimately causing ignition failure. Clean the electrode tips and set them properly.

7. **Electrodes too close to the nozzle.** It has already been outlined that the electrodes set too close to the nozzle will promote spark shorting out from the electrode tip to the nozzle, thus creating a delayed ignition or ignition failure. Set electrode tips according to prescribed procedure.

8. **Spark gap too wide.** If the spark gap is too wide, either there will be no spark at all, or the spark will short out at some other point along the ignition system. Again, set tips as instructed previously. However, we are learning that in many applications today, and due to the changes in fuel oil, a slightly wider than normal gap may result in smoother ignition. Ignition of fuel is not an exact science and so a couple of settings may have to be tried to find the best results.

9. **Insulators not held securely.** In the event the electrode support bracket is loose, or the porcelains do not fit properly in the bracket, it is possible that the electrodes may move out of adjustment because of burner vibrations. Set electrodes and tighten the electrode support bracket securely, but do not overtighten because that may crack the ceramic insulators.

10. **Puffbacks may be caused by lack of draft.** If it is discovered that the ceramic insulators are heavily sooted and/or carbonized and the electrode tips are properly gapped and properly set, then it is

a good possibility that lack of overfire draft is causing the trouble. Refer to Chapter 6—'Chimneys & Draft.' Puffbacks and carbon may be caused by a partially clogged nozzle. See Chapter 5 on Nozzles.

11. **Ignition "on" time should be checked.** This, of course, concerns interrupted ignition primary controls. The ignition "on" time is easily checked by connecting one lead of a 40-watt test light to the ignition wire of the primary, and connecting the other lead to neutral or the white wire. Start the burner while watching the bulb time to determine the length of time it remains "on." With cad cell type controls, it should remain on for the length of time specified by the manufacturer.

Ignition Control

Most burner manufacturers today use interrupted ignition. On commercial/industrial burners, ignition "on" times of greater than 10-20 seconds are seldom found. The purpose of interrupted ignition is to ignite the fuel and shut off the system, prolonging ignition system component life. For example, let us say that a residential burner that consumes 1,000 gallons per year is operating with a 1 GPH nozzle. For this example, let us assume the burner will start 3,000 times per year.

Example 1

Intermittent ignition = ignition is on when burner runs. 1000 gallons / 1 GPH = 1000 hours of ignition on time.

Example 2

Interrupted ignition = timed or sequenced ignition.

Cad-cell type relays

3000 starts x 45 seconds = 37.5 hours ignition on time

3000 starts x 30 seconds = 25 hours

3000 starts x 15 seconds = 12.5 hours

3000 starts x 8/10 seconds = 40 minutes ignition on time

As we can see, we can dramatically lower ignition on-time and prolong the useful life of our ignition systems and reduce service calls.

Delayed ignition is one of the frustrating ignition problems we encounter. Some solutions are covered in the following charts provided by Beckett Corp., Figure 9-14: Ignition Service Help Chart and Figure 9-15: Delayed Ignition Problem Solving, on following pages.

Figure 9-14:
Ignition service
help chart

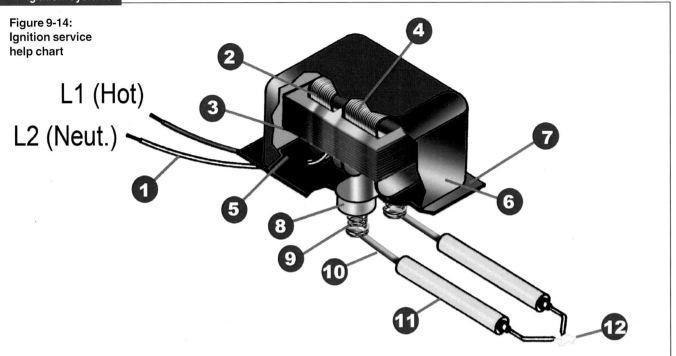

L1 (Hot)

L2 (Neut.)

Designation	Description	Service Hints
1. 120V ac input wires	Brings 120 volt to primary coil	Wires must not be pinched against housing when transformer is closed
2. Primary coil	Current in this coil generates a magnetic field	
3. Iron core	Transfers magnetic field into secondary coil	
4. Secondary coil	Magnetic field from core induces voltage in this coil	
5. Insulating compound	Keeps moisture out, conducts heat	Should not be leaking out
6. Metal cover	Protects internal of transformer	Should not be punctured or severely dented
7. Mounting base plate	Mounts transformer to burner housing	Must not be bent and cause air to leak from around transformer
8. Transformer output ceramic insulator	Insulates high voltage from ground and opposing terminal. Holds ignition spring dimensions	1. Must not be cracked 2. Must be totally clean
9. Ignition spring terminals	Transmits high voltage to electrode rods	1. Must make good, clean contact to electrode rods
10. Electrode rods	Transfers high voltage to electrode tips	Must be clean
11. Electrode insulators	Mounts electrodes and insulates each electrode from ground	Must be clean and not cracked
12. Arc gap and electrodes	Specified gap (1/8" - 5/32") allows arc to jump to other terminal and ignite	1. Too close causes delayed ignition 2. Too wide results in no ignition and possible damage to secondary 3. Clean and properly adjust

Figure 9-15

Chapter 9
Ignition Systems

Delayed Ignition Problem Solving—Electrical

Start the burner and use test meter to measure voltage at the transformer/primary lead junction and the Neutral connection. Do you have a nominal 120 VAC?

 YES

With the burner OFF, attach the leads of a transformer tester to the secondary terminals. Start the burner. Is there approximately 10,000 VAC output?

 YES

Check transformer secondary procelain bushing for crazing, arc tracks, moisture, cracks, pin holes, carbon or other defects. Are they clean and free from defects that could cause short-circuiting?

 YES

When the transformer is in the closed position, do the spring terminals make good positive contact with the electrode rods?

 YES

Check electrode porcelains for crazing, arc tracking, moisture, cracks, pin holes, carbon or other defects. Are they clean and free from defects that could cause short circuiting?

 YES

Are the electrodes set to the manufacturer's specifications? Are the tips in good condition?

 YES

The dimension from the nozzle face to the combustion head flat surface is important. With Beckett burners this is designated the "Z" dimension. Is this set correctly?

 YES

The above procedure should enable you to isolate the source of trouble. However, if these items check positive and delays persist, then the problem may be located in the oil handling system or with improper burner adjustment.

Replace the primary control.
The relay contacts are defective.

  YES

 NO   Measure the line voltage input to the primary control. Is there a nominal 120 VAC?

NO

Check the electrical supply system.

 NO   Replace the ignitor transformer.

 NO   Clean and restore to service if possible, otherwise replace the transformer.

 NO   Straighten, reposition to ensure positive contact. Replace springs if necessary.

 NO   Replace with good quality porcelain insulators.

 NO   Replace worn eroded electrodes. Adjust to manufacturer's specifications.

NO   Adjust to manufacturer's specifications.

MOTORS
FANS
& RELAYS

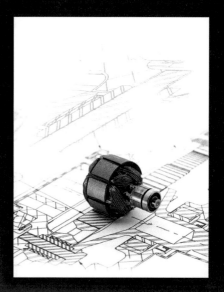

IN THIS
CHAPTER

- **Motor components**

- **How motors work**

- **The types of motors used in heating systems**

- **Diagnosing motor problems**

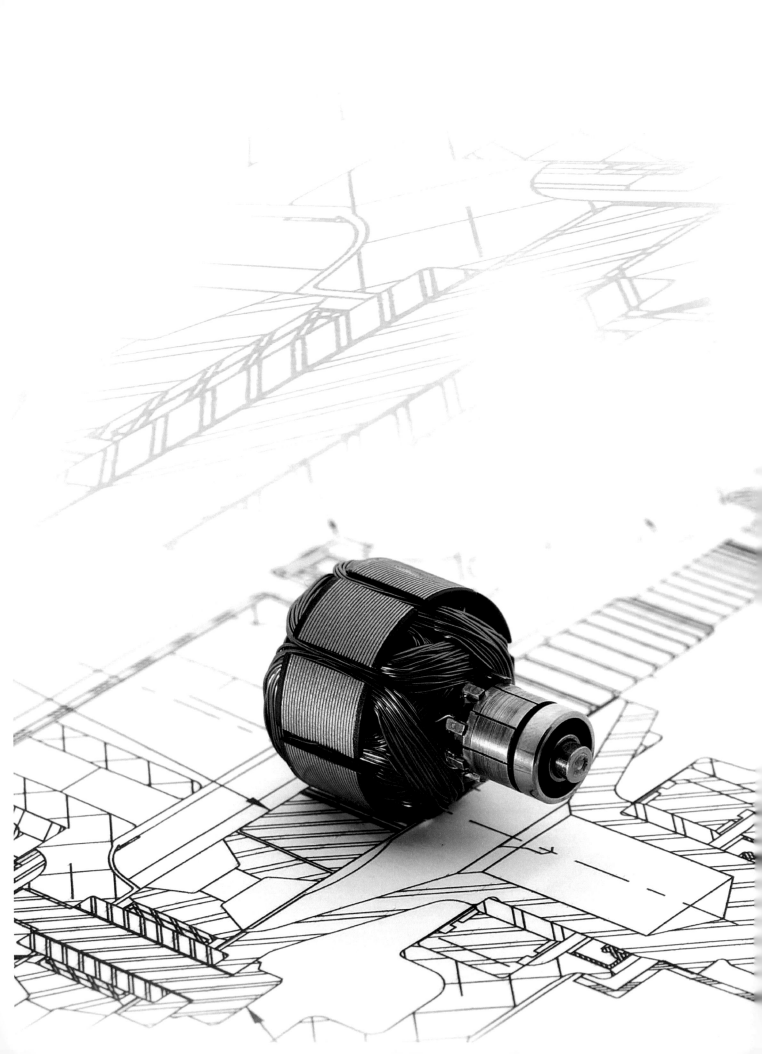

Chapter 10

Motors

Introduction

Electric motors run the fuel unit, run the fan, providing combustion air to the fire, run the circulating pumps in a hot water system, and power the blowers in forced warm air and air conditioning systems. In addition, low voltage motors open and close zone valves and damper motors.

Motor components

Residential and commercial oilburner motors are generally AC motors. DC motors are sometimes used in some specialty applications, such as power washers and road maintenance equipment. Most motors use AC split-phase induction motors equipped with two sets of windings. This type generally has low to moderate starting torque with high amp draw on start-up.

There are basic components of a motor:

Base: the device used to support the motor.

Rotor: The permanent magnets or windings attached to the motor shaft that follow the rotating magnetic field created by the electromagnets in the *stator* and cause the rotation of the motor shaft.

Stator: The stator contains stationary electromagnets and windings that create the field that causes the motor to turn. The start and run windings are wound around the stator. When electricity flows through these windings, it creates the magnetic field.

Start windings: Electric current flowing in these windings provides the extra power needed to start the rotor turning and are turned off when the motor is up to full

**Figure 10-1:
Cutaway of
burner motor**

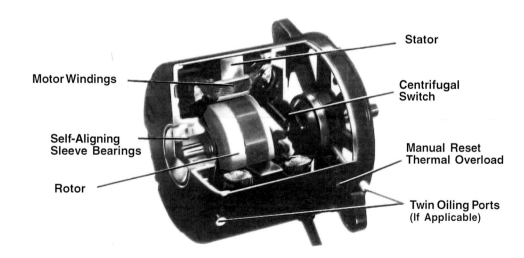

Motor Windings

Self-Aligning
Sleeve Bearings

Rotor

Stator

Centrifugal
Switch

Manual Reset
Thermal Overload

Twin Oiling Ports
(If Applicable)

> Motors are typically rated by voltage, amp draw, direction of rotation, frame size, and horsepower.

speed. Starting windings will draw high current (amps) during the starting phase for a split phase motor.

Run windings: Electric current flow in these windings creates the rotating magnetic field in the stator. This maintains the shaft rotation after the start windings have been disconnected. The starting and running windings are oriented perpendicularly to each other. The windings are designed so that the current in one lags the current in the other. The difference makes the resulting magnetic field rotate, creating a torque that turns the motor shaft.

Start switch: Start windings draw many amps. On split-phase motors, we turn off the power to these windings once the motor has started to turn in order to conserve electricity. The centrifugally operated switch used in split phase and capacitor start motors opens and disconnects the start winding after the motor reaches 75% to 80% of full speed. The power remains connected to the run windings. The centrifugal switch throw-out speed for a 3,450 RPM burner motor is about 2,800 RPM.

The flange end of the motor is sized to bolt onto the oilburner casting. Although most burner manufacturers use the same size flange mount, you may encounter some that are different. Generally, the 3,450 rpm flame retention burner motor has a smaller M flange with a circumference of 6¾". The N flange that can be found on older burners and small commercial motors measures 7¼".

Motors are typically rated by voltage, amp draw, direction of rotation, frame size, and horsepower. The motor rating plate provides this information. The frame sizes

are established by NEMA (National Electrical Manufacturers Association). Some motors have cooling holes in the motor ends called bells, but some bells are totally closed. The end of the motor around the shaft is the shaft bell and the other end is known as the end bell. The type of shaft bell can affect air pressure and flow for a burner. Shaft bells with fewer air holes will generally provide higher pressure. A reduction in pressure and flow can negatively impact burner operating characteristics.

Not all manufacturers refer to rotation in the same manner. Some manufacturers consider rotation when looking at the shaft bell, others by looking from the end bell towards the shaft. Be aware of this when ordering a new motor or when installing a replacement motor that needs to be wired to establish rotation.

Motor oiling

There are two ways motors are lubricated:

1. Permanently lubricated—this type of motor does not have any oiling ports and should not be oiled.

2. Motors that require lubrication are oiled according to their duty cycle using SAE 20 oil.

   Occasional Duty— less than 2 hours a day: Oil every 5 years.

   Intermittent Duty—run 2 to 12 hours a day: Oil every 2 years.

   Continuous Duty—12 or more hours a day: Oil once every year.

   Most oilburner motors see intermittent duty.

Start switch

The start switch of a motor is wired internally in series with the start winding. There are two parts to the start mechanism—the stationary switch, with its contacts—and a governor. The governor holds the switch contacts together when the motor is not running and releases the pressure to open the contacts when the motor is up to speed. This action must

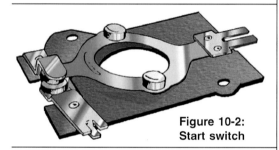

**Figure 10-2:
Start switch**

occur quickly; if not, the start winding can be damaged. The starting switch is a centrifugal switch. Its contacts are weighted and a spring holds them closed. As the motor shaft begins to turn, centrifugal force pushes the weights against the spring, opening the contacts of the switch. Figure 10-2 is a drawing of the centrifugal start switch.

Locked rotor amperage

This is the amount of amperage that can be measured for the brief instant when the motor first starts. A motor will draw substantially more amperage on the start than it will while running. After starting, the motor should only draw the amount of amperage listed on the motor nameplate. The locked rotor amperage (not usually listed on the motor nameplate) is the amount of current present if the motor fails to start after current is delivered to it. A motor may not turn because of bad bear-

ings, bound up fuel pump, or any other reason for the rotor to be "locked in" place.

Motor wiring

Figure 10-3 shows the internal schematic of the split phase fractional horsepower motor pictured in Figure 10-1. It is used in most residential burners. Note the location of the start switch. Apart from the size and voltage shown on the motor nameplate, there is also a frame number. This refers to the type of cradle or mounting the motor has.

Capacitor start motors

We use capacitors to build up an electric charge and store it until it is needed. A capacitor is made of two conducting plates separated by an insulator. A capacitor start motor has a starting *capacitor* inserted in series with the start switch and starting winding, creating a circuit which is capable of a much greater phase shift (and so, a

**Figure 10-3:
Split phase motor,
internal wiring**

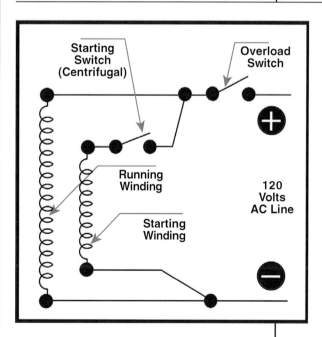

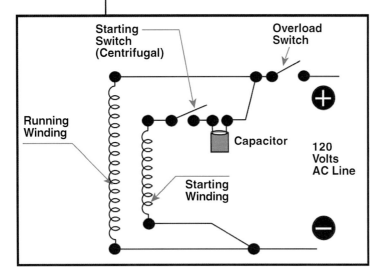

Figure 10-4: Capacitor start split phase motor

much greater starting torque). Figure 10-4 shows the internal connections of a split phase motor with a start switch and also a start capacitor in the line to the start winding. Many circulator and commercial oilburner motors are capacitor start motors.

Thermal or motor overload switch

The thermal or overload switch is wired in series with the motor windings and is activated (opens) when an unusual increase in temperature occurs inside the motor. This switch protects the motor from being damaged by overheating. If the motor overheats, the bimetal in the switch will warp then the switch will open and turn off the motor. There are two types used in oilburner motors:

1. **Manual reset thermal protectors** are most common and must be reset by pressing a reset button. Figure 10-5 shows the operation of a manual reset overload.

2. **Automatic reset;** this type will reset itself (close) after the motor cools down.

Figure 10-6 shows the action of an automatic reset overload. In Figure 10-7, a schematic wiring diagram shows the location of the overload switch in the circuit.

When the thermal overload switch shuts the motor off, it indicates motor overheating. This is caused from either internal failure or external loading conditions.

The following will cause motor overload:

1. The line voltage is too high or too low.

Figure 10-5: Manual reset overload switch

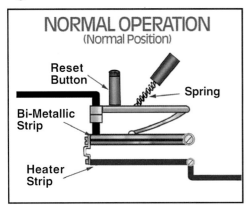
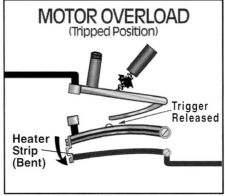

Figure 10-6: Automatic reset overload switch

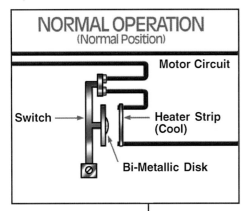
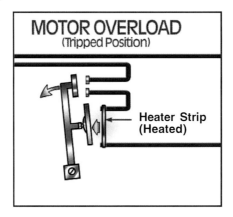

Figure 10-7: Overload switch location

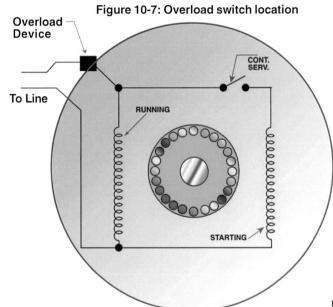

Overload Device

To Line

CONT. SERV.

RUNNING

STARTING

9. The motor is in a very hot environment (the inside of a hot vestibule of a furnace).

10. There is dirt in the motor cooling vents; this will also cause the motor to overheat.

11. The motor is under-sized—if the load requirement exceeds the nameplate rating for horsepower (HP), the motor will eventually overheat. Use a clamp around ammeter (Figure 10-8) to make sure the motor current does not exceed 10% over the motor nameplate current.

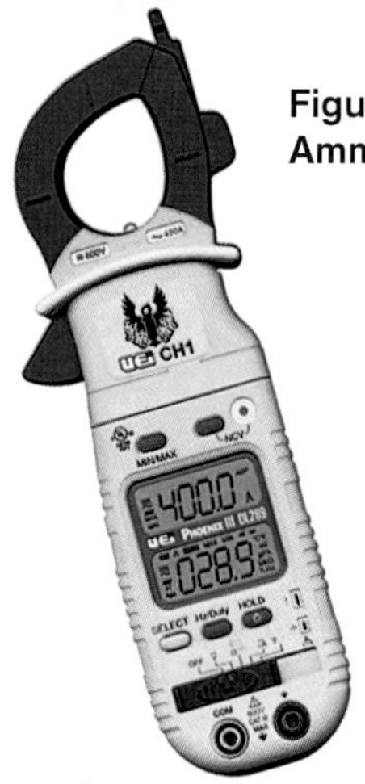

Figure 10-8: Ammeter

2. The oil pump has seized due to rust or debris in the gear set.

3. The motor bearings are bad.

4. The return is plugged.

5. There is misalignment of motor to pump—check to see if any mounting bolts have loosened, causing improper seating of the motor or pump to the burner housing. Also, check to see if the pump coupling is too long, causing pressure on the motor shaft.

6. The start switch is dirty or broken. This prevents electricity from flowing to the starting windings. With this switch open, current will still flow to the run winding, but the motor will not start. The increased amperage will generate heat in the line and cause the overload switch to trip out.

7. The centrifugal start switch has failed to disconnect the start windings from the AC power when the motor has reached approximately full speed; the motor will overheat.

8. The fan or blower wheel is jammed or very dirty.

Wiring connections and reversing rotation

Some oilburner motors have an "S" cord attached to the motor and connected to a junction box. If this is the case, be certain the BX cable or conduit to the junction box is tightly fastened to provide a good bonding to ground. If Romex cable is used, be certain the bonding wire is fastened to the junction box.

The motor rotation on some oilburner and blower motors can be electrically reversed. The instructions may be found on the nameplate of the motor or inside the cover that provides access to the wiring connections.

The rotation of a motor is determined by the direction of the current to the start winding. If we reverse the connections to the start winding we can reverse the rotation of the motor. The instructions with each motor will identify these connections and how to change them. Figure 10-9 shows how to switch the wires to reverse rotation.

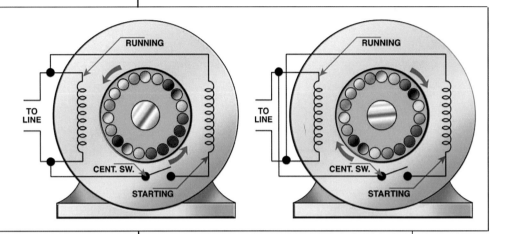

Excessive oil can also be a problem. Follow the recommended lubrication procedure.

Figure 10-10 illustrates the types of bearings. **Ball bearings** consist of a ring of steel balls held in place around the rotor. As the rotor turns, the balls are free to roll, aided by lubricating grease. Because the rotor is attached to the inside ring of the ball bearing assembly, there is no end play (the fan wheel is not free to move away from the motor flange). The gap between the fan wheel and the housing is kept constant, minimizing air leakage and increasing the zero-flow static pressure by as much as .3 to .4 inches of water column, compared to sleeve bearing motors.

**Figure 10-9:
Reversing
rotation of
burner motor
wires**

Bearings

There are two basic types of bearings used on most of the motors in our industry: they are sleeve type and ball bearing type.

Sleeve bearings, also called *bushings* or *self-aligned bearings*, are special metal sleeves around the rotor shaft. Oil is applied between the shaft and the sleeve; the thin film of oil lubricates the shaft and allows it to turn with little friction. Many modern sleeve bearings are permanently self-lubricating and have a sponge like material that continually supplies oil as the rotor turns. Sleeve bearings require increased starting torque if they are contaminated by rust or dirt. Worn, dry, or tight bearings will cause motor overload and possible thermal overload lockout.

Figure 10-10: Bearings

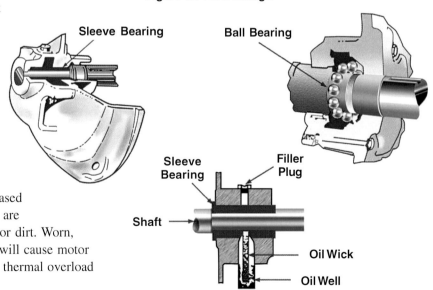

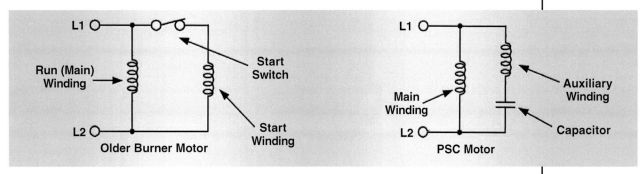

Figure 10-11:
Motor circuits

PSC (Permanent Split Capacitor) motors

Most new oilburners feature PSC motors. A PSC motor uses a capacitor (a device that stores and releases an electrical charge) in one of the windings to increase the current lag between the two windings. Unlike conventional capacitor start motors, PSC motors have no centrifugal starting switch and the second winding is permanently connected to the power source. Both

the capacitor (auxiliary) winding, and the main winding remain in the circuit the entire time the motor is running—hence the name "permanent." PSC Motors perform with better efficiency, offer equal or increased power output and lower starting and running current than conventional split phase motors.

See Figures 10-11 and Table 10-1.

PSC motor

Table 10-1: Heating system motor testing chart (courtesy Beckett Corp.)

Test Parameter	Split Phase	PSC	Comments
Average starting current (locked rotor current)	15-25 Amps	7 Amps	PSC has a decreased starting current, which extends primary control relay life.
Average running current	2.0 - 2.4 Amps	1.5 Amps	PSC draws an average 30% less current.
Approximate starting torque	55 - 70 oz-in	49 oz-in	General mini pump starting torque requirement: 13 - 20 oz-in. [1]
Average electrical power	200 Watts	170 Watts	PSC draws an average 15% less power.
Efficiency	40 - 50%	60 - 65%	Efficiency = output power (mechanical) divided by input power (electrical)
AFG full load speed	3375 - 3450 rpm [2]	3440 - 3460 [2]	PSC: Similar or increased output power.

[1] Most standard oil pumps (for instance, the Suntec A or B models) do not require as much power or starting torque as the larger pumps (for instance, Suntec J and H models), which often are provided with a 1/5 hp motor.

[2] **Rule of thumb:** Air flow (cfm) is proportional to motor speed, and static pressure varies with the motor speed *squared* (if the speed increases by 2%, the pressure increases by 4%).

Diagnosing motor troubles

Typical heating system motors are reliable, but problems can occur. The following should help you quickly pin point a problem. For more details, see Chart on page 10-16.

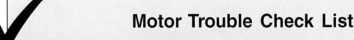

Motor Trouble Check List

1. The motor will not start

a. Is voltage present at the motor? Is it the correct voltage? (It must be within 10% of nameplate.) Are all wiring connections tight?

b. Is the motor off due to overload? If manual reset, push the button. If auto, wait for the motor to cool until it resets.

c. Is the capacitor (if needed) functioning? If in doubt, replace it with a capacitor of the same rating.

d. Is the load on the motor excessive? If the motor starts after the load is removed, this could be the problem.

e. Are the bearings on the motor seized or dry? If so, free up and lubricate.

2. Noises

a. Is motor lubricated? If not, do so, unless it is permanently lubricated.

b. Is the alignment of the motor shaft and the driven device correct?

c. On a belted unit, is the belt OK? Is it too tight or too loose? The belt should have a 1" play.

d. Noise could be caused by shaft end-play (the distance the shaft will move in and out of the motor). A new motor will have no more than .035" of movement. If the shaft end play is more than .060", the motor could be suspect.

3. Motor overheats

a. Is there adequate ventilation? Are the air venting slots on the motor clean and unobstructed?

b. Is the load excessive? Use an ammeter to measure the current draw. If the load or the draw is more than the nameplate rating, the load must be either reduced or a larger more powerful motor must be installed. Make sure that the driven device is unrestricted in its operation.

NOTE: When checking the current draw of the motor, the service factors must be considered. A motor with an amp rating of 4.0 and a service factor of 1.25 can safely be operated at 5 amps.

c. Is the motor located in an excessively hot area?

PSC motors are also frequently used in air handlers, fans, and blowers and other cases where a variable speed is desired. By changing taps on the running winding, but keeping the load constant, the motor can be made to run at different speeds.

Troubleshooting 'dead spots'

'Dead spot' is a common term for a certain orientation of the rotor at which the motor will not start. Two things can cause dead spots. First, there could be a fault in the manufacturing process. If so, the motor may not have enough torque to start the burner. This condition is rare and cannot be repaired. Second, if the start switch of a split phase motor is unevenly worn or has shifted out of position, the contacts may become slightly separated when the rotor is in a particular location. No current will flow through the starting winding and the motor will not start. If this is the problem, the motor should be replaced.

Troubleshooting the start switch

To check a faulty start switch, you need an ohmmeter. The motor starting windings have a much lower resistance than the run windings do. Use this difference to determine if the start switch is defective. When the start switch is functioning properly, both the start and run windings are connected, resulting in lower resistance. If the start switch is faulty, the start windings will not be connected or will intermittently be connected. This results in higher resistance or fluctuating resistance as the motor shaft is rotated.

Set the scale on your ohmmeter at its lowest setting and zero out the meter by touching the test leads together and adjusting the meter to show zero ohms. Turn off the power, disconnect the motor input leads and remove the motor from the housing. Place the motor on its back, shaft up. Connect your meter across the black and white motor input leads. If the start switch is functioning properly, the resistance

should be about 2 to 4 ohms. If the resistance is much higher (in the range of 7 to 10 ohms) then the start switch is probably bad.

To double-check the measurement, pull up on the shaft and note if the resistance drops to the proper 2-4 ohms. If it does, the switch is definitely bad and the motor should be replaced.

The most important function of this test is to make sure the resistance across the motor leads does not change when the motor shaft is pushed down or rotated in a full circle. Rotate the shaft slowly and note the resistance. If it goes up to 7-10 ohms at any point in the rotation, you have found your dead spot. If it is the kind of motor where you can see the start switch, push down on the switch and the resistance should increase from 2-4 to 7-10 ohms.

Troubleshooting PSC motors

PSC motors have two major areas to troubleshoot—the capacitor and the windings. Both are relatively simple to check and require only a multimeter (Figure 10-12) with a capacitance range. On page 10-17, from RW Beckett, is a PSC motor trouble shooting checklist.

Figure 10-12: Multimeter with a capacitance range.

Checking capacitors—A failed capacitor will cause a PSC motor to either stop or run more slowly than designed. The thermal protector will trip if a restart is attempted. To check a capacitor, perform the following steps:

1. Remove power from the burner and carefully disconnect the two leads from the capacitor terminals.

2. Discharge the capacitor. To safely discharge the capicitor follow the instructions on page 8-21 and Figure 8-25.

Caution: Capacitor discharge can cause physical harm due to electrical shock.

3. Using the multimeter on the ohms scale, observe the meter's response when the leads of the meter are connected to the terminals.

Note: Because the meter charges the capacitor slightly in order to make a resistance measurement, if you desire to repeat the measurement, discharge the capacitor first (step 2).

4. The ohmmeter reading should jump immediately to a non-infinite resistance value and then quickly increase again to infinity. This should happen in a fraction of a second since the capacitor will charge quickly and then resist any more charge. If the meter settles to zero ohms, the capacitor has short-circuited. If the meter resistance is infinite the entire time, the capacitor is open circuited. A failed capacitor (open or short circuited) should be replaced by a capacitor of the same capacitance (micro-farads or µF) and a voltage rating at least as great as the original one. In most cases it is best to replace the entire motor.

Test tip: The quick capacitor response is more easily observed with an analog "needle" meter (see Figure 10-13), than a digital meter. With a digital meter, the resistance reading should gradually increase to infinite resistance (either quickly or slowly, depending on the meter).

5. Using the capacitance function of the multimeter, see Figure 10-14, and after shorting the capacitor, determine the microfarad output of the capacitor. The reading should be between 5-10% of the rating.

Checking the PSC motor windings:

1. Remove power from the burner and detach the motor power leads from the burner.

2. Discharge the capacitor and discon-

nect the two leads from the capacitor terminal.

3. Connect one ohmmeter lead to the L1 motor power lead and the other meter lead to each of the capacitor leads, one at a time. See Figure 10-15.

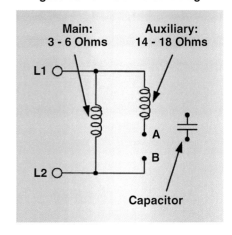

Figure 10-15: PSC Motor wiring

4. Record the two resistance values.

5. Repeat by measuring the other motor power lead (L2) and each of the capacitor leads, one at a time.

6. Check with the manufacturer's instructions. From one of the power leads, you should have measured 3-6 ohms and 9-18 ohms. From the other power lead, you should have measured a short (less than 1 ohm) and 15-25 ohms. If you do not observe these resistances, the motor windings are faulty, and the motor should be replaced.

Miscellaneous things to look for:
• Make sure bearings are in good condition and oiled.

• Check and be sure there is no excessive end play on the shaft. This can cause noise and hard starting.

• Is all the wiring in good condition? If not, replace and secure with appropriate connectors.

• On blower motors check belt size, width, and tension. Remember, over-tightening is as bad as a loose belt.

Figure 10-13: Analog "needle" meter

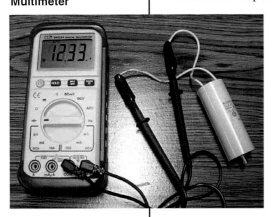

Figure 10-14: Multimeter

• Make sure the motor is aligned with the driven device and the coupling is tightened.

• Make sure the motor is operating within the proper amp ratings.

• Make sure voltage and rotation are correct.

When choosing a new motor

Generally, heating system motors are designed to be non-serviceable items that must be replaced when they fail. When replacing a motor, look for the following:

1. Correct voltage.

2. Correct rotation. Some motors have reversible rotation. Change if necessary. Run the motor without the load to verify rotation is correct before connecting the load.

3. Frame designation, size, and mounting type. Example: most standard 1725 RPM burner motors are frame type 48N and most 3450 burner motors are 48M frame.

4. Is the speed of the new motor the same as the old?

5. Horsepower is at least the same as the old.

6. Shaft diameter and length must be the same as the old, or at least long enough and the proper diameter to securely couple to the driven device. Bushings are sometimes used to increase the diameter of the shaft.

7. Rated amperage must be at least as high as the driven device will require.

Replacing an oilburner motor

The specified motors for most oilburners either are the closed-end type or models with small cooling openings in the shaft bell at the motor shaft end. The small openings

are satisfactory as long as they are covered once the fan wheel is installed onto the motor. The back plate of the fan wheel must be positioned close to the motor end bell according to the manufacturer's gap setting for maximum efficiency and output. See Figure 10-16.

Use of a motor with cooling openings that are not covered will cause a loss of static pressure at the burner retention head due to air leakage and turbulence. Use a thickness feeler gauge to measure the gap between the motor and the blower wheel. Place the gauge on top of the motor and bottom of the blower wheel. The setscrew must be centered on the flat of the motor shaft. Then tighten the setscrew.

Burner couplings

A flexible burner coupling is a mechanical device used to connect two rotating shafts. It permits a small amount of misalignment between shafts. The "Nylo-Flex™" coupling, see Figure 10-17, fits most burners, thereby reducing truck inventory. These couplings are made up of two plastic ends and a center piece that is cut to size. The molded ends are designed to slip over the motor and pump shafts and do not require setscrews. They can be purchased with a variety of ends to match the various pump shaft sizes.

With this type of coupling, it is important to slide the ends on the shaft to the end of the flat portion or the coupling will move. Measure the length needed for the center piece and cut it exactly to that measurement. The center piece is hollow and will slide over any portion of the shaft extending beyond the end piece. Be sure the motor and the pump

Figure 10-16: Beckett AFG motor

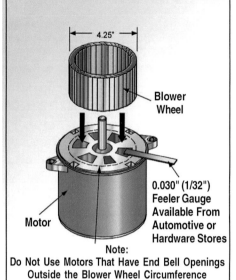

4.25"

Blower Wheel

Motor

0.030" (1/32") Feeler Gauge Available From Automotive or Hardware Stores

Note:
Do Not Use Motors That Have End Bell Openings Outside the Blower Wheel Circumference Reprensented by the Dashed Lines

Figure 10-17: Flexible coupling

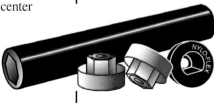

are mounted tight to the burner housing before measuring the center piece. If you cut the center piece too long, when the motor and the pump are bolted in place, the pressure may put an undue strain on the motor and may keep it from starting.

Warm air furnace motors and fans/blowers

The third most common use of motors in our industry is for moving air through warm air and air conditioning ducts. Many are multi-speed motors that can be operated at any of two or more speeds. In the case of multi-speed PSC motors, the speed is dependent on the load.

Three types of blower motors can be found on warm air systems:

1. The split phase, fractional horsepower motor used for belt driven blowers.

2. The capacitor start motor, also used for belt drive.

3. The multi-speed, direct drive motor/ blower assembly. These blowers are often used on systems that also provide air conditioning. They can run at a slower speed for heating and faster speed for the air conditioning. These motors can be either PSC type motors or a newer design called an *ECM*, see Figure 10-18.

The ECM is a DC voltage motor. ECM stands for Electrically Commutated Motor. ECMs have grown in popularity due to their low power consumption, infinite motor speed capability and reliability. The ECM has all the efficiency and speed control advantages of a DC motor with none of the disadvantages, such as carbon brush wear, short life, and noise. The ECM uses 1-phase AC input power and converts it into 3-phase operation. Three-phase motors offer superior efficiency and reduced noise.

**Figure 10-18:
ECM motor**

Belt driven blowers

These are the most common type blowers on older oil-fired furnaces. These motors are mounted to the blower and drive it through pulleys and a "V" belt. Adjusting the size of the pulleys changes the speed of the blower. The larger the pulley on the motor, the faster the fan will turn. The larger the pulley on the fan, the slower the fan will turn.

Variable pitch pulleys can be adjusted to increase or decrease size to change the speed without changing the pulley. When adjusting the speed of this type of motor, it is imperative to take an amp reading to be sure that the increase in speed does not work the motor beyond its rated capacity.

Figure 10-19 shows some of the wide variety of pulleys available. Note how the adjustable pulley opens and closes to vary

Figure 10-19

Standard Pulley   V-Step Pulley

Adjustable V-Pulley

Closed   Open

diameter. Make sure it is not too far open or closed causing poor seating of the V belt. Figure 10-20 stresses the importance of using the right size belt for the pulley being used. Width of belts and pulleys varies so be sure both are the same when changing motor and pulley. Proper tension on belts without over-tightening is important.

Direct drive blowers

These are blowers with the motor mounted inside the wheel of the blower with the shaft of the blower connected directly to the blower wheel. Some of these are multi-speed PSC motors. In this case, speed is adjusted by swapping the wires as indicated on the wiring diagram on the blower.

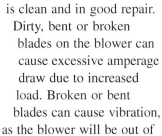

On both types of blowers, it is important that the blower, Figure 10-21, is clean and in good repair. Dirty, bent or broken blades on the blower can cause excessive amperage draw due to increased load. Broken or bent blades can cause vibration, as the blower will be out of balance.

Figure 10-21

Circulator motors

Hot water heating systems rely on circulator pumps to move the hot water through the heating system. There are two kinds: cartridge and three-piece circulators. With cartridge units, the pump impeller is fastened directly to the motor shaft as shown in Figure 10-22.

Three-piece circulators feature a bearing assembly that connects the motor to the pump body. The bearing assembly shaft is connected to the motor shaft by a pump coupling. The pump impeller is fastened to the bearing assembly shaft. Figure 10-23 shows a three-piece circulator. Circulator motors often are PSC motors, as shown on page 10-9.

Circulator couplings

These are used on three-piece circulators to couple the motor to the circulator pump. See Figure 10-23. These can wear and break.

Excessive oiling of the circulator can cause the rubber motor mounts to sag, causing the coupling to break; therefore check motor mounts when replacing the coupling. The motor mounts need to be replaced if they have softened.

On some of these circulators, the coupling has tension pulling the shaft toward the motor with a spring. This holds pressure on the water seal in the circulator. Care should be taken to maintain this pressure during the change, or water will leak out around the circulator shaft. It is best to reduce the water pressure on the boiler while changing this type.

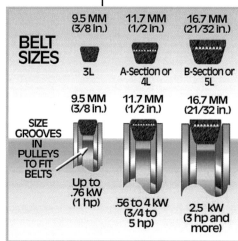

**Figure 10-20:
Pulley belts**

**Figure 10-22:
Cartridge
circulator**

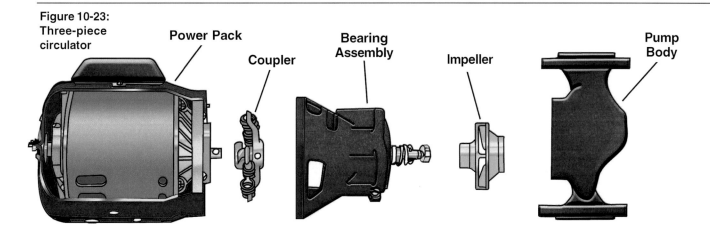

**Figure 10-23:
Three-piece
circulator** **Power Pack** **Coupler** **Bearing
Assembly** **Impeller** **Pump
Body**

Heating system motor troubleshooting chart (courtesy of R.W. Beckett Corp.)

Trouble	Cause	What To Do
Motor fails to start	Blown fuses	Replace with time-delay fuses. Check for grounded winding.
	Low voltage	Check for inadequate wiring or extension cords. Check for low system voltage. Call electric company.
	Improper line connections	Check connections against diagram supplied with motor.
	Overload (thermal protector) tripped	Check and reset overload relay in starter. Check heater rating against motor nameplate current rating. Check motor load. If motor has manual reset thermal protector, check if tripped.
	If three-phase, one phase may be open	Indicated by humming sound. Check lines for open phase. Check voltage with motor disconnected, one fuse blown
	Defective motor or starter	Repair or replace
Motor stalls	Overloaded motor	Reduce load or increase motor size.
	Low motor voltage	See that nameplate voltage is maintained.
Motor does not come up to speed	Not applied properly	Consult motor service firm for proper type. Use larger motor.
	Voltage is too low at motor terminal due to line drop	Use higher voltage tap on transformer terminals, increase wire size. Check for poor connections. Voltage unbalance.
	Starting load too high	Check load motor is carrying at start.
Motor takes too long to accelerate	Excess loading; tight belts. High inertia load	Reduce load; increase motor size. Adjust belts.
	Inadequate wiring	Increase wire size. Check for poor connections.
	Applied voltage too low	Reconnect to a higher tap. Increase wire size. Check for poor connections.
	Defective motor	Repair or replace.
	Inadequate starting torque	Replace with larger motor.
Motor vibrates or is excessively noisy	Motor is misaligned	Realign
	Three-phase motor running single phase	Check for open circuit, blown fuses or unbalanced voltages.
	High or unbalanced voltages	Check wiring connections, transformer.
	Worn, damaged, dirty or overloaded bearings	Replace; check loading and alignment.
	Loose sheave or coupling	Tighten set screw(s); replace.

Is the motor off on overload? If manual reset, push the button. If auto, reset and wait for or assist the motor to cool until it resets.

Is the capacitor (if needed) OK? The simplest way to test the capacitor is to replace it with one of the same rating.

Is the load on the motor excessive? If the motor starts after the load is removed, this could be the problem.

Are the bearings on the motor seized or dry? If so, free up and lubricate.

PSC Motor Troubleshooting

Condition	Cause	Recommended Action
Motor does not start	No power to motor	Check wiring and power from primary control lead. If necessary, replace control, limit controller or fuses (time-delay type).
	Insufficient voltage supply	Check power from primary control.
	Thermal protector has tripped	Determine and repair cause of thermal over-load and reset (if manual re-settable).
	Pump shaft will not turn	Disconnect motor from pump. Turn coupling to ensure free rotation of pump shaft.
	Capacitor or windings have failed	Check capacitor and windings.
	Motor bearings have failed	Turn the motor shaft, which should turn easily.
Motor starts, but does not reach full speed	Motor is overloaded	Disconnect pump from motor. Turn pump shaft to ensure free rotation.
	Insufficient voltage supply	Check power from primary control. Voltage should be 110V - 120V.
	Capacitor or windings have failed.	Check capacitor and windings.
Motor vibrates or is noisy	Bearings are worn, damaged or fouled with dirt or rust	Replace motor.
	Motor and pump are mis-aligned with each other or housing	Check pump to motor, motor to housing, and pump to housing alignment.
	Blower wheel or wheel balancing weight (if ap-plicable) is loose	Check blower wheel and balancing weight (if applicable) for location and tightness.
Motor draws excessive	Motor and pump misaligned with each other or housing	Check pump to motor, motor to housing, and pump to housing alignment.
	Motor is undersized for the application	Increase motor size if needed.
	Motor windings are damaged	Check windings. If damaged, replace motor.

Checking the PSC Motor windings:

1. Remove power from the burner, and detach the motor power leads from the burner.
2. Disconnect the two leads from the capacitor terminals.
3. Connect one Ohmmeter lead to the L1 motor power lead and the other meter lead to each of the capacitor leads, one at a time. See Figure 10-15.
4. Record the two resistance values.
5. Repeat by measuring the other motor power lead (L2) and each of the capacitor leads one at a time.

Chapter 11

PRIMARY CONTROLS

RESET

TO RESET, PRESS AND HOLD 2 MIN.

IN THIS CHAPTER

- **Functions of a primary control**
- **Flame detection**
- **Ignition modes**
- **Types of primary controls**

RESET

TO RESET, PRESS AND HOLD 1 MIN.

Chapter 11

Primary Controls

Introduction

The safe, automatic operation of an oilheat system is dependent on the interaction between:

• The thermostat, which opens and closes a circuit based on temperature changes in the heated space.

• The limit control, which opens and closes a circuit based on temperature or pressure changes in the boiler or furnace.

• The primary control, which regulates the operation of the oilburner.

In a properly designed, installed, and serviced oilheat system, these three components work together to safely satisfy a call for space heating, cooling, or water heating.

In a typical oilheat system, line voltage flows in a series circuit from the fuse or circuit breaker to a remote toggle (on/off) switch located away from the heating unit. From there, it continues to a service switch at the oil-fired appliance, then to the limit controls, and then to the primary control, which distributes power to the oilburner components (motor, igniter and oil valve).

Functions of the primary control

The primary control has three main functions:

1. To respond to the thermostat

2. To respond to the limit control

3. To control the startup, run cycle, and shutdown of the oilburner.

All primary controls, whether old thermo-mechanical or modern microprocessor, operate on the same basic principles.

The primary control accomplishes its mission by:

• Reacting to the presence or absence of flame

• Managing oilburner startup by checking for a flame *before* energizing ignition transformers (or igniters), burner motors, and oil valves.

• Supervising burner shutdown once the thermostat is satisfied or the limit control opens.

All primary controls have line voltage (120 VAC) circuits. In a basic heating system, line voltage is supplied to the primary control through the high limit control when the *temperature*, in a water heater, boiler or furnace, or the *pressure*, in a steam boiler, is below the limit setting. Once the limit control is satisfied, it breaks, or opens the circuit, de-energizing the primary control and shutting down the burner.

Most primary controls also have low voltage circuits (24 VAC) to accommodate thermostats and/or other devices. The low voltage circuit is closed when the thermostat senses the need for an increase in room temperature. When the heat reaches the right temperature and the thermostat is satisfied, it opens the circuit.

For the primary control to activate the oilburner, *both* the line *and* low voltage circuits must be closed. In most cases, that means that if *either* the thermostat *or* the limit control is satisfied (open) the primary control will not activate the oilburner.

In systems with a line voltage thermostat, or with a low voltage thermostat connected to controls other than the primary control, a jumper is placed between the primary's thermostat terminals, permanently closing the low voltage circuit, Figure 11-1. The primary control is activated solely by the limit control.

Some systems have an additional control wired in parallel with the thermostat. In those cases, the primary's low voltage circuit can be completed through either the thermostat *or* the

Figure 11-1:
Parallel wiring for 24v thermostat and aquastat to the primary

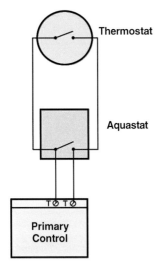

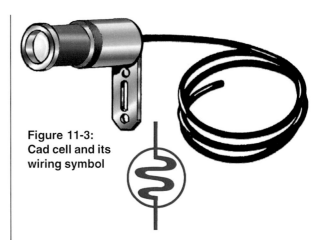

Figure 11-3:
Cad cell and its wiring symbol

additional control. For example, a steam boiler with a domestic hot water coil will normally have an aquastat wired to the low voltage terminals on the primary control. This enables the boiler to maintain domestic hot water even when the room thermostat is not calling for heat.

> *Did you know?*
> Power outages do not affect flame detection. If power is lost during a running cycle, the control will NOT go off on safety and it will normally re-energize the burner after power is restored.

Flame detection

Primary controls detect both the presence *and* absence of flame. A safety feature of primary controls is that they will *not* activate the oilburner for startup if the control senses a flame during the off cycle. This prevents additional fuel being pumped into a unit that has a fire before startup.

Primary controls must react quickly to the presence or absence of flame while the oilburner is running. The primary control must shut the burner off promptly if no flame is established on startup *or* if the flame is lost during the run cycle. If the primary control did not shut off the oilburner in these circumstances, the burner

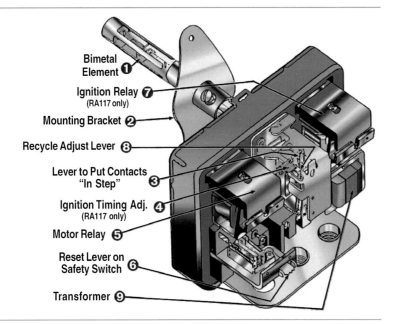

Figure 11-2:
Honeywell RA117a primary control

could continue to pump fuel into the unit, creating a hazardous condition.

When the primary control shuts off the burner because no flame is detected, it is referred to as being "off on safety," "in safety" or "in lock out." Once the primary control goes off on safety, it must be manually reset before it can send power to the burner again, Figure 11-4.

The amount of time that elapses from the start of a cycle in which flame is not detected, to the time the control goes off on safety is referred to as "trial for ignition" or "safety timing." Slight variations from an individual control's *stated* safety timing often exist due to manufacturing tolerances, voltage variations, and temperature changes.

spark across the electrodes that ignites the oil is present whenever the burner is running.

Interrupted duty ignition means the spark comes on for a short time at the beginning of each burner operating cycle and is turned off once flame is established, or for a fixed time—which may include a period of time after trial for ignition, known as a 'Sparkout' period—to insure a stable flame is fully established. Interrupted duty ignition is preferred because it makes for quieter combustion, increases the life of the ignition system, uses less electricity, and generates fewer nitrogen oxide (NOx) emissions.

> **Did you know?**
> Primary controls that are designed for interrupted duty ignition can be adapted for intermittent duty ignition, but primary controls designed for intermittent ignition cannot be used for interrupted ignition.

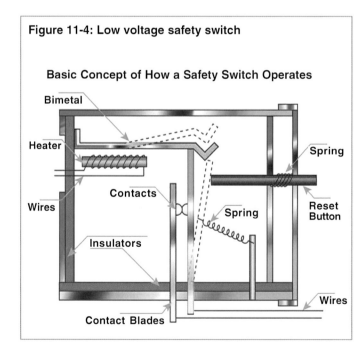

Figure 11-4: Low voltage safety switch

Basic Concept of How a Safety Switch Operates

Types of primary controls

There are two basic types of primary controls commonly found in the field today:

- Thermal-mechanical primary controls
- Cad cell primary controls

Thermal-mechanical controls, commonly called "stack switches" or "stack relays", utilize bi-metals to detect flame and to mechanically open and close electrical contacts to provide burner control. They have spring loaded reset buttons and a thermal safety switch that must cool before the control is allowed to be removed from lockout.

Through the 1960's, stack relays were the industry's standard primary control and

Ignition modes

Oilheat systems operate in one of two ignition modes: *intermittent duty* or *interrupted duty*.

Intermittent duty ignition means that the

there are many types of stack relays still operating in the field today. Fortunately, the manufacturers designed the wiring to be the same regardless of the make and model.

Stack relays are typically mounted in the flue pipe, although you may occasionally find one mounted directly into the flue collector or heat exchanger.

Flame detection

Stack relays employ a bi-metal heat-sensing element for flame detection. This heat-sensing element MUST be in the path of the combustion gases, between the

heating unit and the draft regulator. It should be centered in the flue pipe at a point where it will be exposed to flue gases between 300° and 1000°F. When the burner operates, heat rises and passes over the bi-metal element, which expands and moves a shaft. This closes contacts that enable the burner to continue operating. If the bi-metal is not sufficiently heated, a built-in safety switch shuts the burner off in approximately 75 to 120 seconds and it cannot be started again until the safety switch cools down and is manually reset.

Wiring

- The power or "hot" lead from the limit control is connected to Terminal 1.

- All neutrals are connected to Terminal 2.

- One wire from the burner motor and one from the oil valve, if used, are connected to Terminal 3.

- If the unit operates as interrupted duty ignition, one wire from the trans-former is connected to Terminal 4.

- For intermittent duty ignition, connect the transformer lead to Terminal 3 along with the burner motor lead, leaving terminal 4 empty

- If the control has a green terminal, it should be connected to ground. Figure 11-5.

Thermostat connections

If the control has two low voltage terminals for the thermostat connection, one of the thermostat wires connects to each.

If the control has three low voltage terminals and the system has a two-wire thermostat, it is connected to the W and B terminals. If a 3-wire heat-only thermostat

Figure 11-5: Wiring diagram for RA117A with 24v 3-wire thermostat

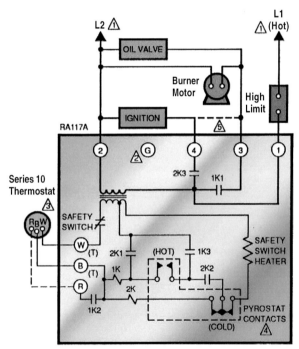

△ Power Supply, Provide Disconnect Means and Overload Protection as Required

△2 Use Green Terminal to Connect Control Case to Ground

△3 If Using a Two-Wire Thermostat, Tape Loose Ends of Red Wire (If Necessary)

△4 Contacts Break in Sequence on Temperature Rise

△5 To Replace an Intermittent Ignition Device, Connect Ignition Leadwire to Terminal 3, Instead of Terminal 4

is used, connect the red wire to Terminal R, white wire to W and black wire to B.

Operation of a stack relay

If all components are functioning properly, the control is in standby mode until:

• Line voltage is applied through the limit control to Terminal 1, AND a call for heat from the thermostat completes the circuit between W and B, or T-T.

• Then Terminal 4 will be powered and Terminal 3 will be powered a split second later.

• The transformer will generate ignition through the electrodes.

• The motor will turn the fuel pump and burner fan. If there's a delayed oil valve installed, it will open based on its delay timing.

• Once flame is established and heated flue gases pass over and expand the bi-metal detector element, the safety switch heater will be de-energized, preventing the unit from shutting off on safety.

• The ignition circuit will be de-energized, shutting off the transformer if the unit operates on interrupted ignition.

• The oilburner will then continue to run until either the thermostat is satisfied, opening the low voltage circuit, or the limit control is satisfied, opening the line voltage circuit. *Either* of these actions causes the primary control to cut power to Terminals 3 and 4, safely shutting down the oilburner. The primary control then returns to standby mode.

Safety check

It is important to check the safety timing of primary controls every time you perform a service call. To check the safety timing:

• Turn off the service switch at the unit.

• Remove the stack switch from the flue pipe or block the flow of oil by installing your pressure gauge in the nozzle port.

• Turn on the service switch.

• Make sure that both the line and low voltage circuits are complete.

• The control should energize and shut off on safety in approximately 75 seconds.

• If the control goes off on safety within 120 seconds, clean the bi-metal and reinstall it.

• If the control does not go off on safety, replace it and be sure to check the timing on the new control.

Cad cell primary controls

Any system still operating with a stack relay is probably a good candidate for replacement with a high-efficiency oilheat system.

While the basic functions of cad cell primary controls are the same as those of stack relays, they feature a much quicker reaction time through visual, as opposed to thermal, flame detection.

The cad cell primary control circuit is made up of two components: the flame detector and the primary control.

Flame detection

The flame detector consists of a cad cell, a holder to secure it in place, and a wiring harness to connect it to the primary control. The detector is installed in the air tube of the oilburner where it can view the flame.

> *Did you know?*
> Cad cell resistance looking into an inactive chamber should be at least 50,000 ohms.

> *Did you know?* Cad cell primary controls, also called "cad cell relays," were introduced in the early 1970's. Modern oilheat systems operate more cleanly, more efficiently and much more economically than systems designed when stack relays were the standard.

Did you know? The burner manufacturer determines the location of the cad cell; if for some reason an alternate location must be used, make sure that:

- The cell has a clear view of the flame

- Ambient light does not reach the cell

- Ambient temperature is below the cell's rating (approx 140°F, see specs)

- Movement, shielding or radiation of metal surfaces near the cell does not affect cell function.

- Avoid extreme changes in flame light reaching the CAD cell, as pass/fail thresholds in the control may not function properly.

The cad cell is a ceramic disc coated with cadmium sulfide and overlaid with a conductive grid. Electrodes attached to the ceramic disc transmit an electrical signal to the primary control. In darkness, cadmium sulfide has a very high resistance to the passage of electrical current. As the cell is exposed to light, its resistance decreases and current is allowed to pass.

For a cad cell relay to start the burner, the flame detector must sense the absence of flame and resist the passage of current. Once the burner starts and flame is established, the cell senses light, resistance drops, current passes through the circuit and the burner continues to run.

If the cad cell does not sense enough light when the burner starts, the control will shut off on safety. It can not be started again until the safety switch cools off and is manually reset. Note that electronic safety switches do not have to cool down before resetting. If

Cad cells can only see yellow and white flames. This is why they are not used on gas controls. New low NOx oil burners burn with a transparent to blue flame and biofuels' flames are also more blue. Manufacturers are using infrared or ultraviolet detectors to see these new flames.

the flame is lost *during* the running cycle, very early model controls will shut the system down after the safety timing (15 to 45 seconds) is reached; later models will make one attempt to restart. Recycle type controls will shut down for 1 minute, then allow startup, for any number of startup attempts.

Wiring

As with stack mounted primary controls, the major manufacturers adopted uniform standards regarding wiring connections for first generation cad cell primary controls.

In place of the numbered screw terminals on stack relays, cad cell relays have color-coded wire leads pre-attached to the solid-state circuitry. These wire leads from the control are connected to the wiring for the system components with wire nuts.

The hot wire from the limit control is connected to the black wire of the cad cell relay. Some postpurge controls have line voltage connected to a red/white wire.

The hot wire of the burner motor, igniter and oil valve are connected to the orange wire. Postpurge controls have the valve connected to the violet wire.

The white wire is connected to the neutral lead along with the neutrals from the burner components.

The low voltage side of cad cell relays typically has two terminals labeled T-T, which can be connected to the thermostat.

The cad cell flame detector leads are connected to the F-F terminals.
Figure 11-6.

Operation

The most common first generation cad cell primary controls you are likely to come across in the field are the Honeywell

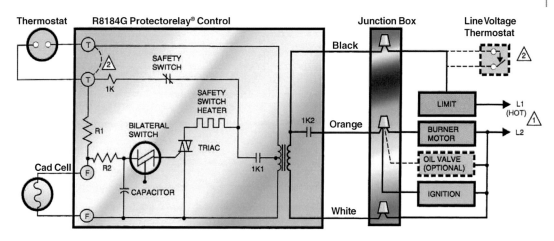

Figure 11-6:
Cad cell
primary control

⚠ 1 Power Supply, Provide Disconnect Means
and Overload Protection as Required

⚠ 2 To Use R8184 with Line Voltage Controller, Jumper T-T Terminals and
Connect Line Voltage Thermostat in Series with Limit Controller.

R8184G or the White Rogers 668. They both feature intermittent duty ignition and operate as follows:

If all components are functioning properly, the control is in stand-by mode until:

• Power is applied through the limit control to the black wire, AND a call for heat from the thermostat completes the circuit between T and T. Then, assuming that the cad cell does NOT sense light…

• The control is energized and the orange wire is powered.

• The igniter generates ignition through the electrodes and the motor turns the fuel unit and burner fan. If there is an oil valve installed, it opens based on its delay timing.

• Flame is established and the cad cell resistance decreases to fewer than 1600 ohms, de-energizing the safety switch heater and preventing the unit from shutting off on safety.

• As long as the cad cell senses flame, the oilburner continues to run until either the thermostat or limit control is satisfied.

Safety check

To check the safety:

1. Turn off the power at the service switch.

2. Install a 1,000 ohm resistor across the F-F terminals to reduce resistance and simulate flame. It is OK to leave the cad cell leads hooked up.

3. Turn on the service switch and make sure that both the line and low voltage circuits are complete.

4. The control should NOT energize, because the resistor connected to the F-F terminals simulates a fire in the chamber. If it does energize, replace the control.

If it does not …

1. Turn off the service switch and remove the resistor.

2. Disconnect one lead from the F-F terminals.

3. Turn on the electrical switch. The control should energize and the burner should lock out based on safety switch timing (15 – 45 seconds.) If the control

does *not* go off on safety, replace it and be sure to check the timing on the new control.

4. If the control does go off on safety, reconnect the lead to the F terminal and press the reset button. The safety is working properly.

Troubleshooting tips

If the oilburner does not start:

Verify that electrical switches are in the 'ON' position and that the thermostat is set

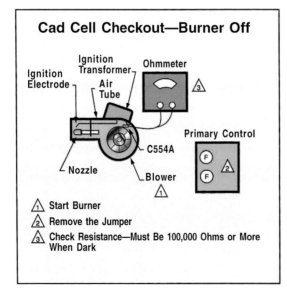

Cad Cell Checkout—Burner On

Ignition Electrode
Air Tube
C554A
Ohmmeter △4
Light Cell Resistance Under 1600 ohms
Primary Control
△2
Nozzle
△1
Blower
F
F
△3

△1 Remove Cad Cell Leadwires From the Primary Control
△2 Start Burner
△3 Jumper (F) (F) Terminals—Allows Burner to Run
△4 Connect Ohmmeter to Cad Cell Leadwires—Must Read Less Than 1600 Ohms

Cad Cell Checkout—Burner Off

Ignition Electrode
Ignition Transformer
Air Tube
Ohmmeter
△3
C554A
Primary Control
F
F
△2
Nozzle
Blower
△1

△1 Start Burner
△2 Remove the Jumper
△3 Check Resistance—Must Be 100,000 Ohms or More When Dark

above room temperature. Be sure that there is not a fire burning in the unit.

Remove the primary control's cover and visually check to see if the spring-loaded mechanism has locked off on safety.

If the primary control is NOT off on safety, check for proper voltage coming from the limit control.

If there is sufficient line voltage, remove one lead from the F-F terminals. If the burner starts, the problem is in the cad cell sensor or wires. The cell may be sensing light or the wires may have been shorted.

If the burner does not start, disconnect all the thermostat leads and install a jumper. If the burner starts, the problem is in the thermostat or its wiring.

Did you know? Leaving the thermostat wiring connected to the control while testing may harm today's computerized thermostats.

If the primary *is* off on safety, check the combustion chamber to be sure the unit is not saturated with oil. If the chamber contains excess oil, follow your company's procedures to eliminate the oil. **Never attempt to fire an oilburner into a saturated chamber!**

If the chamber is free of excess oil, press the reset button.

If the primary control energizes but the burner motor does not turn—shut off the service switch and check the electrical connections and the burner motor reset button.

If the burner runs and flame is established but the control shuts off on safety, disconnect the cad cell leads, press the reset and, before the unit shuts off on safety again, place a 1000-ohm resistor across the F-F terminals. If the burner continues to operate with the

Burner Locks Out On Safety

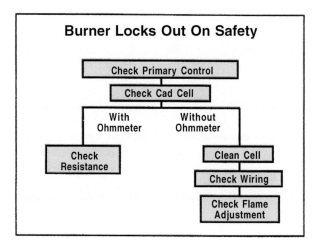

Check Primary Control
Check Cad Cell

With Ohmmeter — Without Ohmmeter

Check Resistance

Clean Cell
Check Wiring
Check Flame Adjustment

Checking Cad Cell and Primary

Ignition Electrode
Air Tube
Ohmmeter
④
Nozzle
Primary Control
F F ③
Blower ②

① Remove Lead Wires From Primary Control
② Start Burner
③ Jumper F-F (With 1500 Resistor)
   Control Locks Out—Replace—
   Burner Runs—Trouble Is Cad Cell
④ Check Resistance—
   Infinite—Open Circuit (Cell Defective or Not Seated)
   Greater Than 1600 Ohms—Cell Dirty
   or Not Sighting Properly

resistor in place, the cad cell relay is operating as designed and the problem is with the cad cell flame detector.

With the unit operating, connect the cad cell leads to your ohmmeter. A reading of zero ohms indicates a short circuit. Check for pinched or shorted cad cell wires.

If the resistance is infinite, check for broken cad cell wires or a loose or defective cell.

On most properly adjusted burners, the reading will be 400 ohms or less. Some burners with large static plates or small openings in the retention head operate in the 400-800 ohm range. Very few burners operate with resistance over 800 ohms.

If the reading is greater than 1600 ohms, there is a serious problem with the fire, the cad cell eye, its holder, its leads or its alignment. Remember the cad cell needs to have a good view through the air tube to the fire.

If the eye is coated with soot, it will not be able to "see" the flame. Clean the eye and continue your trouble-shooting to find out why the eye is dirty.

Cad Cell Check List

Ohmmeter Reading	Cause	Action
0 ohms	Short circuit	Check for pinched cad cell leadwires
Less than 1660 ohms but not zero	Cad cell and application are working correctly	None
Over 1600 ohms but not infinite	Dirty or defective cell, improper sighting or improper air adjustment	1. Clean cell face, recheck 2. Check flame sighting 3. Replace cell, recheck 4. Adjust air band to get good reading
Infinite resistance	Open circuit	Check for improper wiring, loose cell in holder or defective cell

Second generation cad cell primary controls

Second generation cad cell primary controls have the same basic features as first generation controls, but steady advances in technology have led to a number of improvements.

For example, second generation cad cell primary controls have electronic reset mechanisms which are *not* spring loaded. The reset button on these controls does not "pop-up" when the unit shuts off on safety, and the reset doesn't have a thermal component, so there's no cooling time required before the control can be reset. To bring the control out of safety lockout, you simply depress the reset button for three seconds.

Typical second generation cad cell primary controls include:

Safety monitoring circuit

This circuit monitors the contacts of two *separate, redundant motor* relays. Safety lockout occurs if the contacts of either motor relay are found closed when they should be open, thus ensuring shutdown even if one motor relay fails.

Interrupted duty ignition

These controls have an additional wire that is connected to the transformer or igniter. With interrupted duty ignition:

- Electrodes and igniters/transformers last longer

- Electrical consumption, operational noise and NOx emissions are reduced

- Combustion problems leading to dirty boilers and running saturations are minimized

Recycle-on-flame-failure

Recycle-on-Flame-Failure means that instead of shutting off on safety on loss of flame during the run cycle, the burner will shut off within approximately 1.5 seconds. After a wait of 60-90 seconds, the control will attempt to restart the oilburner.

Operation

Second generation cad cell primary controls operate similarly to first generation controls.

If all components are functioning properly, the control is in stand-by mode until—

- Power is applied through the limit control to the black wire, AND the circuit between T and T is closed.

Then assuming that the cad cell does NOT sense light—

- The control is energized and the orange and blue wires are powered.

- The ignition and motor start.

- After the cad cell senses flame, the ignition stays on for another 10 seconds, then shuts off.

As long as the cad cell senses flame, the oilburner continues to run until the thermostat or limit control is satisfied.

If the control does not sense flame within the control's safety timing, lockout occurs. Pressing the reset button for 3 seconds resets the control.

Third generation cad cell primary controls

Third generation primary controls

include a microprocessor in the printed circuit boards. They feature interrupted duty ignition, fifteen-second safety timing and include several new features.

"Valve-delay-on" technology—depending on the manufacturer, this feature may be referred to as "valve-on-delay," "delayed-valve-on," or other similar wording. Through the use of an oil valve, "valve-delay-on" allows the burner motor to get up to speed delivering full flow from the fuel unit and full airflow from the fan before oil flows from the nozzle. This optimizes fuel/air mixing at start up resulting in a significant reduction of soot build-up and increased efficiency.

"Motor-delay-off" technology—may also be referred to as "burner-motor-off-delay," or other similar wording. This feature allows the motor/fan combination to continue delivering full air flow for a period of time after the oil flow through the nozzle has been cut off by an oil valve, resulting in cleaner shut downs.

Did you know? Many people in our industry refer to "valve-delay-on" as "pre-purge" and "motor-delay off" "post purge." This is not correct. The primary controls' operations do not fit the Underwriters' Laboratories (UL) definition of pre- and post-purge.

Dry alarm contacts—These auxiliary electrical contacts close when the control goes into lock out or latch up. Through various added controls (i.e. an auto dialer) can alert the homeowner, alarm company,

and/or service company of the situation.

Limited reset—This feature protects against the repeated pressing of the reset button which floods the chamber with oil.

If the control goes into lockout three times during a single call for heat, it goes into a restricted mode, commonly called "latch up." The control can be reset only twice, regardless of the number of times the reset button is pressed. Instructions for removing these controls from latch-up are printed on the underside of the control where the customer cannot see them.

Limited recycle—This feature limits the number of times the control will attempt to restart if the flame is repeatedly established and then lost, preventing excessive sooting from repeated combustion failure.

Diagnostic LEDs—These small, low-power lights provide a significant amount of information to help the service technician quickly and accurately diagnose the situation.

Conclusion

Primary controls have evolved from simple stack switches to microprocessor based controls that offer greater reliability, safety and efficiency. Control manufacturers continue to develop new products with advanced features that will make the controls in use today seem as obsolete as thermo-mechanical controls are now.

As an oilheat service technician it's important for you to be aware of these new controls so that you can continue to offer professional service to your customers.

Specific Microprocessor-Based Primary Controls
The following section is intended strictly as an overview. While other manufacturers may have similar controls, these are the units that you are most likely to encounter. Also, remember that manufacturers periodically add improvements and additional features to their controls.
It is critical to consult product specific literature to verify information regarding individual controls, even if they are familiar to you.

Carlin

• Model numbers can be found just above the thermostat and flame detector terminals.

• Wiring diagrams are to the left, and the controls timings are listed above the model number.

• For example, this xxx has an xx-second "trial for ignition" an xx-second recycle time, an x second "valve delay on," an xx-second "trial for ignition," and an xx-second "motor-delay-off."

• There may also be a revision designation printed on the lower right side of the label.

Carlin's microprocessor based controls, models 50200 and 60200 feature:

Limited reset—also known as "Service-man Reset Protection." Once these controls go into lockout three consecutive times without establishing flame, the control will go into latch-up. In order to release them from latch-up, depress and hold the reset button. After 10 seconds, the two diagnostic lights will blink alternately. After another 20 seconds, the lights will stop blinking. Release the button to complete the reset procedure.

Recycle-on-flame-failure—in the event of flame loss during the run cycle, within approximately two seconds the 50200 will

Model 50200

shut the burner off and the 60200 will turn off power to the oil valve and complete a "motor-delay-off" cycle. After a wait of 60-90 seconds, the red LED light will flash for 65 seconds, then the control will attempt to restart the oilburner.

If flame is established during the "trial for ignition" period, the burner will resume normal operation. If flame is not established in the "trial for ignition" period—the control will go into lockout.

Diagnostic LEDs—these primary controls have two diagnostic LEDs: one red and one amber.

• Amber-on signals that the control is in self-test.

• Red-on indicates that the control is in lockout

• Amber *and* red-on indicates that the control has locked out three times during a single call for heat and is in latch-up.

• Red flashing indicates that flame has been lost during a run cycle, after trial for ignition.

• Amber blinking-off every 3 to 4 seconds while the control is in the standby mode indicates that the cad cell is sensing light, or a diagnostic fault which disallows startup.

Wiring

Thermostat and cad cell leads connect to the appropriate terminals.

The 50200 is connected in the same way as earlier interrupted-ignition cad cell relays:

- The black wire connects to the limit control

- The white wire connects to all neutrals

- The blue wire connects to the igniter or transformer

- The orange wire connects to the burner motor

The 60200 control has both "valve-delay-on" and "motor-delay-off" features, so the wiring is slightly more complicated:

- The black wire connects to the limit control

- The white wire connects to all neutrals

- The blue wire connects to the igniter or transformer

- The orange wire connects to the burner motor

- The violet wire connects to the oil valve

- The red wire with white tracer (stripe) connects to constant power

Operation
The Carlin 60200 operates as follows:

Each time power is applied to the red wire with white tracer, the control performs a boot up test to verify internal operation.

Model 60200

After about 4 seconds, the amber LED comes on. The test continues for 6 more seconds and, if successful, the amber light turns off. If the test is not successful, the control repeats the test until successful.

When a call for heat is initiated, the amber LED turns on and there is a 3 to 4 second delay while the control performs a safe start check. If no flame is sensed and all internal conditions are correct, the LED turns off and the control enters "valve-delay-on" mode. The ignition is powered and one second later, the motor is powered.

After completion of the "valve-delay-on" cycle, the control goes into "trial for ignition." The oil valve is powered and opens. Flame should be established within the "trial for ignition" period of 15 seconds. If the flame is not sensed by the end of "trial for ignition," the control goes into lockout, the red LED comes on and the dry alarm contacts close. The control must be manually reset by pushing the reset button for one second and releasing.

Once the flame is established, the ignition remains on for a short time to ensure flame stability and then shuts off.

The burner will then run until the call for heat is satisfied, at which time the power to the oil valve will shut off. The motor will continue to operate for the specified "motor-delay-off" period. Once that cycle is completed, the control returns to standby mode.

Specific Microprocessor-Based Primary Controls
The following section is intended strictly as an overview. While other manufacturers may have similar controls, these are the units that you are most likely to encounter. Also, remember that manufacturers periodically add improvements and additional features to their controls.
It is critical to consult product specific literature to verify information regarding individual controls, even if they are familiar to you.

Riello primary controls

Riello primary controls are designed exclusively for use on Riello burners.

The Riello primary control, in combination with the coil of the oil valve and a cad cell, monitors and controls all functions of the burner. An auxiliary tap on the motor windings provides a 46-volt AC power supply to operate the control. The oil valve provides the starting and running circuits for the primary control through a logic board and safety lockout switch. The ignition transformer is integrated into the primary control and provides interrupted-duty ignition.

There are no thermostat terminals on current Riello primary controls. An additional device, such as a switching relay, must be used for low voltage thermostat connections.

The Riello control's safety switch is equipped with a contact allowing remote sensing of burner safety lockout. Should burner lockout occur, 120 Volts AC is supplied to sub-base Terminal 4 to activate any connected remote alarm systems.

Wiring

• All wiring is connected through the control's sub-base terminals.

• A wiring diagram is supplied with each control and serves as an insulator on the underside of the control. This diagram should always be left in place to protect the printed circuit board of the control.

• When working on these controls, most experienced Service Technicians refer to Riello's plastic laminated troubleshooting card or the troubleshooting guide provided in the training manual.

Operation

If all components are functioning properly, the control is in standby mode until 120 volts is supplied through the limit control to Terminal 5. Then assuming that the cad cell does NOT sense light:

• The control is energized and Terminal 6 is powered, providing 120 Volts AC to the motor.

• The auxiliary winding tap provides 46 Volts AC to power the control.

• The motor starts and establishes a 10-second "valve-delay-on."

• The oil valve opens, supplying oil to the nozzle line, and at the same time the ignition is powered.

• Once the cad cell senses flame, the ignition circuit is opened and the spark shuts off.

• As long as the cad cell senses flame, the oilburner continues to run until the demand for heat is satisfied.

• If the control does not sense flame

within approximately 5 seconds after "valve delay-on," the control shuts the burner "off on safety."

• If the cad cell loses sight of the flame at any time during the firing cycle, the control immediately closes the oil valve to prevent oil flow, then goes back into "valve-delay-on" mode and makes one attempt to relight.

Safety check
• Turn off the service switch

• Remove the control box from the sub-base

• Remove the cad cell from the control box

• Replace the control box on the sub-base

• Turn on the service switch and make sure that the line voltage circuit is complete

The control should energize and the burner should "go off on safety" approximately 5 seconds after the "valve-delay-on" cycle. If the control does NOT "go off on safety", replace it and be sure to check the timing on the new control.

Troubleshooting tips
In general, it is good practice to check that the control box spades and sub-base terminals are making good contact, and to verify that there is between 42 and 52 Volts AC between terminals 3 and 7 while the motor is running.

If the burner stays in "valve-delay-on," check for the following before you con-

demn the control:

• Cad cell faulty or sensing light before "trial for ignition."

• Coil wires are reversed on Terminals 1 and 2 or on Terminals 1 and 8.

• Open coil circuit, Terminals 2 and 8. To check this, connect your ohmmeter between terminals 2 and 8; if the coil circuit is open, the reading will be 0 ohms.

• Open coil circuit, Terminals 1 and 2. Reading should be 1235 ohms or less.

• Note—this is for the 530 SE primary control only. An open coil circuit on Terminal 1 will cause the 483 SE control to lock out.

• Insufficient voltage between Terminals 3 and 7. It should read 42 to 52 Volts AC. If you have lower voltage, check the incoming supply. If there is proper incoming voltage, above 102 Volts AC, change the burner motor.

If a burner with a 530 SE control continues to purge and light off with immediate flame dropout, or a burner with a 483 SE control cycles on and off in quick succession, check the following:

• The metal yoke for the coil may be missing or improperly installed.

• Coil wires 2 and 8 may be reversed.

• There may be low resistance on the coil holding circuit, terminals 1 & 2. Resistance should be 1350 ohms, plus or minus 10%. If the resistance is low, change the coil.

The following pages show reference guides for the Riello primary control.

RIELLO BURNERS
TROUBLESHOOTING CHART
40-SERIES OIL BURNERS
530SE/C Control Box

Thermostat closed (Calling for heat) and Operating limits closed

Reset control box (Press red button)

Burner starts

Burner does not start

Check power supply at sub-base (between L & N) to ensure voltage within
range of 102Vac — 132Vac

Burner remains in pre-purge

First check if cad cell may be sensing light during pre-purge by removing cad
cell and checking resistance value — Less than 40,000 ohms with light or
more than 150,000 ohms without light (Alternative is to remove cad cell
and reset burner — If burner locks out, cad cell should be replaced)
Check visually to ensure good contact between control box and sub-base
Then check sub-base for mis-wired terminals
Then check for "open" circuit between terminals 2 & 8 — If "open" circuit found
the coil should be replaced
Then check to ensure voltage between terminals 3 & 7 within range of
39Vac — 51Vac
If the condition persists, the control box is likely faulty and should be replaced

No voltage

First check system fuse and ensure service switch is ON
Then check to ensure all control limits are closed
Then check thermostat or 24V relay for 0Vac

Voltage within range

First turn off power supply
Then place a jumper between sub-base terminals 5 & 6
Then turn ON power supply

Burner continues to cycle through pre-purge and ignition with immediate flame dropout

First check burner settings for compliance with specifications
Then check coil for missing metal yoke/bracket
Then check cad cell by removing cad cell and checking resistance value —
Less than 40,000 ohms with light or more than 150,000 ohms without light
(Alternative is to remove cad cell and reset burner — If burner locks out
the cad cell should be replaced)
Then check sub-base for mis-wired terminals
Then check to ensure resistance of coil on terminals 1 & 2 within range of
1215 ohms — 1485 ohms

Then check pump valve stem condition by removing valve stem and ensuring piston/plunger operates freely — If not operating properly the valve stem should be replaced
If the condition persists, the control box is likely faulty and should be replaced

Motor runs

First check to ensure voltage between terminals 3 & 7 within range of 39Vac — 51Vac
Check visually to ensure good contact between control box and sub-base
If the condition persists, the control box is likely faulty and should be replaced
First check electrical connections
Then check for and replace seized pump/motor
Then check for defective (PSC) motor capacitor — If motor hums the capacitor should be replaced
Then wait until motor cools and reset control box
If the condition persists, the motor likely shut down on a thermal overload and should be replaced

Motor does not run

Burner locks out after trial for ignition

First check oil supply — For possible empty tank, closed valve, dirty filter, damaged supply lines, etc.
Then check coil for missing metal yoke/bracket
Then check if cad cell fails to sense flame during ignition by removing cad cell and checking resistance value — Less than 40,000 ohms with light or more than 150,000 ohms without light (Alternative is to remove cad cell and reset burner — If burner locks out, cad cell should be replaced)
Then check to ensure pump vacuum is within range of 0 — 11" Hg
Then check to ensure oil pressure is within appropriate ranges of 20 — 80 psi in pre-purge mode and 120 — 200 psi in firing mode
Then check connection, settings and condition of ignition electrodes — Clean or replace if necessary
Then check breech or overfire draft — Reduce excessive draft conditions
Then check nozzle and pump strainer and replace if necessary
Then check pump valve stem condition by removing valve stem and ensuring piston/ plunger operates freely — Replace if not operating freely
Then check to ensure resistance of coil on terminals 2 & 8 is within range of 1.3 ohm ± 10%
Then check to ensure pump drive key is in place and in good condition
If the condition persists, the control box is likely faulty and should be replaced

Specific Microprocessor-Based Primary Controls
The following section is intended strictly as an overview. While other manufacturers may have similar controls, these are the units that you are most likely to encounter. Also, remember that manufacturers periodically add improvements and additional features to their controls.
It is critical to consult product specific literature to verify information regarding individual controls, even if they are familiar to you.

The Honeywell R7184

Honeywell's controls differ from Carlin's. It is also extremely important to note that some Honeywell models utilize different wire color-coding.

Standard features of the Honeywell R7184 include:

Limited reset—This control can be reset only two times before it goes into "restricted lockout," or latch-up mode. The reset count returns to zero each time a call for heat is successfully completed. To reset the control from latch-up, press and hold the reset button. The LED will go out. Continue holding the button for approximately 30 to 45 seconds until the light comes on again.

Limited recycle—Should the flame be lost while the burner is firing, the control shuts down the burner, enters a 60 second recycle delay and then attempts a restart. During the recycle delay, the LED will flash slowly—two seconds on, two seconds off. Do not confuse this with the burner being "in lockout." If the flame is lost three consecutive times without successfully satisfying a call for heat, the control goes into lockout and must be reset manually.

Diagnostic LED—The diagnostic LED has four states:
- On—flame present

- Off—no flame

- 2 seconds on, 2 seconds off—recycle

- 1/2 second on, 1/2 second off—lockout <u>and</u> latch-up.

The LED can also be used to check cad cell resistance. When the burner is running after the ignition has turned off, quickly press and release the reset button. Hold it for only a half-second or less. The LED will flash from one to four times depending on the cad cell resistance:

- If the light flashes once—cad cell resistance is normal: 0-400 ohms

- Two flashes means resistance is normal: 400–800 ohms

- Three flashes is normal: 800–1600 ohms

- Four flashes indicate limited resistance of more than 1600 ohms

- Lockout can occur above 4000 ohms.

Pump priming cycle—To facilitate priming, the control can be placed in a purge routine by pressing and quickly releasing the reset button while the ignition is on. If the control has not locked out since its last complete heating cycle, the lockout timing will be extended for up to 4 minutes and the ignition will operate in the intermittent mode for this cycle only.

Communications port—Many Honeywell residential combustion controls have a communications port that allows for data interchange between the control and other products, such as diagnostic tools, modems, zoning systems, and home automation.

Wiring the Honeywell R7184

Currently there are four models of the R7184: A, B, P and U. On each model, the thermostat leads and cad cell leads connect to the appropriate terminals.

R7184A

- The black wire connects to the limit control

- The white wire connects to all neutrals

- The blue wire connects to the igniter or transformer

- The orange wire connects to the burner motor

R7184B

The B model has a 15-second "valve-on delay" feature requiring the installation of an oil valve. This control has an added violet wire that connects to that valve. The other wire from the valve is connected to the neutrals. All other wiring is consistent with the A model.

R7184P

The P model has both a fixed 15-second "valve-on delay" and a "burner motor-off-delay" feature which may be field selected to 30 seconds, 2 minutes, 4 minutes or 8 minutes or fixed at 15 seconds. In addition to the violet wire for "valve on delay," there is a red wire that connects to the limit control, while the black wire connects to constant power to achieve the "burner motor-off delay" feature. All other wiring is consistent with the B model.

R7184U

The U model has all of the features of the P models with selectable on and off delays, plus low voltage dry alarm contacts that are located above the thermostat terminals. On the U model you have the ability to adjust dip switches that enable or disable both the valve on delay and the "burner motor-off delay." This makes the U model control the same as the A control. This way you only need to stock one control on your truck. All other wiring is consistent with the P model.

Model designations and revisions

Honeywell puts the model designations and revision information for the R7184 next to the control part number and/or prints it on the side of the control. Revisions are numerical and indicate which improvements or changes are included in the particular control. For example, Series 1 controls have different cad cell indicator ranges; Revision 2 changed the pump priming cycle from 45 seconds to 4 minutes and added the limited recycle. Some

Honeywell—continued

revisions have wires, while others have spade connectors.

Series 4 and later controls have added safety features. If a Series 4 control detects flame eight seconds into "valve on delay" or 30 seconds into "burner motor-off-delay," the control will go into lock out. This is to prevent poor starts and shut-downs due to bad oil valves. This means that these controls CANNOT be operated without an oil valve. If the fuel unit has to be replaced, you MUST use one with either an integral or external oil valve. It also means that if you are replacing an earlier control with a Series 4 or later control, you cannot simply "cap off" the violet and/or black wires as you could with earlier revisions. There is also a series 5 control. See Beckett's website for details.

Sequence of operation

Currently, the most sophisticated Honeywell R7184 is the U model. Let's take a look at how it operates.

Standby: When a call for heat is initiated, there is a 2 to 6 second delay while the control performs a safe start check. If no flame is sensed and all internal conditions are correct, the control enters "valve on delay" mode—and the ignition and motor are powered for 15 seconds.

Trail for ignition: Then the control goes into "trial for ignition." The oil valve is powered and opens. Flame should be established within the "trial for ignition" timing of 15 or 30 seconds. If no flame is sensed by the end of "trial for ignition," the control goes into lockout and must be manually reset. The dry alarm contacts close and complete the circuit to activate any remote alarm that is connected.

Carryover: Once the flame is established, the ignition remains on for 10 seconds to ensure flame stability, then shuts off. The burner will then run until the call for heat is satisfied, at which time the power to the oil valve will shut down.

Burner motor off delay: The motor will continue to operate from 30 seconds to 8 minutes depending on how the dip switches are set. Once this "burner motor-off delay" cycle has been completed, the control returns to standby mode.

Chapter **12**

LIMIT CONTROLS & THERMOSTATS

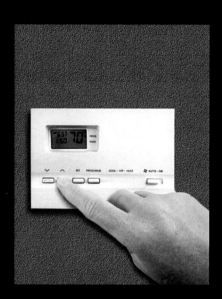

IN THIS CHAPTER

- **The oil-fired heating system control circuit**

- **Thermostats, principles and design, low voltage and line voltage types and heat anticipators**

- **Limit controls, warm air fan limits and electronic fan timer center, steam pressure controls and low-water cutoffs, as well as hot water heating aquastats**

Chapter 12

Limit Controls
and Thermostats

There are a large variety of limit controls, thermostats, and switching relays used in oil-fired heating systems. At first glance, it can be confusing. Remember, these devices are just switches that turn things on and off.

Some of these switches are turned on and off by the warping or flexing action of bimetal blades. Some use magnets and springs. Some are controlled by a fluid that expands and contracts quickly. Some are line voltage and some are low voltage. Some need transformers to change the voltage so that low voltage switches can control line voltage loads. Some controls now use solid-state microprocessors and other electronic devices.

No matter what they look like, limit controls are just switches. You may want to review the section on switches in the basic electricity chapter before you go any further.

Electrical control circuit

The hot (L1) electric power wire for the basic oilburner circuit begins at the service panel fuse, or circuit breaker, travels to the main switch, then to a junction box that is usually located on the ceiling near the burner. Many states and local codes require a thermal or Firomatic® switch at this junction box. From the junction box, the hot line (which is a black wire) runs to the serviceman's switch, through the high limit

Figure 12-1: Basic oil burner control circuit

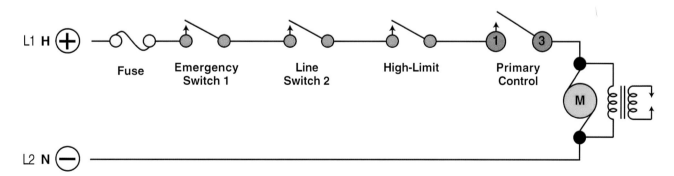

**Basic Oilburner Circuit Showing
Switches, Motor, and Ignition Transformer**

control and then to terminal #1 or the black lead wire of the primary control. From the primary control, wires are connected to the oilburner motor and ignition transformer. All wires up to this point carry 120 volt line voltage.

The neutral white (L2) wire of the control circuit also starts at the main entrance service panel, and passes to terminal #2 or the white lead of the primary control. On a modern circuit, there should never be any switches or fuses in the neutral side of the circuit. Older homes with knob and tubing wiring often have fuses on both the hot side and the neutral side of the circuit. And sometimes switches, limits, and fuses are put on both sides by mistake. Never assume anything when it comes to electricity. Always test!

Also, before doing any wiring, check with the local fire marshal or other authority to make sure that your installation complies with all local requirements. In some areas, only licensed electricians are allowed to install line voltage wiring.

The low voltage (24 volt) side of the oilburner control circuit usually starts at the step down transformer in the primary control. The low voltage circuit turns the burner, circulator, or blower on and off, and opens and closes valves in response to temperature changes in the heated space and the appliance.

See Figures 12-1 and 12-2.

Burner switch

The burner switch is used to shut off the burner in an emergency or as a convenience switch when servicing the oilburner. There

Figure 12-2:
Circuit wiring

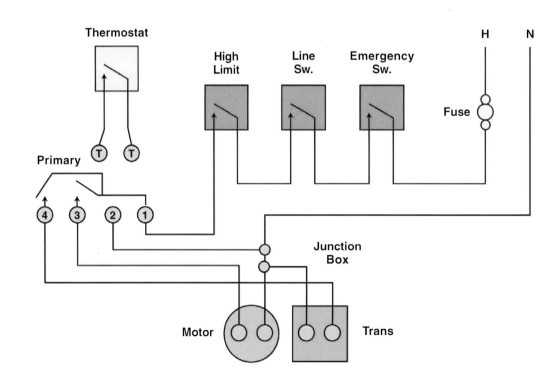

are usually two disconnect switches. The first is called a customer or emergency switch and it is normally located at the head of the basement stairs or at the entrance to the heater room. The second switch is a serviceman's switch and may include a fuse. This switch is located on or near the furnace or boiler.

Thermostats

Principles and design

A thermostat is a mechanical or electronic switch that automatically opens or closes a circuit as room temperature changes. The thermostat's purpose is to start the burner and/or circulator or blower when the temperature is below the established setting, and to shut them off when the heat demand is satisfied. Thermostats must be extremely sensitive to temperature changes. In older thermostats, a bimetal element warps or unwinds in response to temperature change to open or close a switch. In the solid-state thermostat, the room temperature changes the resistance of an electronic device that will act in various methods to open and close circuits.

The majority of thermostats installed in the field still use a bimetal element and mercury switch to function. The following text covers this type of thermostat, Figure 12-3 shows the most common type in use. The replacements are mostly electronic and will be discussed later.

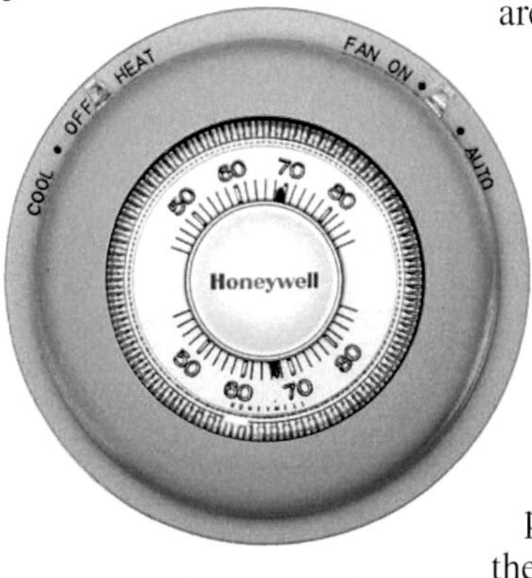

The bimetallic element comprises two dissimilar metal strips, bonded together, which expand or contract with a change in temperature at different rates of speed. This difference in expansion

Figure 12-3

rate will cause the bonded bimetallic element to bend or warp with temperature changes. By bending or moving when heat is applied to it or taken away, it creates a mechanical force that flips a mercury switch to make or break a pair of switch contacts. Making or breaking a contact means closing or opening a circuit. Remember, as with all mercury switches, such thermostats must be installed level. Figure 12-4 shows how to level the T87 thermostat.

3 wire thermostats vs. 2 wire thermostats

Very old style thermostats needed three wires to operate. When replacing an old three wire thermostat with a new two wire, eliminate the red wire. Today there are some three wire thermostats that operate some zone valve motors and dampers. A circuit is necessary to drive the valve or damper open and another circuit must drive it closed. The switching action of these thermostats is single pole, double throw as opposed to a single pole, single throw switch for the two wire circuits. Thermostats of this type are never connected to primary controls.

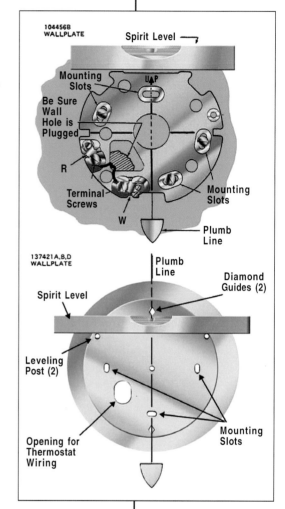

Figure 12-4:
T-87 thermostat

Low voltage and line voltage thermostats

In some older systems, line voltage thermostats were used to directly control the circulator without the use of a switching relay. Line voltage thermostats are not as sensitive as low voltage types and this often leads to wide fluctuations in the room temperature. If open blade contacts are used in the line voltage controller, the contacts will eventually burn, and pitting of the contacts is the result. At this point we can lose control of the room temperature. Line voltage thermostats are mostly used in commercial and industrial applications.

Heat anticipating principle

The differential of a thermostat is the number of degrees temperature change that are required to cause its bimetal or bellows to move the required distance to close or open its electrical contacts. The number of degrees difference between the opening and closing of a thermostat is called the mechanical differential. For example, if a thermostat opened at 70°F, and its contacts closed at 68°F, its mechanical differential would be 2°.

Manufacturers incorporate an anticipat-

ing heater to increase the sensitivity of the thermostat. It reduces the mechanical differential. The heat anticipator is a small electrical resistance heater that fools the thermostat into thinking it is warmer in the room than it actually is.

The heater is wired so that electric current flows through it when the thermostat calls for heat. The anticipator heater creates heat within the thermostat near the bimetallic element. This causes the thermostat to break its contacts prior to the room air reaching the temperature of the dial setting, so the burner is turned off slightly ahead of the time that the room air temperature increases to the dial setting of the thermostat. The blower in a warm air system continues to operate, bringing the room air temperature up to the dial setting. With a hot water or steam system the heat in the radiators or baseboard will raise the room temperature after the thermostat shuts off the burner and circulator.

The anticipating heater must be adjusted to match the current that is supplied to the thermostat. We must adjust for the number of amps supplied to the heater, because the greater the number of amps, the quicker the heater will heat up. Current flow in this 24 volt circuit generally varies from 0.05 amperes to 0.6 amperes, depending on the make and model of control. When setting the heat anticipator, consider the length of the wire and other resistances in the circuit. The current from the control to the thermostat heater circuit should be measured with an amperage meter and the anticipator set to the amps in the low voltage circuit.

If an ammeter is not available, set the anticipator to the amp rating found inside the cover of the control to which the thermostat is directly connected.

Figure 12-5 shows the location of the heat anticipator in a heating and cooling thermostat. Notice the anticipator in the R

Figure 12-5: T-87F heat anticipator

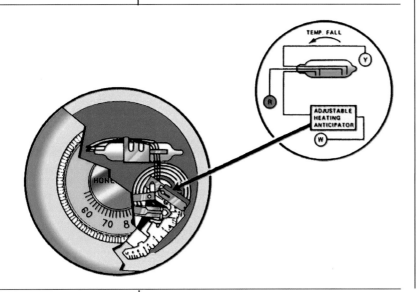

to W circuit. This is because the anticipator is only used for heating and not in the circuit R and Y that would be used if this thermostat were used for air conditioning. Figure 12-6 shows the heater indicator and the scale in a thermostat.

In some installations, longer operations may be needed to assure delivery of heat throughout the house. To lengthen operations, move the heater indicator preferably not more than half a division in the direction of the scale arrow. To shorten operations, move the indicator in the opposite direction.

If the operating control supplies 0.4 amps to the thermostat circuit and the anticipating heater of the thermostat is set at 0.8 amps, the burning cycle will be long. However, if the heat anticipator of the thermostat is set at 0.2 amps while the control is supplying .4 amps, then the burner cycle will be short. In the latter case, the burner will operate on and off for short periods of time (short cycling).

Electronic thermostats

Figure 12-7 shows some examples of electronic thermostats. These thermostats rely on solid-state technology to not only operate the equipment, but to maintain and store temperature settings, day and date, and number of cycles. Unlike the earlier mechanical thermostats that had only one day per operation cycle, many of these thermostats can have four different settings for all seven days of the week.

The difference in electronic thermostats over manual and mechanical clock types is the lack of an adjustable anticipator. Instead the electronic thermostat must be programmed according to 'cycle rate adjustment'. Once these settings are made at the time of installation, the thermostat, and its circuitry accommodate for the correct number of cycles.

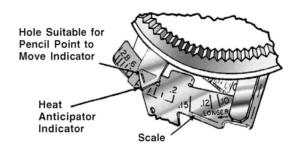

Hole Suitable for Pencil Point to Move Indicator

Heat Anticipator Indicator

Scale

Location of the thermostat

A thermostat should be installed about 5 feet from the floor on an inside living or dining room wall, or a wall where there is good natural air circulation. It may be wise to select several good locations, pointing them out to the homeowner, and then let them choose from the suggested locations.

Some locations that will cause trouble are:
1. Above a TV, stereo, computer, or lamp
2. On or near an outside wall
3. Near a radiator or air register
4. In line with the air stream from a register
5. On a wall containing steam pipes, hot water pipes, warm air risers, or chimneys
6. On a wall with high internal air movement
7. Behind a door or other obstruction to free air circulation
8. In an over radiated or under radiated room
9. Near a window or door frequently opened to the outside
10. In a room with a heat source such as refrigerator, stove, or fireplace
11. On a wall or partition subject to excessive vibration

Figure 12-6: T-87F heater adjustment

Figure 12-7: Electronic thermostats

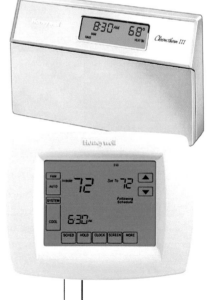

Mounting thermostats

• Servicing or installing a thermostat is a job for clean hands. Do not mar or soil wall surfaces.

• Be absolutely sure that all wires are connected to their proper terminals and that all connections are tight. If a color code is being used, be certain that it is followed.

• If mercury switches are used in the thermostat, be absolutely certain the thermostat back plate and/or the thermostat itself are level.

• All excess wire should be pushed back into the hole in the wall, and the hole should be plugged with putty to prevent cool air drafts from affecting the thermostat performance.

Limit controls

A limit control is a temperature or pressure actuated switch. Limit controls are generally divided into two groups: the high limit or safety controls and the low limit or operating controls. Limit controls are of either the direct acting or reverse acting type. Direct acting controls break (open) their contact on temperature rise while the reverse acting controls make (close) their contacts on temperature rise. Remember, in electricity, open means that there will be no flow of electricity and closed means electricity can flow through the switch.

The high limit is a safety device that turns off the burner should temperatures get too high within the furnace or boiler, or steam pressure become excessive in a steam boiler. This control should be line voltage, wired in series with the primary control so that it can turn off only the oilburner, never the circulator or system fan. The circulator or fan must stay on to remove the excessive heat produced. A low limit or operating control is a limit that is used to control the operation of the burner and blower or circulator.

Remember, in electricity, open means that there will be no flow of electricity and closed means electricity can flow through the switch.

Warm air limit controls

Warm air limit controls protect the furnace heat exchanger from excessively high temperatures and operate the blower. Both the high limit control and the fan control may be operated by a bimetallic element inserted in the plenum, or through an electronic control panel. The line voltage high limit control in series with the primary control may employ either metal to metal contacts or a mercury switch to make or break the circuit.

Fan and limit controls are usually combined into one housing. In this instance, the helix type bimetallic element operates both the fan control switch and the high limit control switch. Figure 12-8 shows a combination fan and limit control. A single dial as shown in Figure 12-9 (old

Figure 12-8:
Combination fan and limit control

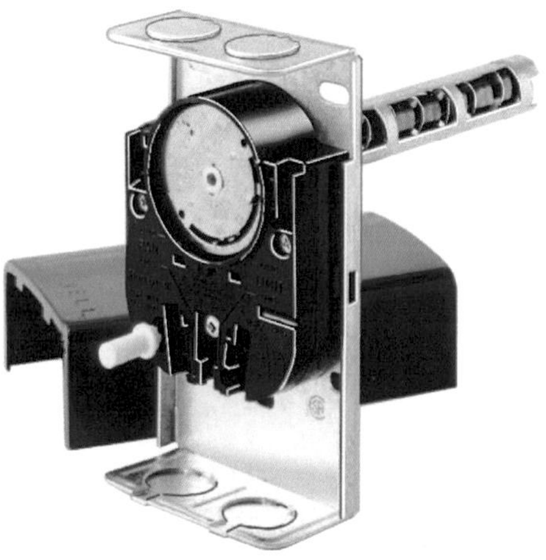

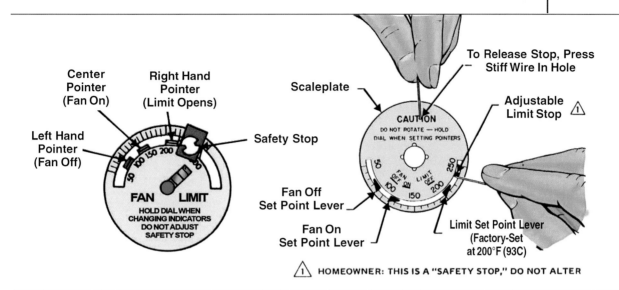

Center Pointer (Fan On)
Right Hand Pointer (Limit Opens)
Left Hand Pointer (Fan Off)
Scaleplate
To Release Stop, Press Stiff Wire In Hole
Adjustable Limit Stop ⚠
Safety Stop
CAUTION
DO NOT ROTATE — HOLD
DIAL WHEN SETTING POINTERS
Fan Off Set Point Lever
Fan On Set Point Lever
Limit Set Point Lever (Factory-Set at 200°F (93C)

FAN   LIMIT
HOLD DIAL WHEN
CHANGING INDICATORS
DO NOT ADJUST
SAFETY STOP

⚠ HOMEOWNER: THIS IS A "SAFETY STOP," DO NOT ALTER

Figure 12-9: High limit

and newer version) has indicators for the fan on position and the fan off position as well as an indicator for the high limit setting.

The function of the fan control is to operate the system blower when the air temperature is within the fan control dial settings. The fan control will permit the fan to operate when the air temperature in the furnace rises above the fan on setting as prescribed for the specific system or the manufacturer's requirements. The fan control will also prevent blower operation in the event the air temperature is below the fan off setting of the fan control. This prevents cool air from being forced into the living area during cold weather.

Many fan controls provide for manual operation to provide for summer air circulation. After the burner has been on for a short period, the element of the fan control will sense the desired amount of heat in the plenum or bonnet of the furnace, and start the blower. The blower will then run as long as there is heat, which can be for some time after the burner has stopped.

Limit terminals and fan terminals (old and new) connect the line voltage wires of the heating system electrical circuit. As shown in Figure 12-10 on following page.

The heat sensing element, or bimetallic element, expands and contracts with a change in furnace temperature. Since the element is helical in shape, it turns with a circular motion, either clockwise or counterclockwise, depending upon whether the furnace air is being heated or it is cooling off.

The operation of the fan switch control as shown in Figure 12-10 is as follows:

1. If the furnace temperature is the same as the room temperature and the fan on indicator is set at 140°F, the fan off indicator set at 110°F and the thermostat then calls for heat, the burner is turned on.

2. As the burner produces heat, the air in the furnace begins to rise in temperature and the helical element reacts to this change in temperature. In its attempt to expand, the bimetal causes the scale plate to turn in a clockwise direction. Once the scale plate

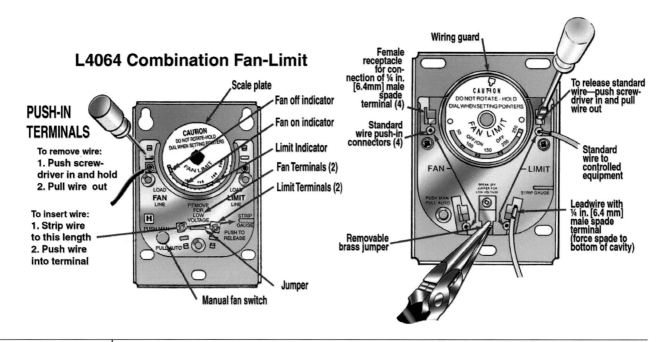

**Figure 12-10:
Limit and fan
terminals**

has reached the fan on position, 140°F, the fan switch will close its contacts and the fan will be turned on, forcing warm air into the living area.

3. The burner will continue to operate until the room thermostat is satisfied, at which time it will turn off. However, the fan will continue to operate until the air temperature has dropped below the minimum setting or the fan off indicator setting. Once this point has been reached, the fan control will then "open" its electrical contacts, and the fan will stop.

The heat exchanger of the furnace is still hot, although the burner, controlled by the thermostat, is not running; warm air currents will continue to rise to the bonnet. Under certain conditions this heat may be sufficient to again elevate the temperature to 140°F, and the fan switch will again operate the fan until all of this heated air is delivered to the living area.

In the event that the fan fails to operate, the air filters are clogged, or a blower belt is broken; the temperature in the furnace would continue to rise, going beyond the fan on position and ultimately reaching the high limit indicator setting of 200°F as shown in Figure 12-10.

Upon reaching this point, the limit control would open its electrical contact and prevent line voltage from reaching the primary control. This in turn would prevent line voltage from reaching the oilburner motor and ignition transformer thus causing the oilburner to go off. The high limit control would continue to hold its electrical switch contacts open until the air temperature in the bonnet had dropped below the 200°F mark minus the differential of the switch. (Normally 25°). The helical element would at the same time cool, rotating in a counter-clockwise direction, causing the limit indicator to also rotate in a counterclockwise direction until the scale plate had traveled below 175°F. Once this point has been reached, line voltage power would once again be restored to the primary control and if the room thermostat is still calling for heat, the burner would once again operate.

Always consult local codes and ordinances or regulations and manufacturer's instructions before installing a fan limit control. The helical element of the fan limit control must be located in the furnace plenum or at a location where it will be subjected to a representative airflow and temperature. It must not be located near cold air returns or the humidifier, nor in a dead air spot where there is poor circulation. It must definitely not touch any internal parts of the furnace.

Figure 12-11 is a schematic wiring diagram showing how a Honeywell L4064B

combination control is wired into the heating system electrical circuit. In this illustration, the limit control is wired directly into the hot line of the line voltage circuit and is in series with the primary control. The high limit control should never be wired to the neutral wire of the furnace unit.

Figure 12-12 lists some typical warm air limit settings and fan control on and off settings; the lower these settings can be

Figure 12-12

Warm Air Limit Settings			
Types of Systems	Limit	Fan = On	Fan = Off
Average furnace, average system	200°F	140°F	110°F
Oversized furnace and/or oversized fan and/or short air ducts	170°F	130°F	90°F
Undersized furnace and/or undersized fan and/or long air ducts	230°F	160°F	130°F

without creating uncomfortably cool air delivery into the living area, the more economical the operation of the heating system will be.

Referring to Figure 12-11, note that the fan motor is wired into the system circuit

Figure 12-11:
Warm air circuit

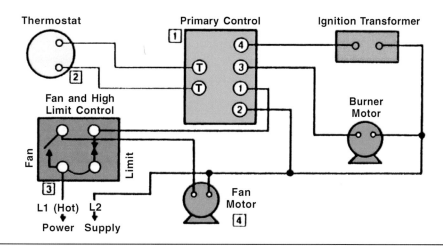

Oil-Fired Forced Warm Air System
Stack Detector

in parallel with the primary control and the high limit control. The fan control should always be connected on a warm air system in this manner to enable the fan motor to operate independently of the burner.

Electronic fan timer center

Most new warm air furnaces incorporate air conditioning, heating, humidification and air cleaning in one unit. They also feature multi-speed direct drive blower motors. To operate all these devices, they need an electronic fan center. A good example of this device is the Honeywell ST9103A Electronic Fan Timer, Figure 12-13. It integrates the control of all burner and system fan operations in an oil furnace.

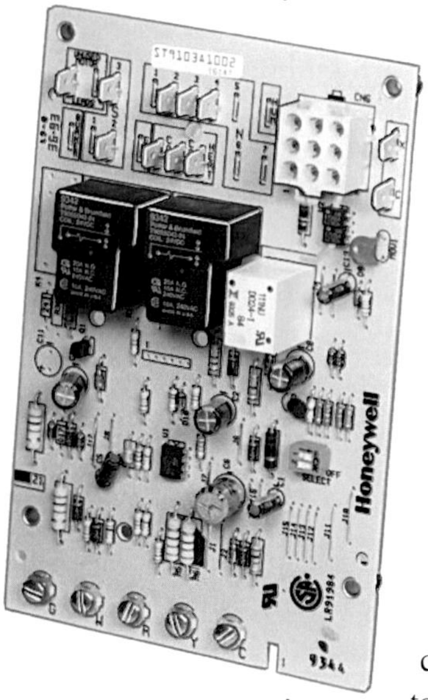

Figure 12-13: Electronic fan timer

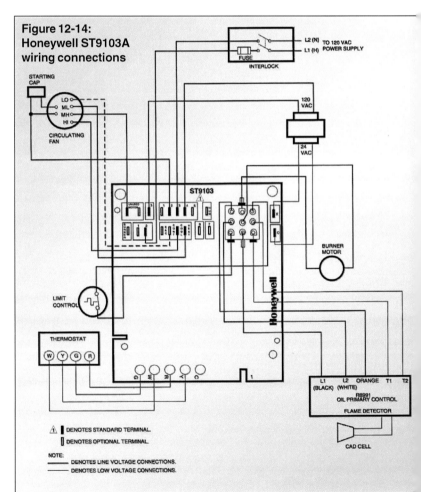

This control serves as the central wiring point for most of the electric components of the furnace. The ST9103A allows the thermostat to control heating, cooling, and system fan demands and run the oilburner primary control as well as up to a four speed circulating fan. It also monitors a limit switch string, which energizes the circulating fan whenever the limit switch opens. Electronic air cleaner and humidifier convenience

terminal connections are provided as an option. A means for operating continuous indoor air circulation is also available as an option. See Figure 12-14 for ST9103A wiring connections and Table 12-1 for the operating sequence.

Steam system controls
Pressure controls

Limit controls that respond to changes in steam pressure are called pressure controls, or *pressuretrols*. As is the case with warm air limit controls and hot water controls,

Figure 12-14: Honeywell ST9103A wiring connections

Table 12-1

Action	System Response
Thermostat calls for heat. (W terminal is energized)	• ST9103A closes oil primary control T-T connections. • Ignition system and oil primary control start the furnace. Oil flows as long as oil primary control senses flame. • Burner motor is energized and heat fan on delay timing begins. When timing is complete, the circulating fan is energized at heat speed and warm air is delivered to the controlled space.
Thermostat ends call for heat	• Oil primary control is de-energized, terminating the burner cycle. • Heat fan off delay timing begins. When timing is complete, the circulating fan is de-energized. • ST9103A returns to standby mode (oil primary control and circulating fan are off.
Burner fails to light	• Oil primary control locks out within lockout timing (timing depends on oil primary control). • Burner motor is de-energized. • If heat fan has started, it continues through the selected delay period.
Established flame fails	• Burner motor is de-energized and oil primary control goes into recycle mode. • If selected heat fan off delay is longer than the recycle delay timing, the heat fan continues to run through the next trial for ignition.
Thermostat begins call for cool (G and Y terminals are de-energized)	• Circulating fan is energized at cool speed. • Cooling compressor turns on immediately.
Thermostat ends call for cool (G and Y terminals are de-energized)	• Circulating fan and cooling compressor turn off immediately.
Thermostat begins call for fan (G terminal is energized)	• Circulating fan is energized immediately at cool speed. • ST9103A may be factory-configured to operate heat speed in this mode.
Thermostat ends call for fan (G terminal is de-energized)	• Circulating fan is de-energized.
Limit switch string opens	• Oil primary controls shuts off burner. • Circulating fan is energized immediately at heat speed. • ST9103A opens oil primary control T-T connections. • Circulating fan runs as long as limit string stays open. • If there is a call for cooling or fan, the circulating fan switches from heat speed to cool speed.
Limit switch string closes	• ST9103A begins heat fan off delay sequence. • Circulating fan turns off after the selected heat fan off delay timing. • ST9103A recloses oil primary control T-T connections. • Oil primary control is energized, initiating burner light off.
Continuous circulating fan is connected	• Circulating fan is energized at low speed when there is no call for heat, cool or fan. • If fan operation is required by a call for heat, cool or fan, the ST9103A switches off the continuous fan speed tap before energizing the other fan speed.
Electronic air cleaner is connected (Optional connectors are available for 120 Vac electronic air cleaner)	• Electronic air cleaner (EAC) connections are energized when the heat or cool speed of the circulating fan is energized. EAC connections are not energized when the optional continuous fan terminal is energized.
Humidity control connected (Optional connectors are available for 120 Vac humidifier)	• Humidifier connections are energized when burner motor is energized.

pressure controls will also complete or break a circuit by opening or closing their contacts. Their contacts may be constructed of the metal to metal design, or they may be of the mercury tube type. The operating range of a pressure control must never exceed the design pressure of the boiler. All residential and most commercial boilers are of the low pressure type with a maximum pressure range not to exceed 15 PSI; therefore, pressure controllers must be limited to the 0 to 15 PSI range.

Occasionally a steam system may be required to maintain pressure and the use of an operating controller may be necessary. In this case, two separate pressure controllers are necessary, one acting as the safety limit and the other as the operating limit. Residential steam systems require less than 2 PSI.

Most pressure controls are not sensitive enough for the low operating pressures required for some residential steam systems. In these systems, you will get better results with a Vapor Control that operates on ounces of pressure instead of pounds.

As the steam pressure changes, an expansion or contraction of a bellows actuates the switching mechanism. The cut-in and cut-out pressures can usually be independently set to meet any requirement. The snap-acting switch type does not require leveling.

If mercury switches are employed, the control must be leveled. Figures 12-15 and

**Figure 12-15:
Vaporstat**

**Figure 12-16:
Pressuretrol**

12-16 show a vapor control and a pressure control.

In both cases the switching mechanism is actuated by a diaphragm—the steam pressure counteracts the pressure exerted by the spring in the control. The tension of the spring is predetermined by the pressure adjustment screw, or main scale set point screw.

It is important to read the pressure adjustment instructions for the particular pressure controller being adjusted. On some controls, the differential is subtractive, meaning that if the pressure cut out is set for 3 PSI and the differential is set for 2 PSI, the cut in point will be 1 PSI. On other controls, the differential is additive and if the cut in point is set at 1 psi and the differential is set at 2 PSI, then added together, it would give us a cut out point of 3 PSI.

The cut out point is the pressure at which the oilburner will shut off. The cut in point is the pressure at which the burner will restart. It is very important to remem-

Figure 12-17:
Mercury tube
pressure switch

ber that if the cut out point is changed and the differential is left the same the cut in point will also change. The same thing happens in reverse, if the cut in point is changed, the cut out point also changes.

Figure 12-17 shows a mercury tube pressure switch with the cover off, indicating various parts and adjustment points.

The pressure control must always be installed above the water level of the boiler, and a pigtail, or siphon, as shown in Figure 12-18, must be installed between the boiler and the control. The siphon loop prevents steam from damaging the control bellows.

The pressure control should be installed in the fitting provided by the boiler manufacturer, or in the pressure control mounting of the low-water cutoff. When

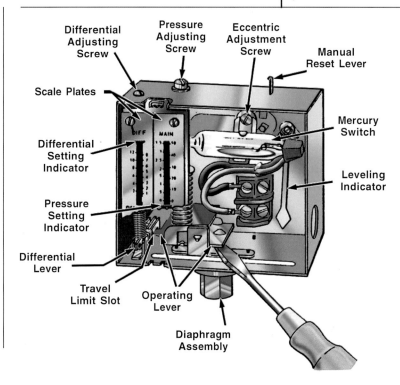

Installation of a Pressure Control

Figure 12-18:
Pressure control,
siphon loop

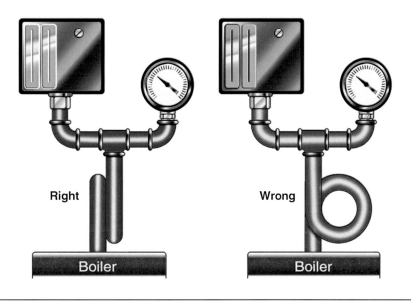

making pipe connections, use pipe dope sparingly. Excess dope may clog the small opening of the pressure control, thus preventing it from operating properly.

When mounting the pressure control and the pressure gauge to the same boiler fitting, follow the method shown in Figure 12-18, previous page. Be certain to mount them in such a manner that their faces are perpendicular to the siphon loop circumference. The reason for this is that the siphon loop tends to expand, thus causing a forward and backward motion that could cause the mercury switch in the pressure control to operate improperly if the faces of these instruments were mounted parallel to the circumference of the loop.

Figure 12-19 is a wiring diagram showing the pressure control. Like all other

high limit controls, it is wired into the hot line in series with the primary control.

Low-water cutoff

The low-water cutoff prevents a burner from operating if the water level is too low in the boiler. This device is required on all steam boilers whether used for space heating or in a process application and may also be required on hot water systems. If a hot water boiler is installed above the radiation, or even at the same level, a low-water cutoff should be used to protect the boiler in the event of a loss of water.

Figure 12-20 shows a cutaway view of an external low-water cutoff. It is a float operated device. There is also an internal low-water cutoff with the float located inside the boiler.

Figure 12-19: Pressure control wiring

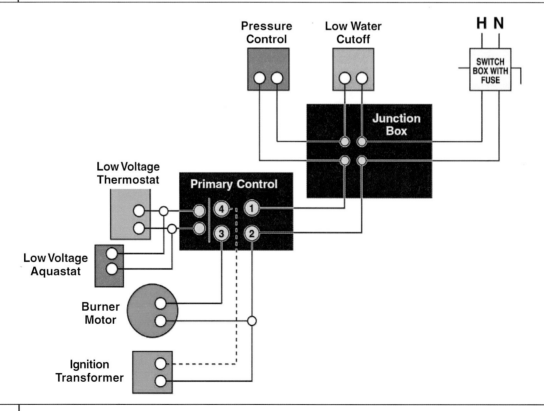

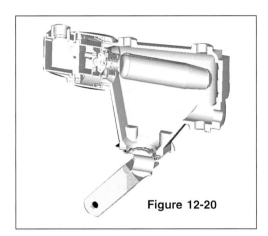

Figure 12-20

With either type, when the float is in a level position, it holds a single-pole single-throw switch in a closed position. In the event the water level inside the boiler drops below the safe operating level, the float will also drop, thus opening the switch and breaking the hot line circuit to the burner.

Probe type low-water cutoffs are becoming very common on most boilers, replacing the float types. These cutoffs may have timing devices to prevent nuisance shut downs should the boiler water surge. Probe type cutoffs send a low voltage charge through the water to ground on the boiler's metal. Don't switch to a probe control without first getting the boiler manufacturer's recommendations as to where it should be installed.

In Figure 12-19 (opposite page), the wiring diagram shows how the low-water cutoff is connected into the main heating plant circuit. The low-water cutoff is connected in the hot line, preceding the pressure control and in series with it and the primary control. Thus, the low-water cutoff may be called a low water line voltage safety device. Low-water cutoffs on steam boilers may be incorporated with, or wired to, electronic solenoid water valves called automatic water feeders.

Hot water limit controls

Hot water limit controls, sometimes called aquastats, control the temperature of the water in the boiler, and the temperature of the domestic hot water. They are all just switches that function automatically. In a basic forced hot water system, these controls must perform three functions:

1. They provide high limit protection against excessive boiler water temperatures.

2. They are employed for the purpose of maintaining a pre-determined boiler temperature, especially in systems that use tankless heaters for domestic hot water.

3. They are used to keep circulators from lowering the boiler water temperature too low.

Figure 12-21 shows a typical single function aquastat, the L4006 with two terminals and Figure 12-22 shows a dual acting L6006 with three terminals.

The high limit protection control prevents the boiler water temperature from rising to unsafe levels that create steam. Low (operating) limit protection means that the boiler water is not allowed to drop below a certain temperature. In the event the boiler water temperature falls below the dial setting of the low limit control, the burner would be turned on. Hot water temperature controls are either direct-acting or reverse-acting. As explained earlier, a direct-acting control will make its contacts, completing an electric circuit, on a drop in temperature

Figure 12-21: Single function aquastat

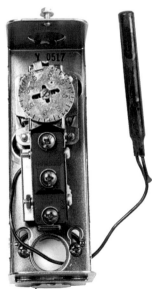

Figure 12-22: Dual acting aquastat

**Figure 12-23:
Hot water limit
(aquastat),
strap on type**

**Figure 12-24:
Hot water limit
(aquastat),
Immersion type**

and it will break its contacts on rise in temperature. Reverse-acting controls make their contacts on a rise, and will break their contacts on a drop in temperature. The letter A after the Honeywell model number normally indicates a control that will open its circuit on a rise in temperature. The B control will normally close its circuit on a rise in temperature for use as a reverse control.

Hot water limits may be of the strap-on type (Figure 12-23, or the immersion type, (Figure 12-24). Normally, the strap-on limit control is installed close to the boiler on the main supply riser. It should never be mounted on a pipe fitting such as an elbow or coupling. The strap-on type control is not as sensitive to temperature change as the immersion type controls and should not be used as a high limit control. Immersion controls should be installed in the tapped holes recommended by the boiler manufacturer.

The temperature sensing element on hot water controls may be electronic thermistors, thermocouples, liquid filled elements, or helical bimetal elements. Liquid filled elements, or capillary sensing bulbs, are the most popular. Volatile liquid expands and contracts dramatically with changes in temperature. This expansion and contraction operates an internal diaphragm to open and close the switch. When installing the heat sensing bulb in the aquastat well, coat the bulb with the heat conductive compound, supplied with the control, to help transfer the heat from the well to the bulb. The immersion control equipped with a

thermistor, (Figure 12-25), will respond faster to rapid temperature changes than the old immersion control of the bi-metal type or the capillary type. A thermistor is a heat sensitive device that increases or decreases resistance based on temperature.

Reverse acting aquastat

When the circulator is turned on by action of the room thermostat, the burner often starts simultaneously. When the circulator starts, it pushes hot water out of the boiler to the radiators, and an equal volume of cool return water from the radiators and system piping flows back to the boiler. This causes a drop in boiler water temperature. Starting the burner at the same time as the circulator helps the burner match its output to the heat content leaving the boiler.

Also, in the event that the water temperature goes too low, the reverse-acting circulator control will function to stop the circulator until burner operation can restore effective boiler water temperature. Then the circulator limit will again close its contacts to turn the circulator on.

Without the reverse acting aquastat, if a thermostat calls for heat while someone is taking a shower, the circulator comes on and sends all the heat in the boiler into the radiation and the boiler temperature drops below what is needed to produce hot water; the result is that the shower water temperature change can be quite noticeable. The reverse acting aquastat shuts the circulator off until the burner can build enough heat in the boiler to keep the tankless coil hot and heat the radiation.

The second reason for a reverse acting aquastat is to keep the products of combustion from condensing in a high

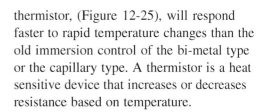

**Figure 12-25:
Thermistor**

efficiency boiler. The new, high efficiency boilers extract so much heat from the products of combustion that they can lower their temperature below the dew point of the combustion gases. At this temperature, the water vapor turns to water. While it does this, it picks up the sulfuric oxides in the gases and creates sulfuric acid. This results in scale build-up on the heat exchanger.

The reverse acting aquastat minimizes the scale build-up. When the boiler water temperature falls below the set point, the aquastat shuts off the circulator and the heat from the burner raises the boiler water temperature. This allows the temperature of the combustion gases to stay above the dew point. See the chapter on combustion theory (Chapter 7) for more detail.

Immersion aquastats should be mounted as follows:

1. When mounting immersion aquastats, try to avoid using bushings on the well. Bushings may prevent the temperature sensing element from extending far enough into the boiler water to be in the direct path of the hot water. Locate the element in freely circulating water.

2. Handle the aquastat with care. Do not damage the sensing element.

3. The bulb of the immersion aquastat should bottom in its well.

4. Be certain that the sealing washer is in place (remote control).

5. Make certain the case is mounted level if a mercury switch is employed.

The domestic hot water

low limit (operating) control used for controlling the domestic hot water supply should be installed on the boiler as close as possible to the hot water generator on a tankless hot water heating unit. In the event a tank is used for hot water storage, it may be installed in the hot water tank. With most hot water producing boilers, this control must be wired in parallel with the thermostat.

The reverse-acting circulator control should be installed in the boiler where the water returning from the circulator will surround the temperature sensing element. Figure 12-26 shows all three types of aquastats wired into a one zone circuit with the use of a switching relay.

Switching relays

Switching relays control a line voltage load with a low voltage thermostat. They are used

Figure 12-26

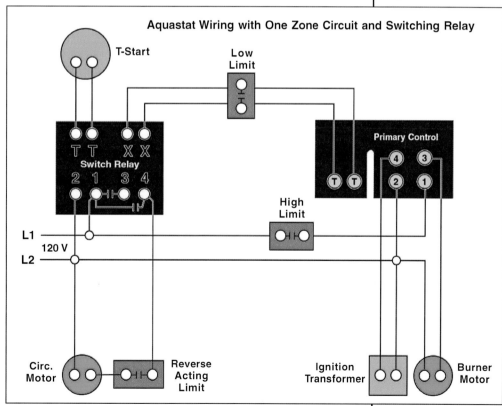

Aquastat Wiring with One Zone Circuit and Switching Relay

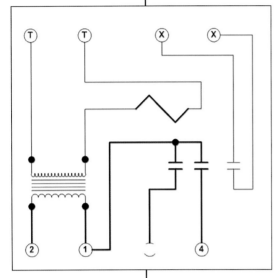

**Figure 12-27:
Double-pole, single
throw (DPST) relay**

**Figure 12-28:
DPDT switching relay**

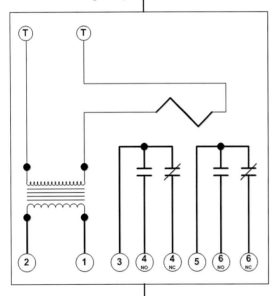

extensively on forced hot water systems to provide for multiple zones. In order for a switching relay to use a low voltage switch (thermostat) to control the line voltage loads (the circulator), it must contain a step down transformer (from 120 to 24 volts), a relay or relays and the necessary line and low voltage connections.

Most of today's switching relays are double-pole, double-throw (DPDT), but relays can be found in several configurations. This is the oldest type and can control only one load without exceeding the contact current capacity of the relay.

Figure 12-27 shows a double-pole, single-throw (DPST) relay that allows for two devices to be switched at the same time. A good application for this type of relay is where the switching relay turns on the circulator and primary control.

Figure 12-28 shows a DPDT switching relay for use with a low voltage, low (operating) limit control. A typical use for this control is to control an additional zone with a combination control package that will provide for high limit, low limit and circulator operation.

Figure 12-29: Panel used with circulators

Figure 12-30: Zone valves panel

Multiple zone switching relays can also be used to reduce costs and simplify wiring when several zones are used. Figure 12-29 shows a panel used with circulators and Figure 12-30 shows a zone valves panel. Note that both panels can work with all makes and wiring configurations of thermostats, zone valves and circulators.

Hydro air fan controls

Figure 12-31 shows a wiring diagram for a typical hydro air fan control. A hydro air system uses boiler water pumped through a fan coil for heating. The fan coil is mounted in an air handler along with the air conditioning coil from the compressor. With these units you can use hot water to heat the air flowing through the same ducts used for summer cooling. The controls are the interface between the thermostat and the air handler. They have an isolated end switch to start the boiler and/or circulator.

When the thermostat calls for heat, the fan control energizes the end switch relay and allows the fan to operate at low speed when the water temperature is above the aquastat setting. When the thermostat calls for cooling, the fan control energizes the condenser and operates on high speed. Many of these relays also allow selectable one, three, four minute delay on fan operation in the heating mode.Many of these relays also allow selectable one, three, and four minute delay on fan operation in the heating mode.

Combination controls

When the controls are separate units and scattered around the boiler, they are referred to as non-integral controls. When they are all in one box, high limit, low limit and circulator controls are called integral controls. They are also available in dual capacity high limit and low limit, or as triple function controls acting as high limit, low limit, and reverse-acting circulator limit.

In older heating systems, non-integrated control systems were used much more than they are now. Today's systems are generally integrated control systems that provide control of both the burner and circulator by

Figure 12-31:
Diagram of typical hydro fan control

(Both HAFC 101 and HAFC 201 are capable of 1 and 2 speed applications)

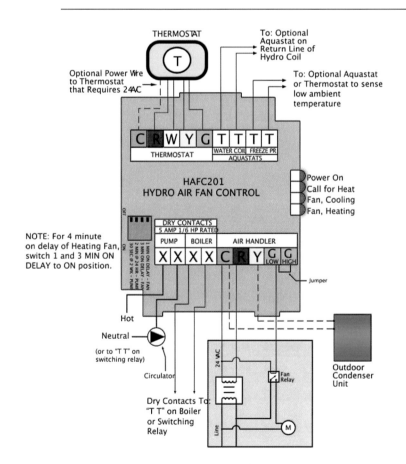

HAFC 201 With 1 Speed Air Handler

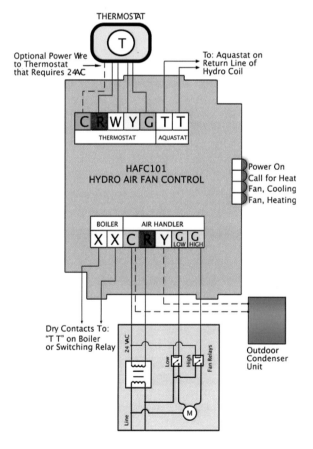

HAFC 101 With 2 Speed Air Handler

the room thermostat, and are preferred because many new boilers have a boiler water capacity of only a few gallons. Since space and accuracy are also factors, these combination controls are almost always now integral packages.

Triple acting aquastat relays

Dual and triple function aquastat controllers incorporate all of the various limit functions. Only one boiler water immersion element is required, simplifying installation. Figure 12-32 is a schematic diagram of a triple acting controller, the Honeywell L8124A. This controller incorporates a line voltage circuit, a low voltage circuit, and a switching relay, and includes all three limit controls: low, high, and reverse.

Assume that the low limit is set to open at 170°F, the high limit is set to open at 200°F, and the differential is set at 20°F. The system may be analyzed as follows:

When the thermostat calls for heat, it closes its switch, energizing the low voltage circuit through the secondary (24 volt) coil of the step-down transformer. The IK solenoid electromagnet is energized, pulling in the relay clapper, making contact IK1, closing the line voltage circuit to start the circulator that also closes contact IK2 in the line voltage circuit to start the oilburner at the same time.

The circulator limit switch in the circulator hot line must be closed to allow the circulator to operate. It will be closed if the boiler water temperature is above 180°F. If this switch is open, only the burner will operate, which will cause the boiler water temperature to increase to 180°F and then the circulator limit switch

will close and the circulator will start. The reason for this is that the low limit has a built in differential of ten degrees. The differential is added to the set point, less the differential. So, you subtract 10 degrees from the 170°F set point to get 160°F and then add 20°F to this number. In the summer, the burner will operate between 160°F and 180°F working off of the 20° differential.

The high limit switch is located in the burner hot line and it must be closed to allow the burner to operate. It will always remain closed unless the boiler water temperature is higher than 200°F. This switch will again close the circuit when the water temperature drops below 190°F based on its 10° fixed differential.

When the thermostat is satisfied, the circulator will stop and the burner may also stop, or it may continue to operate for a short period if boiler water temperature is below 160°F.

This is the control operation during a normal heating cycle, from thermostat on to thermostat off. Now when a hot water boiler also provides domestic hot water, the low (operating) limit functions, to cause the burner to run and heat the boiler water year round to provide adequate domestic hot water through the tankless or the tank type coil installed in the boiler.

The low limit switch closes to run the burner when the boiler water temperature drops below 160°F. It is desirable to open the circulator switch at the same time so that the circulator cannot operate until proper water temperature is again restored. The control manufacturer has incorporated a Single Pole Double Throw (SPDT) switch installed in the hot line to both the circulator and the burner for this purpose.

Figure 12-32:
Schematic diagram
for a triple acting
controller, Honeywell
L8124A

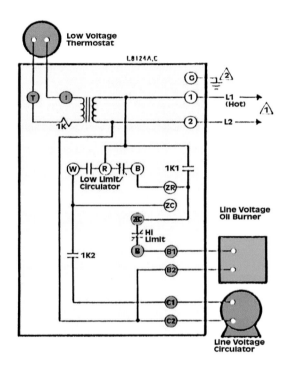

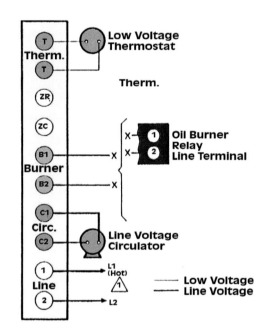

Shows how the external connections will often
appear in the instruction sheet with the control.

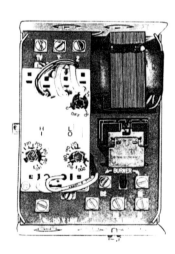

*Note that the hot line, starting at terminal 1, goes directly to a point midway between
the low limit switch and the circulator limit switch. This point is the hot side of a SPDT
switch that is actuated by the heat sensing element immersed in the boiler water.*

If the water temperature is below 160°F, the double-throw switch will close the hot line to the burner by moving its contact up to terminal B, allowing power to pass to B1 and the primary control. The thermostat terminals, T and T of the primary, are now closed so the burner starts and will continue to operate until the water temperature reaches 180°F. Then the double-throw switch will transfer its contact from B to W and the burner stops. The boiler water temperature has now been restored to effectively provide domestic hot water. When the thermostat again calls for heat, the circulator can operate. The burner can be energized in two ways: first by an action of the thermostat and second by action of the SPDT switch even when the thermostat is not calling for heat.

Figure 12-32 (previous page) also shows terminals ZC and ZR. These terminals are used when circulated zones are added to the system. When a call for heat energizes the zone relay, the use of these two terminals enables the control to act as though the main zone circulator was called. The control will start the burner and drop out the circulator if the boiler water temperature drops below the low limit/differential set point. This ensures consistent tankless coil performance.

Caution

Be careful when wiring hot water heating systems with multiple zones not to hook one set of powered terminals to another. The thermostat circuit (usually TT) is powered by the transformer in that control. Never hook wires from TT of one control to the TT of another control or switching relay. This will apply 48 VAC to the circuit and burn out the controls.

Since there may be differences in control models as well as control manufacturers, you are urged to study the operation of the various makes of controllers covered in the data and instruction sheets supplied by the manufacturer of the control.

Testing limit controls
High limit controls

1. With the burner operating and the room thermostat calling for heat, move the limit indicator to the low end of its scale.
2. Allow the burner to operate so that either the temperature or the pressure of the furnace or boiler rises to the limit setting. The burner should shut down. If it does not, then the limit control is either improperly installed or defective.
3. If it does shut down, then set the indicator at the desired temperature or pressure.

Circulator controls

1. Set the thermostat to call for heat.
2. In the event the boiler water temperature is above the circulator switch (reverse acting aquastat) setting, the circulator relay should close its contacts and the circulator should operate.
3. Next, turn the thermostat down below room temperature. This should cause the circulator relay to open its contacts and stop the circulator.
4. If the boiler water temperature is below the circulator switch when the thermostat is turned up and calls for heat, the circulator should not operate until the burner has heated the boiler water to the setting of the circulator control. In the event the circulator does not operate as outlined above, then the circulator control is either improperly installed or faulty.

HEATING SYSTEMS

IN THIS CHAPTER

- Warm air heating systems

- Hot water heating systems

- Steam heating systems

- Oil-powered water heaters

Chapter 13

Heating Systems

This chapter introduces the basic principles of oil-fired heating systems.

Part I

Warm air furnaces

Furnaces create warm air that is distributed through the building through ducts. A warm air furnace utilizes a metal heat exchanger that is designed to absorb heat from the oilburner flame and transfer that heat to the air that circulates through the furnace and into the house.

It accomplishes this by having the burner fire into a combustion chamber which is adjacent to the heat exchanger. The resulting combustion gases are vented to a chimney via the flue pipe. This heated air is then distributed to the house through supply ducts while cold air from the building is brought back to the furnace through return ducts, see Figure 13-1

The advantage of warm air systems is air cleaners, humidifiers, and central air conditioning systems can be incorporated into the unit to provide a total comfort indoor air quality climate control system.

Warm air furnaces have a blower attached to their ducts. The airflow the blower creates is measured in CFM (Cubic Feet Per Minute). It is important that the blower and ducts be properly sized to move enough air across the heat exchanger to remove the heat from the furnace and deliver it to the house.

The normal operation of a warm air furnace is as follows:

1. Thermostat calls for heat and activates the burner through the primary control.

2. Burner runs until a sufficient amount of heat is built up to activate the fan control and start the blower. (Usually 140 degrees)

3. The burner and blower run together until the thermostat has been satisfied and the burner shuts off.

Figure 13-1: Typical warm air furnace

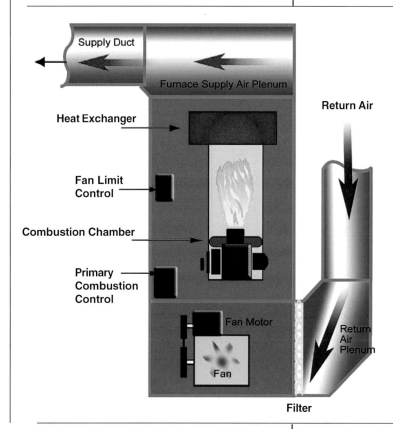

Figure 13-2:
Highboy furnace

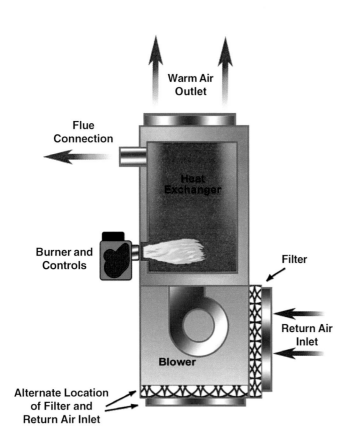

4. The blower continues to run until the heat in the furnace has been dissipated and the fan control shuts it off. (Usually 100 degrees.) The blower may come back on after a minute or two because some residual heat from the combustion chamber and heat exchanger has risen from the furnace to activate the fan control once more.

There are different types of warm air furnaces for different applications. The basic operation of these is similar but the configurations vary.

Highboy furnace: The most common furnace is the highboy. It gets its name because the heat exchanger sits on top of the blower within the furnace cabinet. Return air is pulled in through the bottom of the unit and circulated upward across the heat exchanger and then out through the top of the unit. See Figure 13-2.

Lowboy furnace: Where height constraints are a consideration, a lowboy furnace is often used. The blower is in a compartment next to the heat exchanger, thereby shortening the overall height of the unit. See Figure 13-3.

Counterflow furnace: These units are commonly found in slab type construction and mobile homes and look much like a highboy in outward appearance, but differ in that the blower is located above the heat exchanger. Return air comes in through the top and is distributed out through the bottom of the unit. In this type of furnace an additional fan control is installed below the heat exchanger. The upper control turns the blower on when it

Figure 13-3:
Lowboy furnace

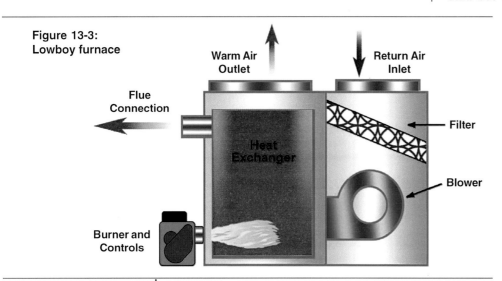

senses the temperature of the air rising in the unit. The lower control turns the blower off when it senses a decrease in the temperature of the air being blown down through the furnace. See Figure 13-4.

Horizontal furnace: A horizontal furnace is often described as a highboy furnace on its side. These units are normally used in crawl spaces or suspended from a ceiling. The air travels through these units in a horizontal pattern with return air entering on one side and supply air discharging through the opposite end. See Figure 13-5.

The distribution system

Figure 13-6 (following page) shows the main components and fittings found in a warm air distribution duct system. The distribution or duct system is comprised of three main parts.

Plenums: These are boxlike chambers connected to the furnace. There are two plenums in the modem furnace, one on the supply side and one on the return. The plenum should always be the same size as

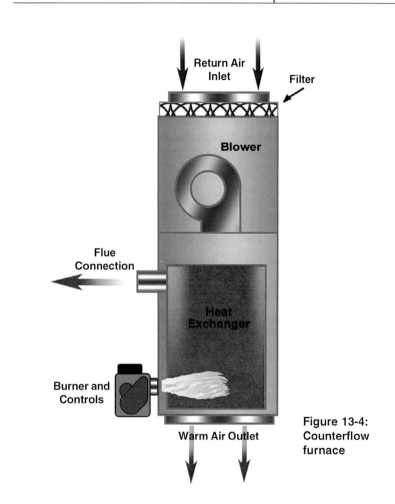

Figure 13-4: Counterflow furnace

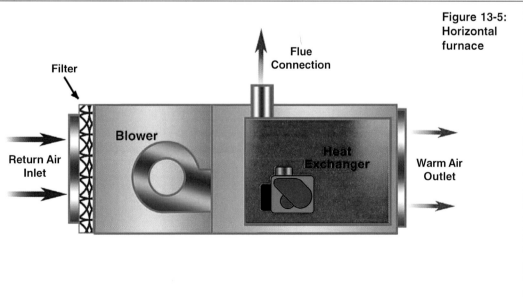

Figure 13-5: Horizontal furnace

the opening on the furnace and be at least 14" long or high.

Trunks: These are usually rectangular ducts that connect to the plenums and are run out through central areas of the house.

Branches: These are smaller ducts, either round or rectangular, which connect the trunk lines to the individual registers. It is a good idea to install locking dampers on each branch to allow for system balancing.

Troubleshooting warm air systems
Not enough heat

When responding to a service call for "not enough heat" or certain rooms in the house "not heating," first see if the burner, controls and blower are operating properly, then look to the distribution system. Some common problems to check are:

1. Is there adequate return air? As a general rule of thumb, there should be an equal amount of return coming back to the furnace as there is going out on the supply side.

As a minimum, the return should never be less than 80% of the supply. (100% is better and with air conditioning 120%.) If the ducts appear to be adequate then check to see if any return grills are blocked by furniture or rugs.

2. Is the system balanced? Turn the system on and open any dampers. Check each register to see that the same amount of air comes out of each.

If an imbalance is found, then the register should be checked to be sure it is open. The individual branches should then be checked to be sure that dampers are properly adjusted.

**Figure 13-6:
Warm air
distribution
system**

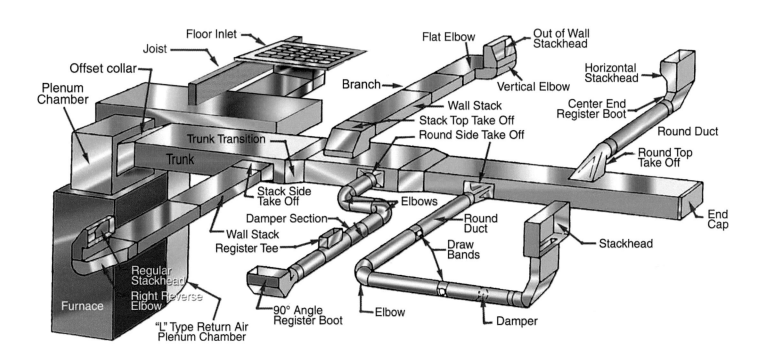

3. Do the ducts run through "cold" areas? Sometimes it is necessary to run ducts in unheated areas such as crawl spaces, garages or attics. When this situation occurs, the heat loss from the bare duct can cool the air coming out of the register. If this situation exists then the ducts should be insulated to stop this heat loss.

Short cycling

If the burner is short cycling or if the unit is regularly shutting off on high limit, the following should be checked:

1. Are controls set properly?

2. Is blower operating?

3. Is fan belt broken or slipping?

4. Are pulleys slipping?

5. Are air filters plugged?

6. Are return air grills and ducts free of restriction?

7. Are supply registers and ducts free of restriction?

8. Is unit over firing?

9. Is the duct system designed to meet the requirements of the furnace?

Part II

Hot water boilers and heating systems

A hot water boiler is a heat exchanger that uses the heat from the oil flame to heat water. This heated water is piped to radiation in the building to supply space heating. The cooled water is then pumped back to the boiler where it is reheated. Figure 13-7 shows a basic hot water heating system.

Usually the heated water leaves the boiler at about 160° to 180°F and returns at 140-160°F.

Boiler designs

Boilers are constructed from cast-iron or steel and can be either "wet base" or "dry base."

A wet base boiler has water surrounding the combustion chamber while a dry base boiler does not.

The most common steel boiler is the "fire-tube" boiler in which hot combustion

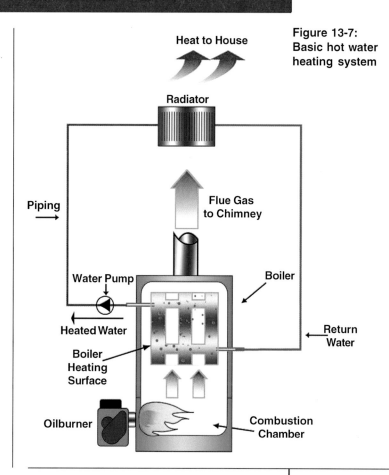

Figure 13-7: Basic hot water heating system

Heat to House

Radiator

Piping

Flue Gas to Chimney

Water Pump

Boiler

Heated Water

Return Water

Boiler Heating Surface

Oilburner

Combustion Chamber

gases flow inside long tubes surrounded by water. These fire-tubes can be arranged vertically (up-and-down) or horizontally within the boiler water. As the combustion gases rise through the tubes, heat passes through the wall of the tubes to the water. Figure 13-8 shows a vertical fire tube boiler.

In horizontal fire-tube boilers, the hot gases travel to the back of the boiler and then pass into the horizontal fire tubes where more heat is transferred to the water. This design is called a "two-pass" boiler because the gases go front-to-back in the first pass, and back-to-front in the second pass before they are transported by the flue pipe to chimney.

Some steel boilers include a third pass through fire-tubes for increased efficiency. Some features of these boilers include low mass construction and reduced water storage for lower heat loss.

Cast-iron boilers are narrow sections of cast iron that are joined to form the boiler. Each section contains boiler water on the inside, while hot gases pass in channels between the sections. The cast sections are joined together with either metal push nipples or non-metallic "O" rings.

Some cast-iron boilers have "wet-legs" or "wet-backs" so that the combustion chamber is partly enclosed by boiler water.

Water is supplied to each casting through a common header at the bottom and top of each section. The water flows upward and it is heated by the hot inner surfaces of the cast-iron sections. The heated water leaves the boiler through the outlet fitting and then it is piped to the radiation.

Extra attention is needed when assembling or servicing sectional boilers to be sure that there is no way for air to leak into the boiler between the sections. These must be sealed tightly to prevent the entrance of secondary air that lowers operating efficiency.

Firebox and combustion chambers

The burner is fired into a combustion area that may be lined with a refractory material that reflects radiant heat back to the flame. The reflected heat helps to

**Figure 13-8:
Dry base vertical
fire tube boiler**

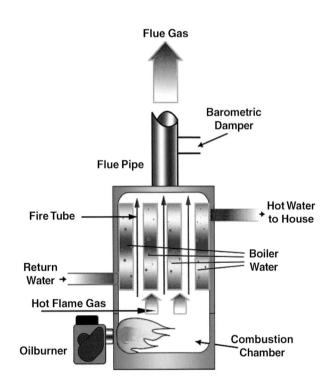

Cross Section View

stabilize the flame by vaporizing the fuel droplets more quickly.

Dry-base boilers require a combustion chamber made of an insulating material such as ceramic fiber to reduce the heat loss through the base of the boiler and to prevent burning out the base. In wet-base boilers the insulating properties of the chamber are less important because the surrounding boiler water recovers the heat.

Heating surface or heat exchanger

The heating surfaces of the boiler are exposed to the hot combustion gases on one side and to the boiler water on the other side. Heat is conducted through these boiler surfaces from the hot gases to the water. Larger surface areas give better heat transfer. Many surfaces are designed with contours, fins, pins or surface projections to increase the outer area and improve the gas-side contact.

The heat transfer surfaces must be kept clean so that good heat exchange can take place. Soot deposits on the heating surfaces act as an insulator.

Baffles or turbulators

Baffles and turbulators are objects placed in heating passages to redirect the gas flow for better heat transfer. In older boilers, baffles were installed at the top of some combustion chambers to improve gas contact with the heating surfaces.

Some older boilers were designed for coal burning with very wide passages for the hot gases. Installing baffles or fire-bricks in the center of these passages

forces the flow toward the boiler walls for better heat transfer.

Fire-tube boilers use turbulators to prevent the flow of hot gases up through the center of the tube. Some turbulators are long narrow strips of metal that are twisted into a spiral to give a spinning motion to the hot combustion gases. Turbulators should always be put back into the tubes after the boiler is cleaned. If they are damaged or badly corroded, they should be replaced with new ones.

Insulation

Boilers and furnaces have thermal insulation on the outside of the heat exchanger to reduce heat loss from hot surfaces. The outer jacket or casing must be securely fastened to minimize heat loss.

Boiler ratings

Cast-iron and steel boilers are tested to verify heating capacity and efficiency. The Hydronics Institute publishes boiler ratings. Listings provided by the Institute show the boiler's Btu output and its Annual Fuel Utilization Efficiency (AFUE). The AFUE is calculated based on a testing procedure specified by the US Department of Energy. The Gross Output is the total heat delivery in Btus per hour that the boiler will deliver. The NET RATING deducts a "piping and pick-up factor" equal to 15 percent of the gross output for hot water boilers. This factor takes pipe heat loss and boiler warm-up time into account. This is important to assure that the boiler will deliver adequate heating at the coldest times of the year. The NET RATING should be used for selecting a boiler.

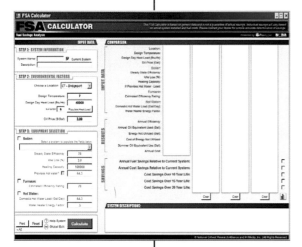

**Figure 13-9:
Image from FSA
Calculator on
NORA's website:
nora-oilheat.org**

NORA has taken the next step and has developed an on-line calculator which allows technicians to compare the efficiency of boilers by inputting the amount of energy to heat the home and provide domestic hot water, Figure 13-9.

Piping systems

One of the features of hot water heat is its flexibility. You will find a wide variety of different hot water piping systems in the field. Each is designed for specific applications and has its advantages and disadvantages. The following is a brief description of some different hot water piping systems you are likely to encounter.

Series loop

The most common is the Series Loop. It

**Figure 13-10:
Series loop**

is the least expensive and easiest to install. See Figure 13-10 for three examples of Series Loop systems. It features a single pipe that goes from the boiler outlet through each piece of radiation and back to the boiler inlet. One of the series loop's biggest advantages is that it will supply heat to each of the pieces of radiation as the heat is pushed around the loop by the circulator with a minimum of pipe and fittings. No special valves or fittings are required. The disadvantage of this system is that heat delivered to the last piece of radiation is less than that delivered to the first piece.

One pipe system

This system also features single pipe that connects the boiler supply to the return while supplying the radiation. What makes it different from the series loop is all of the sections of radiation are connected to the single pipe main by the use of a standard tee and a special tee that form a "branch" of the main circuit. See Figure 13-11. The special tee is called by many names including "One-pipe", "Venturi" "Mono-Flo" and "Jet" and it serves the purpose of directing the flow of water so that each section of radiation is supplied with water at approximately the same temperature. Figure 13-12 shows the special tees required for single pipe systems.

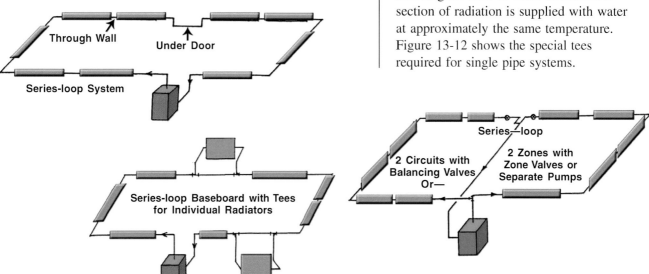

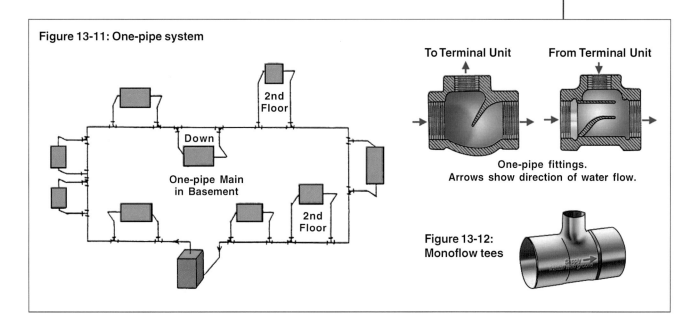

Figure 13-11: One-pipe system

2nd Floor

Down

One-pipe Main in Basement

2nd Floor

To Terminal Unit

From Terminal Unit

One-pipe fittings.
Arrows show direction of water flow.

Figure 13-12:
Monoflow tees

Two pipe system

This system incorporates the use of a separate supply and return pipe from the boiler to each piece of the radiation. The preferred way to pipe this is the first piece of radiation to be taken off the supply is the last returned to the boiler. Likewise, the last supplied is the first returned. This produces a uniform and balanced design that requires no special valves or fittings. See Figure 13-13.

Components of hot water heating systems

Radiation

Hot water is an easily adaptable and transportable medium that lends itself to all sorts of radiation. The five most common types of radiation are the conventional radiator, the convector, the fan-coil unit, baseboard, and radiant panel.

The **conventional radiator** is usually made of cast iron sections that either rest on the floor or mount on the wall. Radiators are normally found in older systems.

The convector is a series of finned-tube

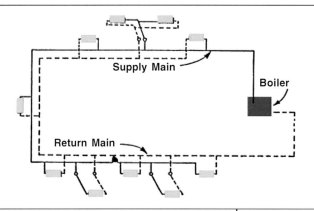

Supply Main

Boiler

Return Main

Figure 13-13:
Two-Pipe
reverse return

sections enclosed within a cabinet. They are constructed of either cast-iron sections or steel.

Baseboard radiation is constructed of cast-iron panels or copper pipe covered with aluminum fins that create surface area for heat transfer. In larger system applications, the pipe and fins can be constructed of steel.

Fan-coil or unit heaters are coils of fin tube element with a fan that blows air over the coils. They are especially suited to rooms where there is little wall space available, such as kitchens and baths. They are also popular in garages and commercial applications.

Radiant or panel heating systems:
These are serpentine loops of non-finned pipe in floor, walls, or ceilings that circulate low temperature water. Residential radiant heat systems are becoming very popular in new homes. The piping can be filled with anti-freeze and run from a

separate heat exchanger or boiler for heating garages, driveways and sidewalks.

Circulators

The circulator is the key to the proper function of today's hot-water heating system. Circulators are centrifugal pumps that create a pressure difference that produces flow in the system. The circulator motor rotates an impeller that pushes water

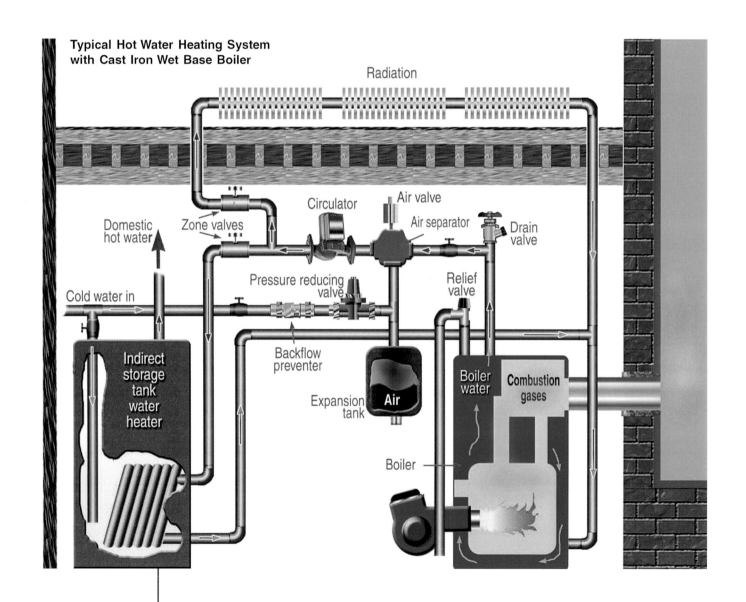

Typical Hot Water Heating System with Cast Iron Wet Base Boiler

Figure 13-14: Pump resistance, TACO "00" circulator

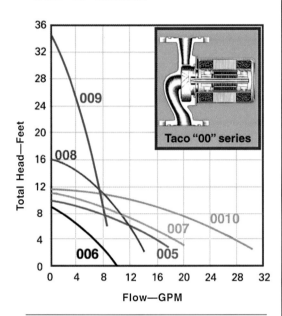

outward to the pump body. As the water is pushed away it pulls water from the system into the impeller. This movement of water creates "head pressure," Figure 13-14.

Pressure reducing valve

The pressure reducing valve allows for the automatic filling and maintenance of system water pressure. This valve takes incoming service water pressure and reduces it to an adjustable pressure. We need pressure to push water out of the boiler and up in the system.

It takes one PSI of water pressure to push water 2.3 feet up a pipe. Typical residential systems operate at 12 pounds pressure because that much pressure will push water up 27.6 feet (sufficient height to heat a radiator up in the attic of a two story home). The factory setting of 12 PSI

is almost always adequate for residential applications. See Figure 13-15.

Pressure relief valve

The pressure relief valve protects the boiler and system from high pressure conditions. Its discharge should be piped to an area where the released water will not scald the occupants. Relief valves should always be sized to boiler manufacturers' specifications. Residential hot water boiler relief valves are set to open at 30 PSI.

Flow control valve

The flow control valve is used to prevent gravity circulation on a forced hot water heating system. It is a check valve opened by the circulator's force so the heated water can travel through the system. See Figure 13-16.

Air elimination or control

Water holds a great deal of air in suspension. Cold water holds more air than warm water and as water is heated, the air is released. If air gets trapped in the system it can stop the flow of water to that part of the system and cause a no heat call. Air vents release air from the system and are often installed at the highest point to keep air from accumulating. In addition, most systems, with the exception of the series loop, have air vents installed in each piece of radiation. Series loop systems typically have air removed through "purge valves" located in the return piping.

Figure 13-15: Pressure reducing valve

Figure 13-16: Flow control valve

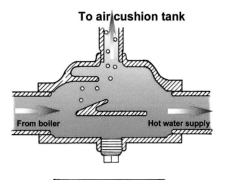

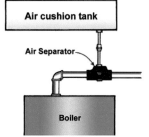

**Figure 13-17:
Air elimination**

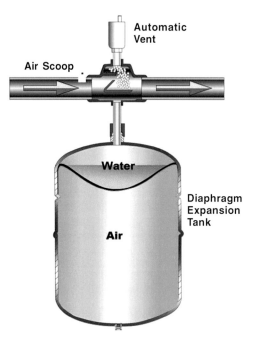

**Figure 13-18:
Expansion tank**

Air separators remove the air from the water being pumped from the boiler and should be located in the supply piping.

Figure 13-17 shows the cross section of an air separator and the installation of one on a steel expansion tank system.

Expansion tank

All hot-water heating systems need an expansion tank. As water is heated, it expands. We cannot compress water, so in a closed system it has nowhere to expand as it is heated, so the pressure increases instead. If we did nothing to address this, every time the burner came

on, the relief valve would open. To fix this problem we have the expansion tank. It is a tank full of air installed in the system, with a flexible diaphragm. When the burner fires, the water expands, pushes against the diaphragm and compresses the air in the tank. When it shuts off, the water cools and the compressed air expands and pushes water back out of the tank.

Originally, all tanks were hollow steel cylinders. These tanks worked on the principle that as the system was filled with water, a cushion of air was trapped in the tank and as the system water expanded, the air compressed. On cooling of the system, the water would contract and the air would decompress. Unfortunately, every time the water cooled it would absorb some air from the tank and carry it to the system. Eventually all the air would be removed and the tank would become waterlogged and require service.

The steel tank has been replaced by the flexible diaphragm design. See Figure 13-18. These tanks are pre-pressurized to 12 pounds per square inch and have advantages over the older design:

1. Smaller size. About 1/3 to 1/2 the size of the older tank.

2. The flexible diaphragm keeps the water and air separated so the cooling water cannot absorb the air from the tank. It cannot become waterlogged unless the diaphragm leaks.

System zones

Hot water systems are easy to zone or break into separate heating circuits or areas. The two primary ways to provide for zone control are circulators and zone valves. Zone valves are 24 volt valves that provide control to either a circuit or piece of radiation. Figure 13-19 shows zone valves. They can also be of the nonelectric type installed on each piece of radiation. Combinations of these two types can be very effective and provide positive, efficient and inexpensive total comfort control.

Figure 13-19: Electric zone valves

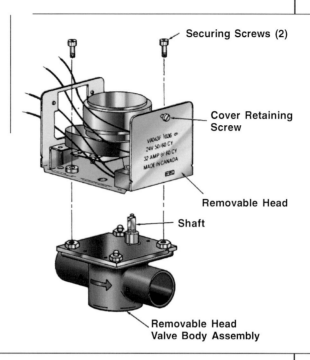

Securing Screws (2)

Cover Retaining Screw

Removable Head

Shaft

Removable Head Valve Body Assembly

Part III

Steam heating systems

Just like hot water boilers, steam boilers are heat exchangers that use the heat from the flame to heat water. A key difference is that steam boilers are only partially full of water, so that when the water is heated it turns to steam and expands by 1,700 times. It is this expansion that pushes the steam into the heating system. All we have to do is get the air that is in the system out of the way and the steam will rush in.

Additionally, it takes a lot of energy to turn water into steam. And, when that steam turns back to water, it releases a lot of energy. Thus, the steam can provide a lot of heat to the residence.

Steam pressure

The job of steam pressure is just to overcome the friction that steam meets as it works its way around the system. We have to supply enough pressure back at the boiler to overcome the system piping friction. The pressure needed is remarkably low, less than 2 PSI. Raising the pressure higher than two PSI will cause problems because steam is a gas.

When you raise the pressure on a gas, you compress it. When you compress steam, it takes up less space. It also begins to move more slowly. It takes longer for high-pressure steam to get out to the radiators than it does for low-pressure steam. Also, high-pressure steam, since it's more tightly packed, will take more water out of the boiler than low-pressure steam. This can lead to low-water problems back at the boiler.

Steam travels through a system because of a subtle difference in pressure. Besides friction, the fire in the boiler and the condensing of the steam in the radiators also leads to a difference in pressure throughout the system. The fire creates the initial pressure. Since all the air vents are open, the inside of the piping system is at atmospheric pressure and steam begins to move from the higher pressure in the boiler to the lower pressure in the system.

As soon as steam begins to move, it also begins to condense into water. When steam condenses into water it leaves a partial vacuum in its place. Since steam occupies about 1,700 times the volume of water, when it condenses it shrinks to 1/1700th of the space it occupied as steam. What we're left with is a partial vacuum that makes the steam travel to the radiators. This is why you don't need pumps to move steam. The

boiler's job is simply to get steam (a gas) out to the last radiator before it turns into water (a liquid.)

The importance of the piping around the boiler

Today's replacement steam boilers contain much less water than the boilers of yesteryear. As boilers became smaller, the piping around them became more and more important. If you want your replacement boiler to work, you have to pay careful attention to the boiler manufacturer's piping instructions.

Here are a few of the things the boiler manufacturers will tell you to do:

• Allow at least 24 inches between the center of the gauge glass and the bottom of the steam header

• Use full-size risers to the header

• Pipe the system take-offs at a point between the last riser to the header and the equalizer

• Pipe swing joints into the header

• Use a reducing elbow to connect the header to the equalizer

The dimension labeled "A" in Figure 13-20 represents the distance you have to maintain between the center of the gauge glass and the bottom of the lowest dry return in the system.

Dimension "A"

In one-pipe systems "Dimension A" must not be less than 28 inches. "Dimension A" provides the force that puts the condensate back in the boiler. Without it, water will back up into the horizontal piping and block the take-offs to the radiators. The house will heat very slowly

**Figure 13-20:
One-Pipe steam
system**

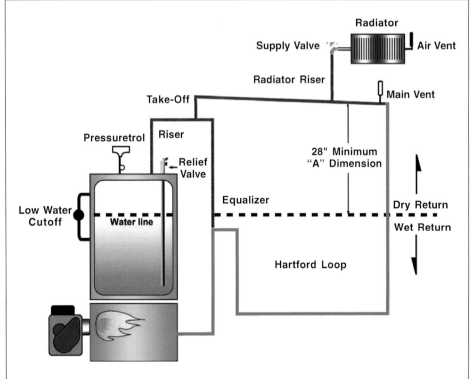

13-16   *Heating Systems*

and unevenly. You'll probably also have water hammer.

New steam boilers must be skimmed

All steam boilers must be cleaned after they're installed to remove substances that can cause foaming and surging of boiler water. It often pays to let the system run for a few days before you clean it to let the cutting oil and dirt have a chance to settle on the surface of the water. Skimming the boiler is the best way to remove cutting oil, grease, sludge, etc., from the system; it includes:

- Inserting a 1 ¼" or larger nipple into a horizontal tapping above the waterline

- Raising the waterline to the midline of the nipple

- Draining water until it runs clear and clean

Before you skim or clean any boiler, check the manufacturer's instructions for their recommendations.

One-pipe steam system

One-pipe steam takes its name from the single pipe that connects each radiator to the steam main. Both steam and condensate travel in this pipe, but in opposite directions. This is what often makes one-pipe steam so difficult to manage. When steam and condensate travel in opposite directions, you have to pay close attention to the size and pitch of the pipes; the pitch must be at least one inch for every twenty feet.

See Figure 13-20 for the layout of a one-pipe steam system.

If you don't follow these rules, you wind up with radiators that bang and air vents that spit. When replacing a steam boiler be sure you maintain the pitch of all the piping.

Relief valve

The relief valve protects the boiler against a runaway fire. On steam boilers the relief valve is set to open at 15 PSI.

Gauge glass

The gauge glass shows where the water is in the boiler. Expect to see some minor movement in the water line. Anything between a half and three-quarters of an inch of up-and-down movement is normal.

Automatic water feeders

An automatic water feeder is sometimes installed to maintain a safe minimum water level. While it's not essential to the system's operation, an automatic water feeder is a useful back-up safety device.

Main vents

Install main vents near the ends of every main so steam will travel very quickly to every radiator in the building. If your main vents are working, steam will arrive at each radiator at about the same time.

Part IV

Domestic hot water

Not only is Oilheat great for space heating, it is also the best way to heat domestic hot water for use in showers, baths, lavatories, clothes washing, and dishwashers. The production of reliable, inexpensive and efficient domestic hot water provides for the health and comfort of our customers and is one of our industry's strong points.

Domestic hot water systems fall into two major groups, *direct* and *indirect*.

A direct system is one in which the water is heated directly by the heat from the flame. There is combustion gas on one side of a heat exchanger and domestic water on the other. With indirect systems we use boiler water to heat domestic water.

There are two types of indirect systems: the *storage system*, where the water is heated and stored for later use in a tank, and the *instantaneous* or *tankless* system, where the water is heated as it is drawn to the fixtures.

Direct fired hot water systems

Direct fired hot water heaters use a tank, which sits over a combustion chamber and is surrounded by insulation and an outer casing. An oilburner fires into the combustion chamber under the tank and the hot combustion gases heat the water in the tank.

There are two designs of water heaters: the rear flue heater where the gases pass around the tank and vent out the back of the heater, as shown in Figure 13-21, and the center flue heater where the gases pass through a freeway in the center of the tank and vent off the top of the heater as shown in Figure 13-22.

Oil-fired direct heaters are typically glass lined steel tanks that are constructed of steel and coated on the inside with a ceramic material. This coating helps protect the tank from rusting and corrosion. However, the ceramic material is not impervious to water and an anode or "sacrificial" rod made of magnesium is immersed into the tank water. This rod will break down and give itself up to protect the tank from the corrosive properties of the air and chemicals present in the water. These anode rods should be checked routinely and replaced when necessary.

Indirect fired water heating
Internal tankless coil

Tankless coils are a copper coil attached to a steel, cast-iron or brass mounting plate. The coil is placed into the water and/or steam jacket of a steam or hot water boiler and the coil plate with a

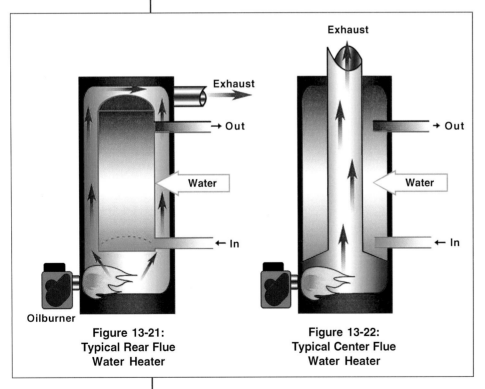

Figure 13-21:
Typical Rear Flue
Water Heater

Figure 13-22:
Typical Center Flue
Water Heater

gasket is then bolted to the boiler shell. This system requires that boiler water temperature be maintained high enough to heat the water as it passes through the coil. There is no storage capacity in this system, and during heavy draw it is unable to provide enough hot water due to its limited capacity. See Figure 13-23.

External tankless coils are copper, cast iron or steel tanks with a coil inside. See Figure 13-24.

Boiler water is piped to the tank and it is kept hot by gravity or forced flow circulation. Many new systems feature an updated version of the external tankless called a plate heat exchanger. It is made of a series of wafers or plates with internal porting. The plates alternate between boiler water and domestic water. See Figure 13-25 on following page.

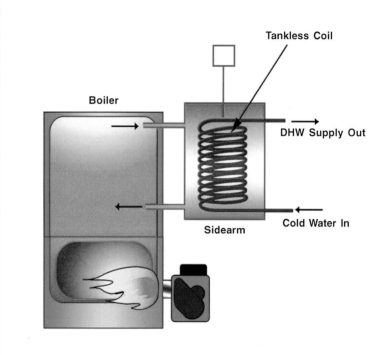

**Figure 13-24:
External tanless coil**

Figure 13-23: Internal tankless coil

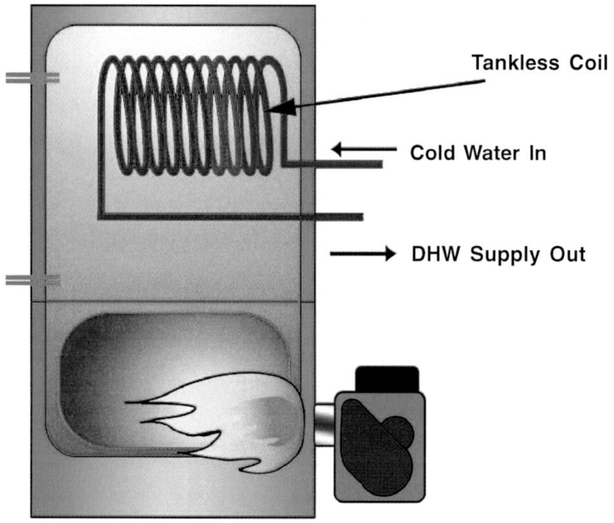

**Tankless coil
with a storage tank**
This system, often called an aqua-booster, is a combination of a storage tank and tankless coil.

Water is heated by the coil and stored in the tank. The tank temperature is maintained by a recirculation loop that allows the water to go back to the coil by forced circulation. Forced circulation is maintained by a non-corrosive circulating pump usually made of bronze or

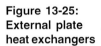

**Figure 13-25:
External plate
heat exchangers**

**Figure 13-26:
Tankless coil
with a storage tank**

stainless steel. The temperature in the tank is controlled by an aquastat installed in the tank. See Figure 13-26.

Indirect-storage type water heaters

The Indirect-Storage type heater also called a "coil-tank" or "indirect fired unit" is a storage tank with a coil of copper inside. The domestic water surrounds the coil and is heated by the boiler water that is circulated through the coil. They are piped and controlled the same as an additional zone to the heating system and may be used on both hot water and steam systems.

Since boiler water is circulated, a standard circulator can be used rather than a more expensive non-corrosive one. The domestic water temperature is controlled by an aquastat that turns the circulator and burner on and off. Although these units are more expensive than tankless coils, their

excellent warranties, improved efficiency, and high recovery rates make them very popular. Figure 13-27 shows an indirect storage type water heater.

Water heater components

A water heater is a closed vessel, filled with water, normally under city water pressure. When the tank is heated, the tank must contain and store two forms of energy: heat and pressure. If the city water pressure is lost, the tank must also be protected against excess vacuum. If adequate protection is not provided then the homeowner has a bomb sitting in the basement.

Relief valves: All water heaters with storage capability should have a temperature/pressure (T&P) relief valve that is spring loaded, which will discharge water (relief) if the temperature and/or pressure in the tank become too high. The valve must be installed into the tank water directly so it will adequately sense the temperature in the tank.

There should never be any type of shut-off devices installed on either the inlet or outlet side of the valve to prevent erroneous shut-off and loss of protection. There should also be a drain line installed on the outlet side of all pressure type valves to direct the hot water to a safe location, in the case of discharge, to avoid damage or injury to any one nearby.

On tankless coil applications where no volume of water is being stored in a tank, a pressure only relief valve is used to protect the coil and piping from excessive pressure

Vacuum relief valves: Protection

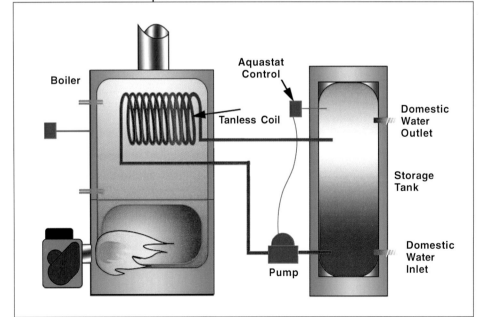

Boiler

Aquastat
Control

Tanless Coil

Pump

Domestic
Water
Outlet

Storage
Tank

Domestic
Water
Inlet

from a vacuum being exerted onto the tank is important since this can lead to a tank implosion. If a vacuum occurs, the vacuum relief valve automatically vents the closed system to the atmosphere and allows air to enter and prevent conditions that could damage the water heater.

A **back flow preventer** is a device much like a vacuum relief valve that will open a vent line to the atmosphere when it senses a vacuum. A back flow preventer should be installed in the cold water feed line above the top of the heater. If there were a leak in the cold water feed to the tank and all the fixtures were closed in the house, a vacuum would be pulled on the system. If the tank or system is not equipped with a back flow preventer or vacuum relief valve, damage to the tank may occur.

A **tempering or mixing valve** is used to control the temperature of the water being delivered to the fixtures. In tankless coil applications, the temperature of the water that has been sitting in the coil immersed in hot boiler water has the potential to scald on an initial hot water draw at the fixtures. As a hot water draw continues, the temperature of the water that has passed through the coil will not be as hot . In order to avoid the potential for scalding and to balance the temperature of the water supplied during a draw, a tempering valve is used.

A tempering valve has three ports for piping connections, one for the hot discharge side of the water heater, one for a cold water connection, and one for the hot water supply to the fixtures in the house. The tempering valve is a simple device that contains an element that senses the temperature of the water being supplied from the water heater and then mixes an appropriate amount of cold water to provide domestic hot water at the desired temperature. These valves are often adjustable so the temperature of the water may be regulated to satisfy individual preferences.

The elements in these valves are susceptible to liming from the minerals in fresh water and require periodic replacement. Rebuilding kits are readily available. When installing a tempering valve they should be installed at a level of 8"-12" inches below the heater so that they will be protected from a heat build-up while not in use.

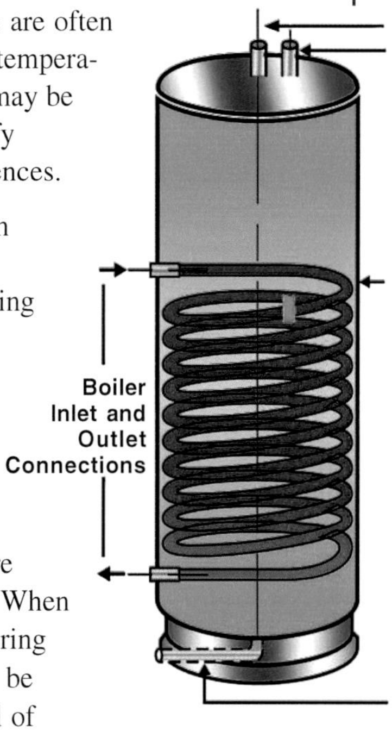

Figure 13-27: Indirect storage type water heater

The **dielectric fitting** protects the water heater or storage tank against the galvanic reaction caused by the use of dissimilar metals and stray current corrosion. These fittings come in many sizes, materials and types and can also be used in place of "pipe thread to solder" adapter or union.

Pressure reducing valve and an expansion tank. Although these items are mentioned here as "optional," they may be required by local codes. Since the domestic hot water heater or storage tank is a closed system it should be protected by an expansion tank specifically designed for the purpose. These expansion tanks should always be installed on the cold water line, before the tank but after all service valves and pressure reducing devices. The use of these tanks will prevent nuisance relief valve discharges and premature tank failures due to excess pressure build-up.

Chapter **14**

PREVENTATIVE MAINTENANCE TUNE-UPS

IN THIS CHAPTER

- The importance of preventative maintenance

- The tools you need to perform preventative maintenance

- A step-by-step procedure for performing a preventative maintenance tune-up

Chapter 14

Preventative Maintenance Tune-ups

The preventive maintenance tune-up is the most important service our industry offers. A properly performed tune-up assures the customer that their heating system is operating at peak safety, reliability, and efficiency.

Four key factors for a proper tune-up

- Safety
- Efficiency
- Reliability
- Cleanliness

Safety

During the tune-up, you will check the system's controls to be sure they work properly and shut the burner off if a problem develops. You will also adjust the burner to reduce the chances of a carbon monoxide build-up.

Efficiency

When you use your combustion analysis kit to adjust the system for maximum efficiency, you're actually helping your customer to conserve oil and save money. The tune-up also gives you the opportunity to recommend new equipment to those customers whose systems are not as reliable or as efficient as today's modern oilheat equipment.

Checking the system

Efficiency test

Equipment integrity

Typically, you may replace certain failed parts (nozzles and filters); look for and correct potential problems; lubricate motors; and check controls.

Cleanliness

Wiping down the boiler jacket

Unfortunately, most of the work you do during a tune-up is not visible to the customer. An important part of every tune-up is to make sure that what the customer does see—the outside of the unit and the area around it—are neat and clean when you've finished.

By focusing on these four factors during the tune-up, you will save your customer money by minimizing their fuel consumption and help to avoid the inconvenience of an oilburner breakdown during the heating season.

Tools of the trade

To successfully perform a tune-up, your truck must have certain tools, instruments,

Keep your tools neat in your truck

parts, and supplies. You need to have at least the following:

A complete set of hand tools including:

• Standard wrenches—depending on the type of burners you service, these can be standard, metric or both.

At a minimum, you will want to have a set of 1/4" through 3/4" standard open and box wrenches.

• Adjustable wrenches—an eight-inch and a ten-inch handle adjustable wrench.

• Socket wrench kit—1/4" to 3/4".

• Pliers—groove joint pliers (commonly called water-pumps or channel locks), linesman pliers, locking pliers (Vise Grips®) and needle nose pliers.

• Allen wrenches (hex keys)— a standard set.

• Screwdrivers—an assortment of slotted and phillips heads.

• Nut drivers—3/16", 1/4", 3/8" and 1/2".

• Wire cutter and stripper.

• Tubing cutters—3/4" regular and mini.

• Flaring tool.

• Flash light with spare batteries.

• Drop light.

• Jumper leads with insulated alligator clips.

• Tape measure—12' minimum.

• Drill and drill bits.

For Riello Burners
you'll also want to have:

- 10mm and 12mm wrenches

- #4 and #5 Torx screw drivers

- 4mm and 5mm Allen wrenches (long and short handle)

Test equipment—pressure gauge, vacuum gauge, electric meter, and complete efficiency kit.

Vacuum cleaner, assorted adaptors and flue brushes.

Supplies—furnace cement, rags, cleaner, drip tray, builder's paper or other floor covering.

As a professional, you should keep your tools and supplies organized and in good condition. Not only will they serve you better, you will project the image of a professional.

Tune-up procedure

The following are the procedures for a typical tune-up. Individual companies often develop tune-up procedures that vary from these, so it is important that you follow your company's policies and procedures.

This is an effective way to perform a tune-up in a thorough, systematic manner. Although there may be circumstances that make it impossible to do all the operations in the suggested sequence, we urge you to follow this outline whenever possible.

Step 1. Customer Interview: Give your customer a friendly and professional greeting. Courteously ask if they have experienced any problems or if they have any questions. Listen carefully and address their concerns.

Ask to see the thermostat and check for obvious problems. Check the heat anticipa-

tor setting, and make sure that it is level and set 10 degrees above the room temperature. Listen for the burner and/or circulator to start and then operate the emergency switch to be sure it works properly. Leave it in the off position.

Step 2. Visually inspect the unit:
Visually inspect the unit while you spread sheets of newspaper or clean drop cloths to protect the work area.

Inspect the heating system

Verify the heat anticipator setting is proper for the control and that limit controls are properly set with the correct differential. Note what kind of filter and pump are installed so you can bring the right replacement parts.

Check the flue pipe to be sure that it is properly screwed together and supported. If it is not, be sure to include a fix in your procedure.

If the unit has not been in operation for some time, turn the burner on for about 5 minutes to dry the heat exchanger surfaces. Check the draft drop by testing at the breech and over-the-fire. If the drop is greater than -.04 inches, there is probably a build up of soot and scale, or you may have air leaks in the unit. Note any problems so that you can repair them during the tune-up and turn the unit off before proceeding.

NOTE: If you run the burner, or if it was operating when you arrived, be extremely careful when vacuuming the unit. Allow it to cool enough to prevent hot embers from entering the vacuum.

Step 3. Inspect the oil tank: NORA recommends that if possible, technicians check the oil tank for water during tune-up. If you find water in the tank report it to your supervisor so arrangements can be made for it to be removed and an investigation made as to the source. Be sure to tighten any tank plugs you may have removed while checking the tank for water when you are finished. See Chapter 3 for tank inspection procedures and more information on tank maintenance.

Fuel line pressure gauge

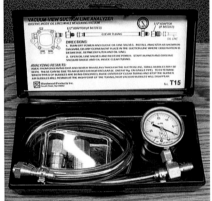

Step 4. Oil lines, valves, and filters: Shut off the oil valve and remove the filter canister—use a pan to collect the extra oil. Clean and check the filter canister and replace the cartridge and gaskets. If you find evidence of excessive sludge or water, notify your supervisor so corrective action can be scheduled.

Inspect the oil line for leaks, kinks or dents. If the line is run underground check to be sure it is made of coated copper or run in protective tubing; if bare copper is run underground, report it to your office. Make sure there are no compression fittings. If you find any, replace them with flare fittings.

Dirty strainer

Step 5. Fuel unit: Clean or replace the pump strainer, carefully scraping off the old gasket before installing a new one.

Open the valve, turn the switch on and bleed the unit. Run oil through a clear tube into a container until there are no visible air bubbles. Check for leaks at the valve stem, filter, and the pump gasket.

Disconnect the nozzle line from the drawer assembly and install your pressure gauge on the nozzle line. Operate the unit until the pressure holds steady and increase the pressure 40-50 PSI above the recom-

Checking pressure gauge on nozzle line

mended setting. Check that the pressure reading changes smoothly as you turn the adjustment screw. A pulsating or bouncing needle could indicate a leaking oil line or a bad pump. After adjusting the pump back to its proper setting, wait until the unit shuts off on safety and verify the primary control's safety timing. When the unit shuts off, the pump pressure should drop no more than 15 to 20% and then hold steady. If the pressure continues to drop, the pump has a bad cut-off and requires replacement.

Step 6. Nozzle or firing assembly: Mark the position of the firing assembly on the burner housing—remove it and note the nozzle type, size and spray angle. Verify that these match the unit data plate or the listing in your manufacturer's OEM guide.

Remove the nozzle and carefully drain the oil into a container. Inspect the nozzle adapter. Replace it if it's stripped, cracked, or if the seat is worn. Flush out the assembly, fill it with clean oil and install a new nozzle.

Clean, inspect and adjust the electrodes using the appropriate gauge.

Clean and inspect the air tube, including

the end cone slots and holes. Verify that the air tube is inserted to the correct position.

Reinsert the nozzle assembly into the air tube and secure it in place, making sure it is in the same position that you marked earlier.

Step 7. Burner motor, housing and fan: Remove the burner motor and check the burner housing for oil that could indicate a loose fitting, cracked flare or leaking fuel pump seal.

Using a fan brush

If there are oiling points on the motor; lubricate each with 3-4 drops of SAE 20 non-detergent oil. Cooling slots should be clear. Check the motor shaft for end play; if it is excessive, replace the motor. Inspect the burner coupling to be sure it is not worn or stripped. Clean the air inlets and fan using a small brush. After you reinstall the motor, spin the fan a few times to make sure that the motor, fan and pump are moving freely and that everything is properly connected. Check all wires and connections at the burner.

Step 8. Transformer and cad cell: Clean and check the transformer bushings and springs. Inspect the ignition wires. Clean the cad cell eye and wires. Make sure the bracket is positioned correctly for good flame sighting.

As you close the transformer, be sure the electrodes are making solid contact with the transformer springs and that no wires are being crimped.

Step 9. Clean the flue pipe: Remove the flue pipe and brush it out, inspect the pipe's condition, replace it if necessary.

Check the draft regulator to be sure it swings freely.

If the unit has a stack relay, inspect and clean the helix and the relay contacts.

Clean out the chimney base and check the chimney for blockages. If there's an accumulation of broken brick or liner, advise the customer to contact a chimney professional and note this information on your service ticket.

Adjusting draft regulator on flue

If the unit is equipped for power venting, clean and check the fan blower wheel. Oil the motor and check the draft-proving switch. Remember to check and clean the outside hood and exterior mechanism.

Step 10. Clean the heat exchanger and combustion area: Remove any baffles and scrub the flue passages, keeping your vacuum hose close to the brush to avoid spreading soot. Look for signs of air or water leaks.

Use a soot snorkel to clean the combustion area, being careful not to damage the chamber or target wall. Inspect the condition of the refractory material and repair or replace it as necessary.

Step 11. Replace, seal and fasten: Reassemble the unit using furnace cement if necessary to seal any air leaks. Double-check

Using a vacuum

to be sure the flue pipe is connected with sheet metal screws and is supported.

Step 12. Fire the unit and check operation: Start the burner, check the appearance of the flame and make sure that there is no impingement. Cycle the burner to check for prompt ignition, smooth operation and clean cut-off.

Disconnect the thermostat leads and install a jumper across the T-T terminals to keep the burner running. Check the operation of the high limit control.

Step 13. Efficiency test and adjustments: Perform a complete efficiency test and record the readings. The readings should be:

- Smoke: zero to a trace

- Draft: Unless the unit is designed for positive pressure, draft over-the-fire should be approximately -.02wc (negative point zero two inches)

- CO_2: 10½ to 12%

- Net stack temperature: over 350°F

When you have finished adjusting the burner, remember to remove the jumper from the T-T terminals and replace the thermostat wiring.

Step 14. The heating system: The following steps will vary depending on the type of heating system you are working on. If there is more than one thermostat, ask the customer to set each one 10 degrees above room temperature.

Hot water system
Check the zone valves and/or circulators to be sure each operates properly. If applicable, lubricate the circulator motor and bearing assembly. Check the circulator couplings and motor mounts. Check the control settings to be sure they'll provide for proper heating, hot water, and circulator operation.

Check the system pressure and the expansion tank.

If there is an indirect water heater, check the circulator and control.

Warm air system
Open the blower compartment to clean, check and lubricate the blower if applicable.

Check the air filters and clean or replace them. Note the filter size on your service ticket and remind the customer to check and clean/replace the filter regularly.

Check the condition and tension of the fan belt, replace, and adjust as required.

Check the blower mountings and bearings for excessive wear. Then properly reinstall the blower compartment door.

Check the blower limit settings.

If there is a humidifier, check it for proper operation, water leaks and mineral build up.

Steam boiler
Check the low water cutoff by draining water from the system until the burner shuts off. Check the automatic water feeder.

Clean the sight glass and replace it and the washers if necessary. If the glass fills with dirty, oily water, skim the boiler until it clears up.

Chapter 14
Preventative Maint./Tuneups

Check the main vents and look for evidence of leaks.

When you have completed these steps, be sure to return all controls to their proper settings and double check to be sure that you removed any jumpers you may have used.

Ask the customer to reset all thermostats to their normal settings.

Step 15. Cleanup the work area: Once you're satisfied that everything is working properly, use a garbage bag to remove old parts, oil absorbent and newspaper or drop cloths so that nothing can fall out on your way back to your truck. Use your vacuum cleaner to clean the area around the system. Return your tools to their proper places in your truck and clean your hands.

Step 16. Double-check your work: Check your work area one last time. Pay

Make it shine before leaving

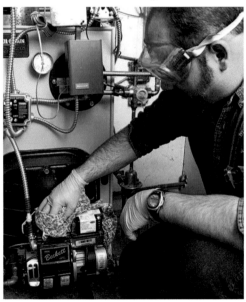

particular attention to potential sources of oil leaks such as the filter canister, pump, burner housing and oil valve.

Step 17. Make it shine: Spend a few more minutes cleaning up. Wipe and clean all of the external surfaces of the boiler or furnace and work area. Use only clean rags so you do not leave an odor behind.

Step 18. Reset and record: Verify that thermostats and controls have been returned to their proper settings. Fill out the service card with the work you have performed, the parts you have replaced, the efficiency readings, the nozzle size, and the safety timing.

Reading the service card

Fill out your company's required paperwork completely, including all of the information on the service card plus the oil level and anything that needs to be followed-up on.

Step 19. Report to the customer: Before you leave, explain what you have done and be sure to follow-up on any concerns discussed during the initial interview. Explain the efficiency test results and advise them about potential energy saving improvements.

If follow up work is required, explain what and why.

Have the customer sign the work order, give them the appropriate copy and thank them for their business.

Chapter 14—Preventative Maintenance Tune-ups 14-9

Chapter **15**

SERVICE
PROCEDURES

IN THIS
CHAPTER

- **A systematic
approach to
troubleshooting**

- **Time-saving
troubleshooting
suggestions**

Chapter 15

Service Procedures

Introduction

The most interesting and challenging part of an Oilheat Service Technician's job is troubleshooting. Think of all the parts that must work together for a system to function properly; if any one of them becomes defective, the system will malfunction. Your job is like a detective's—you must figure out what happened, why it happened, how to fix it and how to keep it from happening again.

Using an electrical meter

The previous chapters have provided you with an understanding of the operation of the various components of Oilheat systems. This chapter explains how to use that knowledge to repair systems without wasting time or replacing parts that are working properly.

Before you get involved with in-depth troubleshooting, remember to check the basics:

- Are all the switches on?

- Is the fuse blown or circuit breaker tripped?

- Is the thermostat set above the room temperature?

- Is there oil in the tank?

- Is the blower door closed? (There is a switch on many blower doors that prevents the system from operating if it's not properly closed.)

- Is there enough water in the steam or hot water system?

- Are the air filters clean?

There are many reasons for a customer to require your expertise, among the most common are:

- No heat

- Insufficient heat

- Too much heat

- No hot water

- Water leak

- Oil leak

- Odors, smoke or soot

- Oil tank and/or piping

- Thermostats, controls or electric supply

- Heat distribution system

- Oilburner components

You need to approach each problem *carefully* and *systematically*.

Carefully—**never do anything that can put you, other people, or property in danger.**

Wear appropriate Personal Protective Equipment and protect your work area with drop cloths, newspaper or builder's paper. Use insulated screwdrivers and avoid working on live electrical circuits. Do not press reset buttons without first making sure that there is not a fire or an oil buildup in the combustion chamber.

Wear protective equipment

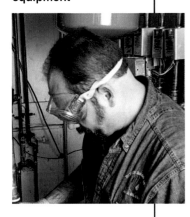

Systematically—**the best Service Technicians develop standard trouble-shooting routines. They go from step to step until they find and correct the cause of the problem.**

A systematic approach starts with logic—looking for the obvious solution and then trying to narrow down the problem. Start with the easy—if the heating system is not working, check that all electrical switches are turned on and that there is enough oil in the tank before you start disassembling the oilburner.

Most importantly, NEVER assume anything. Don't assume that the reset was only pressed once; don't assume that the last service technician installed the correct nozzle; don't assume that your dispatcher told you the correct reason for the call and don't assume that because a customer says they have plenty of oil that their tank isn't empty.

An example of a systematic troubleshooting routine:

Step 1. Information gather- ing: Effective troubleshooting starts before you arrive at the customer's home. When your dispatcher gives you the call, try to get important data such as:

- What problem did the customer report?

- When was the last oil delivery?

- When was the last tune-up?

- When was the last service call, and what was done?

When you arrive at the customer's home, listen to what the customer says and ask questions to clarify the situation. Depending on the type of trouble, you may want to ask if any work has been done recently that might have caused the situation, such as other tradesmen working on the electric or plumbing, or if a chimney sweep has just been performed.

Ask if they have pressed the reset button, how many times and what happened after it was pressed.

Once you think you understand exactly what the problem is, proceed to the appliance area and on your way, check the electrical switch and oil tank gauge. When

Check service card

you get to the burner, read the service card on the unit to see what work previous technicians have performed.

Step 2. The investigation: At this point, you know what the problem is (no heat) and what work has been recently performed. Now is time to narrow down your investigation.

Assume that you find the primary control is off on safety. You know that in an oilheat system, electricity flows from the circuit breaker to a switch to the limit controls to the primary control to the burner components. Since the control is off on safety, you can eliminate everything from the primary control back—the limit controls, switches or circuit breaker cannot have caused the problem.

You have determined that the problem is probably the fuel supply, the primary control or a burner problem. There could also be a low voltage situation. Use your electrical meter to check. If the voltage is correct, move on to the next step.

Step 3. Determine the problem: Next, protect the work area and remove the thermostat wires from the T-T terminals of the primary control (to prevent damage to the thermostat). Install a jumper between the terminals to simulate the thermostat calling for heat throughout the rest of the service call.

Open the observation door to check for a flame or excess oil in the chamber, if there is no flame or oil, leave the door open to allow any excess pressure to escape in the event of a delayed ignition when the burner starts.

Press the reset button and observe what happens:

• If the burner ignites and runs properly but shuts off on safety, you should visually check the cad-cell eye and leads; and check the retention head for carbon build up. If the eye and/or retention head is dirty, clean them and continue troubleshooting to determine why they're dirty.

• If the eye and head are clean, disconnect the cad cell leads from the control, start the burner and install a 1,000-ohm resistor across the F-F terminals to simulate a fire and connect your ohmmeter to the disconnected leads to check the resistance through the cad cell. If the resistance is high, the cell is either defective or is not sighting the fire correctly. If the resistance is below 1,500 ohms check the leads again, either they're crimped or the control is defective.

• If the burner starts but does not ignite, you know the problem is related to the

You can protect the work area with newspaper, builder's paper or drop cloths. Be careful when using drop cloths because they can absorb oil and cause you to bring a mess and odors to your next call.

Ohmmeter connected to leads

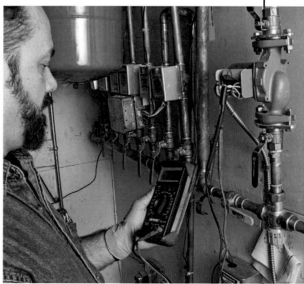

combustion process. It could be an ignition problem, an oil problem or excess air.

• If nothing happens, the control might be sensing flame. The cad cell leads might be crimped together or the F-F terminals might be shorted.

• If the burner hums but does not start, the burner motor might be defective or the pump might be "bound" causing the motor to shut off on overload.

Step 4. The 5 Whys: Professional Service Technicians look beyond the *symptoms* to find the *cause* of the problem. For example, if you press the reset button and the burner starts, you have not fixed anything. You have to find out why the control went off on safety and take corrective action to keep it from happening again.

When you find the cause of a problem, ask yourself "why did this happen?" Continue to ask yourself the same question and eventually you will get to the real cause of the problem. For example, suppose a customer has no heat. During

your systematic troubleshooting routine, you may find the following:

Sometimes you will find the answer with less than five "whys"; sometimes it might take more than five. The key is to keep asking until you are satisfied that you know the reason for the problem and the corrective action to take.

Step 5. The "Hows": Once you know the "whys" you need to correct the immediate problem *and* keep it from happening again. "How" do you do that? In the situation we just reviewed in the "5 Whys" the following steps are required:

1. Replace the vent pipe
2. Remove the water from the tank
3. Clean the oil lines
4. Replace the fuel unit
5. Replace the nozzle
6. Replace the oil filter
7. Reset the primary control (and burner motor if applicable)
8. Fire the unit
9. Adjust the burner and perform an efficiency test

In some situations, you might not have the time, equipment or experience necessary to perform all of the "Hows". In that case, you should troubleshoot the situation to the best of your ability and contact your supervisor for instructions on how to proceed.

Step 6—Paperwork and exit. Once you have completed the "Hows," clean up your work area, remove all debris to a receptacle in your service vehicle and clean your hands.

Complete your company's paperwork and fill in the service card at the unit. Take

The control is off on safety.

The motor will not turn.

The pump is seized.

It is full of rust and water.

The oil tank has water in it.

The vent pipe is rotted and allows rainwater to enter the tank.

a last look around to make sure that the area is clean, that you have taken all your tools, removed all jumpers and returned all controls and thermostats to their proper settings.

Give the customer the appropriate copy of the invoice, explain what you did and the efficiency test results and answer any questions they have. Thank them for their business and return to your vehicle to move on to your next call.

Helpful hint: try to avoid unplugging any electrical appliances when performing service. If you must unplug anything, ask the customer for permission first and leave your truck keys tied to the cord to ensure you will plug it back in before you leave.

Troubleshooting suggestions

The following is intended to help you troubleshoot typical problems that you are likely to encounter. It is not a list of all possible situations or each and every step you should take to troubleshoot problems.

#1 No heat—the unit is cold and the burner is not operating.

If the primary control has no power:

1. Check the limit controls. If the limit control has power coming through it there is a problem with the wiring between the limit and the primary control. NOTE: Make sure you have checked all of the limit controls; for example—on a system with both a high limit aquastat and a low water cut-off, you must make sure that both are allowing electricity to pass through to the primary control.

2. If the limit control has no power coming to it, check the switch. If there is no power to the switch, check the circuit breaker or fuse.

3. If you reset the circuit breaker and the unit runs, do not leave right away

because something *caused* the breaker to trip. Use an ammeter to determine if any of the system components are malfunctioning.

If the primary control has the correct input voltage, but no power is going to the burner motor, igniter or oil valve:

1. Check to be sure that there is not a fire in the chamber. (Cad cell primaries will not energize if a fire is sensed.)

2. Make sure that the thermostat is set well above room temperature and the heat anticipator is set to the current draw of the control circuit.

3. If the burner still does not start, disconnect the thermostat wires from the T-T terminals of the primary control and install a jumper.

If the burner starts, there is a problem with the thermostat or its wiring.

4. If the burner still does not start, disconnect the cad cell leads from the F-F terminals.

• If the burner starts, there is a problem with the cad cell or its leads.

• If the burner does not start, check to be sure that there is not a piece of wire or something else shorting out the F-F terminals.

• If there is nothing shorting out the F-F terminals, the control is probably malfunctioning. Use your ohmmeter to perform the test mentioned earlier.

If the primary control is passing the correct voltage through to the burner components but:

A. Motor runs but no flame

1. Disconnect the nozzle line and check the oil flow. If water is found in the oil, drain it from the tank.

2. If the flow is good and water free, check the nozzle and ignition system (see next section B, on following page.)

3. If there is no flow, check the oil solenoid valve and bleed the pump.

4. If the pump cannot be primed, make sure all valves are open and check for oil (Stick the tank, the gauge may be wrong).

5. If there is sufficient oil, check the oil filter and perform a vacuum test (see Chapter 4), the oil line or tank vent may be clogged.

6. If the vacuum is high, clean the oil line with a push-pull pump.

7. If the vacuum is low, check the coupling.

8. If the coupling is good, check the pump strainer.

9. If everything checks OK, perform a complete pump test (see Chapter 4.)

B. Motor runs with oil flow but no ignition

1. Check the electrodes/porcelains/ignition cables for defects.

2. Check the electrode setting and nozzle position.

3. Check the transformer connections.

4. Verify that correct primary voltage is supplied to ignition transformer/igniter.

C. Motor runs with oil pressure and ignition but no flame

1. Check the nozzle and replace if plugged.

2. Check the oil pressure, set to manufacturer specs.

3. Check the air settings—adjust as necessary (too much air can "blow out" the flame.)

Nozzle gauge

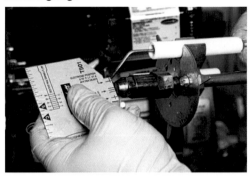

Checking oil pressure

D. Burner fires but shuts off on safety

1. If a stack relay is installed:

- Check the helix, clean and/or reposition as necessary.

- Check that there is sufficient temperature in the flue.

2. If a cad cell control is installed:

- Check the cell, clean and re-position as necessary.

- Check the air tube and end cone, clean/replace as necessary.

3. Check for water or air in the nozzle line:

- If water is found, drain it from the tank and lines

- If air is found, perform pump tests to determine why. (Chapter 3)

4. Check air settings—adjust as necessary.

E. Motor does not start

1. The motor might be off on thermal overload—if there is a reset, press it. If there is no reset, check to see if the motor feels hot; if it does, give it a few minutes to cool down.

2. If the motor still does not start, the trouble is in the motor or motor circuit.

3. If the motor has a capacitor, check it before you condemn the motor.

#2 No heat—the unit is warm but no heat is circulating.

If the oilburner operates properly but no heat comes from the radiation or ductwork, the problem is with the delivery system. Make sure that all thermostats are set to call for heat, verify that heat anticipators are properly set and:

Hot water system

1. Check for closed hand or motorized valves.

2. Check that there is sufficient pressure in the system.

3. Check that the circulator is operating properly.

4. Check the flow control valve.

5. Check that the system is not air bound.

6. Check that the high limit is set properly.

7. Check that the reverse aquastat is set properly.

Warm air system

1. Check that the fan-limit control is set properly.

2. Check that all dampers are open.

3. Check that air filters are clean.

4. Check to see if the blower is operating:

   - If it is, check the drive belt.

   - If it is not, check the motor.

Steam system

1. Check the water level—too much water in the system will prevent steam from rising.

2. Check for closed hand or motorized valves.

3. Check the electrical circuits for motorized valves.

4. Check the main vents.

5. Check the pressuretrol setting.

#3 Insufficient heat—the burner is operating but the house is much cooler than the thermostat setting

Sometimes this occurs because it is much colder than normal and the house just cannot "keep up" with the outside temperature and/or the system (boiler, furnace, piping, radiation, ductwork) might be undersized.

> **The best Service Technicians develop standard troubleshooting routines. They go from step to step until they find and correct the cause of the problem.**

Your job is like a detective's—you must figure out what happened, why it happened, how to fix it and how to keep it from happening again.

Other causes for insufficient heat:
A. Burner trouble

1. The burner might be under-fired. Make sure that the burner's firing rate is properly set for the boiler or furnace.

B. Control circuit

1. Check the heat anticipator settings.

2. Check that the thermostat is properly located. Thermostats are affected by the heat generated by lamps, appliances or fireplaces and should not be located near any heat source.

3. Check that the limit controls and reverse acting aquastats are properly set.

C. Heating systems

1. Check to be sure that the steam vents are operating properly.

2. Check that pipes and/or ductwork are properly insulated.

3. Check that airflow through air filters, radiators, or baseboard is not obstructed by dust, closed air dampers, carpet, furniture or curtains.

4. Check that the water level is adequate in steam systems.

5. Check that hot water systems are not air bound.

6. Check that blowers and their pulleys and belts are functioning properly.

#4 Too much heat

When the customer complains of too much heat the most likely causes are:

1. Thermostat stuck, set too high, improperly located or defective.

2. Limit control defective or set too high.

3. Flow control valve stuck.

4. Motorized valve stuck.

#5 No hot water

Troubleshooting a "no hot water" call with an oil-fired water heater is basically the same as troubleshooting a no heat call; you check the burner and the limit control. When the hot water comes from a domestic hot water coil or storage tank, you should:

1. Check the aquastat settings.

2. Check to be sure the water level in the boiler is above the coil.

3. Check the mixing valve.

4. If there's a storage tank installed:

   • Check the control setting.

   • Check the circulator.

   • If the tank seems to be full of hot water but the water coming from the hot tapping is cool, check the dip tube on the inlet to the tank.

#6 Water leak

Depending on the severity of the leak, this can be a minor inconvenience or a major problem.

1. **USE CAUTION!** Never work on electrical components while they are wet or when you're standing on wet floors.

Helpful hint—Treat all electrical circuits as if they were energized even when you're sure they aren't.

2. If a relief valve is leaking:

Steam system—check the steam gauge and the pressuretrol. Remember that residential steam systems should operate at a maximum of 2 PSI and steam relief valves open at 15 PSI. If the relief valve opens, it is likely either the valve or the pressuretrol is malfunctioning.

Hot water system—a number of things can cause the relief valve to open on a hot water system:

- A full expansion tank.

- A bad diaphragm on a pressurized expansion tank.

- A malfunctioning or improperly set aquastat.

- A misadjusted or malfunctioning pressure-reducing valve.

- A leaking domestic hot water coil.

- A malfunctioning relief valve.

Water heater—check the aquastat and the domestic hot water pressure.

Helpful hint—many municipalities require the installation of backflow prevention devices that can cause heating system relief valves to open. Often the only way to stop the valve from opening is to install a domestic water expansion tank.

Remember that each gallon of oil burned creates a gallon of water in the combustion gases. If the boiler water temperature drops below 130 degrees, the water in the combustion gases will condense in the heat exchanger, mimicking a water leak.

---

3. Circulator flange gaskets can leak. Tightening the flange may stop the leak but it is usually better to replace the gaskets once they start leaking.

4. Older style circulators often had a separate bearing assembly that would leak water from a weep hole when they became defective. With this type of leak, you can either change the bearing assembly or replace the entire circulator with a modern water lubricated model.

5. If the boiler itself is leaking, it is usually beyond repair. Turn off the electric power and the water supply to the unit, drain the remaining water from the system and contact your supervisor for instructions.

Helpful hint—Customers often complain of water leaks during rainstorms. These "water leaks" are sometimes caused by rainwater coming down the chimney and leaking onto the floor.

Remember that each gallon of oil burned creates a gallon of water in the combustion gases. If the boiler water temperature drops below 130 degrees, the water in the combustion gases will condense in the heat exchanger, mimicking a water leak.

#7 Oil leaks

Oil leaks are a serious concern because they can lead to significant damage. Your approach to these calls will depend on the severity of the leak.

Minor leaks typically occur at:

1. **Brass fittings:** If the system has compression fittings, they should be replaced with flare fittings. If a flare fitting is leaking, turn off the oil supply then

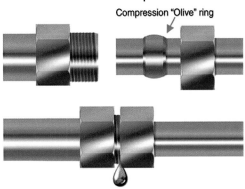

Compression "Olive" ring

Compression fitting

disassemble and inspect the flare. If the flare looks to be in good condition reconnect it, tighten it, clean it with an absorbent rag and run the burner. After several minutes inspect the fitting closely, if there's any evidence of a leak cut out the flare, re-

Flare nut

Flair fitting

flare the copper, reconnect it and keep checking until you're sure the leak has been stopped.

2. **Malleable fittings:** If you find a leak at a malleable fitting, inspect it closely before taking it apart. If the leak appears to be coming from the area where the fitting is threaded, disassemble it, clean it, apply pipe joint compound and reconnect it.

If the leak appears to be coming from a crack or sand hole, replace the fitting.

3. **Fuel unit:** If a leak appears to be coming from a fuel unit, check that all of the fittings, plugs and bolts that hold the cover are tight. If the leak continues, check the gasket; if it is leaking, replace it. If the pump is still leaking, replace it.

4. **Oilburner:** Most burners have a "weep hole" in the bottom that allows oil to drain from the housing. If you find such a leak check:

- The pump seal.
- The nozzle adaptor.
- For an after-drip from the nozzle.

5. **Tanks:** Minor leaks at tanks often appear as drips or wet spots. If the tank has

a minor leak, put a magnet patch on it and call you supervisor for instructions.

6. **Oil lines:** oil lines, especially those in contact with concrete, can develop holes and leak. Do NOT cut out the leaking section and replace it with a new piece of copper. When a leak develops, replace the line from the tank to the burner; if the line is buried in or contacts concrete, install coated copper tubing or install the line in secondary containment.

If you encounter a more serious leak, try to stop the flow of oil, shut off any sump pumps in the area and close off floor drains and any access to groundwater. Contact your office immediately and spread absorbent while you wait for help to arrive.

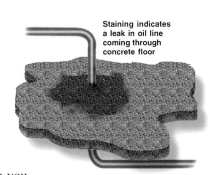

Staining indicates a leak in oil line coming through concrete floor

#8 Odors, smoke, or soot

Several different problems can cause these troubles, among them are:

1. Delayed ignition
2. Combustion problems
3. Dirty or defective chimney or flue
4. Insufficient air in boiler room
5. Air leaks in the boiler
6. Defective heat exchanger
7. House fan sucking air down the chimney

#9 Noise

These calls are often frustrating because the noise can be intermittent. When you arrive, the noise may have stopped and you will have to run the burner through several cycles and raise all the thermostats to get it to start. Some heating system noises originate in the area near the heating system, but can only be heard in the living area.

Noises can come from:

- Worn pump gears
- High vacuum
- Air in oil line
- Oil lines in contact with each other, boiler/furnace jacket, beams, or other items
- Air in a hot water heating system
- Electrical circuit—hum from relays, transformers, motors, etc
- Improper control settings (too much pressure or temperature)
- Circulators
- Blowers
- Zone valves
- Loose covers on controls
- Water pipes
- Heating pipes and baseboard
- Chimneys

Conclusion

Much of what you learn about troubleshooting will be due to your on-the-job experiences. We hope that you will remember the "5 Whys" and always look beyond the symptoms for the cause.

A final piece of troubleshooting advice: "Listen, look and think before you rip, tear and destroy."

The following Troubleshooting charts were provided by Beckett Corp. and Riello. We thank them for allowing us to share them with you.

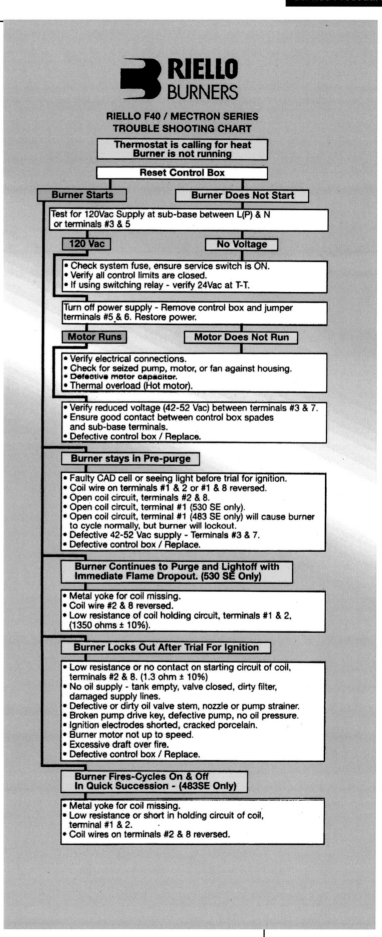

RIELLO BURNERS

RIELLO F40 / MECTRON SERIES TROUBLE SHOOTING CHART

Thermostat is calling for heat Burner is not running

Reset Control Box

| Burner Starts | Burner Does Not Start |

Test for 120Vac Supply at sub-base between L(P) & N or terminals #3 & 5

| 120 Vac | No Voltage |

- Check system fuse, ensure service switch is ON.
- Verify all control limits are closed.
- If using switching relay - verify 24Vac at T-T.

Turn off power supply - Remove control box and jumper terminals #5 & 6. Restore power.

| Motor Runs | Motor Does Not Run |

- Verify electrical connections.
- Check for seized pump, motor, or fan against housing.
- Defective motor capacitor.
- Thermal overload (Hot motor).

- Verify reduced voltage (42-52 Vac) between terminals #3 & 7.
- Ensure good contact between control box spades and sub-base terminals.
- Defective control box / Replace.

Burner stays in Pre-purge

- Faulty CAD cell or seeing light before trial for ignition.
- Coil wire on terminals #1 & 2 or #1 & 8 reversed.
- Open coil circuit, terminals #2 & 8.
- Open coil circuit, terminal #1 (530 SE only).
- Open coil circuit, terminal #1 (483 SE only) will cause burner to cycle normally, but burner will lockout.
- Defective 42-52 Vac supply - Terminals #3 & 7.
- Defective control box / Replace.

Burner Continues to Purge and Lightoff with Immediate Flame Dropout. (530 SE Only)

- Metal yoke for coil missing.
- Coil wire #2 & 8 reversed.
- Low resistance of coil holding circuit, terminals #1 & 2, (1350 ohms ± 10%).

Burner Locks Out After Trial For Ignition

- Low resistance or no contact on starting circuit of coil, terminals #2 & 8. (1.3 ohm ± 10%)
- No oil supply - tank empty, valve closed, dirty filter, damaged supply lines.
- Defective or dirty oil valve stem, nozzle or pump strainer.
- Broken pump drive key, defective pump, no oil pressure.
- Ignition electrodes shorted, cracked porcelain.
- Burner motor not up to speed.
- Excessive draft over fire.
- Defective control box / Replace.

Burner Fires-Cycles On & Off In Quick Succession - (483SE Only)

- Metal yoke for coil missing.
- Low resistance or short in holding circuit of coil, terminal #1 & 2.
- Coil wires on terminals #2 & 8 reversed.

Basic Troubleshooting provided by *Beckett*

Recommended Equipment

1. Electrical test meter (VOLTS, OHMS, AMPS).
2. Ignition transformer tester.
3. Combustion analyzer kit (oxygen or carbon dioxide, smoke, stack temperature, draft, system efficiency).
4. Pressure/vacuum gauge (0-200 psig and 0-30: Hg).
5. Full assortment of standard hand tools.

Preliminary Steps

1. Check oil level in supply tank.
2. Make sure all oil line valves are open.
3. Examine combustion chamber for excessive unburned oil. Clean if necessary.
4. Measure line voltage at primary control input connections. It should be 120 volts. Lower than 105 volts AC may cause operating problems. If there is no reading, check for open switches or circuit breakers.
5. Make sure thermostat or other controlling device is calling for burner operation.
6. Check primary control to see if safety reset switch is "locked out."

Determining Malfunction Causes

1. Disconnect nozzle line connector tube and reposition it so that it will deliver oil into a container. Tighten flare nut at pump discharge fitting.
2. Reset primary control safety switch if it is locked out. Turn power ON. Observe the following:

   - **Contact action of primary relay control.** Does it pull in promptly, without arcing erratically or chattering?
   - **Oil delivery.** You should have an immediate, clear, steady stream. White frothy oil means air in the supply system, which must be corrected. No delivery means severe restriction somewhere.
   - **Ignition arc.** You should hear ignition arc buzzing. If not, test output voltage of transformer. If below 9,000 volts, replace.
   - **Motor.** Does it pull up quickly and smoothly? Listen for RPM change and audible "click" as the centrifugal switch disconnects start (auxiliary) winding.

3. If cause of failure has not been identified:

   - Reconnect nozzle line fittings for burner fire test.

- Reset primary control if necessary. Run several cycles. Observe flame quality. Use a flame mirror, if possible, to see if flame base is stable and close to combustion head. Is flame centered, uniform in shape, and relatively quiet? Are head and chamber free of carbon formations or impingement? Sometimes a defective or partially plugged nozzle can cause trouble.

Additional Procedures:

If the problem still has not been identified, a more thorough evaluation of the basic system must be made. The following procedures may be helpful:

Primary Control System (Cad Cell Type) starts burner, supervises operating cycles, shuts burner off at end of heat call, and locks out ON SAFETY if there is a flame failure.

1. Measure electrical voltage at primary input (usually black) and neutral lead (usually white) connections. It should be 120 volts.
2. Jumper thermostat (TT terminals) or otherwise energize primary control.
3. Control relay should pull in. If not, make sure wiring connections are secure and cad cell is not "seeing" stray light (chamber glow).
4. If relay pulls in, but motor fails to start, measure voltage between neutral lead (usually white) and primary control lead for motor (usually orange). Relay switch contacts may be defective, causing a severe voltage drop.
5. If relay fails to pull in, or is erratic and chatters, even when wiring connections are secure, replace control.
6. Check safety lockout timing by removing one F (cad cell) lead from control. Start burner and count seconds until control locks out. Time should be reasonably close to rating plate specifications on control body.
7. To check cad cell, start burner and unhook both cad cell leads from control FF terminals. Jumper FF screw terminals to keep burner operating. Measure OHMS resistance across cad cell leads **as it views the flame.** It should be 1600 OHMS or less. Preferred reading is 300-1000 OHMS. Next, with meter connected to cad cell leads, turn burner OFF. DARK conditions should give a reading of 100,000 OHMS or infinity. If reading is lower, let refractory cool down, and check for stray light entering burner through air inlet, or around transformer base-plate. If cad cell is not performing within these guidelines, replace it.
8. The control may be governed by a room thermostat. Be sure heat anticipator setting or rating of the thermostat matches the 24 volt current draw.

This information is usually printed on the control body. Erratic operation may be caused by improper anticipator settings. Settings are typically .2 or .4 amps. This value can usually be measured by connecting a multitester in SERIES with one of the TT leads, and reading the value on the appropriate milliampere scale.

The Ignition System is generally comprised of an ignition transformer and two electrodes that deliver a concentrated spark across a fixed gap to ignite oil droplets in the nozzle spray. Delays in establishing spark at the beginning of the burner cycle can result in "puff backs," which can fill the room with fumes. If spark is inadequate, burner may lock out on safety. If transformer is suspect, make the following checks:

1. Measure voltage between transformer/primary lead and neutral connection. It should be 120 volts on the primary input side.

2. Secondary terminals of a good transformer deliver 5000 volts each to ground, for a total of 10,000 volts between the terminals. Measure this with a transformer tester or use a well-insulated screwdriver to draw an arc across the two springs. This should be at least 3/4" in length. Check **each** secondary output terminal by drawing a strong arc between the spring and base. If arc is erratic, weak, or unbalanced between the two terminals, replace transformer.

3. Transformer failures and ignition problems can be caused by the following:

   • An excessive gap setting on ignition electrodes will cause higher than normal stress on the internal insulation system. This can lead to premature failure. Set electrode gap according to manufacturer's instructions (typically 5/32").

   • High ambient temperatures can lower effectiveness of internal insulation system.

   • High humidity conditions can cause over-the-surface arc tracking, both internally and externally, on ceramic bushings.

   • Carbon residue and other foreign materials adhering to porcelain bushings can contribute to arc tracking and subsequent failure.

   • Low input line voltage can cause reduced transformer life. It should be at least 105 volts AC.

   • Ignition electrodes must have good contact with transformer springs. Any arcing here must be eliminated. The only arcing should be at the electrode tips.

   • Electrode insulating porcelains must be clean and free of carbon residue, moisture, crazing, or pin hole leaks. Leakage paths can contribute to faulty ignition.

• Electrode settings must conform to specifications for gap width, distance in front of nozzle face, and distance above the nozzle center line. Improper positioning can produce delayed ignition, spray impingement on electrodes, carbon bridging, and loss of ignition, which can lead to safety lockouts.

• Replace electrodes if tips are worn or eroded. Replace questionable porcelain insulators.

The Burner Motor drives the blower wheel and fuel pump by means of a shaft coupling. To diagnose motor problems, follow these guidelines:

1. Motor fails to start.

   • Check for adequate voltage between motor/primary lead and neutral connection with the motor energized. Line voltage must be within 10% of motor rating plate specified voltage.

   • If motor hums when energized, but shaft does not rotate, the start switch may be defective. With the power turned OFF, rotate blower wheel by hand. If it turns freely, replace motor.

   • If blower does not turn freely, check for a bound fuel unit, jammed blower, dry bearings, or a grossly misaligned shaft coupling. Oil bearings with SAE 20W oil. Or, if permanently lubricated, does not need to be oiled.

2. Other motor-related problems.

   • If overload protection has tripped, start motor and measure current draw. It should not exceed rating plate specifications under load conditions by more than 10%. Excessive amp draw usually indicates an overload condition, defective start switch, or shorted windings.

   • If motor is noisy, check alignment of shaft with coupling. Tighten or slightly loosen motor-to-burner-housing bolts in an alternate sequence. Check for loose blower wheel, excessive radial shaft play or loose start switch parts.

   • It is difficult, and usually not cost effective, to rebuild motors in the field. Replace them, instead.

   • If motor operates normally, but does not drive pump shaft, check coupling for slippage due to stripped end caps.

The Fuel Pump transfers oil from the supply tank, cleans it with a strainer or similar mechanism, pressurizes the oil for good atomization at the nozzle, and provides a good shutoff at the end of the run cycle. Manufacturers provide excellent installation and service information. Please read and follow it carefully. Many burner problems can be traced to incorrect installation of oil piping and fittings.

Chapter **16**

ENERGY CONSERVATION

IN THIS CHAPTER

- The technician's role in increasing equipment sales

- Steady state versus seasonal efficiency

- How oil-fired heating systems lose heat and efficiency: on-cycle losses, off-cycle losses, jacket losses, piping and duct losses, and air infiltration

- Equipment upgrades and replacements to improve efficiency

- How to persuade your customers to invest in energy conservation

Chapter 16

Energy Conservation

The technician as an energy expert

A service technician must ensure that the customer's heating system is operating as efficiently as possible. Efficient equipment is more reliable and cleaner burning. Customers with efficient heating equipment are more satisfied with their oil dealer and with Oilheat. In this chapter, we will examine what constitutes an efficient system, how heating systems waste energy, and what we can do to be sure our customers are getting the most comfort for their energy dollar.

As an energy expert you must:

• **Inform customers of new technology advances**—Customers trust technicians; therefore, we can supply valuable advice to customers.

• **Install and adjust equipment for peak efficiency**—Properly adjusted Oilheat equipment is the safest, most reliable, most efficient, cleanest, most environmentally friendly and most comfortable heat available.

• **Service the equipment**—Take responsibility for the operation of your customer's equipment.

• **Keep track of new technology**

• **Measure and record combustion efficiency**—Use test instruments to ensure customer's equipment is operating at its

peak potential and cleanliness while producing minimal air emissions and carbon monoxide levels.

Combustion efficiency tests

Using instruments improves efficiency, ensures minimal smoke and soot, lowers air pollution emissions, and ensures safe operation. It also cuts call backs, improves our image and increases customer satisfaction.

Steady state vs heating system efficiency

Combustion efficiency tests are vital to proper servicing of equipment; however, they only measure the efficiency when the burner is running. Heating System Efficiency is the actual heating efficiency of the home for the year. (It is also sometimes called Seasonal Efficiency.) You cannot measure it on a service call. It involves the amount of fuel consumed, the total degree days for the year, the temperature the customer heated their home to all year, and the amount of hot water consumed. It is the difference between the Btus purchased and Btus used.

Heat losses in oilheating systems

The purpose of an oilheating system is to transfer the heat from the burner flame to the home. No heating system, regardless of the fuel it uses, can operate at 100 percent efficiency. Some heating energy is lost before it ever reaches the radiators, convectors or supply registers in the house. These losses reduce overall system effectiveness and increase fuel use. It is important we understand the many types of heat loss that reduce efficiency. Figure 16-1. Heat can be lost through:

- Burner on-cycle
- Burner off-cycle
- Jacket or Casing
- Pipes or Ducts, and
- Air infiltration

**Figure 16-1:
Flue heat loss
(on and off
cycles)**

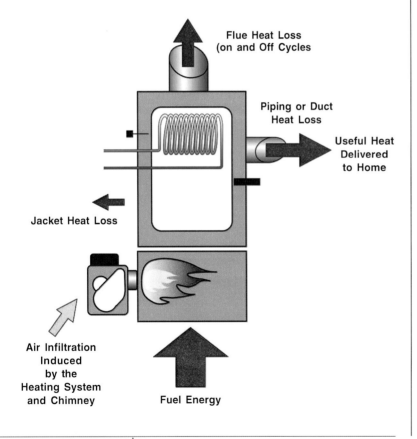

The actual efficiency of an oilheating system is affected by many factors, including:

Installation factors:

- Selection of burner/boiler or burner/furnace
- Chimney design or upgrades
- Boiler or furnace sizing
- Boiler water or furnace air operating temperatures
- Piping or ducting design
- Burner adjustment
- Isolated combustion air.

Service procedures:

- Barometric damper setting
- Sealing air leaks into the boiler or furnace
- Burner adjustment: (excess air and smoke)
- Cleaning boiler or furnace heat transfer surfaces
- Proper nozzle sizing.

Other factors that affect efficiency:

- Location of unit
- Chimney Draft—height, materials, construction
- Source of combustion and draft relief air
- Burner design & operating pressure
- Zoning of distribution system

- Integration of domestic water heating system
- Mass of the boiler or furnace

> **Combustion test equipment must always be used to adjust the burner for peak efficiency**

Service procedures have a significant effect on boiler or furnace efficiency. Even the most efficient heating unit will waste fuel if it is not serviced periodically and if it is not adjusted properly. When the full efficiency of the boiler or furnace is not reached, then oilheat's efficiency advantage is reduced. Routine service using standardized procedures, including vacuum cleaning and precise burner adjustment, are a vital part of good service. Always record efficiency test results.

Burner on-cycle heat loss

One of the biggest heat losses from central heating systems through the flue is the venting of exhaust gases while the burner is operating. See Figure 16-2. Combustion air and fuel enter the burner at room temperature (usually about 65°F) and heated combustion products leave the boiler or furnace, normally between 400 and 700°F. Heat loss can be reduced by better burner adjustment, clean heat exchanger surfaces, or equipment replacement.

Flue heat loss consists of two components; water vapor loss (a fixed property of the fuel) and sensible heat loss (varies with burner adjustment, equipment design and servicing).

The "water vapor" of flue loss is a result

Sensible Heat Loss Depends on Volume of Exhaust Gases

Water Vapor Loss Fixed Property of Fuel

Boiler Or Furnace

Burner Adjustment Affects Sensible Heat Loss

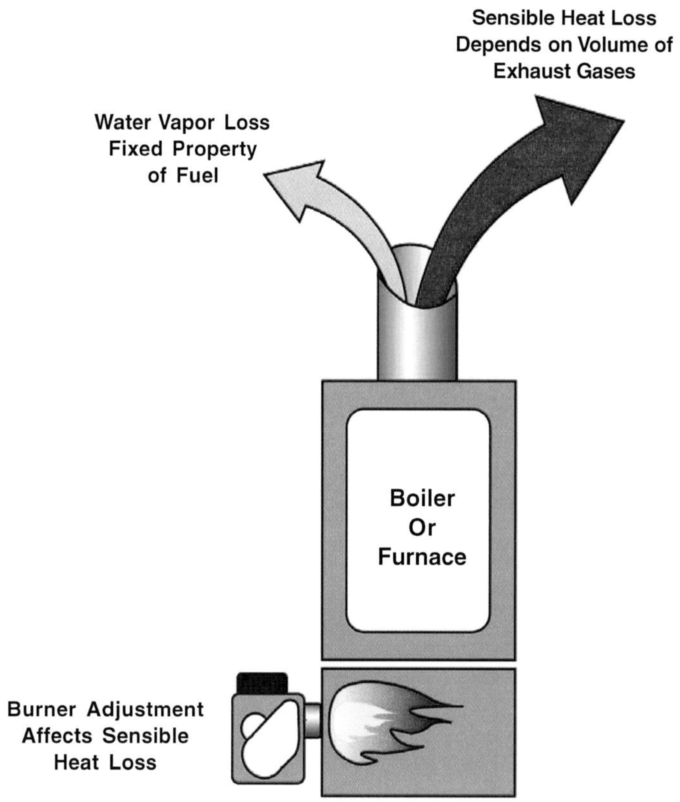

Figure 16-2: Burner on-cycle heat loss

of the water vapor contained in the combustion of exhaust gases. Water is produced when oil is burned. This water is transformed to steam and leaves the heating unit. Eight-thousand Btus are lost with each gallon of water that is vented as steam—or about 6.5% of the total energy in fuel oil. This loss is also called "latent heat loss" (it is the energy required to convert water from liquid to vapor).

It is possible to reclaim the heat contained in the water by lowering the exhaust temperature until the water condenses out of the

FLUE HEAT LOSS DURING BURNER OPERATION

(Percent of Total Heat Content of Fuel Oil)

	Average	Typical Range	Comb. Eff.
Old Oil Heating Units	28	20 - 35	72%
New Oil Heating Units	13	11 - 19	86%
Minimum for Non-Condensing	10	—	89%

**Figure 16-3:
Off-cycle
heat loss**

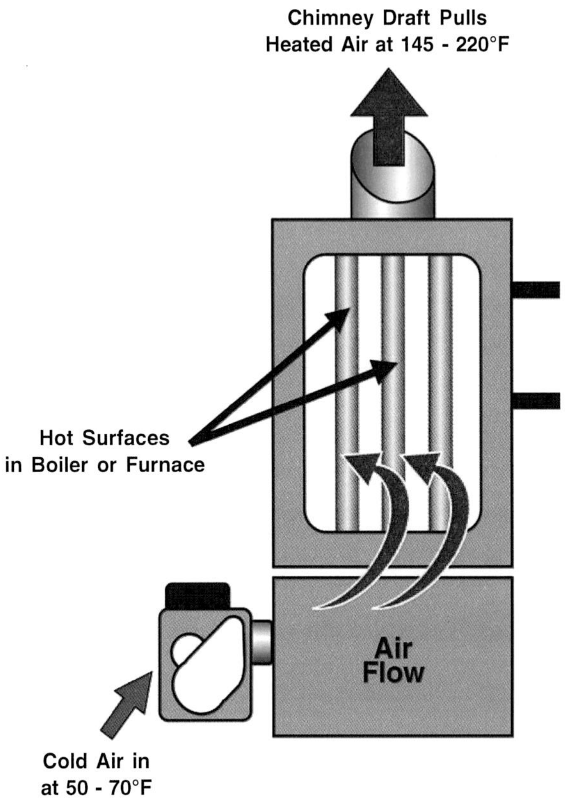

Chimney Draft Pulls
Heated Air at 145 - 220°F

Hot Surfaces
in Boiler or Furnace

Air
Flow

Cold Air in
at 50 - 70°F

flue gases. Condensing equipment, which deliberately condenses the water in the combustion gases, is available in some heating appliance lines. These units are designed to handle the water and the acids that are created in this process.

To prevent condensation in conventional heating units, exhaust gas temperatures need to be 350°F or more. The 350° exhaust gases also produce the chimney draft that is required by conventional systems for normal flue gas venting.

"Sensible heat loss" depends on the temperature of exhaust gases and their total volume. Increased excess air increases the volume of combustion gases, which also increases the velocity of these gases through the heat exchanger. The faster the gases move through the heat exchanger, the less heat can be extracted. This raises stack temperatures and lowers efficiency. Lowering excess combustion air and/or flue gas temperature can reduce sensible flue heat loss.

New oil-powered appliances operate very efficiently, with flue heat losses ranging from 11 to 15%. This is close to the highest value possible for non-condensing systems. Remember that a net stack temperature of about 350°F or more is required to avoid water condensation and to maintain adequate chimney draft. Sidewall vented units can operate with somewhat lower temperatures.

Off-cycle heat loss

Burners in home heating systems do not operate continuously, but cycle on and off. A typical burner will run between 15 to 20% of the time and remain idle for the remaining 80 to 85% of the time.

Burner off-cycle heat loss is caused by air flowing through the heating unit when the burner is idle. The draft of the chimney creates negative pressure in the heat exchanger. It pulls cold air into the boiler or furnace at the burner air inlet and through other leaks in the unit. This air travels across the hot combustion chamber and flue passages where it is heated and carries the heat out of the house through the chimney.

The size of this loss varies with burner design, chimney draft, the operating temperature of the unit and installation. It is an important cause of inefficiency, especially for older and oversized units. Figure 16-3 shows off-cycle loss.

Off-cycle is also affected by the temperature of the boiler or furnace during the burner off-period. The higher the operating temperature, the greater the burner on-period.

Restriction of off-cycle airflow by the burner can reduce heat loss. Generally, older burners were designed with open combustion heads that provide very little restriction to off-cycle airflow. In contrast, high-speed flame retention head burners reduce off-cycle airflow and thereby reduce heat loss. This is a primary reason why oilheating systems have much lower off-cycle losses than typical natural gas heating units.

Natural gas heaters often use open "atmospheric" burners that do not restrict off-cycle airflow through the heating unit. Additionally, traditional gas units have large draft hoods that continuously remove heated air from the home. Oilburners *push* air into the heat exchanger while atmo-

spheric gas burners depend upon draft to *pull* air in. This is why oilheat exchangers can be more restrictive than gas, making them more efficient.

Low mass combustion chambers (including ceramic fibers) will store less heat than high-density firebrick materials, so they will have lower losses. Similarly, small low mass boilers or furnaces store less heat than their older heavier counterparts and will have lower off-cycle losses.

Oversized heating units have longer off periods and off-cycle loss will be higher. A heating unit that is closely matched in size to the building's heating requirements will provide the lowest off-cycle heat loss and highest efficiency.

Proper heating system adjustment and maintenance also affects burner off-cycle heat loss. Three examples are: air leaks into the heating unit, temperature control settings of the boiler or furnace, and fuel firing rate.

Air leaks

Air leaks into the heat exchanger should be avoided whenever possible because they provide a path for off-cycle airflow. Initial start-up and annual servicing procedures should include sealing all such leaks before the final burner adjustment.

Some common locations for air intrusion include the space between the burner air tube and the combustion chamber opening, the connection between the combustion chamber area and heat exchanger, the space between sections of cast iron boilers, heat flanges, and loose-fitting clean out and flame inspection doors. Eliminating these unnecessary air leaks will reduce off-cycle airflow and heat loss.

Temperature settings

The water and air temperature controls also affect heat loss. The blower on a furnace operates until the low temperature limit is reached, but heat remains in the furnace and can be lost during the off period. The low limit set point often is adjustable and lower settings can sometimes prevent unnecessary heat loss. Aquastat settings for boilers have the same effect. Maintaining excessive boiler temperatures increases off-cycle losses.

Excessive firing rates

Fuel nozzles that are too large for the heating requirement of the house increase off-cycle loss. Recall that heat loss varies with the off-period time and that large firing rates produce long burner-off times. The solution to this problem is to reduce the nozzle size, provided that the burner will perform well with the smaller firing rate. With fixed head burners, it may be necessary to change the combustion head if you are drastically reducing nozzle size. Selecting the correct nozzle size is an important part of proper service procedures.

Reducing firing rates on older units works because most of them are oversized. The three exceptions to this are: steam boilers, boilers with tankless coils, and any appliance where the steady state stack temperature is less than 400°F. In these three cases, the units should be fired to their *maximum* rating. New units that are properly sized for the load should be fired to the manufacturers' recommendations.

Older units have high stand-by losses

Older appliances have larger losses than modern units. Replacement of these outdated units is often the best option for homeowners. Several design features of old units promote heat loss, including:

• Open burner head designs (non-flame-retention) that allow air to flow during off-cycle

• Larger more massive heating units that store (and lose) more heat during the off-period.

• Dense combustion chamber materials that can increase stored heat and off-cycle loss

• Heat exchange passages that are less restrictive than modern units, allowing larger off-cycle airflows.

• Steam boilers that operate at higher

Figure 16-4: Heat loss through the boiler or furnace jacket

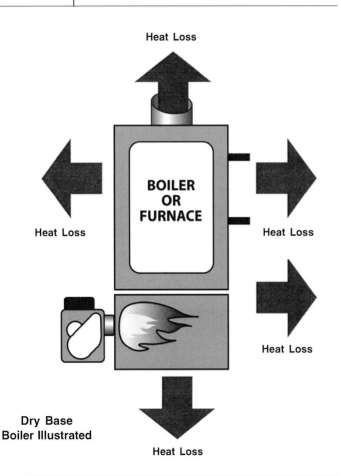

temperatures than hot water systems. The off-cycle heat losses for old units, especially steam boilers may be more than 20%.

Jacket heat loss

Useful heat is lost through the walls of the boiler or furnace. This is referred to as "jacket" or "casing" loss and it reduces the amount of heat delivered to heated areas of the home, Figure 16-4. The size of this loss depends on the heating unit design and the location of the boiler or furnace within the house.

Jacket heat loss is largest when the burner is operating and heat from the flame passes through the combustion chamber and out of the unit through its outer jacket. Heat losses through boiler jackets were measured at Brookhaven National Laboratory and ranged from about 1% to 12% of the fuel's heating value. Generally, wet-base boilers had the lowest losses and dry-base units had the highest. Old boilers, especially coal-conversion units with large firebrick combustion chambers, had the largest jacket heat loss.

Pipe and duct heat loss

The heat from a boiler or furnace is transported to the home through hot water (or steam) pipes or warm air ducts. Heat loss that occurs between the heating unit and the living space causes system inefficiency (see Figure 16-5). The level of efficiency depends upon how and where the pipes or ducts are installed, the size of the distribution system, the amount of thermal insulation and the location of the pipes and ducts within the building.

Hot water piping that is not insulated adequately can increase fuel use. The water in pipes leading to the radiators is generally between 180° and 200° Fahrenheit. These pipes often are located in cool basements and in other unheated spaces. If these pipes are not insulated, heat will be lost from the boiler water before it reaches the radiators in the house. More fuel must be consumed to compensate for these heat losses.

Similarly, heat loss from warm air ducting reduces the useful heat output of a furnace. Furnace ducts typically waste more heat than piping losses. There are two reasons for this. First, warm air ducts have a

**Figure 16-5:
Heat loss from
warm air ducts and
hot water pipes**

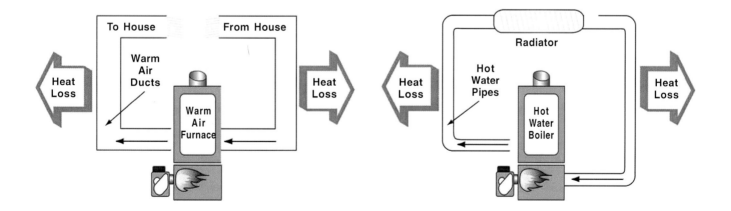

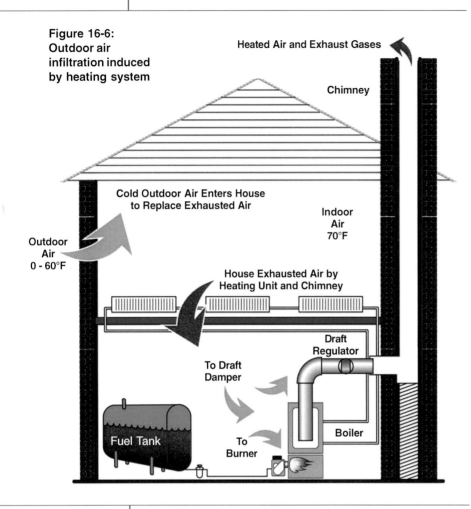

Figure 16-6:
Outdoor air infiltration induced by heating system

Heated Air and Exhaust Gases

Chimney

Cold Outdoor Air Enters House
to Replace Exhausted Air

Indoor
Air
70°F

Outdoor
Air
0 - 60°F

House Exhausted Air by
Heating Unit and Chimney

Draft
Regulator

To Draft
Damper

Fuel Tank

To
Burner

Boiler

large surface area through which heat can be lost. Second, warm air can escape directly from leaky joints in the ducting. According to studies by the US Department of Energy, ducting losses can be as high as 40%.

The level of heat loss is different for each system and it depends upon the placement of ducts within the house. Warm air ducts in cold areas such as unheated basements, attics, or crawl spaces must always be insulated and all joints must be sealed.

Outdoor air infiltration

The air that goes up the chimney must be replaced by cold outdoor air drawn into the building. This cold air must be heated to indoor temperature, Figure 16-6. The amount of heat needed to heat this cold

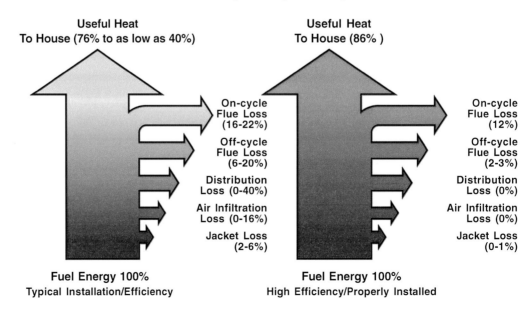

Typical Heat Losses For Oil-Fired Hydronic Boilers
Actual Losses Vary From System To System

Figure 16-7:
Typical heat losses for oil fired heating units

Useful Heat
To House (76% to as low as 40%)

Useful Heat
To House (86%)

On-cycle
Flue Loss
(16-22%)

Off-cycle
Flue Loss
(6-20%)

Distribution
Loss (0-40%)

Air Infiltration
Loss (0-16%)

Jacket Loss
(2-6%)

On-cycle
Flue Loss
(12%)

Off-cycle
Flue Loss
(2-3%)

Distribution
Loss (0%)

Air Infiltration
Loss (0%)

Jacket Loss
(0-1%)

Fuel Energy 100%
Typical Installation/Efficiency

Fuel Energy 100%
High Efficiency/Properly Installed

air depends upon on-cycle airflow through the heating unit (boiler-burner or furnace-burner design). If the unit is outside or is in a non-heated portion of the home that has plenty of excess air, air infiltration is not important. Air infiltration loss is greatest for heating appliances that operate with large quantities of excess combustion air, units with air leaks into the heat exchanger, or units that have large off-cycle airflows. Efficient boiler-burner or furnace-burner combinations will operate with low air infiltration losses.

Air infiltration heat loss for oilheating systems is usually about 2% of the total fuel energy, but some studies indicate that it can be as high as 12%. This figure is considerably higher for propane and natural gas-fired heating units, and it is one of the efficiency advantages of oil-fired equipment. The best solution for air infiltration is isolated combustion, whereby outdoor air is piped directly to the burner air intake.

In summary

New, highly efficient oilheating units

transfer more than 85% of the fuel energy directly to the home. Old units may operate in the 60 to 76% range. See Figure 16-7.

Equipment modifications to improve efficiency

New oil boilers and furnaces are often more efficient than their gas counterparts. While older oil boilers and furnaces are less efficient than the newer units, they can be "modernized," and their operating efficiencies can be improved. Heating system modifications to improve efficiency range from low-cost adjustments such as adjusting for proper combustion and sealing excess air leaks to equipment replacements such as installing new flame retention oilburners or new boilers or furnaces. The table below summarizes the efficiency gains from those improvements.

This next section will identify a number of equipment modifications that save energy. These are:

- Flame retention burners

- Replacement boilers or furnaces

Savings For Every $100 Fuel Costs by Increase of Combustion Efficiency
Assuming Constant Radiation and Other Unaccounted-for Losses

From an Original Efficiency of:	To an Increased Combustion Efficiency of:								
	55%	60%	65%	70%	75%	80%	85%	90%	95%
50%	$9.10	$16.70	$23.10	$28.60	$33.30	$37.50	$41.20	$44.40	$47.40
55%	—	8.30	15.40	21.50	26.70	31.20	35.30	38.90	42.10
60%	—	—	7.70	14.30	20.00	25.00	29.40	33.30	37.80
65%	—	—	—	7.10	13.30	18.80	23.50	27.80	31.60
70%	—	—	—	—	6.70	12.50	17.60	22.20	26.30
75%	—	—	—	—	—	6.30	11.80	16.70	21.10
80%	—	—	—	—	—	—	5.90	11.10	15.80
85%	—	—	—	—	—	—	—	5.60	10.50
90%	—	—	—	—	—	—	—	—	5.30

- Pipe or duct insulation
- Heating systems tune-up
- Thermostat set back
- Combining equipment modifications

Flame retention burners

The main difference between old non-flame retention and flame retention burners is the way the combustion air and fuel are combined. The flame retention burner has a specially designed burner head (end cone) and a high-pressure fan that produces more recirculation within the flame for better fuel-air mixing. The swirling air pattern increases the contact between the fuel droplets and the air. In addition, a recirculation zone is formed within the flame.

This recirculation pattern draws some of the hot combustion gases back toward the burner head. This helps to vaporize the oil droplets by direct contact with hot gases. Recirculation also provides a longer path length through the flame. This adds to the time available for the fuel and air to react, promoting complete combustion. This swirling and recirculation pattern also reduces smoke formation, requires less excess combustion air, and provides higher efficiency.

The flame is more stable in flame retention burners. It forms a tight shape that is held near the burner head. That's where the name "flame retention" comes from. Flame retention burners can operate efficiently in heating units where marginal chimney draft or where oversized combustion chambers could cause problems with older burner designs.

With flame retention, the flame is stabilized by the high velocity airflow and it does not need radiant heat reflected back from the combustion chamber for stable operation. This eliminates some of the flame problems experienced by older burner designs. A drawing of non-flame retention and flame retention combustion is shown in Figure 16-8.

Figure 16-8: Non-flame retention and flame retention combustion.

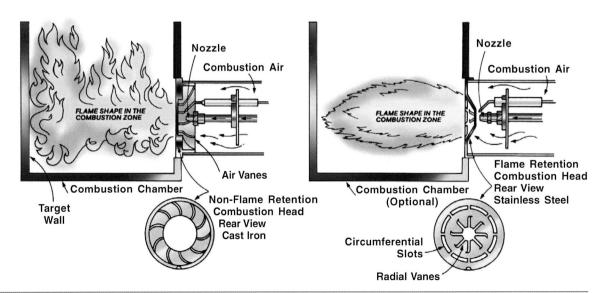

Excess air reduces efficiency and flame retention burners operate with less excess air than older burner designs. Flame retention burners require 20 to 30% excess air while older burners need 50 to 100% more to achieve low smoke numbers. The difference in the flue heat loss for these burners is often about 10%.

The second advantage of flame retention burners is reduced off-cycle heat loss. The flow of off-cycle air through the heating unit is reduced by the narrow openings of the air band and the flame retention head. Therefore, off-cycle heat loss is less. This improves the heating system efficiency. See Figure 16-9.

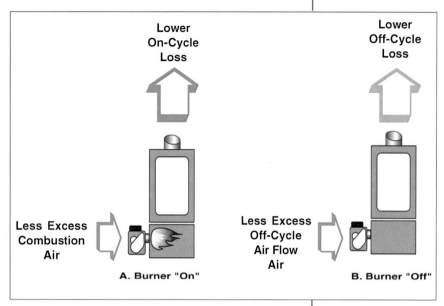

Figure 16-9: Flame retention burners operate with less heat loss.

Installation requirements

Be sure to check the condition of the combustion chamber before installing a new burner. Many older chambers are not suitable for the flame produced by a flame retention burner. Modification of the combustion chamber may be required. See Chapter 5 for more details about chamber upgrades.

Be extra careful when installing new burners into dry-base boilers and older furnaces because it may be possible to burn through the base.

Important considerations in an installation procedure include:

• Select the most efficient fuel nozzle size for the job. Many boilers and furnaces are overfired and operate at lowered efficiency. Remember that flame retention burners operate with higher efficiency and a smaller nozzle is usually advisable.

• Inspect the combustion chamber and repair or replace it. Add a high temperature ceramic liner insert if needed.

• Install the new burner. Carefully follow the recommendations of the burner manufacturers.

• Seal all air leaks around the heat exchanger, and the burner air tube. Air leaks can increase both on-cycle and off-cycle heat loss.

• Adjust the burner using combustion test equipment to an efficiency of 80% or higher. Some burners have adjustable head positions. Use the setting recommended by the manufacturer for the installed fuel nozzle size. If a fixed retention head is used, be sure that the head is the correct size. Use the head size that matches the fuel nozzle rating.

• Test all safety controls for proper operation.

• Perform final checks of burner operation.

Installation of flame retention head burners as replacements for older units can be an effective and economic means for conserving heating oil if the old boiler or furnace is suitable.

Expected energy savings

Most homeowners with older oilburners can reduce their fuel cost substantially, with savings from 15% to as high as 25%. The combination of low burner cost and high fuel savings make retention head burners one of the best conservation investments available to homeowners. Your service department can also benefit. New burners usually require fewer service calls.

Note: AFUE, Annual Fuel Utilization Efficiency, is a US Department of Energy standard for measuring the efficiency of heating appliances. AFUE ratings are used to compare the efficiency of different makes and models of furnaces and boilers.

Replacement of boilers or furnaces

Many older heating units are inefficient and oversized and replacement with a new oil-fired boiler or a furnace is better than any add-on modification. New high efficiency oil boilers and furnaces have Annual Fuel Utilization Efficiencies (AFUE's) from 82% to 95%. Replacing old and outdated heating units will cut fuel consumption and increase customer satisfaction.

No simple method can evaluate the efficiencies of older units. However, some design features of older systems tend to increase heat loss and lower efficiency.

Some of these are:
Designs that allow substantial jacket heat loss by:

- Dry-base combustion chamber

- Poor or missing jacket insulation

- Side arm hot water coils

- Massive combustion chambers constructed of heavy firebrick

- Many older burner designs use "open" end cones that cannot restrict off-cycle airflow. Secondary air openings and leaks increase off-cycle heat loss.

- High stack temperatures increase on-cycle heat loss. This is caused by wide open flue passages without baffling designed for burning coal. If the stack temperature is excessive for a clean unit with the correct firing rate and burner adjustment, then the design of the boiler or furnace is the problem.

Combustion efficiency testing can help to identify low efficiency boilers and furnaces that need to be replaced.

Expected energy savings

Replacement of obsolete boilers and furnaces with modern, highly efficient models can reduce fuel cost more than any other single option available to homeowners, even insulation and storm windows. Field studies show that replacing a boiler or furnace will often save between 18 to 32%, with typical payback periods of 3 to 6 years.

Pipe and duct insulation

Hot water pipes and warm air ducts often waste large amounts of energy when not insulated. These losses reduce system efficiency and increase fuel consumption. Pipe and duct loss is avoidable with the use of thermal insulation. All heating system distribution lines that run through unheated spaces should be protected against heat loss.

Boiler pipes

The heat loss from this piping system depends upon several factors:

- Temperatures of the hot water or steam within the pipes

- Length of piping system

- Degree of thermal insulation

- Temperature of the air (or other material) surrounding the pipes

Warm air ducts

Ducts that distribute heated air to the house lose heat in two ways.

- Heat flows from the heated duct walls to the colder surroundings

- Heated air escapes from leaky duct joints

Both of these losses reduce the useful heat delivered to the house and increase fuel consumption. Many warm air ducts pass through unheated areas, such as attics or crawl spaces. Because of the cooler surroundings, heat loss into these areas is large. Inspect all warm air ducts for leaks and proper insulation. Use seamless insulated ducts on new installations.

Expected energy savings

Boiler Piping:
Insulating piping may save 5-10 percent.

Warm Air Ducts:
Insulation and sealing leaks may save up to 40 percent.

Heating systems tune-up

Periodic cleaning and adjustment of all heating systems assures the highest level of efficiency, safety, and fewest service calls. Service routines save fuel and prevents equipment breakdowns that are a nuisance to both homeowners and service departments. See Chapter 14 for more details on proper tune-up procedures.

You may wish to develop a checklist to be filled out during each tune-up. Good

service procedures involve a number of steps that include (but are not limited to):

> **Service routines save fuel and prevents equipment breakdowns that are a nuisance to both homeowners and service departments.**

- Visually inspecting the entire heating system

- Performing a combustion efficiency test; be sure to check the draft drop through the heat exchanger by comparing the draft over fire and at the breach.

- Vacuum cleaning of all heating surfaces including the boiler or furnace flue passages (when required).

- Checking to be sure the flue pipe and chimney flue are clear and in good condition

- Cleaning all burner parts including the air fan and housing, ignition electrodes, and burner head.

- Replacing fuel and air filters.

- Sealing air leaks around the burner and heat exchanger.

- Using combustion test equipment to measure efficiency.

- Adjusting the burner for high efficiency and low smoke number.

- Modifying system and readjusting until peak efficiency is obtained.

- Recording final combustion efficiency for tuned system.

- Checking all combustion safety controls.

Heating system tune-ups reduce on-cycle flue heat loss and assure good long-term efficiency. Reduced excess combustion air lowers flue heat loss and low smoke settings avoid soot accumulations and

If there is a significant bout of severe cold weather, customers using setbacks may not be able to get the house back to a comfortable temperature. Having customers not use the setback or switch to manual in extreme cold is a good idea.

gradual efficiency loss. The combustion tests give a sound basis for recommending various efficiency modifications. New equipment sales should be recommended once the efficiency is determined to be below standard.

Expected energy savings

Typical savings from a tune-up are about 3% for systems that are regularly adjusted. If a heating system has been infrequently tuned or is out of adjustment due to equipment malfunction, then the fuel savings will be higher. For example, the efficiency of a boiler or furnace with a partially plugged fuel nozzle and sooted heating surfaces can be improved by 10% or more after a tune-up.

Thermostat set-back

The thermostat is the single best device homeowners can use for energy conservation. The greater the difference between indoor and outdoor temperatures, the more energy it takes to maintain it. For every degree you lower the thermostat setting, up to 3% can be saved on the heating bill.

It is possible to save some energy by lowering the thermostat setting if the building is empty for long periods during the day and again at night when all the occupants are sleeping. Set back thermostats are available that do this automatically.

If the set back is too great in sub-freezing conditions, the heating system may be shut

off long enough for water or heat pipes in outside walls to freeze up. Additionally, if the setback is too great, it will take a long time to get the home back up to a comfortable temperature. This may require more energy than you saved by setting the temperature back. A maximum of five degree setback is recommended.

Combining equipment modifications

It is difficult to estimate fuel savings when more than one modification is applied to the same heating system. The expected savings cannot be determined by simply adding together the savings for each individual modification as more than one of them may address the same losses. The most economical first cost retrofit is the one that saves the most fuel for the lowest cost.

Steps for advising your customer

- Measure combustion efficiency

- Inspect the heating system

- Evaluate primary equipment upgrades

- Recommend secondary energy saving options

- Present recommendations to customer

Today's heating equipment is greatly improved over the old equipment. Replacing an old inefficient oversized boiler or furnace is one of the best investments our customers can make.

Where else can they get over a 20% tax free return on investment; abundant hot water; a more comfortable, cleaner, quieter home; help improve the environment;

lower their cost of living; and increase the value of their home? This is such a great deal, the new equipment should be selling itself. Unfortunately, oilburners cannot talk. They need our help.

Advantages of new equipment

- High Efficiency—saves energy which saves customers money.

- Clean Operations—easier to service and better image as clean modern fuel.

- Low Air Pollution Emissions— properly adjusted new oil equipment has the lowest emissions.

- Improved Reliability— requires less emergency service.

- Greatly increases customer satisfaction.

Additionally, if customers invest in new oil-fired equipment, they will not be tempted to switch to gas heat. The new equipment will save them so much money and be so reliable, they will brag about it to their friends. You will keep your old customers and they will help you get new ones.

How to sell new equipment

It is vitally important that we install new oil-fired heating equipment in all of our customer's homes. New equipment makes customers satisified and insures a bright future for the Oilheat Industry. If your company has equipment sales people or your service manager does the selling, your job is to identify equipment that should be upgraded and recommend the customer

speak to your sales people about investing in conservation.

As the one who services their heating equipment, you have established credibility with your customer. By suggesting an upgrade may be in order, you are extending this trust to the sales person and have given them a great running start.

If you recommend that a customer consider new equipment, you must be sure that you tell the sales person about it. When you recommend new equipment you have given your customer a problem. He thought his system was OK, now you are telling him that it is not. Your sales person had better get to the house right away to solve the problem before the customer solves it himself with some other heating contractor or a switch in fuel.

> **It is vitally important that we install new oil-fired heating equipment in all of our customers' homes. New equipment makes customers satisified and insures a bright future for the Oilheat Industry.**

If your company does not have sales people and it is your job to sell the equipment, you need to learn all you can about the art of selling. There are many good books, tapes and seminars on selling. Selling is a skill you can learn and, like any skill, it improves with study and practice.

NORA has published a book on this topic titled *Efficient Oilheat, An Energy Conservation Guide*. It is the basis for the NORA Gold Technician Certification Program. The book, as well as all of NORA's books and tapes, is available at norastore.org.

Chapter **17**

CUSTOMER SERVICE

IN THIS CHAPTER

- Why providing great customer service is important to you, your company, and oilheat

- What customers want when something goes wrong

- Solving customer problems and handling complaints

- Helping angry or upset customers

- Hot tips for successful service calls

Chapter 17

Providing Astounding Customer Service

Service technicians—oilheat's ambassadors

As a service technician, you will have more face-to-face contact with customers than any one else in the oilheat industry. Therefore, you are one of your industry's most important ambassadors. What you say, how you say it, what you do, how you act, and how you look all determine how customers feel about you, your company and oilheat. Your customers trust you to take care of their problems and keep them comfortable. Your company's and your industry's reputation is in your hands. A good attitude and good people skills are just as important as your technical ability. Providing exceptional service is important and this chapter has tips on how to deliver it.

What's in it for you?

When a customer requests a specific technician, writes a letter of recommendation, or tells their friends good things about your company, it is because of your technical skills, your attitude and your people skills. Raises and promotions are often based on people skills too; your managers know when you deliver good service.

Why extraordinary service is so important

Many interesting studies have been conducted to determine what impact service has on customers' attitudes. One popular study examined why customers leave one company for another. Of the customers leaving, 66% said they switched because lack of interest in the customer by the company's service providers. Fourteen-percent left because of unanswered complaints. Whether customers leave or stay depends on your work.

One important customer satisfaction study found that most customers do not complain. For every one complaint you hear you have 20 unhappy customers and 6 very angry ones who do not call. Complaining is too much trouble and they do not know who to complain to. However, they do get even. Seventy percent of disappointed customers would rather punish the service provider than complain. They take their business elsewhere and then tell their friends about it.

The average upset customer will tell ten friends and 18% of them will tell more than 20 people! This means for every complaint you get from an unhappy customer, at least 270 people have heard something bad about your company.

The good news is that whenever you exceed your customer's expectations, they will be pleased. Happy customers will tell at least five friends about the experience. The only way to be sure that your customers are saying nice things about you and your company is to make sure every customer is thoroughly satisfied.

The key to successful customer relations is to put yourself in your customer's place—to treat your customers as you would like to be treated. Do the job right

THE
GOLDEN
RULE:
Do unto others
as you would
have them do
unto you

the first time. It means being helpful, friendly, thoughtful, tactful, and polite. As you know, customer service is a unique and challenging profession. You are often the only link a customer has with your company. The few moments you spend with a customer is all it takes for them to form an opinion—good or bad—about your company. What you say and how you say it, will determine if the customer stays or goes. It also determines if they tell their friends good things about your company—or bad things.

It's a relationship

Your company's relationship with your customers is very close. Many of your customers will buy from your company for as long as they live in their homes. Naturally, they expect more than a "take the money and run attitude"—they expect your company to keep its promises.

Customer disappointment is usually based on bad customer relations rather than bad technology. They won't leave if the burner breaks, but they will leave if you let them down by not fixing the problem or failing to let them know what is happening. Many technicians tend to take complaints personally and then feel a need to defend themselves. It's important to remember that the customer usually isn't upset with you; they're upset with the situation. To the customer, the service call is an interruption and many of them have to adjust their schedules, miss work and lose wages just to wait for their system to be repaired.

Keep promises

Breaking promises is the fastest way to lose a customer. Never make a promise you can't keep. If you tell a customer you are going to do something—do it. As a service technician, your job usually requires keeping promises made to customers by your company. The most common promises are appointment times for service calls. Your customers want to know exactly when you are coming to their home.

You have to communicate with your dispatcher so he/she can judge the arrival times for your future calls. The ultimate beneficiary of good communications and accurate promises is the service technician. Isn't it nicer to work for a customer who is delighted that you arrived on time rather than one who is angry because you are late?

If, for some reason, you find that you must break a promise, do it as quickly as possible. The sooner you give your customer the bad news, the less they will be inconvenienced.

Moments of truth

It is helpful to think of customer relations in terms of "Moments of Truth." Every time you come in contact with a customer, you have a chance to make either a good or a bad impression. Each customer contact is a one-time opportunity to distinguish yourself from the competition. Successful customer relations mean making all the "Moments of Truth" good ones. If the service provider gets it wrong, they may be erasing all memories of good treatment. If they get it right, they can undo all the mistakes that happened before.

You can make all of your moments of truth good ones by being patient, understanding and professional. If there is a problem, you need to acknowledge it and apologize for the inconvenience. Be sure to use your customer's name, confirm you are listening, and if authorized, give the customer a choice in the resolution.

What customers want when things go wrong

Customers want their heating system to function properly. When there's a problem, they want it taken care of quickly. When something goes wrong, they want action, NOT excuses. They want you to fix the problem and let them get on with their day. They want you to be respectful of them, their property and their time.

Instead of quietly taking their business elsewhere, the complaining customer is telling you, "I care enough to tell you something is wrong. I am willing to stay if I get some satisfaction." It may sound strange, but the first thing to say to a complaining customer is, *"Thank you for telling us about this problem. Your satisfaction is very important to us and I will do all I can to set this right."*

Customers want to be treated in a way that suggests that the company cares about them and about fixing the problem. Customers generally do not expect service providers to be perfect, but they do expect us to care enough to repair the problem with a minimal amount of inconvenience.

The steps to problem solving

- **Listen to the complaint:** If the customer is upset, let them vent. You have to deal with emotions before you can solve

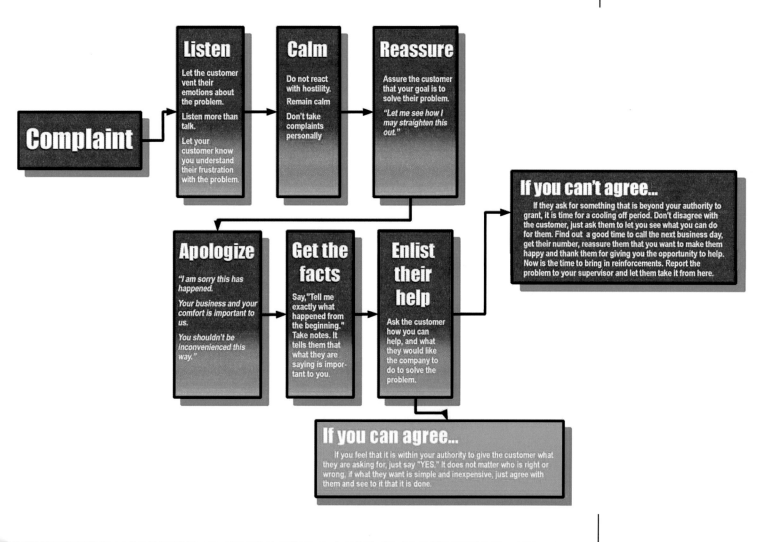

problems. Be prepared to listen more than talk. Say things like, *"I understand why you are upset; I would be angry too."* Never disagree with the customer. Remember, this is not a personal assault. Do not react with hostility. Remain calm. The idea is to separate the problem from the customer's emotions so you can both work together for a solution.

> Ask yourself:
> "How did I leave their heating system?" and "What did I say about my fellow employees and company?" Make your "moments of truth" good ones. You hold our reputation in your own hands.

- **Calm them, reassure them, apologize, and get the facts:** Say to your customer, *"I am very sorry this has happened. Let me see what I can do to straighten this out. Tell me exactly what happened from the beginning."* This will get them into a rational, problem-solving mind-set.

- **Enlist their help:** Ask them what you can do to set it right. Ask them what the company must do to satisfy them.

- **Cooling-off Period:** Inserting a "cooling-off" period in the middle of the problem solving process may be helpful. You can "cool-off" the situation by saying you want to review some manuals in your truck or discuss this with someone in the company who has solved a similar problem. At this point, you may also decide that the service manager should step in and help solve the problem.

- **Investigate:** Now is the time to thoroughly troubleshoot the situation to find the cause of the problem.

- **Offer the Solutions:** Explain the cause of the problem and offer the customer a solution.

Abusive customers— when is it time to leave?

At some point, you will encounter an abusive customer who may push you to the limit, make you angry, and cause you to respond poorly. When you are in this frame of mind you are no help to your customer, your industry, or yourself. If you start to become angry, tell the customer that you need to go to your service van. This will give you a chance to calm down, decide whether you can solve the problem, or if you need some help from the office.

Explain to the customer, *"I am sorry, but if you continue to yell at me, I can't do my job. Please let's both calm down so that I can help you."* If all your attempts to calm the customer and yourself fail, it is time to leave. Quietly gather up your tools and leave. Do not say anything that can make the situation worse.

Never criticize the work of others

Never criticize the work of anyone, regardless of whether they work for your company or another company. If the customer says something like, "Gee, the man that was here last time didn't go to this much trouble," explain that everyone has their own approach to problems, every problem is different and you are doing your best to solve this particular problem. If one of your fellow technicians has made a mistake, take the matter up with him privately so he will not make the same mistake again.

Do not criticize your customer's heating equipment. Remember, your company may have sold and installed it. If the equipment is obsolete, suggest an upgrade. Your customer may be pleased to hear they can save money and avoid more service calls.

No one in your industry can build customer goodwill as well as you can. Remember, you are usually the only person from your company that your customer sees. You are the person whom the customer trusts with his family's safety, warmth, and comfort. Keep this in mind at all times.

Image is everything

Surveys indicate that many people think oilheat is dirty. This is why your appearance is so important. You have to focus on clean trucks, neat uniforms, clean shoes, clean toolboxes, and leaving the customer's homes and heating systems cleaner than you found them. Cleanliness implies a higher level of quality in the service rendered.

The airline industry has done extensive customer satisfaction research and found that people believe that if they find coffee stains on the food trays, then the airline must not do a good job on engine maintenance. The same applies to our industry—customers often judge the quality of your service by the appearance of the system after you have finished your work.

The importance of details can not be overemphasized, especially details that are crucial to creating a positive impression on the customer.

Focus on your customer's heating system

Unfortunately, the condition of their furnace and the area around it is the reason so many people think that oilheat is dirty. To insure a bright future for our industry, you have to make cleaning-up of the heating systems a top priority. The customer will judge the quality of the work you have done by the appearance of his heating equipment after you have left.

When one of your customers sells their home, the condition of the heating system becomes your best salesperson—or your biggest sales problem. The new homebuyer will look at the condition of the system and draw conclusions about what kind of company left their sticker on it. If the unit is nice and clean, they will probably call you to set up an account. If the unit is a mess, they might not want to buy from the company that left this mess in their nice new home.

What do you look like to your customer?

What about your image? Is your truck clean? Remember, your truck is a rolling advertisement for your company.

What about the inside of your truck? Customers might look-in when you open the doors. What about your tools and toolbox? Customers believe if your tools are in good shape, you are probably a good technician who will show the same respect to their equipment.

What about your appearance? Check your appearance before each call and have enough pride in yourself to appear as presentable as possible. It is a good idea to carry an extra uniform shirt in your truck in case the one you are wearing gets dirty. You may want to have a pair of coveralls to protect your uniform on particularly dirty jobs.

Try to avoid using your customer's facilities to wash up. Keep a can of hand cleaner in your truck, consider using protective gloves to keep your hands clean.

A word about tobacco

Never use tobacco when you are on your customer's property.

Conclusion

The extra value that you provide to your customers is what sets your company apart. Your professionalism and dedication are the most valuable things you have to sell. You make your company unique and special.

Hot Tips

for Successful Service Calls

— Be on time. Being late, without notification, is the quickest way to get off on the wrong foot with your customer.

— Prepare... ask the dispatcher if your company has been to the residence recently and gather appropriate information.

— Be careful where you park. Don't block the customer's car, drive on the lawn or walk through the flowerbeds.

— Set yourself up with a well-organized toolbox. This will reduce the number of trips you need to make to your truck.

— Keep track of your calls with a service card hanging near the system. Write the date, your initials, a brief explanation of what you did, the parts you used and the efficiency readings. This card can be a big help with troubleshooting.

— The most important service call is the preventative maintenance tune-up. It gives you a chance to look for potential problems and fix them before they occur. This is also a great time to talk to your customer about the possibilities of investing in new energy saving heating equipment.

— Do not let the problems of the previous call affect your attitude on this call.

— Some customers like to watch you work. It helps to explain what you are doing and make recommendations. Getting the customer involved may sound like trouble, but they deserve to know what is happening. You may be able to show them how they can avoid problems in the future. Involving the customer improves customer relations and may help avoid complaints.

— If an expensive part is broken and not covered by the service plan, get the customer's approval before replacing it.

— Always look beyond the symptoms for the cause of the problem. For example, a "bound" fuel unit is often a symptom of water in an oil tank and water in the tank may be a symptom of a

rotted fill or vent pipe. Be sure to find and fix the cause, not just the symptom.

— Do not discuss one customer's problems, home condition, or cleanliness with other customers.

— Keep a clean, well-organized service truck (photo). It will go a long way to making your day more pleasant.

— Be sure to notify your manager about calls that require follow-up for immediate attention.

— Pay attention to your personal appearance. Clean and neat projects a professional image.

— Keep your "library" of service information and literature up-to-date.

— Answer questions from customers honestly and thoughtfully.

— The easiest way to upset a person is to discuss controversial subjects such as politics and religion, so do not do it.

— Never make a promise you cannot keep. Check first with the service manager, dispatcher or other personnel before making a promise to a customer.

— Concentrate on solving the problem at hand. Do not boast of the problems you have solved in the past.

— When you are finished, leave the areas around the heating system cleaner than you found them. Tell the customer what you did, show them the parts you replaced, and thank them for the opportunity to be of service.

Glossary

AFUE (Annualized Fuel Utilization Efficiency): A measure of the efficiency of the heating unit (burner and boiler/furnace) including standby losses during the off-cycles, given on an annual basis. See also "Steady State Efficiency."

Air: A mixture of nitrogen, oxygen and slight traces of other gases. For purposes of combustion analysis, we say air is 79% Nitrogen and 21% Oxygen.

Air Change: The number of times in an hour the air in a room is changed either by mechanical means or by the infiltration of outside air leaking into the room through cracks around doors and windows, etc.

Air Cleaner: A device designed for the purpose of removing airborne impurities such as dust, fumes and smoke.

Air Conditioning: This is the process of simultaneously controlling temperature, humidity, cleanliness and distribution of air to meet various requirements of the conditioned space.

Air Infiltration: The leakage of air into a house through cracks and crevices, doors, windows, and other openings, caused by wind, pressure, and/or temperature difference.

Alternating Current: In the case of alternating current, electrons are made to move first in one directions and then in the other. The direction of current flow reverses periodically in cycles.

Ammeter: An instrument for measuring the amount of electron flow in amperes.

Ampere: A measure of current flowing through a conductor having a resistance of 1 ohm and a difference of potential of 1 volt.

Aquastat: A term applied to a control which may be inserted in, or attached to, a vessel for the purpose of controlling the temperature of water within the vessel.

Atmospheric Pressure: The pressure of the atmosphere at a given elevation, the atmospheric pressure at sea level is 14.7 pounds per square inch, allowing water to boil at 212°F.

Atomization: The reduction of a substance to minute particles. In oil burning, atomization produces a fine mist of fuel.

Available Heat: The quantity of useful heat per unit of fuel available from complete combustion, after deducting dry flue gas and water vapor losses.

Biofuel: A renewable, biodegradable combustible liquid fuel. Manufactured by processing vegetable oils such as soy and rapseed (canola). Also made from waste cooking oil and trap grease, tallow, and animal fats such as fish oil.

Bioheat Fuel®: A blend of 95% or more #2 oil and 5% or less B100 biofuel.

Boiler: A closed vessel in which steam is generated or in which water is heated by fire.

Boiler Efficiency: The ratio of heat absorbed per pound of fuel fired, to the heat of complete combustion of one pound of fuel.

Boiler Heating Surface: The area of the heat transmitting surfaces in contact with the water (or steam) in the boiler on one side, and the fire or hot gases on the other.

Boiler Rating: The guaranteed output of a boiler in Btus per hour, or in square feet of radiation, as determined in a test laboratory such as the Institute of Boiler and Radiator Manufacturers (IBR) or the American Society of Mechanical Engineers (ASME).

British Thermal Unit (BTU): The quantity of heat required to raise the temperature of 1 lb. of water 1°F. This is somewhat approximate but sufficiently accurate for any work discussed in this manual. Here is how the Btus of the various fuels compare:

No. 2 Heating Oil = 138,690 Btus per gallon

Natural Gas: Averages 1,027 Btus per cubic foot, about 135 cubic feet equals one gallon of oil.

Kerosene: 131,890 Btus per gallon, 1.05 gallons of kerosene equals the heat content of one gallon of 2 oil.

Propane: 91,330 Btus per gallon, 1.53 gallons of propane equals one gallon of 2 oil.

Electricity: 3,412 Btus per kilowatt hour (kwh), 40.6 kwh equals one gallon of No. 2 oil.

Wood: one full cord of wood has the heat value of between 95 and 140 gallons of oil.

Anthracite Coal: has 12,000 Btus per pound. About 12 pounds of coal equals the heat content of one gallon of No. 2 oil.

Cad Cell Relay: See "Primary Control."

Carbon Dioxide (CO$_2$): A gas which, in heating practice, indicates the complete combustion of carbon in the fuel and is found through analysis of the flue gas.

Carbon Monoxide (CO): A gas which, in heating practice, indicates incomplete combustion of the carbon in the fuel and is found through analysis of the flue gas.

Centigrade: See "Celsius."

Celsius: A thermometer scale at which the freezing point of water is 0° and its boiling point is 100°. In the United States it is only used in scientific and laboratory work.

Chimney Effect: The tendency of heated air or gas in a vertical passage to rise due to lower density compared to that of the surrounding air or gas. In buildings, the tendency of the cold, denser outside air to replace the heated air results in the "chimney effect."

Circuit (Electrical): The complete path of an electric current from the source through a switch to a load and back to the source.

Circuit Breaker: A thermal device which opens a circuit when the current in the circuit exceeds a predetermined amount.

Cloud Point: The temperature at which wax crystals begin to form in fuel, typically 10 to 20 degrees above pour point.

Combustion: Defined as the rapid reaction of combustible material with oxygen, with the resultant generation of heat. For combustion to take place, the fuel must be heated to its ignition temperature and brought into contact with oxygen.

Combustion Chamber: The refractory or metal lined area within a boiler or furnace in which the combustion of fuel takes place. When no chamber is present (as in wet base boilers) the area is often referred to as "combustion space."

Comfort Zone (Average): The range of effective temperatures over which the majority of adults feel comfortable.

Condensate: Liquid formed by the condensation of a vapor,;in steam heating, water condensed from steam.

Conduction: The process of diffusion or flow of heat energy through a mass, or body of matter, by particle of molecular contact from the warmer to the colder parts.

Conductor (Thermal): A material capable of readily transmitting heat by means of conduction.

Conductor (Electrical): Any material suitable for carrying electric current.

Convector: A concealed radiator. An enclosed heating unit located (with enclosure) either within, adjacent to, or exterior to, the room or space to be heated, but transferring heat to the room or space mainly by the process of convection.

Converter: A piece of equipment for heating water with steam without mixing the two. It may be used for supplying hot water for domestic purposes or for a hot water heating system.

Cycle (Electrical): One complete positive and one complete negative alternation of a current or voltage.

Degree-Day (Standard): A unit which is the difference between 65°F and the daily average temperature, when the latter is below 65°F. The degree days in any one day is equal to the number of degrees F that the average temperature for that day is below 65°F.

Dew Point: The temperature below which water vapor contained in flue gases turns to a liquid. This change is referred to as condensation. To prevent condensation, stack temperature should range from 270°F to 370°F above ambient air temperature.

Dielectric: An insulator. The insulating material between the plates of a capacitor. The insulating porcelain of an ignition electrode.

Direct Current: An electric current that flows in one direction only.

Direct Return System (Hot water): A two-pipe hot water system in which the water, after it has passed through a heating unit, is returned to the boiler along a direct path, so that the total distance traveled by the water, from each radiator, is the shortest feasible.

Direct Venting: The mechanical exhausting of the flue gases of a heating unit in a structure that does not have a suitable chimney.

Down Feed System: A heating system in which the supply mains are above the level of the heating units which they serve.

Draft: In heating systems, draft refers to the pressure difference which causes a current of air or gases to flow through a combustion chamber, flue, chimney or space.

Efficiency: In a heating unit, it is that percentage of the heat energy input which is useful energy output. The ratio of output power to input power is generally expressed as a percentage.

Electromagnet: A magnet made by passing an electrical current through a wire wound on a soft iron core.

Electromotive Force (emf): The force that produces an electric current in an electric circuit.

Electron: A negatively charged particle of matter.

Energy: The ability or capacity to do work.

Fahrenheit: A thermometer scale at which the freezing point of water is 32°F and its boiling point is 212°F above zero. It generally used in the United States for expressing temperature.

Flame Velocity (Rate of Flame Propagation): is the speed with which a flame travels through a given fuel-air mixture. It varies with the fuel, fuel-air mixture ratio and temperature of the mixture.

Flash Point: Maximum temperature at which fueloil can be safely stored and handled without serious fire hazard. ASTM minimum for No.1 and No.2 is 100°F).

Flue Gas: Includes all gases which leave the furnace combustion chamber by way of a flue. Flue gas consists of nitrogen, gaseous products of combustion, water vapor and oxygen.

Frequency: The number of complete cycles per second existing in any form of wave motion; such as the number of cycles per second of an alternating current.

Fuel: May be defined as any substance, solid, liquid or gaseous, which may be relatively easily ignited and burned to produce heat. Practically all fuels consist of carbon and hydrogen.

Furnace: That part of a boiler or warm air heating plant in which combustion takes place. Sometimes it is also the complete heating unit of a warm air heating system.

Gauge Pressure: The pressure above that of the atmosphere. It is the pressure indicated on an ordinary pressure gauge. It is expressed as a unit pressure such as pounds per-square inch (PSI) gauge.

Generator: A machine that converts mechanical energy into electrical energy.

Grille: A perforated covering for an air inlet or outlet usually made of wire screen, cast iron or other material.

Gross Heating Value: Is the total amount of heat produced by the complete combustion of the fuel at atmospheric conditions.

Ground: A metallic connection with the earth to establish ground potential. Also a common return to a point of zero potential.

Heat: That form of energy into which all other forms may be changed. Heat always flows from a body of higher temperature to a body of lower temperature.

Heat of Combustion: The heat evolved when the substance combines rapidly with oxygen.

Heat Exchanger: Any device which is used for transferring energy from one fluid or gas to another.

Heat Unit: In the foot-pound-second system: the **British Thermal Unit (BTU):** in the centimetergram-second system: the calorie (cal).

Heating Medium: A substance such as water, steam, or air used to convey heat from the boiler, furnace, or other source of heat to the heating units from which the heat is dissipated.

Hot Water Heating System: A heating system in which water is used as the medium by which heat is carried through pipes from the boiler to the heating units.

Humidistat: An instrument which controls the relative humidity of the air in a room.

Humidity: The amount of water vapor within a given space, generally measured in pounds-per-cubic foot.

Hydronics: The science of heating and cooling with water.

Ignition: The act of starting combustion.

Ignition Point: Lowest temperature at which rapid combustion of a fuel will take place in air. For No.2 oil, the ignition point is over 500°F.

Insulation: A material which is used to minimize the heat losses from a given space.

Kilowatt Hour: It is 1000 Watts per hour of electrical energy and is equivalent to 3,412 BTU.

Latent Heat: The energy involved to change the physical state of a substance, (from a liquid to a gas) without changing its temperature.

Magnetic Field: The space in which a magnetic force exists.

Master Control: See "primary control."

Milliammeter: An ammeter that measures current in thousands of an ampere.

Nitrogen (N_2): Is present in air in a large quantity and does not serve any purpose in the process of combustion.

Ohm: The unit of electrical resistance.

Ohmmeter: An instrument for directly measuring resistance in ohms.

One-Pipe System (Hot Water): A hot water heating system in which one pipe serves both as a supply main and also as a return main. The heating units have separate supply and return connections to the same main.

One-Pipe System (Steam): A steam heating system consisting of a main circuit in which the steam and condensate flow in the same pipe. There is but one connection to each heating unit, which must serve as both the supply and return.

Over Head System: A heating system in which the supply main is above the heating units.

Oxidizing Flame: A flame produced by the burning of a fuel with more than the amount of oxygen required for burning under stoichiometric conditions.

Oxygen (O_2): The lesser quantity of air that is necessary in the combustion of any fuel. When found in large quantity in flue gases, it is an indication of excess air being introduced to the unit.

Panel Heating: A method of heating involving the installation of the heating units (pipe coils) within the wall, floor or ceiling of a room.

Plenum Chamber: An air compartment maintained under pressure and connected to one or more distributing ducts.

Pour Point: Lowest temperature at which fuel will flow. The ASTM standard for untreated No. 2 oil is 17°F.

Primary Control: In an oil burner circuit, it is the control responsible for the proper sequencing and safety of the operation of the burner. It is often referred to as the cad cell relay, protectorelay, stack switch or master control.

Pressure: The force-per-unit-area measured in pounds-per-square-inch, inches of water or millimeters of mercury.

Pressure Reducing Valve: A piece of equipment for changing the pressure of a gas or liquid from a higher pressure to a lower one.

Pressuretrol: A pressure controller often used to identify the control used to limit the pressure in a steam system.

Proportioning: Can be applied to the maintenance of the ratio between fuel and air supply throughout the operating range of the burner.

Protectorelay: See "primary control."

Radiant Heating: A heating system in which the heating is by radiation only. Sometimes applied to a panel heating system.

Radiation, Equivalent Direct: The amount of heating surface expressed in square feet which will deliver 240 Btu/HR for steam, and 150 BTU/HR for hot water systems operating at design conditions.

Radiator: Heated and exposed to view, radiator transfers heat by radiation to objects "it can see" and by conduction to the surrounding air, which in turn is circulated by natural convection.

Recirculation: A strong, swirling air pattern that recirculates combustion products for more complete mixing of fuel and air.

Register: In heating and air conditioning, it refers to a grille for the distribution of air which most often contains a built-in damper or shutter.

Relative Humidity: The amount of moisture in a given quantity of air compared with the maximum amount of moisture the same quantity of air could hold at the same temperature. It is expressed as a percentage.

Relay: An electromechanical switching device that can be used as a remote control.

Return Mains: The pipes which return the heating medium from the heating units to the source of heat supply.

Reverse Return System: (Hot Water) A two-pipe hot water heating system in which the water from the several heating units is returned along paths, arranged so that all radiator circuits of the system are practically of equal length.

Sensible Heat: Heat which only increases the temperature of objects as opposed to latent heat.

Series Loop System: A hot water heating system in which a single pipe connects from the heating unit to the first distributing unit then on to the next distributing unit, continuing this way until it returns to the heating unit. All distributing units would then be connected in series.

Solenoid: An electromagnetic coil that contains a movable plunger.

Square Foot of Heating Surface: See "Radiation, equivalent direct."

Stack Switch: See "Primary control."

Stack Temperature: The stack (flue gas) temperature is the temperature of combustion gases leaving the appliance, and reflects the energy that did not transfer from the fuel to the heat exchanger.

Static Pressure: The pressure necessary to overcome the frictional resistance to flow. In an oil burner, it will refer to the pressure within the burner tube as developed by the fan. In an air distribution system, it refers to the pressure necessary to overcome the total resistance created by the duct work.

Steady State Efficiency: A measure of the carbon dioxide in the flue gases, expressed as a percentage, to determine the level of completion of the chemical reaction during combustion taken at "steady state" conditions, meaning there is no further change in the reaction process.

Steam: Water vapor found when water has been heated to a boiling point, corresponding to the pressure it is under.

Stoichiometric: Describes a condition in which the reactants of a chemical reaction are present in the exact quantities, as predetermined for the chemical equation of the reaction. It describes perfect combustion when the reactants are fuel and oxygen.

Sulfur Dioxide (SO_2): It is present in small quantities in fuel oil. It is the product of the combustion of sulfur.

Supply Mains: The pipes through which the heating medium flows from the boiler, or source of supply, to the run-outs and risers leading to the heating units.

Therm: A quantity of heat equal to 100,000 Btus.

Thermistor: A resistor that is used to compensate for temperature variations in a circuit.

Thermocouple: A junction of two dissimilar metals that produces a voltage when heated.

Thermostat: An instrument which responds to changes in temperature and which directly or indirectly controls the room temperature.

Transformer: A device composed of two or more coils, linked by magnetic lines of force. In transferring energy from one source to another, it can increase or decrease voltage.

Two-Pipe System (Steam or water): A heating system in which one pipe is used for the supply main and another for the return main. The essential feature of a two-pipe system is that each heating unit receives a direct supply of the heating medium which cannot have served a preceding heating unit.

Up-Feed System (Hot Water or Steam): A heating system in which the supply mains are below the level of the heating units which they serve.

Vacuum Heating System (Steam): A two-pipe heating system equipped with the necessary accessory apparatus to permit the pressure in the system to go below atmospheric pressure.

Vapor Heating System (Steam): A two-pipe heating system which operates at pressures at or near atmospheric and which returns the condensate to the boiler or receiver by gravity.

Ventilation: Air circulated through a room for ventilating purposes. It may be mechanically circulated with a blower system or it may be natural circulation through an open window, etc.

Vent Valve (Steam): A device for permitting air to be forced out of a heating unit or pipe and which closes against steam.

Vent Valve (Water): A device permitting air to be forced out of a pipe or heating unit, but which closes against water.

Viscosity: The measure of a liquid's resistance to flow, generally measured in terms of Saybolt Universal or Saybolt Furol Seconds.

Volt: The unit of electrical potential.

Voltmeter: An instrument designed to measure a difference in electrical potential, in volts.

Warm Air Heating System: A warm air heating plant consists of a heating unit (fuel burning furnace) enclosed in a casing, from which the heated air is distributed to the various rooms of building through ducts. If the motive heat producing flow depends on the difference in weight between the heated air leaving the casing and the cooler air entering the bottom of the casing, it is termed a gravity system. If a fan is used to produce circulation and the system is designed especially for fan circulation, it is termed a forced warm air system.

Watt: The unit of electrical power.

Wattmeter: An instrument for measuring electrical power in watts.

Wet Return (Steam): That part of a return main of a steam heating system which is completely filled with water or condensation.

Index

Index